AF541254

BALANCE OF PAYMENTS
Theory and Policy
The Indian Experience

Dedicated to

My Teacher

PROFESSOR BISWAJIT CHATTERJEE

Contents

Preface

This book emerges out of my earlier thoroughly revised Ph.D. work done at Jadavpur University, Kolkata in the summer of 1997 under the guidance of Professor Biswajit Chatterjee of Economics Department, Jadavpur University as well as the work done during 2005-07 for UGC-Sponsored Minor Research Project entitled "Balance of Payments and Macroeconomic Behaviour in India Since the 1990s" under the SEED Support of Potential for Excellence. The book covers everything one needs to know to understand the evolution of Balance of Payments in India right from Independence to the present day along with various theories on balance of payments as well as India's trade and payments policies thereof and researchers' contribution on the theme.

Of interest to academics studying India's international trade, this book is also guaranteed to be extremely useful for students studying at different colleges and universities, researchers, professional economists and those involved with policy-making in different developed, and developing countries. There is very little research that employs a fully specified holistic or integrated framework for open economies so as to include the insights of alternative theoretical strands and use it to identify the major factors that influenced India's balance of trade and balance of payments over time. This book attempts to fill this gap.

I record my deep sense of gratitude to my teacher Professor Biswajit Chatterjee, Department of Economics,

Jadavpur University, also the Dean, Faculty Council of Arts, Jadavpur University (to whom the book is dedicated) for his valuable advice, constructive suggestions and painstaking guidance towards the preparation of the book. Bereft of his conscientious and highly meticulous guidance, the present book might not have been completed in the present form.

In the course of different seminars and conferences, I have received valuable suggestions, comments, and critical inputs at various stages from distinguished economists of our country and abroad, which have helped me in shaping my ideas. While I am indebted to all of them, I must specially mention the encouragement received from: Professor Mihir Rakshit, Professor V.R. Panchamukhi, Professor D.M. Nachane, Professor Basudev Biswas, Dr. Mathew Joseph and Late Professor P.R. Brahmananda, Late Dr. M.J.M. Manohar Rao and Late Professor Amaresh Bagchi.

I owe a great deal to Shri Bimal Bhusan Chakraborty, Shri Manab Sadhan Biswas, Shri Mrinmoy Chatterjee, Srimati Soma Chatterjee, Srimati Chameli Chakraborty, Srimati Mandira Roy Karmakar and Srimati Anamika Choudhury. Srimati Sangeeta Kundu and Sk. Abdur Rahman, Sr. Technical Assistant, Department of Economics, Jadavpur University who helped me in computation and running of regressions. I express my thanks and respect to all of them.

Last of all I thank Shri G.S. Bhatia of Deep and Deep Publications Pvt. Ltd., New Delhi for his help in publishing this book.

Needless to say, all the errors and omissions that may still lie in the present book obviously remain my own responsibility.

DR. ASIM K. KARMAKAR
Department of Economics
Jadavpur University
Kolkata

I

Introduction

One of the major economic problems faced by the Indian economy since Independence has been the chronic and periodic balance of payments (BoP) difficulties. This necessitated policy interventions not only in the external front, but also at the levels of domestic macroeconomic management of the economy. Though the Government of India had intervened to curb and contain trade deficits through various programmes and policy changes from time to time, the problem has not been eliminated as yet. In a growing economy like ours, the recurrence of such problems may not totally be unexpected, but the continued nature of the problem adversely affects the growth process. Since deficits in the current account trade balance constitute the major component of our BoP deficits, the policies aimed at export promotion and import control are linked with policies to manage the flow of foreign exchange in the economy. Naturally, the problem is basically macroeconomic in nature, and therefore, the influence of domestic macroeconomic variables on the country's trade balance and balance of payments cannot be denied.

However, the problem is not unique to India. Most of the developing countries which tried to industrialize and achieve a structural change in their production pattern during the post-World War II period had faced similar problems. In fact, one may extend the list and include countries which are developed at present, and some of them perhaps enjoy surpluses in their international transactions, but who had also experienced the phases of balance of payments deficits during the process of their economic growth and development. The problem becomes serious in case of developing countries for whom the ability to grow fast depends on the availability of foreign exchange reserves which limit their ability to import crucial capital goods and intermediate inputs from rest of the world. This may threaten to slow down the growth prospects of these economies in the medium run. This is compounded by a sluggish growth of exportables, and a high degree of rigidity in factor proportions between domestic and foreign resources. As a result, countries like India often had to rely on foreign borrowings on a bilateral basis and loans from the International Monetary Fund. Such loans and borrowings often stipulated conditions on policy options and made the growth profiles of such economies to follow a given path. There are also the associated problems of repayment obligations and servicing of external debt. But the source of all these problems happens to be the ever-increasing gap between imports and exports over time. A study on balance of payments in a growing economy like India therefore must focus on the factors that contributed to the growth of her import surplus over time.

Estimates of the determinants of India's trade balance have given rise to several controversies depending upon the framework chosen. Theoretical researches on balance of payments have emphasized that current account trade balance is basically the difference between a country's national income and domestic absorption. Policy experiment to improve the current account trade deficits must involve policies aimed at controlling domestic expenditure or absorption. This needs to be suitably blended with specific policies designed for export promotion and import substitution so as to initiate a process of long-run structural adjustment in the economy with higher surplus in its current account. We need a holistic integrated macroeconomic framework to assess the importance of the interplay of different variables, domestic as well as foreign, in influencing the size of import surplus of the economy over time. Such a framework should be flexible enough to analyse the movements of capital accounts variables as well in shaping the overall balance of payments of the country. In the existing literature on India's balance of payments, scholars have more or less concentrated on one or two major factors, assuming other factors to be insignificant. In our analysis, we shall adopt a holistic approach to test the significance of alternative set of factors including the factors that were hitherto neglected. Our result will strengthen or modify some of the findings of the existing studies on India's balance of payments.

In particular, the plan of the book is as follows:

In *Chapter 2*, a critical review of the theoretical literature on balance of payments in its different dimensions has been attempted. In *Chapter 3*, an analytical survey of the economic researches on India's balance of payments over the period has been discussed. This enables us to identify the major determinants of a country's balance of payments over time as per alternative theoretical approaches, and access the extent to which some of these factors have been used in Indian economic research to explain the behaviour of India's balance of payments and trade balance over time. This is followed by a detailed account of the actual behaviour of India's balance of payments from the very inception of First Plan period to the present phase of trade and payments liberalization since 1991. The ups and downs in the country's trade balance in response to the various constraints that emerged during the process of planned economic development in India, and the policy changes that affected these periodic movements have been discussed in great detail in *Chapter 4*. *Chapter 5* analyses the various aspects of trade, payments and other policies that were introduced from time to time to meet the difficulties in our external payments position and their effectiveness and implications are discussed in great detail. In *Chapter 6*, we take up some multiple regression analysis to identify the major factors that influenced India's trade balance as well as balance of payments in terms of holistic integrated macroeconomic framework for open economies.

The data for the present study have been taken from several sources. For relevant data on India's balance of payments and its components over time, exchanges rate, terms of trade, value of exports, imports, government's budget deficits, GDP at market prices, money supply, etc., we have used Reserve Bank of India's Hand Book of Statistics on the Indian Economy (various years) as well as Reports on Currency and Finance, its various Annual Reports, the Finance Ministry's Economic Surveys, various issues, CSO's National Accounts Data, in addition to the India Data Base, published by H.L. Chandhok and the Policy Group (1990). We have used various issues of IMF's Balance of Payments Statistics Yearbook, OECD's World Economic Outlook, GATT's Trade Policy Review, World Bank's World Development Report, and World Debt Tables with respect to trade balance and balance of payments for different years as are available. The huge data set has been processed at the computer to formulate the relevant tables, some of which constitute the basis of our multiple regression exercises reported in *Chapter 6*.

2

Balance of Payments Theory and Economic Development—A Survey of Literature

The adjustment of an economy and its policies to balance of payments disequilibrium (surplus or deficit) is not always smooth, and in a developing country like India with so many structural and institutional rigidities, adoption of optimal policies to tackle balance of payments disequilibrium often leads to other domestic economic problems particularly in the immediate run. In order to comprehend the adjustment mechanism that a country facing balance of payments deficit usually obtains under alternative specifications and to assess the efficacy of the policies adopted, we need to have a close look at the theoretical underpinnings of such adjustment behaviours particularly in a developing economy. The implications of the various studies to assess India's balance of payments positions and policies can be evaluated in the proper perspective only when we make a comprehensive review of the important theoretical developments in balance of payments, economic interdependence, exchange rate variations and macroeconomic policies in general, and their implications for economic growth and development process in particular.

The present chapter deals with a critical review of the theoretical literature on balance of payments and macro-economic management in an open economy under alternative exchange rate regimes, including the implications of such theoretical insights for the study of economic growth and development.

2.1 ALTERNATIVE APPROACHES TO BALANCE OF PAYMENTS

There are different theoretical approaches to the study of balance of payments adjustments, each pointing to the significance of different adjustment variables in ensuring policy-induced corrections in the disequilibrium of balance of payments. The reliance on price adjustments in equilibrating demand for and supply of foreign exchange is reflected in the famous Elasticity Approach to Balance of Payments, and the derivation of the Marshall-Lerner condition under specific assumptions. The Keynesian revolution in macro-economic theory has emphasized the importance of income adjustment in a situation of macroeconomic disequilibrium, and the open economy extensions of this framework has led to the emergence of Absorption Approach to Balance of Payments. The integration of elasticity and absorption approaches has also been attempted in the literature to review the impact of devaluation on trade balance and real income in terms of both income and substitution effects of such variations in the exchange rate. While these two approaches primarily focus on adjustments in flow variables to policy shocks or exogenous changes, the disequilibrium in a country's balance of payments has the twin dimensions of flows and stocks adjustments, and the Monetary and the Portfolio Approaches to Balance of Payments emphasize the need to integrate both the dimensions and also relate the interactions between the current account and the capital account, and the effectiveness of alternative policy interventions. While there is an urgent need to evolve an integrated framework and evaluate the relative strength of alternative adjustment variables, we shall discuss the four alternative approaches mentioned above separately so as to obtain insights into the operation of these different macro-variables in balance of payments adjustments.

2.1.1 The Elasticity Approach to the Balance of Payments

The elasticity approach to the BoP provides an analysis of what happens to the current account balance when the country devaluates its currency. In other words, can devaluation improve the balance of payments? If so, what are the precise conditions under which such a policy will prove successful? These were some of the fundamental questions that preoccupied some theorists in the 1920s and the 1940s and which led to the development of an approach that came to be known as the elasticity approach to BoP. Among the most cited contributions to the early development of the elasticities approach are Bickerdicke (1920), Marshall (1923), Lerner (1944), Robinson (1947) and Metzler (1949). The standard model analyses the effect of an exchange rate change on the current account in terms of separate markets for home-produced and foreign produced goods, typically abstracting from the existence of any non-tradable goods. The following streamlined exposition of the model draws heavily on Bickerdicke (1920).

We start with the trade balance:

$$BOT = Ex - Im = Pex.ex - Pim.im \tag{2.1}$$

with BOT = balance of trade, Ex = value of exports, Im = value of imports, Pex = price of exports, Pim = price of imports, ex = export volume, im = import volume.

Taking the total differential yields:

$$dBOT = dEx - dIm \tag{2.2}$$

or,

$$\frac{dBOT}{Im} = \frac{dEx}{Im} - \frac{dIm}{Im} \tag{2.3}$$

We define,

$\eta BOT = \left(\frac{dBOT}{\text{Im}}\right) / \left(\frac{de}{e}\right) =$ the elasticity of the trade balance with respect to the rate of exchange (e).

$\eta Ex = \left(\frac{dEx}{Ex}\right) / \left(\frac{de}{e}\right) =$ the elasticity of the supply of foreign exchange.

$\eta \text{Im} = \left(\frac{d\,\text{Im}}{\text{Im}}\right) / \left(\frac{de}{e}\right) =$ the elasticity of the demand for foreign exchange.

Now dividing both the left-hand term and the right-hand term of equation (2.3) through by de/e:

$$\eta BOT = \left(\frac{Ex}{\text{Im}}\right) \eta Ex - \eta \,\text{Im} \qquad (2.4)$$

We trace the demand and supply elasticities of imports and exports underlying this equation. Demand and supply depends on prices. Assuming equilibrium in the market for export goods:

ex = Sex(Pex.e) = Dex(Pex) (2.5)

With S = Supply and D = Demand

Taking differentials, we obtain

dex = (∂Sex/∂Pex) (e.dPex + Pex.de) = (∂Dex/∂Pex) dPex (2.6)

or

dex/ex= (∂Sex/dPex) (1/Sex) (e.dPex + Pex.de) = (∂Dex/∂Pex) (1/Dex)dPex (2.7)

Dividing through by de/e and multiplying both the numerators and the denominators by P results in:

$$\frac{\frac{dex}{ex}}{\frac{de}{e}} = \left[\frac{\partial Sex.Pex}{\partial Pex.Sex}\right]\left(\frac{\frac{dPex}{Pex}}{\frac{de}{e}} + 1\right) = \left[\frac{\partial Dex.Pex}{\partial Pex.Dex}\right]\frac{\frac{dPex}{Pex}}{\frac{de}{e}} \qquad (2.8)$$

The expression within square brackets on the left-hand side is the price elasticity of export supply, Sex, and the expression within square brackets on the right-hand side is the foreign price elasticity of demand for import goods, η_f. For equation (2.8) we may, therefore, write

$$\frac{\frac{dex}{ex}}{\frac{de}{e}} = sex\left(\frac{\frac{dPex}{Pex}}{\frac{de}{e}} + 1\right) + 1 = \eta_f \cdot \frac{\frac{dPex}{Pex}}{\frac{de}{e}} \tag{2.9}$$

From equation (2.9) we derive the relative change in export prices in terms of foreign currency with respect to the exchange rate change:

$$\left(\frac{dPex}{Pex}\right) / \left(\frac{de}{e}\right) = \frac{Sex}{(\eta_f - Sex)} \tag{2.9A}$$

As the supply elasticity is zero or positive and the demand elasticity, abstracting from Giffen goods, is zero or negative, this expression must have zero or negative value.

For small variations, the change in export earnings may be represented as the sum of the change in volume and the change in price:

$$\eta Ex = (dex/ex)/(de/e) + (dPex/Pex)(de/e) \tag{2.10}$$

Substituting equations 2.9 and 2.9A in 2.10, we obtain

$$\eta Ex = (\eta_f Sex)/(\eta_f - Sex) + Sex/(\eta_f - Sex)$$
$$=(\eta_f+1)/[(\eta_f/Sex)-1)] \tag{2.11}$$

For the import goods we, again, start off with the equilibrium condition

$$Im=Sim\ (Pim)=Dim(Pim.e) \tag{2.12}$$

and find in a similar way as in the use of the export goods the elasticity of the demand for foreign exchange with respect to the rate of exchange.

$$\eta Im=(Sim+1)/[(Sim/\eta_d) - 1] \leq 0 \tag{2.13}$$

with Sim = the supply elasticity of imports and
η_d = the domestic price elasticity of import demand.

Substituting equations 2.11 and 2.14 into 2.4, we obtain for the elasticity of the trade balance:

$$\eta BOT=(Ex/Im) . \{(\eta_f + 1)/ [(\eta_f / Sex) -1]\} - (Sim + 1)/ [(Sim/ \eta_d) -1] \quad (2.14)$$

This is often referred to as Bickerdicke-Metzler-Robinson condition, derived by Bickerdicke (1920) and exposited by Robinson (1947) and Metzler (1949).

In the case of rigid prices and infinitely elasticity supply elasticities, equation (2.14) simplifies to

$$\eta BOT=(Ex/Im) (-\eta_f -1) - \eta_d \quad (2.15)$$

If we start from equilibrium, that is Ex=Im, we find the Marshall-Lerner condition. Alfred Marshall in 1879 and Abba Lerner again and independently in 1944, developed the principal theorem of this approach and it is with the two names that the theorem is now identified. [For an analytical review of Alfred Marshall's contributions, one may see Karmakar (1996)]. If $\eta_f + \eta_d < -1$, $\eta BOT > 0$, then the current account improves. If Ex/Im<1, that is, if we have a trade deficit to start with, the Marshall-Lerner condition is a sufficient but not necessary for the trade balance to improve.

We now analyse the effects of devaluation on the terms of trade. For small variations, we may write the elasticity of the terms of trade (TOT) with respect to the rate of exchange rate as:

It means :

$$\eta ToT = Sex/(\eta_f - Sex) - \eta_d/ (Sim - \eta_d)$$
$$= (Sex.Sim - \eta_f\eta_d)/[(\eta_f - Sex) (Sim - \eta_d)] \quad (2.16)$$

A devaluation then makes the terms of trade improve if $\eta_f \eta_d >$ Sex.Sim

If $\eta_f\ \eta_d$ = Sex. Sim, the terms of trade do not change.

If $\eta_f\ \eta_d$ < Sex. Sim, the terms of trade worsen.

There are two effects in play once a currency is devalued:

(i) *The price effect*—exports become cheaper measured in foreign currency. Imports become more expensive measured in the home currency. The price effect contributes to a worsening of the current account.

(ii) *The volume effect*—the fact that exports become cheaper should encourage an increased volume of exports and the fact that imports become more expensive should lead to a decreased volume of imports. The volume effect contributes to improving the current balance. The net effect depends on whether the price or the volume effect dominates.

The elasticities approach has a number of limitations. First, the import demand functions and export supply functions depend only on the nominal prices of the goods in equilibrium, rather than on relative prices and appropriate scale variables such as real income and productive capacity. Second, the very concept of a trade imbalance implies that goods are paid for with an asset that has not been explicitly included in the analysis. Third, changes in the trade balance correspond identically in the national income accounts to changes in the difference between domestic production and domestic absorption, neither of which enters the model explicitly. The equations provide only a partial equilibrium framework for analysing the BoP effects of exchange rate changes since the analysis is concentrated on the foreign exchange market whose supply results from exports of goods and services and whose demand is derived from imports of goods and services. Fourth, elasticity pessimists are vociferous by saying a devaluation may work better for industrialised countries than for developing countries. Many developing countries are heavily dependent on imports so that the price elasticity of demand for imports was likely to be very low. While for industrialized countries that had to face competitive export markets, the price elasticity of demand for their exports may be quite elastic. The implication of the Marshall-Lerner condition was that devaluation might be a cure for some countries' BoP deficits but not for others.

In spite of the shortcomings of the elasticity approach to devaluation and the unrealistic assumptions on which the entire analysis is based, those (the elasticity optimists) who defend the use of currency depreciation to rectify BoP deficits still cling strongly to favour evidence relating to price elasticities of demand for exports and imports in support of their case. It is interesting to note that equilibrium in international transactions will be stable if the Marshall-Lerner condition is satisfied no matter whether trade is barter or monetary in nature. This implies neutrality of money in the international context as well, definable only in equilibrium.

To sum up the above discussion we must underline the fact that this elasticity approach is very simplistic and essentially static; it has very little to say about the forces at work that eliminate balance of payments disequilibrium and whether these forces are *dynamically stable.* All it does is to indicate the initial trade balance (TB) in response to a change in the exchange rate.

A general consensus accepted by most economists is that elasticities are lower in the short run than in the long-run, in which case the Marshall-Lerner condition may not hold good in the medium to long run, since export and import volumes take time to react to changes in relative prices in the short run. Moreover, to explain the slow responsiveness of export and import volumes in the short-run, the most important are: (i) a time lag in consumer response, (ii) a time lag in producer response, and (iii) imperfect competition.

The possibility that in the short run the Marshall-Lerner conditions may not be fulfilled although it generally holds over the long run, connotes to what is popularly known as the J-curve effect which is illustrated in Figure 2.1. The curve plots the balance of payments current account balance against time.

The idea underlying the J-curve effect is that in the short run export volumes and import volumes do not change much so that the country receives less export revenue and spends more on imports leading to a deterioration in the current account balance, ultimately resulting in destabilising falls in the

FIG. 2.1
The J-curve Effect

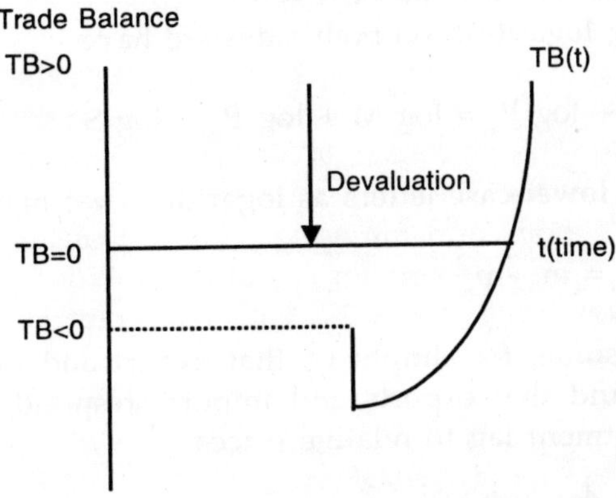

exchange rate and so on. However, after a time lag export volumes start to increase and import volumes start to decline. Consequently the current account deficit starts to improve and eventually moves into surplus.

The J-curve phenomenon may be stated as follows:

> A once-and-for-all fall in the exchange rate will cause the current account to worsen in the short run until higher export volumes and lower imports eventually generate the conventional favourable current account response, assuming that the Marshall-Lerner conditions hold. Thus the dynamic pattern of the current account traces out a J-curve.

To elaborate these dynamics, we introduce the following notation and a simple model of the current account. The current account may be written as:

$$CA = X.P_x - MP_m/S = 0 \quad (2.17)$$

where X = Volume of exports
M = Volume of imports
P_x = Price of exports (home currency)
P_m = Price of imports (foreign currency)
S = Exchange rate (foreign currency per unit of domestic currency).

We assume that there are no capital flows and that there is no foreign exchange intervention implying that the current account must balance, i.e., CA = 0

Taking logarithm on both sides we have

$$\log X + \log P_x = \log M + \log P_m - \log S \tag{2.18}$$

Using lower-case letters as logarithms we may write:

$$x + p_x = m + p_m - s \tag{2.19}$$

We assume, for simplicity, that export and import prices are given and that exports and imports respond with a first order adjustment lag to relative prices:

$$x = -\frac{\lambda_1}{D+\lambda_1}\eta_1 \left(p_x + s - p_x{}^*\right) \tag{2.20}$$

$$m = -\frac{\lambda_2}{D+\lambda_2}\eta_2 \left(p_m + s - p\right) \tag{2.21}$$

where p = Domestic price level,

P* = Price of competitor's exports (foreign currency)

D = d/t (differential operator),

η_1 is the long-run price elasticity of demand for exports, and

η_2 is the corresponding elasticity of demand for imports. $\lambda_1$and λ_2 are expotential lag parameters. Fulfilment of the Marshall-Lerner conditions implies $\eta_1+\eta_2>1$.

If the exchange rate is flexible it must move over time to balance the current account. Thus the BoP identity given in (2.19) acts as market-clearing condition in the foreign exchange market. Incipient current account deficits depress the exchange rate and *vice-versa*. To determine the dynamic implications for the exchange rate we may substitute equation (2.20) and (2.21) into (2.19) and solve the second-order differential equation that is obtained. We do so under the assumption that P_x and P are perfectly correlated, that P_m and P_x^* are similarly related and that P and p_m^*m are constants. The differential equation of the system is:

$$(-D^2 + \alpha_1 D + \alpha_0)\ S = -\alpha_0\ (P - P_x^*) \tag{2.21A}$$

where $\alpha_1 = \lambda_1\ (\eta_1 - 1) + \lambda_2\ (\eta_2 - 1)$ e″ 0

$$\alpha_0 = \lambda_1\ \lambda_2\ (\eta_2 + \eta_1 - 1) > 0$$

The general solution that describes the dynamic path of the exchange rate is:

$$S\ (t) = A_1 e^{r1t} + A_2 e^{r2t} + p_x^* - p$$

where A_1 and A_2 are arbitrary constants and r_1 and r_2 are the roots of the system

$$r_1 = \left[-\alpha_1 \pm \sqrt{\alpha_1^2 - 4\alpha_0}\right]/2$$

Necessary and sufficient conditions for stability are that both α_1 and α_0 be negative. However, the Marshall-Lerner condition that $\alpha_0 > 0$ rules this out. The J-curve phenomenon sends the exchange rate into a nose-dive from which it recovers. For example, a fall in the exchange rate worsens the current account in the short-run which in turn causes the exchange rate to fall further. Although export volumes rise continuously and import volumes fall continuously, import volumes grow faster than export volumes and thus the exchange rate instability persists. However, this instability may be neutralized by speculative behaviour that reflects rational expectations. (Beenstock, 1990)

A very interesting J-curve phenomenon followed the decline in the dollar from early 1985. In fact, the US current account deficit, rather than declining, continued to grow (both in dollars and as a percentage of GNP) through 1987. Did this mean that the traditional adjustment mechanism no longer worked? Krugman (1991) argued that it worked pretty well as expected, but with a rather long lag. As the estimated sum of the average long-run price elasticity of US import demand (1.1) and that of exports (0.8) exceeded unity, they were sufficient to ensure that devaluation, cet par, should work to correct a current account deficit. However, the corresponding short-run elasticities were much lower. The combination of price and volume effects, in the short-run, served to raise spending on imports more than dollar export earnings rose and accounted for some of the J-curve effects. Moreover, several other factors contributed to the J-curve effects of 1985-87. First, the dollar had sharply appreciated to the prior years' level. Secondly, 'other things were not equal': during the period, GNP in the USA grew at high rate as fast in Germany and Japan which, given the income elasticities served to worsen the US current account deficit

Senhadji (1998) after examining 30 developing countries had found a remarkable robustness of a S-curve (the curve that shows negative correlation between trade balance and current and future movements of terms of trade and trade balances' positive correlation with past movements of terms of trade). It does not appear to be typical of developing countries, but it applies to developed countries also.

2.1.2 The Absorption Approach to the Balance of Payments

The early expositors of the elasticities approach recognised its limitations. By the beginning of the 1950s, the effects of a devaluation on national income and/or employment had been modelled formally by Robinson (1947), Harberger (1950), Meade (1951), and Alexander (1952), among others. This new body of analysis—sometimes referred to as the 'Absorption Approach'—was properly perceived not as a rejection of the Marshallian focus on price elasticities, but rather as an attempt to integrate the elasticities approach with the Keynesian theory of effective demand about national income. The absorption approach emphasized that a devaluation of the home currency, by lowering the relative price of the home good and thereby inducing a shift in the composition of demand, would lead to an increase in home output and a decline in foreign output. It was also recognised that the effects on home output and income would have feedback effects on trade flows, and accordingly, a devaluation that improved the trade balance would do so by less than the amounts suggested by a simple elasticities approach in which these feedback effects were ignored. Hence the absorption approach is more macroeconomic since it takes into account the market for domestic goods with both income and price adjustments.

The static elasticities-absorption model of the current account received a new thrust of attention in the early 1970s. The exchange rate changes that followed the collapse of the Bretton Woods system, including in particular the depreciation of the US dollar, renewed interest in the time profiles of the responses of traded good prices and quantities to changes in the exchange rate and gave birth to the concept of the 'J-curve' discussed earlier. The more sophisticated analysis suggested that the set of feasible time profiles of the current account following a devaluation resembled 'alphabet soup' (Magee, 1973).

The following exposition of the absorption model draws heavily on IMF economist Sydney Alexander (1952). The absorption approach to BoP states that a country's balance of trade will only improve if the country's output of goods and services increases by more than its absorption, where the term 'absorption' means expenditure by domestic residents on goods and services. The novelty of this approach may be appreciated by considering the particular question. 'Will a devaluation improve a country's balance of trade?' The elasticities approach, we know, answers the question by focusing on the price elasticities of supply and demand for exports and imports. It holds that the devaluation will be successful if the price elasticities of demand for exports and imports are large enough so that the increase in exports sold to foreigners and the reduction in imports bought by domestic residents together more than offset the terms of trade loss caused by the devaluation (A special case of this result is formalized in the Marshall-Lerner conditions). The absorption approach argues, in contrast, that the devaluation will only be successful if it causes the gap between domestic output and domestic absorption to widen. In effect Alexander criticised the elasticities approach on the ground that it gave an overfacile view of the ease of correcting a trade deficit by devaluation and it focused on the movement along given supply and demand curves in the particular markets for exports and imports (a microeconomic approach), instead of looking at the production and spending of the nation as a whole which shift these curves (a macroeconomic approach).

Alexander's criticism of the elasticities approach is valid. Let the symbols Y, C, I, G, X and M stand for output, consumption, investment, government expenditure, exports and imports respectively. Then the Keynesian income expenditure *identity* states that

$$Y=C+I+G+X-M \tag{2.22}$$

which may be written

$$X-M=Y-(C+I+G) \tag{2.22A}$$

This *identity* states precisely that trade balance (CA) will improve, if output Y increases by more than absorption (A = C+I+G). Transferring equation (2.22A) into first difference form yields:

$$dCA=dY-dA \tag{2.23}$$

What the equation (2.23) implies is that the effects of a devaluation on the current balance will depend upon how it affects national income relative to how it affects domestic spending. If devaluation raises domestic spending relative to domestic income the current account deteriorates. Understanding how devaluation affects both income and absorption is, therefore, central to the absorption approach to BoP analysis.

Absorption can be divided up into two parts: a rise in income will lead to an increase in absorption which is determined by the marginal propensity to absorb, a*. There will also be a direct effect on absorption, which is all the other effects on absorption resulting from devaluation denoted by AD. Thus the change in total absorption dA, is given by:

$$dA = a^*dY + dAD. \tag{2.24}$$

Substitution yields:

$$dCA = (1\text{-}a^*)\ dY - dAD \tag{2.25}$$

Equation above reveals that there are three factors that need to be examined when considering the impact of devaluation. A devaluation can affect the current balance only by changing the marginal propensity to absorb (a*), changing the level of income (dY) and by affecting direct absorption (dAD). The condition for a devaluation to improve the current balance is:

$$(1\text{–}a^*)\ dY > dAD \tag{2.26}$$

that is, any change in income not spent on absorption must exceed any change in direct absorption.

Overall, the effects of a devaluation on the income of the devaluing country are ambiguous. Even if there are increased net exports earnings (which relies on the Marshall-Lerner condition being fulfilled), the negative terms of trade effect works to reduce national income.

Even if income rises overall, it is still not clear what the implications of a rise in income are for the current account; this will depend upon the value of the marginal propensity to absorb. If this is less than unity then an increase in income generated by the increase in net exports leads to an improvement in the current balance because income rises by more than absorption. Alexander speculated that unemployed workers who obtain jobs are likely to have a high propensity to consume and that an increase in income may well stimulate a great deal of investment. Similarly as the economy expands, firms' expenditure may exceed their revenues. Hence it is conceivable in the short-run that marginal propensity to absorb could be greater than unity, so that a rise in income leads to a deterioration in the current account.

The other effects that we need to consider are the impact on direct absorption.

Real Balance effect: A simple formulation of the demand to hold money is that it is a demand to real money balances. Algebraically a money demand function can be expressed as:

$M/P_1 = k$, where k is some constant and P_1 is an aggregate price index.

To consider whether the above condition is likely to be fulfilled it is worth distinguishing two possible states of an economy: below full employment so that income may rise, and full employment so that national income cannot rise.

There are two important effects on income that need to be examined, the employment effect and the terms of trade effect.

Employment effect: If the economy is at less than full employment, then provided the Marshall-Lerner condition is fulfilled, there will be an increase in net exports following a devaluation which will lead to an increase in national income via the foreign trade multiplier. However, if the Marshall-Lerner condition is not fulfilled, then net exports will fall implying that national income falls. Hence it is not clear whether the employment effects will raise or lower national income.

Term of trade effect: A devaluation [a rise in exchange rate (e) in the equation of terms of trade = P/ep^* where P is the domestic price of exports, p^* is the price of imports and e is the exchange rate (domestic currency units per unit of foreign currency)] tends to make imports more expensive in domestic currency terms which is not matched by a corresponding rise in export prices. This means that the terms of trade deteriorates. A deterioration in the terms of trade represents a loss of real national income. Hence the terms of trade effect lowers real national income, which for constant absorption implies a bigger trade deficit.

Given the unchanged money stock and the assumption that economic agents aim to maintain a given amount of real money balance as depicted in equation above, then a devaluation by raising the overall price index means that economic agents have to maintain their real balances by cutting down on direct absorption. Economic agents will attempt to increase their money balances by selling bonds; this pushes down the prices of bonds and raise the domestic interest rate. The rise in interest rates will reduce investment and consumption, so reducing direct absorption.

Income redistribution effect: The rise in the general price index resulting from a devaluation is likely to have a number of effects on the income distribution. However, it is extremely difficult to say whether the income redistribution effects will raise or lower direct absorption. There is money illusion effect as well as expectational effects. Laursen-Metzler (1950) noted that the deterioration in the terms of trade following a devaluation will have two effects on absorption, an income effect and a substitution effect. While the deterioration in the terms of trade lowers national income and thereby income related absorption also makes domestically produced goods relatively cheaper compared with foreign produced goods, which implies a substitution effect in favour of domestically produced goods. Since domestically produced goods become relatively cheaper this will tend to raise direct absorption. If the positive substitution effect outweighs the negative income effect, Laursen and Metzler noted that a deterioration of the terms of trade could lead to a net rise in absorption.

Hence, the effects of a devaluation on direct absorption are ambiguous. While the real money balance effect works to lower direct absorption all the other effects may raise or lower direct absorption. Overall, the approach suggests that a devaluation will have many diverse and conflicting effects on the current account.

Despite above limitations, the absorption approach has some important lessons for policy makers. Its central message is that raising domestic income relative to domestic-absorption will improve the current balance. In this respect, a devaluation is more likely to succeed if it is accompanied by economic policy measures that concentrate on raising income while constraining absorption. It is noteworthy that IMF stabilization programme designed to deal with a payment deficit typically involved deflationary fiscal and monetary measures as well as devaluation.

Initially, it was thought that the absorption approach was an alternative to the elasticities approach. While the elasticity approach concentrated on price effects, the absorption approach concentrated on income effects. However, authors such as Tsiang (1961), and Alexander (1959) himself showed that the two models are not substitutes, rather they are complementary.

To understand this complementarity, we may consider the effects of a devaluation on income. Exports will increase more than imports, so raising income only if Marshall-Lerner elasticities condition is fulfilled. If the Marshall-Lerner condition is not fulfilled, then exports will rise by less than imports implying that income will fall. Hence, the Marshall-Lerner condition is clearly relevant to the absorption approach.

It is true that both elasticity and absorption models are essentially static in nature. But the merit is that they both point to the importance of dynamic forces and a time dimension to the eventual outcome. This is plausible as we have seen the possible J-curve effect alongside the effects of devaluation on income and absorption that can spread over time.

The absorption approach essentially deals with flow of expenditure in determining trade balance. It ignores the stock dimensions of balance of payments disequilibrium, and concentrates only on the current account transactions. But when a country's balance of payments is in disequilibrium, both stocks and flows are altered affecting transactions in current and capital accounts together. In the words of Harry Johnson (1961): "Two sorts of aggregate decision leading to a balance of payments deficit may be distinguished in principle . . . between 'stock' decisions and 'flow' decisions: a (stock) decision to alter the composition of the community's assets by substituting other assets for domestic money, and a (flow) decisions to spend currently in excess of current receipts. Since both real goods and securities are alternative assets to domestic money, and current expenditure may consist in the purchase of either goods or securities the balance of payments deficit resulting from either type of aggregate decision may show itself on either current or capital account. . . . The importance of the distinction stems from the fact that a 'stock' deficit is inherently temporary and implies no real worsening of the country's economic position whereas a 'flow' deficit is not inherently temporary and may imply a worsening of the country's economic position."

It may be noted that a stock disequilibrium can be related to a flow disequilibrium with the help of intertemporal budget constraint, and hence it is useful to visualize an integrated framework of an open economy when both the dimensions and their relations are captured in a coherent manner. The Monetary Approach to Balance of Payments is an attempt in this direction. Initially it was conceived of an extension of the full employment quantity theory of money into a global economy context drawing on 'Hume's idea of 'price-specie-flow mechanism', but later the framework has been extended in various directions, integrating it with the general equilibrium theory of international trade developed by Heckscher, Ohlin and Samuelson among others. When non-traded goods are included, a devaluation has resource allocation effects via the Rybczynski and Stolper-Samuelson theorems; but the change in the real balances following a rise in the price of tradeables owing to devaluation adjusts the flow of expenditure to result in a trade surplus in the short-run. In the long-run the flow of money from the deficit to the surplus countries leads to another rounds of expenditure adjustments resulting in zero trade balance for each country in the long-run.

2.1.3 Monetary Approach to the Balance of Payments (MABP) Theory

Though the absorption approach provides us a useful perspective from which to view the trade balance; it is not a theory to get an answer to the question like: what determines absorption and of what determines output? It only deals with the trade balance: a full theory of the BoP requires a theory of capital account movements and a discussion of how the exchange rate itself is determined. The absorption approach does not deal with monetary conditions. For example, a devaluation because it raises prices, may initially also cause higher interest rates which helps to curtail absorption. But if the improvement in the trade balance caused by the devaluation is allowed to lead to an expansion of the domestic money supply, then gradually interest rates will fall, absorption will rise and the effects of the devaluation may turn out to be temporary. This issue has been analysed succinctly not by the absorption approach but by the Monetary Approach to the balance of payments, which predicts, as for example, that a disequilibrium in the money market creates a disequilibrium in the Balance of Payments.

The MABP adjustment explanation was developed by classical economists primarily at the University of Chicago. This monetary approach relies on a mechanism similar to David Hume's spicie-flow analysis, but it is not tied to nation's operating on the gold standard. Johnson (1976) succinctly summed up this monetary approach by claiming there all 'BoP deficits or surpluses are by this nature transient and self-correcting, requiring no deliberate policy to correct them'. The reason is simply that deficits reduce money supply and surpluses build up the stocks. Johnson has loaded the deck by postulating that trade deficits are always the result of an excessive supply of money, and by assuming that there must exist a Walrasian price vector that assures the simultaneous clearing of all markets when goods trade for goods. Given the above conditions, trade imbalances are always eliminated by relative price level movements between the trading partners. The entire problem is resolved by assuming gross substitution adjustment and the absence of any income effect. Thus, it appears that this MABP is firmly based on the classical axioms of gross substitution and the neutrality of money. However, the modern revived of MABP originated in the writings of James Meade followed by Harry G. Johnson and Robert A. Mundell in the 1960s.

The fundamental basis of the modern monetary approach is that the BoP is essentially a monetary phenomenon since deficits or surplus is defined by changes in the international reserves by Central Bank. Not only is the BoP a measurement of monetary flows but such flows can only be explained by a disequilibrium in the stock demand for and supply of money. Since this approach is basically a supply and demand analysis of the money market in an economy, any excesse stock demand for or supply of money is exactly reflected in flows through the BoP. If changes in the money supply are not matched by equivalent changes in demand, then a stock disequilibrium arises. In the open economy changes in the money stock can arise from domestic credit creation as well as from the foreign exchange operations of the monetary authorities. As a result, the monetary approach to the BoP stresses that money market disequilibrium are reflected not only in changes in nominal income but also in the country's overall BoP, as represented by changes in the foreign exchange reserves. Thus, the monetary approach to BoP theory focuses on the relation among prices, output, interest rates and the BoP.

A simple example will make it clear. Let us consider first the familiar balance sheet of the Central Bank:

Assets	Liabilities
D	
F	H

Where H is high powered money, F is the foreign-backed component of H and D is the domestic asset component of H. The domestic money supply is then determined as some multiple of H:

$$M \equiv hH \equiv h\,(F+D) \tag{2.27}$$

where h is the conventional money multiplier, we assume that $h = 1$.

On taking first differences of (2.27) and rearranging:

$$\Delta F = \Delta M - \Delta D \tag{2.28}$$

where clearly ΔF is the change in reserves, ΔD is the change in the domestic component of money supply or domestic credit expansion and ΔM is the change in the money stock which in the MABP literature is the flow demand for money, or hoarding. Now it is known that with a fixed exchange rate system the change in reserves is equal to the sum of the current and capital accounts of the BoP, i.e.,

$$\Delta F = B+K \tag{2.29}$$

where B represents the current account balance (a flow) and K is the capital account balance (also assumed to be a flow). Thus if both the current account and capital account are in deficit the country must be losing reserves. Equation (2.28) explains why, for the country to be losing reserves, domestic credit expansion must exceed hoarding. Thus to control BoP deficit domestic credit expansion has to be controlled relative to the flow demand for money. Alternatively, if ΔM is greater than ΔD then there is an excess flow of demand for money which in an open economy can be satisfied by the public bonds and goods for reserves i.e., the country will run a BoP surplus.

It is now shown that the monetary approach identities, in an *ex post* accounting sense, should give the same result for the change in reserves as the elasticities and absorption approaches.

From the national income accounting it is known that *ex post*.

$$Y = A+B \qquad (2.30)$$

when A represents aggregate absorption and B represents the trade balance. The elasticities approach utilizes the relationship:

$$B = X-M \qquad (2.31)$$

and assuming that the Marshall-Lerner condition holds, a devaluation leads to an improvement in the balance of trade. The absorption approach draws, on the other hand, attention to the fact that the balance of trade can only be improved if income is increased relative to absorption and a country may require a combination of expenditure switching (devaluation) and expenditure—reducing policies:

$$B = Y-A \qquad (2.32)$$

Using (2.28), (2.29) (assuming for simplicity that K = 0), (2.30) (2.31) and (2.32) and taking all variables as *ex post* identities, then

$$\Delta F = B = X - M = Y - A = \Delta M - \Delta D \qquad (2.33)$$

Thus, in an *ex post* sense the three approaches are equivalent. The identity (2.33) does highlight the question that, if the three different approaches are potentially reconciliable why do proponents of the MABP favour using equation (2.28) rather than (2.31) or (2.32)? This is clear from the fact that the overall aggregate budget constraint of a closed economy in which there are goods, bonds and money, would necessarily imply that the sum of the excess demand equals zero. Thus

$$EDg + EDb + EDm = 0 \qquad (2.34)$$

where ED represents an excess demand and the subscripts g, b and m represent goods, bonds and money respectively. In an open economy such an excess demand will be reflected in different net international flows in the BoP accounts. If the country is not small but has some influence on world prices, it can be expected that excess demand will be eliminated by both price changes and international flows. The BoP flows will be constrained by

$$(Xg - Mg) + (Xb - Mb) + (Xm - Mm) = 0 \qquad (2.35)$$

where X and M represent exports and imports respectively. Thus the three accounts the current, capital and money must sum to zero.

The budget constraint implies that if two of the markets are in equilibrium, so also must the third market be. With the elasticities approach, with no capital account, attention is concentrated on the current account and the money market is ignored. But this will be valid only if the crucial nature of the money market is ignored. Thus money is a stock concept and the demand for money is a demand for a stock, not for a continuing flow of money.

The money identity of equation (2.27) shows that in an open economy residents of that country can have an influence on the total quantity of money via their ability to convert domestic money into foreign goods and securities. In this context, proponents of the monetary approach argue that it is arguable to concentrate directly on the underlying disequilibrium in the money market. A direct consequence of analysing the BoP as a monetary phenomenon is that it is clearly seen to be a stock phenomenon and not a flow phenomenon.

In order to assess the major implications of the monetary approach to the BoP, it is useful to present a simplified model within a small, fully employed country operating under a fixed exchange rate system, with full integration of domestic and foreign goods and capital markets. Perfect arbitrage determines the prices of domestic commodities and of financial assets.

Because of its concentration on the money market, the monetary approach to the BoP involves the explicit specification of the money supply process and of a demand for money function. The supply of money (M^S) is the product of the stock of high-powered money (H) and the money supply multiplier (m) where the latter reflects the behaviour of asset holders and the banking system:

$$M^S = mH \quad (2.36)$$

By definition, the stock of high powered money is equal to the domestic currency value of the stock of international reserves, eR (where e is the exchange rate defined as the domestic currency price of foreign exchange and R is the foreign currency value of international reserves), and the domestic asset holdings of the monetary authorities (D):

$$H = eR + D \quad (2.37)$$

The demand for real money balances is specified as the positive function of real income and a negative function of the opportunity cost of holding money. The opportunity cost is usually represented by rate of interest.

The demand for money in nominal terms (M^d) can be written as :

$$M^d = Pf\ (Y, i) \quad (2.38)$$

where P is the domestic price level, Y is the level of domestic real income, and i stands for the domestic nominal interest rate.

Money market equilibrium implies that $M^s = M^d$. Under the assumptions the mechanism operates through changes in international reserves. Accordingly, using s(2.36), (2.37) and (2.38) the stock of international reserves can be specified as:

$$R = g\ (P, Y, i, m, D) \quad (2.39)$$

Equation (2.39) represents the key relationship implied by the monetary approach and the BoP under a fixed exchange rate system. The assumed specifications of M^s and M^d imply that an increase in real income and in (world) prices raises R, while an increase in i, in the money multiplier, and in the domestic asset of the central bank reduces the stock of international reserves. These changes in R are reflected in BoP surplus or deficits. In this simple model, a rise in the money supply brought about by an open market purchase (an increase in D) is completely offset by a corresponding fall in R.

The simplified model presented above may be seen as a prototype of the monetary approach to the BoP and can be regarded as a representation of its long-run equilibrium characteristics, when all adjustments have taken place. In the circumstances, monetary imbalances tend to offset primarily the BoP. In the short run, monetary imbalances also offset prices, output, and interest rate and the relative importance of these effects depends on various factors such as the nature of exchange rate management, the degree of openness of the economy and so forth.

Extensions of the basic framework have considered the effects of exchange rate changes on prices and on the BoP. In contrast with other approaches to the BoP analysis, (notably elasticity and absorption approach), the monetary approach stresses that the effects of a once-and-for-all exchange rate adjustment in a small economy are transitory. A devaluation (a rise in e) raises the price of internationally tradeable goods. This increase in price reduces the real value of the nominal money stock and in order to restore money market equilibrium, a BoP surplus is generated as foreign exchange reserves flow into the country. As monetary equilibrium is restored, the flow of reserve stops.

We can examine the effects of income growth and of external shocks. As shown by the equation (2.39), changes in the level of income have a direct impact on the BoP through their effect on the demand for money. Therefore, an acceleration in a country's rate of growth, by increasing the demand for liquidity, tends to improve the BoP provided that domestic credit policy does not expand accordingly.

Another criticism is that no attention is paid to the composition of a deficit and surplus. If there is a large deficit in the current account which is financed by an offsetting surplus in the capital account the monetarists argue that this means that there is no need for any policy concern with regard to the BoP. Indeed, because any surplus or deficit is necessarily a transitory feature representing a stock disequilibrium in the money market which is necessarily self-correcting, a policy with regard to BoP is unnecessary. Such an approach ignores the dangers of increasing indebtedness due to current account deficit being financed by capital inflows. In the real world it is the increase in such indebtedness that causes much concern for policymakers of the countries concerned..

In spite of the shortcomings, the monetary approach provides a distinctive and clear analysis of the effect of a devaluation and monetary expansion on the BoP. Its emphasis on disequilibrium in the BoP being a flow response to stock disequilibrium in the money market represents an important contribution to the research on international economics. Nevertheless this approach marks the beginning of a new perspective, an asset approach to determining the exchange rate, which has proved fruitful in explaining volatile behaviour of current markets.

Another significant contribution of the monetary approach is that it provides a rich set of policy recommendations. A country that opts to fix its exchange rate will lose its monetary autonomy and a monetary expansion can lead to temporary BoP deficits, whereas a country that allows its currency to float will have monetary autonomy but a monetary expansion then leads to a depreciation of its currency. Hence, it provides a warning to policy makers that reckless monetary expansion can lead to BoP problems under fixed exchange rates or a currency problem under floating exchange rates also affect the BoP through the same mechanism. The basic model can also be used to determine the effects of commercial policies such as an import tariff. A tariff affects the BoP by raising the domestic price level and thereby by lowering the real value of the outstanding money stock. These changes are likely to induce an excess demand for money which, cet par, results in an inflow of international reserves.

Some critics, however, argue that the BoP as a monetary phenomenon is only true in that the BoP measures monetary flows between domestic and foreign residents. They argue that it is quite wrong to regard the BoP deficits and surpluses as exclusively due to monetary decisions, because the question of causation is an open issue. Curie (1976) criticizes the MABP for not taking explicit account of the government budget constraint. The value of his analysis lies in bringing out the analogy between the budget constraint and the external constraint.

A survey of the monetary approach by Boughton (1988) has argued that nearly every assumption made by the proponents is empirically open to question. There is an ample evidence that money demand functions can be highly unstable, economies are rarely at full employment and purchasing power parity is useless as a guide to exchange rate movements. Although these assumptions hold reasonably well in the longer run, they are very rarely fulfilled in the short run. The empirical violation of these key assumptions must bring into question the policy relevance of the monetary approach.

2.1.4 Portfolio Models of Balance of Payments Theory

In the monetary models of exchange rate determination the exchange rate was seen as the relative price of domestic and foreign assets, where the emphasis is on money. Portfolio models incorporate specially a greater number of assets: money as well as domestic and foreign bonds. In this sense, portfolio models which depict demand for several assets. can be seen as broader than the monetary models. Portfolio models have a number of key distinguishing features.

First, it is assumed that Uncovered Interest Parity (UIP) does not hold. In other words, assets are not assumed to be perfectly substitutable. This could be for a number of reasons: differential political risk, differences in the liquidity characteristics of assets, default risk, etc. Whatever the cause, the fact that UIP does not hold implies that there exists well-defined demand functions. Wealth-holders are assumed to hold a diversified portfolio of assets. The demand for an asset is hypothesized to be function of expected rates of return as well as of wealth. Thus, expectations of exchange rate movements are also important in portfolio models. Many authors like Dornbusch and Fischer (1980), Allen and Kenen (1980) and Branson and Henderson (1985) introduced a variety of possible methods of expectations formation including rational expectations.

A second feature of portfolio model is that they often model the exchange rate in a macroeconomic model of an open economy.

Thirdly, portfolio models distinguish between short-run and long-run exchange rate determinations. Usually, the exchange rate in the short-run is determined solely by wealth-holders preferences for foreign and domestic assets. In the long run, there is a role for the real sector of the economy and in particular, the current account. The short-run equilibrium exchange rate determines the current account which, in turn represents net foreign asset accumulation. This accumulation again causes exchange rate changes. Long-run equilibrium is reached only when the current account is in equilibrium.

The final feature of portfolio models is their emphasis on the distinction between stocks and flows. In particular, in portfolio theory, current account surpluses (deficits) imply an increase (decrease) in domestic holdings of overseas assets. If exchange rate are floating, then a current account surplus must accompany a capital account deficit (so that the BoP sum to zero). A capital account deficit (or a capital out-flow) increases wealth-holders holdings of foreign assets. If the long-run equilibrium of portfolio models is to be characterized as a stock equilibria, then this implies that the exchange rate in the long-run must ensure that the current account is in balance and hence that the stock of foreign assets held by residents is unchanging.

The portfolio balance model of exchange rates was pioneered by William Branson (1976, 1977, 1985) and Pentti Kouri (1976), and it has been subsequently modified and extended in various directions by Maurice Obstfeld (1980), Girton and Henderson (1977), Allen and Kenen (1980), Kenen (1982), etc. The model we shall look at is based upon Branson (1976) and Kouri (1976). This model is a simple version of many portfolio balance models because it utilizes the assumption of static exchange-rate expectations, that is, the exchange rate is not expected to change, i.e., $s^e = 0$. We assume that domestic price and output are fixed following a policy disturbance. This means the focus of the analysis is on the accumulation or decumulation of foreign assets resulting from imbalances in the current account following an operation to influence the exchange rate. A current account surplus means that the country is building up a stock of claims on the rest of the world as represented by an increased holding of foreign bonds. The operation of the portfolio balance model is depicted in Figure 2.2.

FIG. 2.2
The Operation of the Portfolio Balance Model

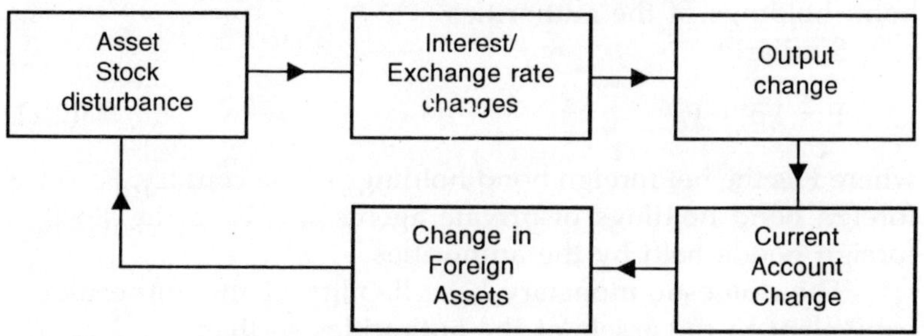

In the portfolio balance model, an open market operation (defined as an exchange of domestic money base for domestic bonds or *vice-versa*), foreign exchange operation (which is an exchange of domestic money for foreign bonds or *vice-versa*) or sterilized foreign exchange operation (which is an exchange of domestic bonds for foreign bonds) creates a disturbance in asset holders' portfolios requiring a change in the exchange rate and domestic interest rate. These changes then lead to effects on the current account.

A current account surplus/deficit leads to an accumulation/decumulation of foreign assets. This leads to further change in asset-holders' portfolios with implications for the exchange rate and domestic interest rate and so on until the model is restored to long-run equilibrium.

The Model

Three assets are held in the portfolios of the private agents and the authorities. They are:

1. Domestic monetary base, M.

2. Domestic bonds denominated only in the domestic currency, B.
3. Foreign bonds denominated only in the foreign currency F.

The net supply of domestic bonds, is assumed to be fixed as:

$$B = Bp + Ba \quad (2.40)$$

where B is the fixed net supply of domestic bonds, Bp is the domestic bond holdings of the private agents, Ba is the domestic bond holdings of the authorities.

Similarly,

$$F = Fp + Fa \quad (2.41)$$

where F is the net foreign bond holdings of the country, Fp is the foreign bond holdings of private agents and Fa is the stock of foreign bonds held by the authorities.

The domestic monetary base liability of the authorities is equivalent to the assets of the authorities so that:

$$M = Ba + eFa \quad (2.42)$$

where e is the exchange rate defined as domestic currency per unit of foreign currency and eFa is net overseas assets.

Total private financial wealth (W) at any point of time is given by the identity

$$W = M + Bp + eFp \quad (2.43)$$

The demand to hold money by the private sector is inversely related to the domestic Interest rate, inversely related to the expected rate return on foreign bonds and positively to domestic income and wealth. This yields:

$$M = m\,(r, \acute{s}^e, Y, W).\ m_r<0,\ m_{\acute{s}}e<0,\ m_y>0\ \&\ m_w>0 \quad (2.44)$$

where r is the domestic nominal interest rate, $\acute{s}^e$ is the expected rate of depreciation of the domestic currency, Y is the domestic income, m_r, $m_{\acute{s}}e$, m_y and m_w are partial derivatives.

The demand to hold domestic bonds as a proportion of private wealth can be written as:

$$Bp = b\,(r,\ \acute{s}_e,\ Y,\ W)\quad b_r>0,\ b_{\acute{s}}e<0,\ b_y<0 \text{ and } b_w>0 \qquad (2.45)$$

where br, bŝe, b_y and b_w are partial derivatives.

The demand to hold foreign bonds as a proportion of total wealth can be written as:

$$eFp = f\,(r,\ \acute{s}^e,\ y,\ w)\quad f_r<0,\ f_{\acute{s}}e>0,\ f_y<0,\ f_w>0 \qquad (2.46)$$

where f_r, $f_{\acute{s}}e$, f_y and f_w are partial derivatives, since f_r, $f_{\acute{s}}e$ f_y and f_w are partial derivatives.

Since an increase in wealth is held as either money, domestic bonds, or foreign bonds, the sum of the partial derivatives with respect to wealth must sum to unity.

$$m_w + b_m + f_w = 1 \qquad (2.47)$$

The balance sheet identify is coupled with the assumption that assets are gross substitutes implying the following constraints on the partial derivatives.

$$m_r + b_r + f_r = 0 \qquad (2.48)$$
$$m_{\acute{s}}e + b_e + f_e = 0 \qquad (2.49)$$

The current account balance is crucial to the dynamics of the system because the current account surplus gives the rate of accumulation of foreign assets. That is:

$$C = \frac{dfp}{dt} = T + r^*(Fp + Fa) \qquad (2.50)$$

where C is the current account surplus measured in foreign currency, T is the trade balance measured in foreign currency and r* is the foreign interest rate. This implies that there is a significant role for the current account to play in the determination of the exchange rate over time.

The current account is made up of two components: the revenue from net exports (the trade balance) and interest rate receipts from net holdings of foreign assets.

Net exports are assumed to be like this:

$$T = T\,(e/P,\ Y)\ T_e>0 \text{ and } T_y<0 \qquad (2.51)$$

where P is the domestic price level, T_e and T_y are partial derivatives.

We now proceed to analyse the effects of open market operations, foreign exchange operations and sterilized foreign exchange operations on the exchange rate and domestic interest rate using a comparative static framework. Taking the total differential of equation (2.43) we obtain

$$dW = dM + dB + Fpde + edFp \qquad (2.52)$$

Taking the total differentials of the asset market functions given by equations (2.44) to (2.46) we obtain.

$$dM = m_r dr + m_{\acute{s}} ed\acute{s}_e + m_w\ (dM + dBp + Fpde + edFp) \qquad (2.53)$$

$$dBp = b_r dr + b_{\acute{s}} ed\acute{s}_e + b_w\ (dM + dBp + Fpde + edFp) \qquad (2.54)$$

$$dFp = f_r dr + t_{\acute{s}} ed\acute{s}_e + f_w\ (dM + dBp + Fpde + edFp) \qquad (2.55)$$

Setting the LH.S. of the above equations to zero and noting that because of static exchange expectations, $d_{\acute{s}}e = 0$, we can obtain the slope of the various asset market schedules in the interest-rate -exchange-rate plane like the slope of the money market schedule (keeping dM = 0 and since $d_{\acute{s}}e = 0$)

$$dr/de = -(m_w\ Fp/m_r) > 0,$$

The slope of the foreign bond market schedule (keeping dBp = 0 and since $d_{\acute{s}}e = 0$

$$dr/de = -(b_w Fp/b_r) < 0,$$

the slope of the bond market schedule (keeping dFp = 0 and since $d_{\acute{s}}e = 0$)

$$dr/de = (1-f_w)Fp/f_r < 0.$$

It follows that the asset market of the model is in equilibrium when all three asset markets clear at the appropriate domestic interest rate and exchange rate. This is depicted in Figure 2.3.

Empirical testing of portfolio model of exchange rate

FIG. 2.3
Equilibrium in the Portfolio Balance Model

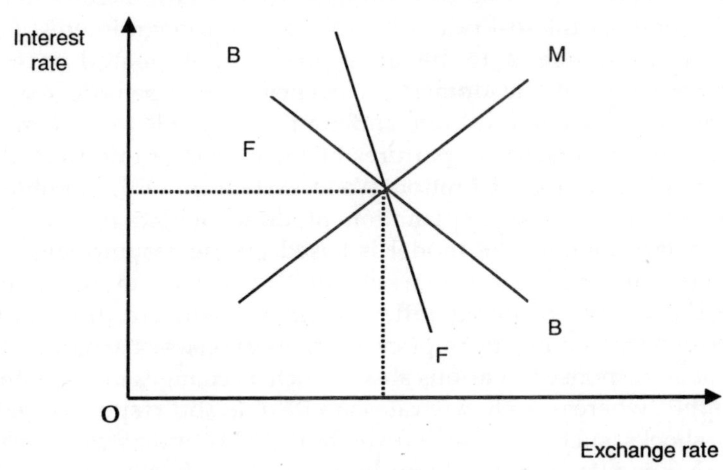

determination is beset with a number of econometric problems. The results of Branson *et. al.* (1977, 1979), Backus 1984) find little support for the model, including Meese and Rogoff (1983, 1984) who tested the Portfolio model with respect to forecasting. However, the test conducted by Kearney and MacDonald (1985, 1986) to estimate the portfolio model using a structural model rather than the usual reduced form provide some support for the portfolio model. On the whole, therefore, it is difficult to come to any firm conclusion about the validity of the portfolio approach. Its contribution, however, has been to highlight the importance of asset demands and supplies as determinants of the exchange rate.

The approach, therefore, attempts to provide a macroeconomic framework for an open economy with integration between commodities, money and assets markets.

2.1.5 Dornbusch's Sticky-Price Monetary Model and Overshooting of Exchange Rate

Rudigar Dornbusch (1976) provides a highly influential model of exchange rate dynamics that significantly advanced the monetary theory of exchange rate formation by Jacob Frenkel (1976). Flexible-price monetarist models as presented by Frenkel are constrained by the assumption that Purchasing Power Parity (PPP) holds continuously meaning thereby that if the domestic interest rate is lower than the foreign interest rate, then there needs to be an equivalent expected rate of appreciation of the domestic currency to compensate for the lower domestic interest rate and are thus not able to explain the large and prolonged departures of the exchange rate from PPP seen after the fall of Bretton Wood system in 1973. Dornbusch model provides an explanation of these deviations within a monetary model. The model is based on the assumptions that wages on the labour market and the prices in the goods markets—both relatively inflexible (in a downward direction)—are determined in 'sticky price' markets and slow changing over time in response to various shocks such as changes in the money supply, whereas exchange rates are flexible and respond rapidly to shocks such as new informations. This indicates that the exchange rate is free to jump in response to shocks, while price levels are constrained to be non-jumping slowly-adjusting variables. Thus, movements in the exchange rate are not accompanied by compensatory shifts in price movements, giving rise to deviations from the PPP. This is often called exchange rate 'Over-shooting' and the model is termed 'Sticky Price' monetarist model.

We focus upon a 'small country' in that it faces a fixed world interest r^* which it cannot influence. The money market clearing condition is

$$m - p = \eta y - \sigma r \tag{2.56}$$

where m is the log of the domestic money stock, p is the log of domestic price level, y is the log of domestic real income, and r is the nominal domestic interest rate and η and σ are positive constant coefficients of the money demand function. Here the demand for real money balances is assumed to depend positively on the level of domestic real income (output) and negatively on the domestic interest rate and the real supply of money is given by m—p.

We assume that the domestic and foreign bonds are perfect substitutes so that the uncovered interest parity condition (UIP) holds, that is, when the exchange rate can change, and interest rate differential equal to the expected rate of depreciation of the home currency can persist. Symbolically this means that

$$\acute{s}^e = r - r^* \tag{2.57}$$

where $\acute{s}^e$ is the expected rate of depreciation of the home currency.

Since the model allows for departures from PPP, it is necessary to specify an equation for the expected rate of change of the exchange rate. This model thus specifies regressive exchange expectations given by:

$$\acute{s}^e = -\varphi\,(s - \hat{s}) \text{ where } \varphi > 0 \tag{2.58}$$

Equation (2.58) says that the expected rate of depreciation of a currency is determined by the speed of adjustment parameter φ, and the gap between the current exchange rate s and its long-run equilibrium value $\hat{s}$:

The Model postulates that the rate of price inflation is determined by the gap between aggregate demand and aggregate supply. That is:

$$\dot{p} = \Pi(y - \hat{y}) \tag{2.59}$$

where $\dot{p}$ is the rate of domestic price inflation, Π is the speed of adjustment of prices, and y is the log of aggregate demand. Equation (2.59) is an assumption about the process of price adjustment.

Aggregate demand is assumed to be a function of exogenous expenditure βo, a positive function of the real exchange rate expressed in log form as $(s - p + p^*)$, a positive function of domestic income and a negative function of the domestic nominal interest rate. This yields:

$$y = \beta o + \beta_1 (s-p + p^*) + \beta_2 Y - \beta_3 r \quad \beta_{0,} \beta_{1,} \beta_{2,} \beta_3 > 0 \quad (2.60)$$

This demand function is closely related to the Mundell-Fleming demand function. Thus s − p + p* term captures the effects of the real exchange rate on the trade balance and hence aggregate demand. The y term reflects the effect of income on expenditure magnitudes such as consumption. The r term reflects the effects of the interest rate on domestic absorption and thus an increase in r results, ceteris paribus, in a fall in aggregate demand. The βo term is a shift parameter.

Substituting equation (2.61) into equation (2.60) we obtain:

$$\dot{p} = \Pi [\beta_1 + \beta_1 (s-p+p^*) + (\beta_2 - 1) y - \beta_3 r] \quad (2.61)$$

At zero inflation, that is = 0, we find the slope of the goods market schedule. For that we must substitute solution for r from equation (2.57) into equation (2.62) to obtain:

$$\dot{p} = \Pi [\beta_1 + \beta_1 (s-p+p^*) + (\beta_2 - 1) - \beta_3/\sigma (p-m+\eta y)] \quad (2.62)$$

Then by setting equation 2.63 to zero we find the slope of the goods market equilibrium schedule in the price-level-exchange rate plane. Along the goods market equilibrium schedule aggregate demand equals aggregate supply implying zero price inflation. The slope of this schedule is given by:

$$dp/ds\ (\dot{p} = 0) = \beta_1 / (\beta_1 + \beta_3/\sigma) \quad (2.63)$$

From the above equation it follows that this schedule is upward sloping and has a slope less than unity.

The rationale behind the goods market equilibrium schedule is that a depreciation (rise) of the exchange rate leads to an increased demand for exports and this increase in demand can only be offset by a rise in the domestic price level. However, because the rise in the price level increases money demand it is accompanied by a rise in interest rates which further reduces demand. This means that the percentage depreciation of the exchange rate has to exceed the percentage rise in the price level to keep the aggregate demand in line with aggregate supply.

To derive the money market schedule which shows different combinations of the price level and exchange rate that are consistent with equilibrium in the money market, we first of all invert the money demand function (2.57) to solve for the domestic interest rate. This yields :

$$r = (p - m + \eta y)/\sigma \quad (2.64)$$

We then substitute the solution for s'e in equation (2.57) and replace the solution for r in equation (2.64) to obtain—

$$s = \hat{s} - (1/\sigma\varphi)[p - m + \eta y - \varphi r^*] \quad (2.65)$$

This means that the slope of the money market schedule is given by:

$$dp/ds = -\sigma\varphi \quad (2.65)$$

Hence the money market schedule is shown to have a negative slope in the price level-exchange-rate plane.

Equilibrium of the model occurs when both the goods and money markets are in equilibrium and the exchange rate is at its PPP value.

It is convenient to rewrite equation (2.60) as

$$y = \alpha[\beta_0 + \beta_1 + (s - p + p^*) - \beta_3 r] \text{ where } \alpha = 1/(1 - \beta_2) \quad (2.67)$$

and to combine (2.57) and (2.58) into

$$r = r^* - \varphi(s - \hat{s}) \quad (2.68)$$

(2.56), (2.59), (2.60), (2.67), (2.68) can be used to describe the relationship between the price level, output, and the exchange rate, both in the steady state and along the path of convergence to the steady state. Noting that $r = r^*$ in the steady state, and letting p denote the steady state level of p, the market-clearing condition (2.56) and (2.67) imply the following two steady state relationships:

$$\hat{p} = m - \eta\hat{y} + \sigma r^* \tag{2.69}$$

$$\hat{y} = \alpha\,[\beta_0 + \beta_1(\hat{s} - \hat{p} + p^*) - \beta_3 r^* \tag{2.70}$$

In addition, the relationship between prices, output and the exchange rate during the adjustment to the steady state can be described by subtracting these two relationships from (2.56) and (2.67) respectively, using (2.68). Thus,

$$(p - \hat{p}) = -\eta(y - \hat{y}) - \sigma\varphi\,(s - \hat{s}) \tag{2.71}$$

$$(y - \hat{y}) = \alpha\,(\beta_1 + \beta_3)\,(s - \hat{s}) - \alpha\,\beta_1(p - \hat{p}) \tag{2.72}$$

The two conditions, in turn, can be solved simultaneously to yield

$$(y - \hat{y}) = -\,z\,(p - \hat{p}) \tag{2.73}$$

$$(s - \hat{s}) = -\,[(1 - \eta\alpha\beta_1/\square]\,(p - \hat{p}) \tag{2.74}$$

where

$$\square = \eta\alpha\,(\beta_1 + \varphi\beta_3) + \varphi\sigma \tag{2.75}$$

$$z = [\alpha\,(\beta_1 + \varphi\beta_3) + \alpha\,\beta_1\varphi\sigma]/\square \tag{2.76}$$

Furthermore, substitution of (2.73) into (2.59) yields

$$p = -\,\Pi z\,(p - \hat{p}) \tag{2.77}$$

It may be noted from (2.73) to (2.77) that the convergence paths for p, y, and s depend on the parameter φ, which describes the expected rate of change of the exchange rate. It is important to note in this connection that since exchange rate expectations are formed simultaneously with, and depend upon, expectations about other variables, hence in the spirit of rational expectations macroeconomics we can say that Dornbusch model ignores some other practical problems like the possibility of peso problems. This happens because Dornbusch model, like many other exchange rate model virtually assumes that the model consistent with expected path of the exchange rate corresponds to the perfect foresight path. Dornbusch like many economists in formulating the exchange rate theory has ignored the scope for rational market participants to form inaccurate expectations about exogenous variables (r^*, p^*, $\hat{y}$, m). These variables, however, can be a source of imprecision and inaccuracy in his model-consistent expectations about endogenous variables. The logic of the model thus implies that the model-consistent expected path of the exchange rate is unique and corresponds to the perfect foresight path.

To solve for the expected path of the exchange rate that is consistent with the model, with the observed state of the economy at initial time 0, and the implicit assumption that the exogenous variables (r^*, p^*, $\hat{y}$, m) will remain constant forever, we note from (2.58) that the expected value at time 0 of the time-t exchange rate can be expressed as

$$s^e(t) = \hat{s} + [s(o) - \hat{s}]\, e^{-\varphi t} \tag{2.78}$$

Similarly, from (2.59), the price level at time t can be written as

$$p(t) = \hat{p} + [p(o) - \hat{p}]\, e^{-\Pi z t} \tag{2.79}$$

Substitution of (2.79) into (2.74) gives the actual path of the exchange rate when all the exogenous variables remain constant

$$s(t) = \hat{s} - [(1 - \varphi\alpha\beta_1)/\square]\, [p(o) - Þ]\, e^{-\Pi z t} \tag{2.80}$$

and hence

$$s(t) = \hat{s} + [s(o) - \hat{s}]\, e^{-\Pi z t} \tag{2.81}$$

Accordingly, from (2.78), (2.81) and from the value of □ and z, model-consistent expected path of the exchange rate is given by the solution of the equation:

$$\Phi = \Pi z = \Pi[\alpha\,(\beta_1 + \varphi\beta_3) + \alpha\beta_1\varphi\beta_3]/\ [\eta\alpha\,(\beta_1 + \varphi\beta_3)] \quad (2.82)$$

The basic motivation for the Dornbusch model was "to develop a theory that is suggestive of the observed large fluctuations in the exchange rates while at the same time establishing that such exchange rate movements are consistent with rational expectation formation (*Dornbusch*, 1976, p. 116). To illustrate that his model was capable of generating large fluctuations in exchange rates in response to unexpected stocks ('news'), Dornbusch analysed the process of adjustment to an unanticipated change in the money supply, demonstrating that the initial jump in the exchange rate exceeded the adjustment in the long-run equilibrium exchange rate. This predicted pattern of 'overshooting' is the most celebrated implications of the sticky-price model of exchange rate dynamics.

The overshooting response of exchange rate to a monetary shock is illustrated by Figure 2.4 where overshooting refers to the tendency for the exchange rate to overshoot its new equilibrium level following some exogenous shocks to the system. The negatively-sloped M_1M_1 line which describes the set of combinations of p and s that clear the money and goods markets simultaneously. Prior to the monetary shock, the economy is in a position of steady state equilibrium at (s_0, p_0).

Fig. 2.4

The Dornbusch Model of Exchange Rate 'Overshooting'

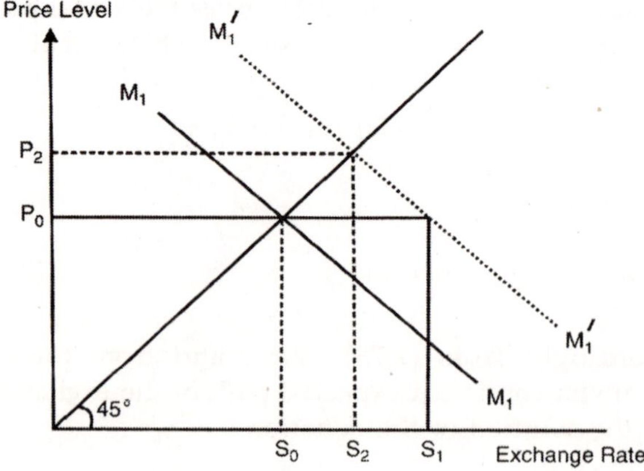

Let us now suppose that the authorities unexpectedly expand the money supply. With exogenous variables unchanged, the new steady state value of s and p must lie along a positively-sloped 45^0 line through (s_0, p_0) (The 45^0 line reflects the assumption that money is neutral in the long run) and the steady state value of p must increase by the same amount as the (logarithm of the) money supply in the long run. Accordingly, the M_1M_1 curve shifts upward to $M_1'M_1'$, leading to a new steady state equilibrium at (s_2, p_2).

The major feature of the Dornbusch model is that in the short run domestic prices are sticky, while money markets are in continuous equilibrium as indicated by the UIP condition. In the context of Figure 2.4 this means the economy is always on the new money market equilibrium schedule $M_1'M_1'$. As domestic prices do not initially change the price level remains at p_0 and this is consistent with a jump in the exchange rate from s_0 to s_1 on the money market equilibrium schedule $M_1'M_1'$. The fact that the short-run equilibrium exchange rate s_1' (determined by interest rate parity) overshoots the level in the long-run equilibrium exchange rate s_2 (determined by purchasing power parity) is known as the phenomenon of exchange rate overshooting. The ultimate reason for the "overshooting" phenomenon is the fact that adjustment speeds are different in the financial and goods markets. A disequilibrium in the financial markets is eliminated immediately by movements of interest rates and exchange rates. However, a disequilibrium in the goods markets persists for a long time because of price rigidities.

Let us now consider what happens in this model when the quantity of money is permanently reduced by say, 10 per cent. In the long-run the price level will fall by 10 per cent and the exchange rate will rise by 10 per cent on account of PPP. Equilibrium money market condition and the demand for money function imply that interest rate will rise by e.g. 2 percentage points p.a. But equation $s'^e = r - r^*$ implies that this will trigger an expected rate of depreciation of 2 per cent p.a. If the exchange rate is expected to be 10 per cent higher than it originally was, the initial jump in the exchange rate must have been 12 per cent. So the exchange rate must overshoot its long-run value.

The important point that comes from the Dornbusch model is that it helps explain why observed exchange rates are usually even more volatile than the money supply, one of the supposed determinants. Since the exchange rate initially depreciates by more than x per cent in the short run in response to an x per cent increase in the money supply, it follows that the exchange rate will be more volatile than the domestic monetary policy.

Further the model represented a major advance in the exchange rate literature. The major innovation of the model is its emphasis on capital market rather than goods market arbitrage being the major determinant of exchange rate in the short-run. It also explains why exchange-rate movements have been large relative to movement in international prices and change in international money stocks.

Lastly, the Dornbusch model has served as the basis for a number of other models of the overshooting type. In many cases, these later models are extensions of the Dornbusch story which sometimes arises from criticisms of the original version of the model. For example, Frenkel and Rodriguez (1982) extend Dornbusch's model to incorporate a low degree of capital mobility. We can note here that Bhandari, Driskill and Frenkel (1984) present a similar model to that of Frenkel and Rodriguez (1982). The key difference is that the former examines the relationship between capital mobility and overshooting in a stock equilibrium of the capital account. Returning to later model, we find an expression for BoP equilibrium:

$$\lambda(s - p - \hat{s}) + \varepsilon\,[r - r^{*} - \varphi\,(\hat{s} - s)] = 0 \qquad (2.83)$$

where the first part represents the trade balance with (s – p) is the actual real exchange rate, and $\hat{s}$ is the long-run equilibrium exchange rate and the second part is the capital flow equation with ε representing the degree of capital mobility.

Here in this model if the capital is highly mobile then MM is negatively sloped. The rationale is as follows: If there is a price level falls, then there will be two effects. Firstly, the capital account effect arises from the increase in the money supply and the fall in the domestic interest rate. This causes a capital account deficit. The second effect is on the current account. The fall in the domestic price level causes the current account to improve and this offsets the capital account deficit to some extent. Hence to restore overall BoP equilibrium, the depreciation of the exchange rate need not be so great.

It is interesting to mention that there are several other modifications to the Dornbusch model that generate similar results, that is undershooting like Dornbusch model with highly mobile and immobile capital. There is another extensions of the Dornbusch model that examine the impact of imposing rational expectation on the model like perfect foresight model of MacDonald (1988). Buiter and Miller (1981) developed a model which enables us to consider the impact of monetary policy designed at reducing the rate of growth of the money supply. The model is in the same spirit as Dornbusch in that it assumes that money is neutral in the long-run, but that in the short-run the goods market adjusts much more slowly than asset markets.

Thus it appears that the Dornbusch model has played a dominant role in shaping the literature on exchange rate dynamics through the early 1990s. The classical assumption of perfectly flexible prices is strongly rejected by the advancement of Dornbusch model and its subsequent development in empirical test. At the same time two handicaps of the Dornbusch model—in particular, its *ad hoc* specification of the price determination process and its failure to provide an explicit role for the current account in exchange rate determination may have contributed to its poor performance and have greatly limited its relevance in policy-oriented discussions of exchange rate dynamics. In this connection it is noteworthy to mention that recent models on an inter-temporal optimization approach have made progress in overcoming the two major handicaps and may ultimately be regarded as a major conceptual advance (*Israd,* 1995).

2.1.6 Frankel's Real Interest Rate Differential Model

The sticky price monetary model of Dornbusch represents a major advance on the flexible price monetary exchange-rate model but unlike the former, the Dornbusch model does not explicitly take into account inflationary expectations. However, the 1970s period of floating exchange rates was dominated by inflation. In a bid to combine the inflationary expectations element of the flexible price monetary model with the insights of the sticky price model, Jeffrey Frankel (1979) provides a general model for analysing the impact of changes in the interest rate on the exchange rate and he refers to this as the 'real interest differential model'.

Frankel's model assumes uncovered arbitrage but modified the Dornbusch expectations equation for the exchange rate by adding a term reflecting relative expected secular inflation ($\Pi - \Pi^*$). The expectations equation is:

$$s'^e - s = \theta\,(\hat{s} - s) + (\Pi - \Pi^*) \qquad (2.84)$$

and uncovered interest parity yields

$$s'^e - s = r - r^* \qquad (2.85)$$

The expected rate of depreciation ($s'^e - s$) depends upon the deviation of exchange rate from its equilibrium value, which as we know gives Dornbusch type results. In addition, if $s = \hat{s}$, the expected rate of depreciation is given by the expected inflation differential between the domestic and foreign currency.

Combining equation (2.84) and (2.85) and rearranging we have

$$\hat{s} - s = (1/\theta)\,[(r - \Pi) - (r^* - \Pi^*)] \qquad (2.86)$$

Equation (2.86) states that the gap between the current real exchange rate and its long-run equilibrium value is proportional to the real interest rate differential as given by the term in brackets. In other words, the movement in the spot rate around its equilibrium value is determined by the relative real interest differential.

By invoking long-run PPP the long-run equilibrium exchange rate s can be expressed in log form as the difference between the long-run price levels:

$$\hat{s} = \hat{p} - p^* \qquad (2.87)$$

In the long-run the expected real rates of interest are equalized so that any long-run nominal interest rate differentials are explained by differences in the steady-state inflation rates:

$$r - r^* = \Pi - \Pi^* \qquad (2.88)$$

By combining (2.89) and (2.87) with equation $m - m^* = (p - p^*) + \eta (y - y^*) - \sigma (r - r^*)$ where m is the log of the domestic money stock, p is the log of the domestic price level, y is the log of domestic real income, and r is the nominal domestic interest rate, where an asterisk over m^*, p^*, y^* and r^* represents a foreign variable, we can obtain an expression for the long-run steady-state equilibrium exchange rate given by:

$$\hat{s} = (m - m^*) - \eta (y - y^*) + \sigma (\Pi - \Pi^*) \tag{2.89}$$

Equation (2.89) states that the long-run equilibrium exchange rate is determined by the relative supply $(m - m^*)$ and relative demands as given by $\eta (y - y^*) + \sigma (\Pi - \Pi^*)$ of the two national money stocks.

In the Frankel generalization of the Dornbusch model, the speed of adjustment of the goods market is relevant to the determination of the short-run exchange rate, so that the equation (2.86) has to be taken into account, when solving for the short-run exchange rate. Combining equation (2.89) and rearranging terms yields the following solution for the short run exchange rate.

$$\hat{s} = (m - m^*) - \eta (y - y^*) + \sigma (\Pi - \Pi^*) \cdot ^{-1/q} \\ [(r - \Pi) - (r^* - \Pi^*) \tag{3.90}$$

The Frankel formulation makes it clear that if there is a disequilibrium set of real interest rates, then the real exchange rate will deviate from its long-run equilibrium value. If the real domestic interest rate is below the real foreign interest rate then the real exchange rate of the domestic currency will be undervalued in relation to its long-run equilibrium value, so that there is an expected appreciation of the real exchange rate of the domestic currency to compensate.

The fully flexible price monetarist school argues that all markets clear instantaneously so that the speed of adjustment parameter θ, in equation (2.90) is infinite, so that the solution for the short-run exchange rate is given by equation (2.89). In the real interest rate model as portrayed by equation (2.90) the goods and the labour markets prices are assumed to be slow to adjust to stocks so the speed of adjustment parameter θ is finite. Thus, rational expectations hold for the foreign exchange market but not for domestic markets. In such circumstances, an unanticipated monetary expansion leads to a fall in the real domestic interest rate. The result according to equation (2.90) is that the short-run exchange rate overshoots its long run equilibrium value, depreciating proportionately more than the increase in the money stock so that there are expectations of a future real appreciation of the currency.

Regarding implications of the monetary views of exchange-rates determination we can say that whichever monetarist model one adopts, a clear implication is that monetary policy is the only predictable and effective means of influencing the exchange rate. Furthermore, because domestic and foreign bonds are assumed to be perfect substitutes there is no distinction to be made between the effects of an open market operation and a foreign exchange market operation. It follows that there is no scope for the authorities to pursue a sterilised foreign exchange operation that will have exchange-rate effects.

In a flexible price monetarist model, while the authorities can influence the nominal exchange in a predictable fashion by monetary policy, they cannot do likewise with the real exchange rate. If there is an once, and, for all x per cent increase in the money supply, this will lead to an once-and for all x per cent depreciation of the home currency and a simultaneous x per cent increase in both the domestic price level and wages. This is a case of complete neutrality of monetary policy with respect to the real economy. Monetary policy influences only nominal not real variables.

Within the context of the 'sticky price' monetarist approach the authorities can exploit the finite speed of adjustment of domestic markets to influence the real exchange rate in the short run, provided that real output is fixed. The Frankel model makes it clear that the overshooting of the exchange rate is proportional to the deviation of the real domestic interest rate from its equilibrium value.

Whichever monetarist view one adheres to, the clear implication is that monetary policy is the most effective means of managing the exchange rate. Furthermore, in the long-run the authorities should abandon any attempt to influence the real exchange rate because real exchange rate is determined by real and not by monetary factors. Thus, in the long-run the authorities should direct exchange rate policy at stabilizing the domestic price level. Whether stabilizing the domestic price level will stabilise the nomianal exchange rate depends on the stability of the foreign price level and therefore upon the monetary policies of foreign countries as well.

A common characteristic of the three monetary models of exchange rate determination—the flexible price monetary model, the Dornbusch sticky price monetarist model and the Frankel real interest rate diffential model—is that what matters for the exchange rate is the money supply in relation to money demand in both the home and foreign countries. The exchange rate is the relative price of two national monies and is consequently a monetary phenomenon.

All the monetary models are built upon PPP. The flexible price monetary model assumes that PPP holds continuously and maintains that the price level adjusts instantaneously to changes in the supply and demand for money. This then leads to an immediate exchange rate adjustment to maintain PPP. Changes in real income and inflation expectations induce changes in the exchange rate because they affect the demand for money. In the sticky price monetary models, the asymmetric speeds of adjustment in goods and asset markets can lead to divergences from the PPP in the short-run, although PPP reasserts itself in the long-run.

The sticky price monetary models provide an explanation of both exchange rate volatility and misalignment. Exchange rates can become misaligned in relation to PPP because of the phenomenon of exchange rate 'overshooting' while instability in monetary policies can result in even greater instability in exchange rate. An important point made by the sticky price models is that both divergences from PPP and highly volatile exchange rates can be explained by rational expectation. In Frankel's view, the equilibrium exchange rate model provides a good description of what happens during hyperinflation, when prices are extremely flexible, whereas the Dornbusch model would be relevant in the case of a low and stable inflation differential.

Perhaps the most noticeable omission of the monetary models of exchange rate determination is the explicit role for the current account to influence the exchange rate. Furthermore, domestic and foreign bonds are regarded as perfect substitutes—that is, they are regarded as equally risky so there is no role for risk perceptions to play a part in the determination of exchange rates. The portfolio balance model of exchange rate determination that we have already examined in the section 2.1.4 has an explicit and important role for both of these factors to influence exchange rates.

2.1.7 Stabilization Policies in Open Economies

The extension of Keynesian macroeconomics to the open economy, in addition to underscoring a need to integrate the elasticities approach with national income analysis in modelling the current account, stimulated new perspectives about the conduct of stabilization policy. Meade (1951), however, revived the simultaneous analysis of internal and external balance. Following Meade, the policy-makers and economists focused simultaneously on the relationship between balance of payments and exchange rate to determine the level of domestic output or employment.

Another important contribution to the literature during the 1950s was a paper by Trevor Swan (1963). Swan stimulated by the debate over full employment in Australia, posed the central issue as follows:

Is there any automatic mechanism to ensure external and internal balance, or what kind of conscious action by the authorities is required?

To analyse the issue, Swan introduced a diagram that soon became popular (Figure 2.5). The starting point of the analysis was to recognise that internal balance (defined as full employment) and external balance (defined as BoP equilibrium) could each be achieved under various combinations of the level of aggregate domestic real expenditure (absorption) and the cost (or price) of foreign goods relative to that of home goods. The downward sloping internal balance schedule shows combination of monetary and fiscal ease consistent with full employment. On the assumption, that monetary ease improves the current account by depreciating the currency (or by a rise in the relative cost of foreign goods), the external balance schedule which shows policy setting consistent with some current

Fig. 2.5

The Swan Diagram

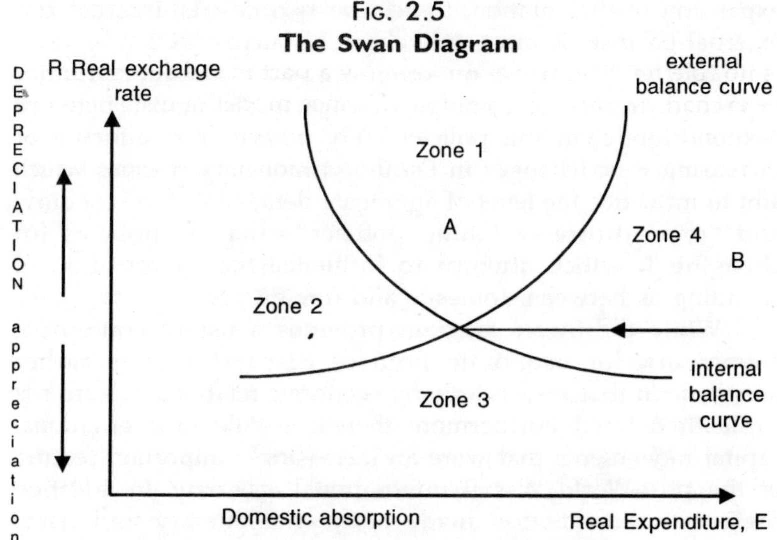

Zone 1: Over full employment and BoP surplus.
Zone 2: Under full employment and BoP surplus.
Zone 3: Under full employment and BoP deficits.
Zone 4: Over full employment and BoP deficits.

account target, slopes upward. The intersection of the two schedules shows how policies should be set to achieve both the goals in the short-run.

Swan emphasized that changes in the economy will shift the two curves over time. In the case the authorities will devise such policies for influencing R and E in a manner that would keep the economy as close as possible to the intersections of the curves, where internal and external balance are simultaneously achieved.

For example, to move from point B to point A, the authorities need to both deflate the economy and undertake a devaluation by appropriate amounts. The deflation will control inflation and the devaluation improve the current account so that the two objectives can be met. The idea that a country generally requires as many instruments as it has targets was elaborated by the Dutch economist Jan Tinbergen (1952) and is popularly known as Tinbergen's instruments-targets rule. Thus a major lesson is that the use of one instrument, be it fiscal expansion or devaluation, to achieve two targets, internal and external balance, is most unlikely to be successful.

As the literature on open-economy macroeconomics expanded, it become common practice to distinguish between "expenditure-changing policies", i.e. poliices for reducing or increasing E or (changes in fiscal and monetary policies which aim to influence the level of aggregate demand in the economy) and "expenditure-switching policies"—that is, policies for changing R which attempt to influence the composition of spending as between domestic and foreign goods.

While the Swan diagram provides a useful conceptual framework for economic policies discussion it is rather simplistic in that the underlying economic relationships are not explicitly defined. Furthermore, there is no rule for international capital movements that were an increasingly important feature of the post-World War II international economy. In addition there is no distinction made between monetary and fiscal policies as means of influencing aggregate demand and output in the economy. The so-called Mundell-Fleming model, to which we now turn, attempts to integrate such features into a formal open economy macroeconomic model.

By the start of the 1960s, the evolution of the world economy had stimulated interest in formulating models in which BoP included endogenous private capital flows in addition to merchandise transactions. This gave rise to a series of remarkable contributions by Mundell (1960, 1961a, 1961b, 1962, 1963) and Fleming (1962), exploring the policy implications of international capital mobility.

The Mundell-Fleming framework combined a simple Keynesian model of the goods and money markets for an open economy with the assumption that net international capital flows into the economy depended positively on the home rate of interest. The analysis took foreign prices and interest rates as exogenous, focusing on either the home interest rate or the home money supply as the instrument of monetary policy, and often on the budget balance as the instrument of fiscal policy.

However, the Mundell diagram differed from the Swan diagram in several respects. In conformity with the standard model of closed economy, Mundell chose to analyse equilibrium in terms of the levels of home-money income and the home interest rate rather than home real expenditure and the relative price (cost) of foreign and home goods. In Mundell's analysis, the trade balance depended on home income, while the overall BoP also reflected the relationship of the capital account balance to the home interest rate. Let us see how it happens in the Mundell Model.

Mundell's paper on 'The International Disequilibrium System' (1961) criticized the Keynesian model's failure to account for the dynamic effects balance of payments imbalance poses. Even in a Keynesian world, Mundell argued, an income-specie-flow mechanism, analogous to Hume's price-specie-flow mechanism, ensures long-run BoP equilibrium. A five-fold increase in a country's money supply, for example, depresses domestic interest rates, stimulates investment spending, and creates a deficit in the BoP. As the Central Bank loses reserves however, the interest rate gradually rises and reduces investment; the process comes to an end (for a small country) only when the domestic money supply, the interest rate, investment and output have returned to their original levels. The introduction of dynamic adjustment made it clear that sterilization could have only limited success as a policy response to permanent BoP disturbances. One source of dynamic effects, however, was not explicitly analysed in Mundell's work. The omitted effect was the real-balance effect on expenditure, relevant as Pigou had shown under Keynesian conditions as well.

In line with the increasing international capital mobility that followed the European move toward currency convertibility in 1958, Mundell gave the capital account a prominent role in his models. The presence of capital mobility suggested a solution to the policy dilemmas that could arise under fixed exchange rates when the goals of internal and external balance appeared to conflict. Mundell showed that by gearing monetary policy to external balance and fiscal policy to internal balance, governments could simultaneously attain both goals. The key to the arguments is the observation that monetary and fiscal expansion both raise output but have different effects on the capital account, monetary expansion causing capital outflows (by driving down the home interest rate), and fiscal expansion causing capital inflows (by raising the interest rate). With two independent instruments, both internal and external policy targets can be attained simultaneously.

One of the major inferences from the Mundell-Fleming model was that the relative effectiveness of monetary and fiscal policies very much depended on both the choice of the exchange rate regime and the degree of capital mobility. Mundell (1963) considered the case of perfect capital mobility in which the elasticity of the capital account with respect to the home interest rate was infinite. With perfect capital mobility and fixed exchange rates, a change in the money supply through the open market operations would give rise to an equal change in the level of foreign exchange reserves, with no impact on home output or employment, while an expansionary fiscal policy would stimulate home output, and have a negative effect on the balance of trade. With perfect capital mobility and flexible exchange rates, a change in the fiscal balance would give rise to an equal change in the trade balance with no impact on home output or employment, while monetary expansion, despite having no effect on the home rate of interest, would depreciate the exchange rate, have a positive effect on the trade balance, and stimulate home output and employment (*Israd,* 1995, p. 102).

With a major step forward, the Mundellian argument for a policy mix suffered from two drawbacks. First, the theoretical specification of the capital account as a function of international interest-rate levels was weak; it seemed unlikely that capital would flow at a uniform level for ever. The second problem with the policy mix was its definition of external balance. Would any policy-maker view with satisfaction a permanently high interest rate that brought about BoP equilibrium by crowding out domestic investment and encouraging build-up of external debt? Key considerations omitted from Mundell's model were the stock of net foreign claims and the associated flows to interest payments. Mundell himself (1968, p. 207) recognised that in many contexts, the definition of external balance as BoP equilibrium again might be inadequate.

Although the Mundell-Fleming model has many limitations, it nonetheless focuses attention on the difficulties and dilemmas faced by policy-makers in an open economy.

Perhaps its most significant contribution is that it focuses on the important role that international capital flows can play in determining the effectiveness of macroeconomic policies under alternative exchange-rate regimes.

2.1.8 Target Zone Approach and Speculative Attacks in Exchange Rate Behaviours

The experience with floating exchange rates and, in particular, the failure to deliver all the benefits promised by its proponents led many industrial countries to adopt increasing intervention to manage their exchange rates. By the mid-1980s, the policymaking community was actively discussing proposals for replacing the system of flexible exchange rates among major currencies, with a system of target zones, and by the end of the decade economists were actively developing models of exchange rate dynamics within a target zone framework. The European Monetary System set-up in 1979 represents one of the formal attempts at monetary integration. Less formal arrangements involve the Group of Seven Countries and their management of the dollar *vis-à-vis* the Deutschmark and the Yen in the latter 1980s after the so-called Plaza and Louvre Agreements. These experiences with exchange rate management have led to various models about how managed exchange rates behave and the problems which the authorities might face in determining an exchange rate within a band or zone.

A definition of target zones was provided by Frenkel and Goldstein (1986, p 635). Perhaps the easiest way to think of them is as a hybrid exchange rate system that combines some of the attributes and characteristics of both fixed and flexible exchange rate systems. We begin with the issue of target zones and how an exchange rate within a target zone is supposed to behave. We then go on to discuss the problem of speculative attacks in fixed or managed exchange rate regimes.

Flood and Garber (1991) describe a target zone as a compromise between fixed and floating exchange rates. Explicit margins are set for exchange rate fluctuations and while the exchange rate is within the bands, policy can be directed at the domestic economy; when the exchange rate reaches the outer limits of the bands, then intervention and policy changes are required to keep it within the bands.

The main concern of the literature on target zones is how the exchange rate might be expected to behave when agents know that it is being kept within bands. The key result of the literature is that the existence of a target zone will alter expectations within the zone. In particular, a change in fundamentals which might normally have led to a 10% change in the exchange rate will now have a smaller effect on the exchange rate. Hence an exchange rate operating within a target zone is expected to exhibit less volatility than a freely floating exchange rate. And exchange rate expectations, if the zones is fully credible, lie within the target zone bands.

Krugman (1991) provides the basic model of exchange rate behaviour within a target zone. The actual exchange rate is a linear function of fundamentals and the expected future exchange rate. In Krugman's Model, the fundamentals included the money supply and velocity:

$$s \equiv m + v + a\, E\,(ds)/dt \qquad (2.91)$$

where s is the spot exchange rate, m is the domestic money supply, v represents shocks arising from changes in velocity, and E (ds)/dt is the expected rate of depreciation. All variables are in logarithms. Equation 2.91 states the familiar flexible price monetary model propositions that: (a) if the money supply rises, then the excess supply of money sill generate a BoP deficit and hence the exchange rate will depreciate (s will rise); (b) if money demand rises, velocity falls, then an excess demand for money will ensue leading to the BoP surplus and an exchange rate appreciation (s will fall). In addition to these fundamentals, the expected change in the exchange rate will also affect that actual exchange rate by an amount determined by a.

Krugman makes two assumptions, *First,* the target zone is assumed to be completely credible. *Secondly,* the central bank intervenes only at the margins. If we relax those assumptions, we get completely different result.

Empirical tests of the basic Krugman model have not tended to be supportive. The target zones model suggests that exchange rates should be non-linearly related to fundamentals. Floodsteal (1991) plot EMS exchange rates against a derived fundamental. The groups show that the relationship appears to be linear. One possible explanation is that the target zone is less than credible and that the degree of credibility changed over time.

If target zones are not credible, then they face a major problem which all fixed exchange rate systems face, namely, the potential for speculative attacks. Flood and Garber (1991) examine the relationships between speculative attacks and target zone models. Their paper is essentially a technical contribution in that they seek to show that target zone models are the mirror image of speculative attack model. In doing so, they also discuss how a target zone could suffer from a speculative attack. We now move to the literature which discusses this problem.

The speculative crisis literature owes its roots, like the target zone literature, to Paul Krugman. In a path-breaking paper Krugman (1979) presents a deterministic model of BoP crisis under fixed exchange rates. The Krugman's model is based on the premise that countries have limited resources for defending their exchange rates and must abandon their currency pegs when foreign exchange reserves are exhausted. The central result of the model is that in a situation where the central bank has finite resources/reserves and it is creating domestic credit at a constant rate, the fixed exchange rate regime will break down following a speculative run. Flood and Garber (1984) and Obstfeld (1986) both extended the basic Krugman model to the stochastic case where there is uncertainty about the rate at which credit is expanding.

Blackburn and Sola (1993) use the following equations to illustrate the structure of these models. We start with the deterministic case, where the speculators have perfect foresight:

$$M_t/P_t = \alpha_0 - \alpha_1 i_t \alpha_0 \ , \ \alpha_1 > 0 \tag{2.92}$$

Equation (2.92) represents money market equilibrium. It states that the real money supply (M/p) is equal to real money demand (which depends on the interest rates i). The t subscripts refer to time.

$$P_t = S_t \ P^* \tag{2.93}$$

that is, PPP holds. P and P^* are the domestic and foreign price level respectively; S is the exchange rate.

$$i_t = i^* + S'_t/S_t \qquad (2.94)$$

Equation (2.94) is UIP where i^* is the foreign interest rate (assumed constant) and S'_t/S_t is the expected rate of domestic currency depreciation.

$$M_t \equiv D_t + F_t \qquad (2.95)$$

The money supply is defined as domestic credit (D) and the value of foreign currency reserves (F).

$$D_t = \mu \quad \mu > 0 \qquad (2.96)$$

Domestic credit is assumed to be growing at a constant exogenous rate equal to μ.

Using these, we can show that excessive domestic credit creation will be reflected in a loss of reserves. If we take equation (2.92) and substitute it from equation (2.93) for P and then substitute in for i from (2.94) we can derive:

$$M_t/P_t = \alpha_0 - \alpha_1 i \Rightarrow M_t/S_tP^* = \alpha_0 - \alpha_1(i^* + S'_t/S_t) \qquad (2.97)$$

Multiplying through by S_tP^* and rearranging gives us equation (2.98)

$$\Rightarrow M_t = \alpha_0\ S_tP^* - \alpha i^*\ S_tP^* - \alpha_1 S'_t P^*$$

$$\Rightarrow M_t = \beta_0 S_t - \beta_1 \dot{S}_t \qquad (2.99)$$

where $\beta_0 = (\alpha_0 - \alpha_i^*)\ p^*$ and $\beta_1 = \alpha_1 P^*$

If the exchange rate is fixed, $S_t = \hat{S}$ and $\hat{S} = 0$, and hence equation (2.98) becomes:

$$M_t = \beta_0\ \hat{S} \qquad (2.100)$$

From equation (2.95) we know that $M_t = D_t + F_t$, and hence we can rewrite equation (2.100) as

$$F_t = \beta_0\ \hat{S} - D_t \qquad (2.101)$$

Since $\hat{S}$ is constant because we are assuming a fixed exchange rate regime, equation. 2.101 implies that the rate of change of F must be equal to minus the rate of change of D. So if domestic credit is *increasing* at the rate μ, then F must be *falling* at the same rate.

Following Flood and Garber (1984), we find, before time t_0, D is rising at a rate μ and F is falling at a rate μ. Now if no attack occurred, then the central bank would eventually run out of reserves at time t. After t_0 the exchange rate floats and the money supply continues to grow at a rate equal to μ. The lower section of Figure 2.6 shows the time path of the exchange rate. It is initially fixed S. But in the post-speculative attack regime, we assume that currency floats, and hence after t_0, it depreciates at the same rate μ.

FIG. 2.6

A Speculative Attack in a Fixed Exchange Rate Regime

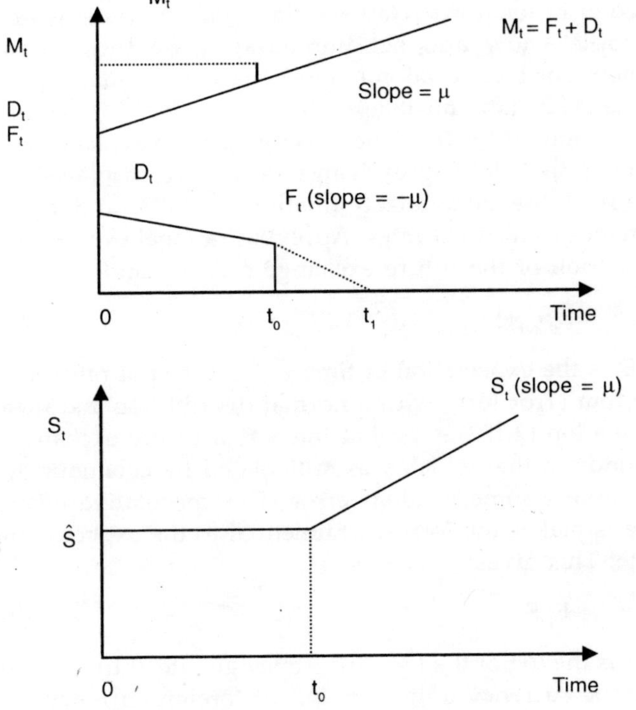

Changing the degree of capital mobility can change the timing of attacks. For example, if capital is not perfectly mobile yet goods prices continue to adjust, then the timing of attacks will be delayed because reserves fall at a slower rate.

In conclusion, the models of BoP crises essentially offer us a different way of showing that monetary authorities cannot follow monetary policy which is inconsistent with the fixed exchange rate target. If they do, then a speculative attack and the abandonment of the exchange rate target is inevitable.

2.1.9 The Rational Expectations Hypothesis of Exchange Rate Determination

This hypothesis is also known under the name of the 'Market Efficiency' or 'speculative efficiency' hypothesis of the exchange rate. The hypothesis often assumes rational expectations. Under floating exchange rate, with frequent daily movements of exchange rates, one would expect to find evidence of rational expectations. Rational expectations assume that people know and act immediately on the systematic components of their economic environment, so that they need not make systematic mistakes.

The origin of the hypothesis is the need to explain the large fluctuations that floating exchange rates have displayed in the aftermath of the generalized floating of 1973, and the poor performance of forward rates. Applying rational expectations to the prediction of the future exchange rate we find:

$$S_{t+1}=E_tS_{t+1}+U_{t+1} \tag{2.102}$$

where E_t is the expectation at time t, S is the spot rate, and U_{t+1} is a random error term with a normal distribution and mean of zero. Equation (2.102) says that the actual future exchange rate corresponds to that which was anticipated by economic agents plus or minus some random error. The speculative efficiency hypothesis makes the forward rate equal to the expected future spot rate; This gives:

$$F_t = E_t\, S_{t+1} \tag{2.103}$$

where F_t is the log of the forward exchange rate at time t defined as domestic currency units per unit of foreign currency.

Substituting equation (2.103) into (2.102) we obtain:

$$S_{t+1} = F_t + U_{t+1} \tag{2.104}$$

Equation (2.104) says that provided economic agents have rational expectations and there is no risk premium in the foreign exchange market, then the future spot rate should be equal to today's quoted forward rate plus a random error.

Various forms of this equation (2.104) or rather $S_{t+1} = a+bF_t+U_t$, have been tested by many economists like Levich (1978) and Frenkel (1982), Meese and Singleton (1982) and Cumby and Obstfeld (1984), Taylor (1988). The results of the tests have not always been encouraging. In general, the speculative hypothesis is rejected as the tests become more powerful. In developing countries the absence of forward markets and arbitrage means this model can hardly be applicable. Unfortunately, the assumptions behind the theories of exchange rate determination of perfect capital mobility and interest rate arbitrage, with efficient money and capital markets or asset markets, does not fit the reality of LDCs.

2.1.10 The News Approach to Exchange Rate Modelling

As we have seen that following the collapse of the Bretton Woods system in the early 1970s, economists tried to refashion their asset equilibrium models of the BoP into models of flexible exchange rates. The usual practice, at first, was to simplify the exchange rate models by assuming that exchange rate expectations were based on the current or past values of relevant economic variables. After a few years of renewed experience with a flexible exchange rate, it was widely realized that regardless of how well expectations about future exchange rate could be summarized *ex ante* by prevailing spot or forward exchange rates, each of the latter provided very poor predictions of the exchange rates that were actually observed *ex post*.

In fact, the recognition that the observed variation in exchange rates far exceeded the variation predicted *ex ante* by prevailing forward premiums or interest rate differentials suggested the importance of designing models in which exchange rate expectations were related to expectations about other variables in a forward-looking manner.

The news approach may be viewed as an extension of the efficient markets model and it emphasizes the importance of expectational revision in explaining why the forward exchange rate may be a poor predictor of the future exchange rate.

The new information or 'news' approach may be illustrated in the following way. If the vector Zi contains all variables—relevant for the process of exchange rate determination, then our equation for the evolution of the exchange rate change is

$$\Delta S_{t+1} = \alpha Z_{t+1} + \beta_{t+1} \quad (2.105)$$

where β_t is a serially uncorrelated error. In forming their (rational) expectations, agents will use this model and hence their expected change in the exchange rate from t to t + 1 will be

$$\Delta S^e_{t+1} = \alpha Z^e_{t+1} \quad (2.106)$$

Subtracting yields

$$\Delta S_{t+1} - \Delta S^e_{t+1} = \alpha(Z_{t+1} - Z^e_{t+1}) + \beta_{t+1} \quad (2.107)$$

which says that the error in forecasting the exchange rate change is driven by new information about the fundamental determinants of the exchange rate and a random error term. On using the definition of the forward premium we may rewrite the above equation as

$$\Delta S_{t+1} = fPt + \alpha(Z_{t+1} - Z^e_{t+1}) - \lambda_t + \beta_{t+1} \quad (2.108)$$

which simply reinforces the point made above that in periods when there is a lot of new information about fundamentals (i.e. the term in parenthesis is large), there will not be a close correspondence between ΔS_{t+1} and fP_t.

In the Dornbusch (1980) and Frenkel (1982) studies that pioneered the *'news'* approach, the results were found to be highly supportive. Generally, the unexpected change in the 'news items' were found to be significant determinants of the unexpected change in the exchange rate.

Apart from the original Dornbusch and Frenkel studies, MacDonald (1983) tests a news type model for six currencies against the US dollar over the period 1972 Q1 to 1979 Q4. He finds that unexpected monetary developments are sometimes statistically important but occasionally with the wrong sign!

An interesting finding by both Edwards (1983) and MacDonald (1983) is that in some regressions past news (i.e. lagged news terms) can have a significant effect on the unexpected exchange rate change. In sum, the results of the news item approach are not particularly robust across different currencies and the news items are sometimes statistically significant but wrong signed.

Overall, the news approach that combines the concept of exchange-market efficiency with conventional exchange-rate models provides a relatively fruitful area for research on exchange rate.

The news approach we have discussed focuses mainly on the issue of exchange rate volatility. However, the floating exchange rate period has been characterized by a tendency for exchange rates to become misaligned, that is, to move away from their long-run fundamental equilibrium value for an extended period. Two very recent theories have focused on this issue. The first is the literature on rational speculative bubbles; the second is the work of Frankel and Froot (1989) on heterogenous expectations (Chartists and Fundamentalists). Chartism or technical analysis is a popular method of exchange rate forecasting, it is so named because it makes no use of the economic and financial fundamentals deemed relevant to exchange rate determination. By use of graphical representation, it focuses on prices and seeks to detect repetitions of past price patterns. One primary method for detecting this pattern is Chartism, that relies on the charts to find recurring price patterns. The key to successful Chartism is the accurate and consistent determination of current trends. The aim is not to explain but to identify trends from careful examination of past data, including analysis of moving averages, past peaks and troughs. Exchange rates are often influenced by support and registance points, that is, specific rates which are hard to breach, because at that rate the market tends to consider the exchange rate too low or too high. For example, a falling currency will often receive a support from the market after a certain level of decline has been reported. Chartists tend to forecast by extrapolating recent trends as if they have 'bandwagon expectations'. If chartists predominate the foreign exchange market, they can exacerbate (or 'destabilize') swings in the exchange rate. The reason is that they will buy on upswings, thus driving the price up, and sell on downswings, thus forcing the price down. In that case the exchange rate deviates and gives rise to bubbles (when we find that frenetic and apparently irrational price surges were followed by a massive price collapse, we use the bubble analogy). Bubbles like bandwagons also affect the currency market. Much forex dealings defies rational expectations. Investors move in because everyone else is doing so. But all investors in bubbles are not necessarily irrational. It may make good sense to invest in a bubble, provided the investor knows when to sell out ! The time horizon of the investor is a critical variable, many traders and investors take a very short-run view. Fundamentalists, on the other hand, look at the macroeconomic fundamentals of exchange rate determination, such as interest rate differentials and purchasing power parity. The co-existence in the foreign exchange market of chartists and fundamentalists, the former relying on technical analysis and the later relying on analysis of economic fundamentals, can give rise to considerable instability of its own. Some experiments have been made to apply chaos theory to explain exchange rate gyrations. Work in this area is still in its infancy.

The rational bubble literature seeks to explain persistent departures of asset prices from their fundamental determinants while still assuming rational behaviour on the part of market participants (Blanchard and Fischer, (1989)). This is possible if one notes that the price of an asset today (P_t) is a function not only of the return one expects whilst holding the asset (the dividend) but also of its expected resale value. This is represented in equation 2.109:

$$P_t = [E\ (D_{t+1}/I_t) + E\ (P_{t+1}/I_t)]/\ (1 + r) \qquad (2.109)$$

D_{t+1} is dividend in period (t+l); I_t is the information set available at time t; P_{t+1} is the price of the asset in period t+l (its resale value); and r is the discount rate. If we assume that investors have rational expectations, the equation (2.109) can be solved to generate:

$$P_t = \sum_{i=1}^{\infty} E\left(D_{t+i} / I_t\right) / (1+r)^i + B_t \qquad (2.110)$$

B_t can be interpreted as the bubble component and could take the following form:

$$B_t = E\ (B_{t+1})/(1+r) \qquad (2.111)$$

that is, the bubble in this period is equal to the discounted value of the expected bubble next period. Rearranging equation (2.111) and given rational expectations, we get:

$$B_{t+1} = (1 + r)\ B_t + Z_t \qquad (2.112)$$

where Z_t is a random error serially uncorrelated with a mean of zero. Equation (2.112) states that bubbles grow in each period at the discount rate, r. If, as is likely, the bubbles have a probability of bursting in each period, then provided investors are a risk neutral, the bubbles must grow at an expected rate equal to r.

Thus, in the speculative bubble literature, in fact, investors weigh the probability of a continued rise in the rate of exchange against the probability of crash. There is an ex ante uncovered interest rate parity. The interest rate differential between home and abroad reflects the expected exchange rate changes, that is, the mathematical expectation of the change in the rate of exchange. As long as bubble does not bursts. Uncovered interest parity does not hold *ex post.*

2.1.11 Intertemporal Models of Open Economies

The empirical estimates of the integrated elasticities and absorption approaches to balance of payments reveal an important role of time in explaining the relationships between the macro-variables governing internal and external balance of a country. In fact, the use of time series data on trade balance, national income etc. to estimate the static Keynesian type of macro-econometric models has often resulted in specification errors and deviations of predicted values from the true values. Attempts have been made primarily in the 1980s to develop inter- temporal optimization models of external balance as a prelude to macro-econometric forecasting using time series data. The inter-temporal approach builds on micro-economic foundations in viewing the current account as the outcome of rational forward-looking decisions of economic agents about savings, investment and borrowing, and as a channel through which a country can optimally modify the time-path of its absorption relative to its production in response to various types of demand and supply shocks. The inter-temporal substitution effect of a parametric change can be viewed as the sum of consumption-smoothing and consumption-tilting by the optimizing agents through adjustments in discount/interest rate such that future is linked to the present.

The trade balance at any time 't' is given by:

$$BOT(t) = Y(t) - C(t) - G(t) - I(t) \tag{2.113}$$

where BOT is trade balance, Y is GDP, C is consumption expenditure, G is government purchases and I denotes domestic investment. Usually, investment is disregarded in these models, and real income and its temporal distribution are taken to be exogenous. The intertemporal budget constraint defined over an infinite time horizon implies that present value of the current account balance is zero and early period borrowing must be matched by later-period lending. Equations (2.114) below states that the present value of the current account is zero, such that the present value of consumption equals the difference between the present values of real income and of government purchases. Thus:

$$PV(BOT) = 0, \tag{2.114}$$
$$C = Y - G \tag{2.115}$$

where C = PV(C(t)), Y = PV[Y(t)] and G = PV[G(t)]. Optimization of inter-temporal, utility function by the agent requires for a two period case <t, t+1> the following condition to be satisfied:

$$\frac{U^1(C_{t+1})}{U^1(C_t)} = \frac{1+r}{1+d} \tag{2.116}$$

where r = rate of interest and d = discount rate

Using (2.116) & (2.114) one can relate C(t) to (Y – G) as :

$$C(t) = a(Y - G) \tag{2.117}$$

such that the trade balance BOT(t) becomes

$$BoT(t) = Y(t) - G(t) - a[Y - G] \tag{2.118}$$

When there is exogenous disturbance, say a terms of trade change, represented by Z(t), we have

$$\frac{dBoT(t)}{dZ(t)} = \frac{dY(t)}{dZ(t)} - \frac{dG(t)}{dZ(t)} - a\frac{d[Y-G]}{dZ(t)} \tag{2.119}$$

When output is given, a change in fiscal policy parameters affecting government expenditure will affect trade balance if:

$$\frac{dBoT(t)}{dG(t)} = -1 + a\frac{dG}{dG(t)} \tag{2.120}$$

One can use the inter-temporal framework to explain the relation between current account deficit and the budget deficit of the government. Frenkel and Razin (1987) have used this inter-temporal optimization framework to explain the effects of bond-financing *vis-à-vis* money creation in financing of government's budget deficit on current account trade deficits, and they have also related the expectation changes in the interest rate to integrate the current account with the capital account of balance of payments. The model can also be extended to include tradable and non-tradable goods in a dynamic framework to study the inter-temporal variations in terms of trade and real exchange rate variations. One such attempt is done by Stephen Turnovsky (1995).

One of the underlying assumptions of the inter-temporal approach is the ability of a country to borrow or lend unlimited amounts at an exogenously given world rate of interest, subject to the inter-temporal budget constraint. For all practical purposes, such an option does not exist for many industrial as well as less developed economies, as the debt crisis of the 1980s clearly demonstrates. Moreover, the effects of shocks in either demand or supply on current account balance are often found to be country-specific and not general in nature, except for the case of United States where the effects of fiscal shocks on the world macroeconomic variables are often found to be statistically significant. This is not surprising in view of the importance of the U.S. economy and its policies on the world economy in large, particularly after the World War II. The interesting aspect of the inter-temporal optimizing models in open economies is to generate testable propositions linking fiscal stimulus, current and capital account balance and productivity shocks, that can suitably use the modern techniques of time-series econometrics, like stationarity and persistence, etc. in making future forecasts.

Another inter-temporal optimizing approach based on different optimizing rules, that has recently gained its importance is the NATREX (Natural Real Exchange Rate) approach of Stein (1990, 1995, 1999). This approach has been able to satisfactorily explain the medium-to-long run dynamics of the real exchange rate in several industrial countries. Assuming perfect international capital mobility, and rejecting the standard hypothesis of perfect knowledge and perfect foresight and allowing expenditure to be separated between consumption and investment, which are decided by different agents, the NATREX guarantees both the long-run internal and external equilibrium, since the NATREX is measuring the inter-cyclical equilibrium real exchange rates ensuring BoP equilibrium in the absence of cyclical factors, speculative capital movements and movements in international reserves.

Here the focus is on the real part of the economy. That is, $r = r_R (p_f/p_h)$ where r is the nominal exchange rate, r_R is the Natural Real Exchange rate. p_f/p_h is the ratio of foreign price level to domestic price level. Hence differential rates of inflation produce offsetting changes in r. In fact, the Natural real exchange rate is the adjustment variable in equation S–I= CA=0 (long-run external equilibrium condition). To illustrate the dynamics of this approach, let us suppose a situation that compels to make S–I< 0. In that case, the interest rate cannot play the role of the adjustment variable since we have assumed perfect capital mobility, Rather the difference between national investment and national saving originates a corresponding inflow of long-term capital. The NATREX appreciates accordingly, leading to deterioration in the current account. In fact, NATREX is the benchmark against which we can measure the misalignment of the actual real exchange rate. If we find that actual real exchange rate is somehow lower than the NATREX, we may then say that the domestic currency is undervalued.

2.1.12 Growth, Development and Balance of Payments

One possible mechanism through which trading performance is connected to sustainable rates of economic growth is the balance of payments, which can act as a fundamental constraint on the rate at which the output of any economy can expand. The idea behind the balance of payments constraint can be traced back to Harrod's foreign trade multiplier. Further, the ideas have been advanced by Kaldor and more recently by Thirlwall (1979), McCombie and Thirlwall (1992, 1994), Kaldor (1979), however, stressed the importance of 'outside' demand in determining the growth of a national or regional economy. A simple exposition of the idea behind the balance of payments constraint can be explained as follows: economic growth creates a variety of demands which cannot be satisfied by domestic production alone; in general, therefore, the faster is the rate of demand (output) growth, the faster is the growth of imports. It would be natural to think of these imports in terms of natural resources that cannot be produced at home—especially fuel and raw materials—but the idea is broader than that and today the import of 'technology intensive' or sophisticated consumer goods may be far more important. However, any excess of imports over exports (a trade deficit) that is generated needs to be financed by borrowing from overseas or from a rundown of an economy's stock of overseas assets, and over long period of time this situation is not a viable one. Of course, other economies may also be growing and this stimulates the demand for exports, so the constraint will tend to operate as a constraint on the rate of growth relative to that occurring amongst the economy's major trading partners. It follows that the rate at which the economy can grow (without running into a problem of debt accumulation) depends essentially on its international competitiveness—its ability to export as well as its propensity to import. In other words, in the context of a simple Keynesian model with rigid prices and fixed exchange rates, and given exogenously the time path of exports, growth for internal causes has an unfavourable effect on the BoP. In fact, the more income growth the more imports grow, so that, given the path of exports, the BoP is effected unfavourably. It follows that growth finds a limitation in the BoP restraint or, more precisely, in the international reserves restraint. But under flexible exchange rates, the BoP constraint can be eased by appropriate variation in the exchange rate (*McCombie and Thirlwall*, 1994).

In 1933, Harrod demonstrated that if the only component of autonomous demand was exports, then there could be a foreign trade multiplier such that:

$$Ya = (1/mpm)\ (Xa) \tag{2.121}$$

where Ya is the change in aggregate income in nation A, Xa is the change in A's exports and mpm is the marginal propensity to import by A's residents. After the General Theory this Harrod formulation was recast into a Keynesian foreign trade multiplier mechanism. In the resulting Keynesian foreign trade multiplier analysis, the Harrod's emphasis on exogenous exports was lost. The Keynesian trade multiplier literature indicated that a domestic policy to stimulate effective demand would induce some increase in imports relative to exports, thereby creating a BoP problem. The expansion of domestic effective demand spilled over into a demand for imports. This growth in imports would stimulate some economic expansion in the nation's trading partners; thereby inducing some expansion of the nation's exports. This feedback effect merely reduced the magnitude of the BoP problems.

Thirlwall (1979) developed a demand driven model of international payments from Harrod's trade multiplier insight. His analysis provides guidelines on the rate of economic growth a nation can achieve without suffering deterioration in its payments balance. A demand driven model is a Keynes model where employment is determined by the point of effective demand. It does not employ the classical presumption of continuous full employment. Demand driven models do not assume that long-run economic growth is exogenously determined by technological progress and labour force growth.

In Thirlwall's model, export and import functions are represented by:

$$Xa = (P_d / P_f)^z Y^{erw} \tag{2.122}$$
$$Ma = (P_d / P_f)^u Y^{ea} \tag{2.123}$$

where Xa and Ma are exports from nation A and imports into A; (P_d/P_f) is the ratio of domestic prices to foreign prices expressed in terms of the domestic currency of A; z is the price elasticity of demand for A's exports, u is the A's price elasticity of demand for imports, ea is A's income elasticity of demand for imports; and erw is the rest of the world's income elasticity of demand for A's exports.

If z and u are small and/or relative prices do not change significantly, then substitution effects can be ignored. The analysis concentrates on income effects.

Using the natural log form of above two equations and ignoring substitution effects, one obtains Thirlwall's Law of the growth of income that is consistent with an unchanged trade balance as:

$$Ya = X/ea \tag{2.124}$$

where Ya is the rate of growth of nation A's GNP, X is the rate of growth of A's exports and ea is A's income elasticity of demand for imports. Since the growth of exports for A depends primarily on the rest of the world's growth in income (Y_{erw}) and the world's income elasticity of demand for A's exports |erw|, i.e.

$$X = (erw)\,(yrw) \tag{2.125}$$

Then equation (2.124) can be written as:

$$Ya = (erw\ .\ yrw)/ea \tag{2.126}$$

If a nation starts from a position of international payments balance, then there is only one rate of growth that a nation can sustain without running into a BoP deficit. This sustainable growth rate, as shown in equation (2.126) depends on the rest of the world's growth and relevant income elasticities for imports and exports.

If the growth in the value of imports is to exactly equal the growth in the value of exports, i.e. erw. Yrw = Ya. ea (2.127)

$$\text{then } (Ya/Yrw) = (erw/ea) \tag{2.128}$$

Equation (2.128) is called Thirlwall's Law. This Law indicates that the ratio of the growth of income in nation A to the growth rate in the rest of the world is equal to the ratio of the income elasticity of demand for A's exports by the rest of the world to A's income elasticity of demand for import. In other words, this Law indicates that a sustainable current account balance can be achieved only if the income growth of a nation is equal to the ratio of income elasticities of demand for exports to imports multiplied by the rate of income growth of the nation's trading partners. Differences in income elasticities can therefore, through a BoP constraint force nations with trade deficits to reduce this growth rate to one. If erw/ea < 1, and if growth in A is constrained by the need to maintain a balance of payments equilibrium, then nation A is condemned to grow at a slower rate than the rest of the world.

For example, if LDCs of the world have a comparative advantage in the exports of raw materials and other basic commodities while the LDCs have a high income elasticity of demand for the manufactured products of the developed world, then for these LDCs, $e_{rw} / e_{LDC} < 1$

If economic development and the balance of payments equilibrium is left to the free market and a balance in the current account is required, then the LDCs are condemned to relative poverty, and the global inequality of income will become larger over time.

Moreover, if the rate of population growth in the LDCs (P_{LDC}) is greater than the rate of population growth in the developed world (P_{DW}), that is if $P_{LDC} > P_{DW}$, then the future of the LDCs is even more dismal. The rate of growth of GNP per capita of the LDCs will show a greater relative decline (or slower increase) compared to the standard of living of the developed world, i.e.

$$(Y_{LDC}/P_{LDC}) << (Y_{Dw}/P_{Dw})$$

As long as the developed world's population growth rate is less than this long-term economic growth rate, these nations will enjoy a rising living standard. Moreover, the slower the rate of growth in income of the rich developed nations, the more rapidly the poor nations are likely to sink deeper into poverty.

However, modern exposition tells a different story. The basic idea behind the constraint (in the hands of Thirlwall, McCombie,) can be explained more formally as follows: if movements in the price levels prevailing in different economies are, over time, counterbalanced by movements in the exchange rate, then the growth rate of an economy consistent with BoP equilibrium, Gb, can be expressed as $\alpha W/\Pi$, when W is the rate of growth of income in the. 'rest of the world', α is the world income elasticity of demand for exports, and Π is the domestic income elasticity of demand for imports. Thirlwall (1979), shows that Gb predicts actual rates of growth around the world with reasonable accuracy.

Some of the difficulties LDCs faced in obtaining enough foreign capital inflows for financing development were approached via the so-called 'two gap models' of aid, trade and development (*Chenery and Bruno*, 1962). The strategic importance of exports and other sources of foreign exchange in stimulating savings and import propensities was first formalized in the two-gap model of economic growth. This model influenced policy-making, in both national governments and international financing agencies. This model was used to show that and extra dollar of foreign aid would relax the binding import constraint and activate unutilized potential savings to raise the rate of growth. In these models, on plausible assumptions about desired rate and pattern of growth, a gap between *ex ante* exports and imports and a parallel gap between ex ante investment and savings were estimated. Since exports of most underdeveloped primary commodity producing countries are price and income-inelastic and many of them also face non-price barriers in trade, whereas their planned investment is often relatively import-intensive, it was often found that the *ex-ante* trade gap was larger than *ex ante* investment savings gap. It was argued then that planning authorities of the country concerned should plan to borrow or canvas for aid to cover the larger of the two gaps, and the development could proceed as planned. Few countries were, however, in the happy position of being able to borrow or receive as aid. Now when the foreign trade is dominant, for example, it is appropriate to allow savings to go down, in order to make the investment-saving gap rise to the export-import gap rather than stimulate investment and increase the trade gap further. The contribution of the Chenery model is in identifying which of these gaps is the effective constraint on growth. However in the two-gap model, the growth rate and BoP are the two key endogenous variables, and emerge as a consequence of domestic and foreign savings gaps.

The basic two-gap model can be summarized as follows. We make the following assumptions:

(i) There exists a fixed maximum propensity to save out of income, such that max $S = sY \# 0 < s < 1$ (2.129) where s is the average and marginal propensity to save.

(ii) Certain capital goods can only be obtained from foreign sources.

(iii) Exports are exogenous and that neither exports nor imports could be changed by altering exchange rates or relative prices.

(iv) The amount of imports of machinery and equipment, intermediate inputs and other essential items needed to sustain a level of output and investment, and therefore a rate of growth, are fixed.

(v) There is a lack of substitutibility between domestic and foreign resources. There is always a minimum amount of foreign exchange required to sustain growth. Thus, we can write

$$Y = \min (K_d/k_1 , K_f/k_2) \quad (2.130)$$

where $k_1 = K_d/Y$ is the amount of domestic capital required to produce one unit of output and $k_2 = K_f/Y$ is the amount of foreign capital required to produce one unit of output.

Given the lack of substitutibility between domestic and foreign resources, the production function implies that growth will be constrained by either K_d (domestic capital) or K_f (foreign capital), whichever is the minimum.

We can assume for simplicity that the country in question imports capital goods only, so that:

$$M=I_f \quad (2.131)$$

where M is the quantity of imports and

$$I_f = \Delta K_f / \Delta t = K_f \quad (2.132)$$

Let us further assume that imports are a fixed proportion of GNP, such that

$$M = mY \qquad (2.133)$$

From the supply side, export possibilities depend on the economy's output capacity, so that

$$\max X = xY \quad 0 < x < 1 \qquad (2.134)$$

Let us suppose that the growth rate permitted by foreign exchange is less than that permitted by domestic savings. Thus, from the production function, we have

$$Y = K_f/K_2 \qquad (2.135)$$

Differentiating both sides of the above equation with respect to time t, we obtain:

$$\frac{\Delta Y}{\Delta t} = \frac{1}{k_2} \cdot \frac{\Delta K_f}{\Delta t}$$

or,

$$\dot{Y} = \frac{1}{k_2} . K_f \qquad (2.136)$$

Substitution yields,

$$\dot{Y} = \frac{m}{k_2} . Y$$

therefore, $\frac{\dot{Y}}{Y} = \frac{m}{k_2}$ (2.137)

That is, the growth of output is equal to the ratio between the import-output ratio m and the incremental foreign investment goods-output ratio k_2.

Similarly, if domestic savings is the limit to growth, we shall have

$$\frac{\dot{Y}}{Y}=\frac{s}{k_1} \qquad (2.138)$$

If the planners set a target growth rate say, g*, the required saving ratio s* and import ratio m* can be calculated from equations (2.137) and (2.138) as:

$$s^* = g^* k_1 \qquad (2.139)$$
$$\text{and } m^* = g^* k_2 \qquad (2.140)$$

If the maximum domestic savings is found to be less than the level required to achieve the target growth then there is said to exist an investment-saving gap equal to

$$I_d^* - \max S = S_d^* - \max S \qquad (2.141)$$

(Since in equilibrium I_d must equal S_d *)

$$I_d^* - \max S = s^*Y - sY = k_1 g^*Y - sY \qquad (2.141A)$$

Similarly, there is said to exist an import-export gap equal to:

$$M^* - \max X = k_2 g^*Y - xY \qquad (2.142)$$

It follows, therefore, that the investment-saving and import-export gaps *(ex ante)* can be written as:

$$k_1 g^*Y - sY \leq F \qquad (2.143)$$
$$\text{and } k_2 g^*Y - xy \leq F \qquad (2.144)$$

where F is the foreign capital (exchange) inflow.

It is thus intuitively clear that if the target growth is to be achieved, foreign capital inflow must fill the larger of the two gaps so that the bottleneck can be avoided.

Initially, the two gap-saving and trade-models [*Chenery and Bruno* (1962); *Chenery and Strout* (1966); *Mckinnon* (1964) and *Weisskof* (1972)]—were used to identify and analyse the binding constraint on the growth. Later, a third gap—fiscal—was also explored for its independent constraining influence on the economic growth of an economy. To an extent a fiscal gap can directly constrain economic growth, it can also influence the trade gap and, therefore, makes an indirect impact on the economy. However, the fiscal constraint in a three gap model is often predicated on the assumptions that the public and private investments (*Blejer and Khan,* 1984; *Barro,* 1989) are complementary to each other and savings are forced through inflation. Using a three-gap simulation analysis of foreign resource flows, Taylor, (1993) finds that a "substantial realignment in international payments would be required to accelerate growth for developing nations overall" (p. 35). Bacha (1990), using these assumptions and taking two gaps at a time, finds that foreign transfers are more important than foreign savings. He finds that a fiscal constraint might also crowd-out investment, even with excess net capital inflows, in a country with a low import content of investment. These results rest crucially on two assumptions already mentioned earlier. While the complementarity assumption has become a regular feature of the macroeconomic investment analysis, the latter assumption that there does not exist a market for government bonds, (*Bacha,* 1990, p. 284) leaves one hundred per cent monetization of fiscal deficits or inflation tax as the only source of financing them. Such an extreme assumption continues to be invoked by the researchers contrary to the ground realities, though budget deficits continue to be monetised in varying proportions in several countries. This explains why the IMF, and the World Bank continue to emphasize on how to contain the inflationary pressures and fiscal deficits through tight monetary and fiscal policies. In LDCs, there exists a market for government bonds however limited it may be. The governments, which can tap the capital market through open market operations, also often resort to the practice of a partial monetization of budget deficits. In short, public sector borrowing continues to be a major source of financing fiscal deficits. (*Downes and Vaez-Zadeh,* 1991).

Most of the works on identification of constraints on growth in LDCs, usually fail to identify the dominant constraints and the interactions between the three gaps as like 'gaps' for domestic saving, foreign savings and government savings. An exception has been made in the paper by S. Sundararajan and Ganti Subrahmanyam (1995) where the interactions between capital flows, investment and output and between binding gaps and national economic policies have been analysed in terms of a three-gap macroeconomic model of a small open economy. Let us briefly sketch the working of this three-gap model.

The model has four classes of actors: (1) a private sector that includes households—they buy factor services, produce, buy and sell commodities, save, invest and pay taxes; (2) a foreign trade sector that imports and exports goods. Capital inflows and outflows also take place; (3) A central bank that regulates the money stock, conducts open market operations and accommodates deficit financing by the government; (4) A government sector that also competes in private sector activities and the finances for which come from taxes and market borrowings including from the central bank.

The economy produces a distinct good that is both consumed and traded abroad. It also imports goods for consumption purposes. Prices and capital stock can change only through time. There is no developed money market, although the fiscal deficit is financed through both open market operations and deficit financing. Export prices, import prices, foreign prices, and interest rates are exogenously determined. The economy operates under a fixed exchange rate regime.

The Model

The model is set out as follows:

$$C_P = C_P\,(i, Y_P, F, [e+P^*-P])\; C_{YP}, C_{PF}, C_{P(.)} > o, C_{P1} < 0 \qquad (2.145)$$

$$I_P = I_P(i, i^e, Y_P, K, CR, F, I_G)\; I_{Pie}, I_{PYP}, I_{PK}, I_{PCR}, I_{PF}, I_{PG} > 0, \quad I_{Pi} < 0. \qquad (2.146)$$

$$X = X(Y^f, [e+XP-(e+P)], e^v)\; X_{yf} > 0,\; X_{(.)}, X_v < 0. \qquad (2.147)$$

$$M = M(Y, (e+MP - P)\, e^v, I)\; M_Y, M_v, M_1 > 0,\; M_{(.)} < 0. \qquad (2.148)$$

$$C_G = C_G\,(T, (e+ P^* - P))\; C_{GT,}\, C_{G(.)} > 0 \qquad (2.149)$$

$$Y = C + I + (X - M) \qquad (2.150)$$

$$S^* = S\,(Y, F, i, [e+P^*-P])\; S_Y, S_{i,} > 0,\; S_{(.)}\, S_F < O. \qquad (2.151)$$

$$F = M-X \qquad (2.152)$$

$$S\, £S^* = Y - C \qquad (2.153)$$

$$C = C_p + C_G = C(Y, i, F, [e+p^* - P])\; C_Y, C_{(.)}, C_F > 0, \quad C_i < 0 \qquad (2.154)$$

$$Y^d_P = Y - T \qquad (2.155)$$
$$Y_G = T + T^f \qquad (2.156)$$
$$D = Y_G - (C_G + i^e + B_{t-1}) \qquad (2.157)$$
$$(S_P - I_P) = D\ B(i,w) + H(P,m),\ B_i,\ B_W,\ H_P > 0,\ H_m < 0. \qquad (2.158)$$
$$I_n = I_P + I_G \qquad (2.159)$$
$$S_P = Y_P - C_P \qquad (2.160)$$
$$I = I_n + kK \qquad (2.161)$$

All the quantity variables are expressed in logarithms of real value. The variables are denoted as follows: C_P is the private consumption, 'i' is nominal interest rate, Y_P is the disposable income, 'e' is the exchange rate, I_P is the private investment, 'i^e' is the equity rate of interest, F is the net capital inflow, CR is the commercial bank credit, K is the capital stock, I_G is the government investment, X is the exports, M is the imports, Y^d and Y are the real domestic as well as full employment incomes, Y^f is the world real income, 'exp(emp)' is the export (import) prices in domestic currency, p^* is the world prices, 'e^v' is the exchange rate volatility, I is the gross investment, I_n is the net investment, P is the domestic prices, C_G is the Government consumption, 'T^f' is the transfer payments, 'i^eB' is the return on the bonds, D is the fiscal deficit, B is the bonds, H is the high-powered money, W is the wealth, 'k' is the rate of depreciation, S^* is the *ex-ante* savings defined as the real gross savings potentially available for investment and 'm' is the real money balances.

Equation (2.145) posits private consumption as a negative function of the nominal interest rate, and as a positive function of private disposable income and relative prices. Private investment in equation (2.146) is expressed as a function of interest rates, disposable income, capital stock, credit, net capital flows. It is also assumed that private investment is proportionate to government investment. Equation (2.147) explains exports as a positive function of the world real income and as a negative function of relative prices and exchange rate volatility. Equation (2.148) can also be defined analogously for the import function. While equation (2.149) states that government consumption is positively related to total tax revenues and relative prices equation (2.151) defines the functional relationship with income capital flows and nominal interest rates.

Equations (2.150), (2.152) to (2.157), (2.159) and (2.160) are the identities. Equation (2.158) constrains the excess of private savings over private investment to the fiscal deficit, which is postulated to be financed by both open market operations and deficit financing. Equation (2.161) states the gross investment as the sum of net and replacement investments.

Solving the Model: At this stage, the model consists of 17 equations in 34 variables, of which 17 are exogenous, while leaving the other 17 variables to be solved simultaneously in the system. In order to study the implications of the constraints on investment, and growth, we also specify the following non-negativity constraints.

$$Y \leq Y^* \tag{2.162}$$

$$F = M - X \leq F^* \tag{2.163}$$

$$I > 0 \tag{2.164}$$

where Y^* is the potential output and equation (2.163) states F to be an exogenously given F^* for independently binding constraints.

Solving the equation system, we obtain the impact effect solutions for savings (I_s), trade (I_T), fiscal (I_D), savings-trade (I_{ST}), savings-fiscal (I_{SD}), trade-fiscal (I_{TD}), and savings trade-fiscal (I_{STD}) constrained investment regimes.

The main findings of this paper based on the above mentioned equations are as follows:

First, a tight monetary policy (an increase in 'i') produces a *contractionary effect* on saving constrained investment. This suggests that any attempt to force savings through a tight monetary policy produces a fall in investment and output. At the same time, it produces an expansionary effect on I_T, I_{ST}, I_{SD} and I_{STD} through a capital flow induced increase in investment. These results also indicate that if capital inflow is a criterion for growth, an increase in 'i' would unambiguously increase investment and growth. In short, as far as interest rate as a policy instrument is concerned, saving is the most binding gap on investment.

Second, devaluation produces an expansionary effect on I_S, I_F, I_{ST} and I_{STD} along the traditional lines. Its effect on the fiscal constrained investment is *contractionary*. Therefore, if the *fiscal gap* is a binding constraint on investment (this may be the case in many developing countries), devaluation may unconventionally produce a contractionary effect.

Third, an easy monetary policy (an increase in the availability of CR) produces an expansionary impact on I_S and I_D, while creating a *contractionary* effect under I_T, I_{SD} and I_{STD} regimes. The negative CR effect may imply that when an economy undergoes macroeconomic reforms, the industries will have an easy access to cheap capital at home and abroad. This would reduce the demand for CR and lead to surplus funds in the inter-bank money market, and a fall in the money market rate, etc. Therefore, any attempt to revive investment through a lowering of the liquidity ratio may create surplus funds in the inter-bank money market. Under these conditions the *trade gap* also becomes a binding constraint on growth.

Fourth, the trade-fiscal constrained regime produces an ambiguous effect on investment and growth, irrespective of the policy choice. This is due to the influence of M_1 on investment.

Fifth, as far as the effect of fiscal policy (an increase in T) is concerned, it produces a positive effect on I_T, I_D and I_{SD} while its effect under I_S and I_{STD} is *contractionary*. When the governments increase 'T' as a part of the adjustment programme, all the *three gaps* would be a binding constraint on investment and growth.

Sixth, coming to the impact of capital flows on investment, if M_1 is low, the *trade (savings) gap* is the most binding constraint on investment in response to a (n) fall (increase) in capital inflows. On the other hand, a high M_1 would indicate that a binding *fiscal gap* will decrease investment.

Seventh, the results of the relationship between F, Y and I indicate that the trade fiscal gaps together become binding constraints when the governments try to take the output and investment to their potential levels. Any fall in F below these constrained levels would produce a negative effect on Y and I. This result indicates that LDCs may not possibly achieve significant growth if they considerably depend on *capital inflow*. Therefore, those countries that are constrained by the *saving-*

fiscal and *savings-trade-fiscal gaps* cannot achieve significant investment and growth. If the LDCs were to take Y and I above their potential levels, the *savings-trade gaps* would alone be jointly binding for growth.

The identification of the regimes of constrained investment and growth and the policy choices involved as revealed through the discussion of the three-gap models point to the importance of devising policies in less developed economies towards management of their balance of payments which take into account specific features of these economies. In fact, the structuralist approach to macroeconomics developed with the background of the experiences of many countries of Latin America with chronic balance of payments deficits, emphasizes the various forms of supply and demand constraints on real output in many LDCs and the institutional and policy-induced distortions in the functioning of different markets that make the operation of standard policy packages on balance of payments adjustments not only difficult but quite often irrelevant and defunct. It is possible to imagine a situation in many LDCs where devaluation of national currency may have contractionary effects something which the standard Keynesian framework of absorption approach to balance of payments will usually consider to be counter-intuitive. The structural bottlenecks in the short run may cause inflation to occur when there is an expansion of domestic demand, and when the government devalues its currency to wipe out the trade deficit; there may be redistributive mechanisms at work which will not only contract domestic output but may also end up with the greater trade deficit (*Krugman and Taylor*, 1978). A lot therefore depends on the combinations of alternative instruments of government policies used on the basis of specific constraints within which an economy is operating, and not on blanket stabilization programmes as are suggested by the IMF for all countries experiencing balance of payments deficits. In fact, lagged supply responses, market imperfections, institutional rigidities and absence of well developed financial markets make the tasks of macroeconomic policy management in open economies much more challenging than are comprehended in many analytical models of balance of payments adjustments based on simplistic assumptions. Our discussions above, however, point out the analytical issues involved in the adjustment process both in the short and the long-run, and the need to integrate various elements into a holistic framework that suits the candid conditions of developing economy like India and makes the alternative projections about the future state of the economy and its balance of payments position meaningful. The chapter three reviews critically the various studies on India's balance of payments made by different scholars in the light of analytical insights discussed above.

The discussions in the above Chapter provide some useful insights. First of all alternative approaches to the theory of balance of payments emphasize the importance of different macroeconomic variables in shaping the adjustments to disequilibrium situations in a country's balance of payments—one needs a holistic or integrated approach to assess the importance of these factors, price, income, money supply, asset composition, inflation, exchange rate, etc., to name a few, in the balance of payments adjustments of a nation. The importance of the interactions between commodity, money and asset markets, the role of exchange rate expectations and interest-rate differentials have also been emphasized in the literature, and a truly macroeconomic framework for an open economy needs to consider all these aspects. The fact that we can assess alternative models to focus on one/two aspects usually, is prompted by the need for simplification—a full scale macro-model with variables capturing all possible repercussions in current and capital accounts of balance of payments, is difficult to handle even for analytical purposes. Secondly, the policy dilemma facing a nation between internal balance and external balance has been discussed to highlight alternative policy choices by the national governments for balance of payments management. The target zone approach and models of exchange rate behaviours are particularly important in this context, and informational asymmetries between agents in foreign exchange markets often provide sources of cyclical behaviours. Thirdly, the inter-temporal framework links balance of payments adjustments to the process of economic growth and development, and for a developing country like India, perception of foreign exchange constraint and its relation with saving-investment and fiscal gaps constitutes important insights regarding interdependence of alternative economic policies in open economies.

3

Balance of Payments in India—A Review of Existing Literature

The existing literature on the subject is wide and varied. But most part of the literature deals either with problems which have arisen in the short run, or with selected aspects such as the analysis of the export performance, the progress of import substitution or of external assistance, evaluation of international trade policies, etc. and the relevant policy implications for the purpose. We have selected major studies from amongst these, which throw light directly on the balance of payments crisis resulting either from balance of trade or balance of payments deficits and hence contain insights about the determinants of the balance of trade and balance of payments in our country.

Some authors have analysed the export performance. Some other scholars have vigorously searched for the extent and efficacy of import substitution that has taken place particularly after the initiation of Feldman-Mahalanobis strategy in India in 1956. Some other authors have examined the efficacy of various policy instruments that have been adopted from time to time for dealing with India's balance of payments problems. When categorized, we find that the published works since 1950s are numerous. For our purpose, among many we take the major ones. The variety of the studies on India's balance of payments reflected the complexity of the issues involved:

(i) Studies on the analysis of India's export performance
(ii) The progress of import substitution
(iii) Devaluation and its impact on the Indian economy
(iv) BoP problems associated with the foreign trade and payments policies.

3.1 EXPORT PERFORMANCE

During the 1950s India's export earnings were almost stagnant. The presumption was that this stagnation was created mainly due to external factors operating on the demand side only, and it was beyond India's control to cope with the situation. Even the official document of India's Second Five-Year Plan put that tea, jute and cotton which accounted for nearly one-half of the total exports, met increasing competition from abroad, which resulted in creating overall deficits in the BoP. The view that the stagnation of India's export was a reflection of an inelastic foreign demand for India's major exports was supported by a study of Dr. S.J. Patil (1959). The view was not completely correct as some years after, authors like Manmohan Singh (1964) and B. Cohen (1964) had shown somewhat different pictures compared to Patel's argument. On the basis of a large number of commodity studies covering the bulk of India's traditional exports, Singh (1970) has explained how the domestic factors, including the ill-conceived planning strategies, had greatly contributed to a decline in India's share of world trade for many of these products. So severe was the bias against exports with the ushering in of import substitution under the Mahalanobis plan that India from being the second largest exporter of textiles in world markets (about 18 per cent share) reached a level of 1 per cent in the course of five to six years. This was due to faulty textile policy, argued Singh. In many other products too, India lost its markets, he showed. Similar results had been obtained by Cohen. In this connection, a study of Bhabatosh Datta, S. Chakraborty, M. Bhattacharya and Gouri Ghosh (1962), seeking to analyse the impact of Indian economic development on the country's export is also worth-mentioning.

In the early post-reform period, India witnessed a considerable buoyancy in exports (during 1993-94 to 1995-96 period) when the annual growth rate of exports averaged at nearly 20 percent in US dollar terms. This unprecedented growth rate of India's exports during the mid-1990s has received a lot of attention to the researchers. That growth of world trade and sharp depreciation of the external value of the rupee following the reform were the driving factor towards this growth of exports were highlighted by many of the most analysis of the researchers [*Brahmbhatt et. al.* 1996; *Marjit* and *Ray Chaudhuri,* 1997; *Srinivasan,* 1998, among others].

Study by Kumar (1998) has shown that India's growth in the exports since 1996 was a combination of many factors. At one hand there had been a decline in the growth of world trade, on the other the East Asian Crisis of 1997-98 had put a tremendous pressure over India's exports thus shrinking its demand adversely affecting international competitiveness of India's exports due to sharp depreciation of East Asian currencies. Further the author argued that abolition of dual exchange rate and consequent introduction of unified market determined exchange rate management in March 1993 might affect the India's competitiveness. And in real terms, rupee would be appreciated in value.

That India's failure to diversify the commodity composition of her exports in the late 1990s has adversely affected her exports was studied by Sinha Roy (1998[a]) and Ganesh Kumar *et. al.* (1999). In another study, Sinha-Roy (1998[b]) showed that India's exports responded to growth in world demand, while at the same times, the exchange rate, a player in the game, played at the most, only a facilitating role during reform period. In fact export performance during liberalization could not be attributed to exchange rate movements alone. Further, the depreciating rupee was to be effective in promoting exports only in situations of growing demand. Lall (1999) observed that the slowdown of exports in 1998-99 by 4 percent was of short duration, while exports thereafter had rebounded to 11.5 percent in dollar terms in 1999-2000. He emphasized that export slowdown after the mid-nineties was driven mainly by external condition.

3.2 ANALYSIS OF IMPORT SUBSTITUTION

In so far as the question of measurement of import substitution in Indian industries was concerned, we may name Padma Desai (1972) and V.R. Panchamukhi (1976) among others. Using four different measures of import substitution, Padma Desai has analysed the pattern of import substitution in Indian industries during the period 1951 to 1963 in each type of industries; consumer goods, intermediate goods and investment goods. This study brings out that for the entire period import substitution in the investment goods sector seemed to predominate. Using a Chenery type approach, in terms of technical change, the change in size and composition of final demand etc., Panchamukhi (1965) has sought to explain growth in output in the Indian economy during 1959-61. Manmohan Singh (1976) on the other hand in the same context argued that import-substitution strategies was not wholly bad. The faulty programming of import substitution coupled with the poor performance of the public sector enterprises producing capital goods in India, led to considerable unutilized capacity and put India in jeopardy. According to him, it was faulty in that due care was not taken at all to discourage non-essential domestic production, though balance of payments problems often led to severe restrictions on those goods. Similarly, very often import controls rather than tariffs have been the principal instrument of protection.

3.3 ELASTICITIES OF DEMAND FOR FOREIGN GOODS

Some workers such as M. Dutta (1964) and G.C. da Costa (1965) have estimated income and price elasticities of demand for Indian exports and imports. M. Dutta's work covered the period 1951 to 1960; he analysed the behaviour of India's merchandise private imports and exports. He found that the demand for Indian exports was fairly elastic with respect to world industrial production. Moreover, relative price played insignificant role in explaining both exports and imports. Like Dutta, G.C. da Costa found the same result as for the price elasticities of demand for Indian exports. The period of his study covered from 1953 to 1962. However, unlike Dutta, da Costa did not find the demand for Indian exports to be elastic with respect to world real income. Moreover, unlike Dutta, his results showed that relative prices of our exports should be considered as one of the crucial variables in the export performance, (as his estimation showed high elasticities of substitution between India's exports and those of her competitors). da Costa's estimation deserved special attention because following Marshall-Lerner condition the success or failure of devaluation in improving a country's balance of trade depended on the magnitude of the elasticities,. But these studies are beset with some methodological and statistical limitations. All the studies analysed a period of ten years, and as such were exposed to biases associated with a small sample. It is interesting to note that some studies in recent years have shown that the Marshall-Lerner condition does not seem to be satisfied in India. The export-price elasticity had been found to be less than the import-price elasticity and together they did not add up even to three-fourths of one percent because there existed supply side rigidities which affected our exports and a built-in inelasticity in the demand for imports. Besides, during the 1950s imports were severely controlled and they fluctuated to a greater extent depending on the availability of external assistance. So it is reasonable to doubt whether the statistics could at all be used to establish a meaningful relationship between import and other variables such as national income, industrial and agricultural production. In spite of the limitations, such estimates helped to some extent for purposes of policy formulation.

In the late 1980s, using disaggregated data Lucas (1988) estimated demand functions for India's manufactured exports and found that of the 18 groups for which the demand functions were estimated, in as many as (i.e., sugar, steel, non-ferrous metals, railway equipment, motor vehicles and cycles), the price elasticity is greater than two: in twelve it was greater than one. In this way he had challenged the thesis of export pessimism.

3.4 IMPORT CONTROL

Although devised originally as emergency measures for dealing with BoP difficulties, throughout the post-war years import controls was the go of the Indian economic life. Mainly this was accounted for by the persistence of BoP difficulties. However, it is well-known that import controls had significant costs. These costs had been analysed by Jagdish Bhagwati and Padma Desai (1970). In their pioneering study they argued that comprehensive import controls maintained until 1966, excepting a period of progressive liberalization with the First Five Year Plan (1951-56) gave rise to many distortions including important protective effects. Moreover, import controls, if imposed only for correcting imbalances in the BoP, might have the effect of granting protection to the wrong type of domestic industries. Therefore, the practical question was not of dismantling of import controls, but of finding some practical means of minimising their adverse effects.

The effect of heavy reliance on import controls has jeopardized the atmosphere on the use of tariff policy as a deliberate protective device. A study by Padma Desai (1969) contained a comprehensive description and evaluation of the working of the tariff bodies in India. This study brought out that, with the emergence of industrial licensing and import controls in India, the status of the Tariff Commission greatly waned. D.T. Lakdawala (1964) held the same view.

Pursell (1992) finds that during the period from 1957-58 to 1975-76, imports substitution policies were followed with little or no regard to costs. They resulted in an extremely diverse industrial structure and high degree of self-sufficiency, but many industries had production costs. By the mid-seventies, industrialists themselves found this strict regime counterproductive and started pressing the government for relaxations of controls. A domestic lobby in the absence of counter lobby came to the fore in favour of liberalization of imports of raw materials and machinery.

Another study by Pursell (1996) showed that during the period May 1992-May 1995 India's trade reforms since 1991 focused on manufacturing while agriculture was largely ignored. Consequently one might observe that the share of value added in the manufacturing sector, protected by quantitative restrictions declined heavily (from ninety percent to thirty six percent) for those periods. The corresponding decline was much less in agriculture from 94 percent to 84 percent during the same period.

Mehta (1998) estimated that only one-third of the value of India's imports in 1998-99 was subject to some type of Non-tariff barriers (NTBs).

3.5 EFFECTIVE RATES OF PROTECTION

Economists are unanimous in that nominal rates of protection are incapable to analyse the effects of trade restrictions on the allocation of resources. In this regard, effective rates of protection do so by estimating the amount by which value added in any given activity is raised by the whole set of tariffs and quotas. It is noteworthy that effective rate of protection of exportables and importables bear indirect linkage with BoP problems. And one of the major problems faced by the policy-makers in developing countries is that the trade regime is in fact often very complicated. Typically there are different tariffs on final products and intermediate goods: some goods are controlled by quotas, others may be subsidised. V.R. Panchamukhi, Jagdish Bhagwati, and Padma Desai (1970) have jointly estimated the effective rates of protection in the Indian organised sector for 18 industries for 1961 and 1962 under eight alternative assumptions. The authors note that their results are fairly sensitive to alternative assumptions with respect to the tariff rates chosen for both tradables and non-tradables. Their estimates indicate a wide range of effective rates that prevail among different industries. They also show that a high effective rate of protection indicates the vigour of restrictions on new investment, where investment is regulated through industrial licensing during the time.

The Chelliah Committee (1992) recommended seven different rates of tariff, viz, 5, 10, 15, 20, 25, 30 and 50 percent to be achieved by 1997-98. Joshi and Little (1994) showed that the suggested multiple tariff rates by the Committee would provide scope for effective protection rate that would be much higher than the nominal tariffs on finished goods. When QRs on consumer goods were removed, a 50 percent duty on imports of consumer goods combined with 25 percent duty on tradable inputs would lead to a high effective rate of protection close to 100 percent on consumer goods.

3.6 EXCHANGE RATE CHANGES

During the 1950s and the 1960s, Indian economists initiated a lively discussion regarding the effectiveness of exchange rate variations as instruments of BoP policy. The economists who had contributed to this heated discussions included D.T. Lakdawala (1964), B.R. Shenoy (1958), D.R. Gadgil (1958), Jagdish Bhagwati (1962), A.K. Dasgupta (1962), Pranab Bardhan (1962), Manmohan Singh (1964), B.N. Ganguli (1966), K. Marwah (1969), and V.C. Shah (1970). However, most of the discussions except Ganguli, Marawah and Shah, have centred around to explain the relative efficacy of exchange rate on much too general a plane. B.N. Ganguli sought to examine the circumstances leading to the devaluation of 1966 and the conditions necessary for making it a success. Using an econometric model for India to compare two sets of solutions—one with a devaluation and the other without, Marwah showed that the devaluation could be expected to slightly reduce real consumption (0.2 per cent in 1966-67 and 0.3 per cent in 1967-68) and total output lagged by a year (0.2 per cent in 1967-68). In addition, he predicted that substantial improvement (nearly 50 per cent) could be expected in the balance of trade. The study was not without its flaws. First, this is not a fully specified model. Secondly, ascribing the decline in consumption to the devaluation-induced price rise and the reduction in output to the decline in real capital formation caused by the rise in the price of imported machinery, was spurious and unexpected.

V.C. Shah (1970) followed the absorption approach to devaluation and examined the trends of domestic output and real domestic absorption and attempted to explain the observed relationship in terms of factors exogenous to the devaluation. The conclusions which he reached were as follows: (a) a devaluation in India could affect the BoP primarily by its effect on exports since a rise in the landed price of imports would mainly reduce importer's premia without affecting domestic prices substantially; (b) the devaluation had a negligible impact on the Indian economy, with the predominant influence being that of drought; (c) given the crucial role of the agricultural sector in India's export structure, the timing of a devaluation was vital to its success; (d) despite the ineffectiveness of the devaluation, it was a desirable policy in-so-far as it led to a greater rationalization of the complex tariff/subsidy system. In the view of Shah, therefore, although the expected positive influence of a devaluation on exports and production did not materialize due to the drought, yet it was a good and desirable policy step.

A serious empirical analysis of the net effects of devaluation of 1966 is comprehensively provided by Jagdish N. Bhagwati and T.N. Srinivasan (1975). They started out by observing that the period under consideration was characterized by the following features:

(i) The impact of the two consecutive droughts as reflected in the fall in real income originating in agriculture in 1965-66 and 1966-67 as compared with 1964-65;
(ii) the continued rise in the wholesale price index, a process that began in a *sus*tained fashion from 1962-63;
(iii) a rise in the relative price of food articles as compared with the prices of manufactures in general and prices of equipment in particular;
(iv) a shift away from investment toward consumption in public sector expenditure;
(v) a drastic fall in non-food aid disbursements net of debt service payments after 1965-66;
(vi) a fall in exports as well as imports, particularly imports of complete machinery, and
(vii) a fall in the ratio of tax receipts to national income and gross domestic savings to gross domestic product (*Bhagwati and Srinivasan, 1975,* pp. 111-13).

They then proceeded to analyse this picture using a combination of descriptive and analytic techniques, a major point of concern in their analysis being to separate the effects of the drought from that of the June 1966 liberalization-policy package—'an attempt made nowhere-else in the literature with this degree of rigour' (Pronab Sen, 1986).

Bhagwati and Srinivasan examined the effect of the drought on prices of manufactures over the period 1951-61 and 1962-71, the (short-run) effect of the devaluation-cum-liberalization package of June 1966 on overall production, distinguishing the later by four areas of activity like : (a) effect on agricultural output (period 1949 to 1965); (b) effects on agricultural-based industrial outputs (period 1952 to 1970); (c) effects on the output of import-intensive industries, other than capital goods (period 1965-70); and (d) effects on the output of capital loads industries (period 1960 to 1971).

Their analysis suggests that the drought was the major explanatory factor for a large part of the observed facts. For example, the price rises were caused by the drought; the recession in production was also induced by the drought and not by the concomitant 'stabilization' policy aimed at an excessive deflation. In particular, the acceleration of the inflation rate, the fall in export volumes and the reduction in government expenditures could be traced primarily to this cause. Appropriate correction for this factor, they conclude, indicates that the June 1966 devaluation-*cum*-liberalization package did indeed give rise to favourable results. Moreover, that package, far from showing that exchange rate adjustment was unworkable, suggested the opposite conclusion. Domestic output and investment increased, although marginally, as a result of the policy, as did exports. The improvements in the BoP, which was due in large part to the reduction in imports, could also be attributed to it although the drought-induced recession certainly played its part. The causal assignments, seemingly were that non-capital goods imports decreased due to substitution, whereas capital goods imports declined with the drought-induced reduction in investments, both public and private.

In this connection, the article by Pronab Sen (1986) deserves attention. He re-examines the 1966 devaluationary episode in India in the light of the new theoretical propositions of the structuralist school. In this article he decomposed the observed aggregate changes into those attributable to the devaluation package, and those determined by other concurrent parametric changes. It was found, contrary to popular belief, that the Indian devaluation was contractionary in terms of aggregate output and consumption, and there was little evidence of an inflationary outcome. Moreover, there appears a paradoxical result that the expansion of the Indian economy in 1966-67 was not the outcome of the devaluation package, but of the drought. The temporary rise in domestic real aggregate demand caused by drought helped to ameliorate the contractionary pressures of the policy package without fully negating its balance of trade effect.

The question "Is devaluation is working in the face of economic liberalization" has been answered by Chaudhuri (2005). Using monthly data for the period from January 1991 to December 1998, he offers an empirical analysis to examine the relationship between devaluation of the Rupee and the real trade balance with India's major trading partners. Exploiting the recent advances in panel-data time-series econometrics, he reaches the conclusion that devaluation may not be effective in improving trade balance in the long run. Success will follow if and only if the policy makers of the country view devaluation as a short-run tool to improve the trade balances. Nominal devaluation is unable to alter real effective exchange rate (REER) and hence, the inflationary impact of devaluation is large in India.

3.7 DETERMINANTS OF TRADE BALANCE

The article by Deepak Nayyar (1982) reviews the BoP situation in India in the decade of 1970s placing it under the wider context of the entire planning with observations about the shifts in emphasis and the change in direction of trade policies and industrialization over the decades of 1950s, 1960s and 1970s. According to Nayyar, India's BoP crisis and the trade deficits reappeared towards the late 1970s after the oil shock of 1973-74 as a result of the unprecedented rise in import bill. The two components of the increase in import bill were (1) the import of crude oil and petroleum products, and (2) import of edible oils, fertilizers, iron and steel, paper and cement. Yet levels of output and investment remained low. After the hike of 1973-74, the oil prices stabilized to a certain degree while the world prices of other commodities were on the increase. To reverse the resulting declining trend in oil prices in real terms, OPEC countries trebled the price of oil and petroleum in 1979. Along with this, the domestic production of crude oil fell substantially on account of the violent agitation in Assam so as to compound the increase in oil imports.

According to Nayyar, rising import bill was the major underlying factor for the trade deficit in a situation where export growth was sluggish and could also be expected to remain sluggish because: (i) supply conditions in the world market were unfavourable; industrialized countries were faced with stagflation and protectionism was on the increase; and (ii) supply condition at home also constituted a constraint in so far as exportable surpluses on wage goods were limited, and the infrastructure required by the non-traditional manufacturing sector would take time to materialize.

As regards the trade policy, policy-makers attitudes towards the promotion of export sector particularly after 1976 as a potential leading sector in industrialization and development was welcomed by Nayyar as steps in the right directions. But he advocated that steps should be taken at the same time to expose the Indian economy to the forces of international competition by reducing the level of protection to domestic industry. To facilitate such outward-oriented industrialization he suggested that trade policies should be amended suitably: export promotion should be designed to encourage production for the world market and the process of import liberalization should be carried further. In his view, the domestic factor which constrained India's exports were the high costs of production, the pressure of domestic demand and infrastructural or supply bottlenecks which, coupled with non-price factor such as quality, have adversely affected the competitiveness of our exports.

The article by G.C. da Costa (1986) entitled 'India's Trade Balance during the Seventies' investigates into the determinants of India's balance of commodity trade with the objective of explaining the movements in it. He also investigates into the determinants of the individual components of the balance like volume of exports and volume of imports over the period 1970-71 to 1981-82. He takes four explanatory variables—the net barter terms of trade, India's gross national product at current prices, gross domestic product at constant prices of industrial countries and a dummy variable to capture the effects of oil price hikes of 1973-74, 1979-80 and the import liberalization of 1980-81. He carries out a multiple regression of trade balance on these four explanatory variables. His hypothesis was that a fall in the net barter terms of trade, other things given, would cause an increase (decrease) in expenditure on imports relative to earnings from exports result in an increase (decrease) in the trade deficits. A positive association between the level of economic activity in the industrial countries, as indicated by the gross domestic product at constant prices of these countries and a negative association between domestic money income—India's gross national product at current prices and the trade balance is also hypothesised. da Costa uses GNP at current prices to bring out implicitly the role of money supply on the trade balance.

His findings are that while the co-efficient of India's GNP at current prices and of the GDP of industrial countries at constant prices are statistically significant, the co-efficient of the terms of trade is not. Replacing terms of trade with the dummy variable, he finds a strong relation between the balance of trade, and each of India's GNP and GDP of industrial countries as explanatory variables. The co-efficient of the dummy variable also has positive sign and is found to be statistically significant. So, he concludes that the dominant factors determining India's balance of trade over the period 1970-71 to 1981-82 were India's GNP at current prices which also implicitly incorporates the role of money supply, and the GDP of the industrial countries at constant prices. Terms of trade had played a secondary role and were strong only during the specific years of the oil price hike as the co-efficients of the dummy variables showed.

G.C. da Costa (1988) in another article argues that a clear understanding of the factors which have been at work on India's commodity trade balance is necessary, since this case provides the basis for the formulation of an effective policy geared to achieve the objective of more moderate trade deficit. And an analysis of India's commodity trade balance over the fifteen year period, 1970-71 to 1984-85, indicates that trade balance depends upon the volume of exports, the volume of imports and their relative prices—that is, the net barter terms of trade. Hence he posed the following questions: First, what factors 'explain' movements in the volume of imports? What factor 'explain' changes in the net barter terms of trade of India? His conclusions have been that the volume of exports, the volume of imports and the net barter terms of trade, are the proximate determinants of the trade balance on the one hand. On the other, he considers the determinants of the volume of exports, of the volume of imports and of the net barter terms of trade as the ultimate determinants of the trade balance. Therefore, he makes the trade balance recursively dependent on the determinants of the volume of exports, of the volume of imports, and of the net barter terms of trade, the last one being explained by the real growth in the economies of the industrial countries, inflation rates in these countries and country's exchange rate.

In this article he asks a pertinent question: Does the drought in the Indian economy not enter into the explanation of the country's exports? He answers that droughts do effect exports in lowering the volume of exportable supplies and at the same time in raising domestic price and eroding the export competitiveness. Considering the fact that the volume of exports fell as a consequence of the drought in 1977-78 in the Indian economy, he argues that increases in domestic prices enter the analysis of exports via the real exchange rate. Hence he hypothesizes, that the volume of India's exports, over the same period, were influenced by trends in the real income in the industrial countries, movements in the real effective exchange rate which embody both nominal exchange rates and relative prices, and by the crude petroleum imports in the terminal years. And since by the end of the seventies, the policy of import liberalization which led to a rise in the real import-GNP ratio for the country, and ultimately resulted in a greater import-dependence of the Indian economy, he hypothesized that the volume of imports for the same period were associated positively with trends in India's real income and with the more liberal import policy, and negatively with the relative price of Imports.

In the light of above hypotheses, G.C. da Costa explains the trade situation, articulating thereby that the contribution to the satisfactory trade balance in the seventies, and to the unsatisfactory trade balance in the eighties, came largely from the two proximate determinants of the trade balance, viz, the volume of exports and the volume of imports rather than the terms of trade. And eventually he draws the conclusion that India's trade balance, which has been the dominant factor in the country's BoP over the 1970-71 to 1984-85 years, was influenced by several factors, in particular, real growth and inflation rates in the industrial countries, trends in India's real income, movements in the real effective exchange rate of the country, and import liberalization. These determinants ultimately comprise both external and domestic factors.

In the revised and updated version of his earlier paper, he, in 1990, extended the earlier period for one year. Taking annual time series data, period covers from 1970-71 to 1985-86. Within these sixteen year period, he chooses six explanatory variables for the commodity trade balance (B) function, i.e. value of commodity exports minus value of commodity imports. They are:

(i) Y_1 India's GDP at factor cost at 1970-71 prices, thousand crores of rupees.

(ii) $\dot{Y}_{IC}$ growth rate of GDP of industrial countries at 1980 prices.

(iii) $\dot{P}_{IC}$ annual percentage change in GDP deflator of industrial countries, i.e. inflation rate.

(iv) R^e index of real effective exchange rate of the rupee, base 1970-71 = 100; exchange rate is defined as number of units of foreign currency per rupee.

(v) D_1 dummy variable for import liberalization—assigned value zero from 1970-71 to 1978-79, and one from 1979-80 to 1985-86.

(vi) D_0 dummy variable for export of crude petroleum—assigned value zero from 1970-71 to 1981-82 and in 1985-86 and one from 1982-83 to 1984-85.

The functional form is:

$$B = f\left(\dot{Y}_{IC}, Y_1, \dot{P}_{IC}, R^e, D_1, D_0\right)$$

He employed a multiple regression model, in which he regressed the dependent variable (commodity trade balance) on the explanatory variables, using the Ordinary Least Squares (OLS) technique. The statistical findings affirm the hypothesis that India's trade balance is associated positively with the growth in real income of the industrial countries ($\dot{Y}_{IC}$) and with the exports of crude petroleum (D_o) and negatively with India's real income (Y_1), the real effective exchange rate of the rupee (R^e) and import liberalization (D_l)

His statistical findings are summarized in Table 3.1.

From his analysis of India's trade balance the following observations can be made:

(a) India's commodity trade balance is the dominant actor in the country's BoP. It, over the period 1970-71 to 1985-86, was influenced by several factors: in particular, real income growth and inflation rates in the industrial countries, trends in India's real income, movements in the real effective exchange rate of the country and import liberalization. These determinants comprise both external and domestic factors;

(b) The proximate determinants of the trade balance viz. the volume of exports and the volume of imports played a major role in shaping the satisfactory trade balance in the *1970s* and to the unsatisfactory trade balance in the eighties. The terms of trade played a minor role in this connection;

(c) The real effective exchange rate has emerged as an important determinant in the movement of exports, and of the trade balance over the fifteen-year period;

(d) The basket arrangement introduced in the mid-seventies to provide stability to the exchange rate of the rupee, succeeded in doing so in 1976-77 through 1983-84, but failed in subsequent years;

(e) The phenomenon like the incidence of protection is captured, albeit implicitly. This is so, since increased protectionist stance is a feature of the early eighties when, in response to the recessionary trends in the industrial countries, world trade stagnated. This protectionism is linked with low or no growth in the

TABLE 3.1

Summary of Statistical Findings, 1970-71 to 1985-86

Dependent variable	Constant term	Coefficient of explanatory variables									$\dot{R}^2$	F-statistic	DW-statistic	SEE as a percentage of means of dependent variable
		Y_{IC}	$\dot{Y}_{IC}$	Y_1	$\dot{P}_{IC}$	Um/P_I	R^e	R	D_1	D_0				
(1)	(2)	(3)	(4)	(5)	(6)	(7)	(8)	(9)	(10)	(11)	(12)	(13)	(14)	(15)
Quantum of exports	115.53	1.25** (6.05)					-1.40** (-4.95)			-16.67* (2.93)	0.955	128	1.44	4.16
Quantum of imports	-15.96			4.48** (7.35)		-0.3633** (-3.13)			46.40** (4.35)		0.953	123.5	2.29	6.57
Terms of trade	175.54		2.59a (2.11)		-3.53** (-4.13)			-7.23** (-5.30)			0.772	22.3	1.67	7.58
Trade balance	18.06		0.2397** (3.20)	-0.2732** (-9.05)			-0.0899** (-5.22)		-2.60** (-6.06)	1.63** (4.09)	0.975	116.7	2.98	16.44

Note : Figures in parentheses are the t-values of the estimated coefficient. The letter a and * and ** indicate 10, 5 and 1 per cent levels of statistical significance of the estimated coefficients, respectively.

Source : G.C. da Costa (1990).

industrial countries, and growth, or absence of it in these countries, features importantly in his analytical frame.

The policy implications of the model are that emphasis must be given to domestic factors rather than on external factors (like terms of trade) because external factors are outside the control of the policy makers in the country. Fortunately, development of exports and imports has contributed to a favourable balance of trade inspite of the severe deterioration of India's terms of trade and its adverse contribution to the trade balance. So, in his opinion, the policy focus should be on the three priority areas: India's real income, import policy, and the country's inflation rate relative to that of the industrial economies. And the policy should gear to the fulfilment of policy objectives of (i) monitoring with great effectiveness the export- import linkages, (ii) imposing fiscal discipline and keeping inflation rate down, and (iii) ensuring of growth of the Indian economy commensurate with the needs of her people.

G.C. da Costa agrees that the dominant actor on the balance of commodity trade scene has been the volume of imports. However, he attributes the serious balance of payments difficulties as a consequence of rising trade deficits to the uneven growth rates of India and the industrialized countries. India's trade imbalance is due to her decision not to keep pace i.e., not to grow in line with the industrialized countries. But this conclusion is not based on an integrated theoretical framework, it makes *ad hoc* assumptions and leaves little space for analysing the impact of policy measures to adjust the imbalance.

G.C. da Costa's use of GNP to bring out implicitly the role of money supply on the trade balance also gives rise to some doubt. GNP is primarily an income variable and to what extent it reflects the role of money supply on trade balance is a matter of guesswork. Further, trade balance can itself be a determinant of money supply, but at the very start, da Costa asserts that "commodity trade balance" by itself is not a determinant of money supply. This is apart from the fact, in general, since it is the domestic credit base which has dominated the money supply. It may be pointed out, in this context, that out of the different factors affecting money supply, the three most important factors are: (i) net bank credit to government, (ii) bank credit to commercial sector, and (iii) the net foreign exchange assets of the banking sector. The last factor is necessarily affected by the commodity trade balance that plays a major role in determining the movements in foreign exchange. This is especially true of India's foreign trade sector where commodity trade balance is the dominant balance. Hence, to deny that the commodity trade balance can impart influence on money supply is naive.

G.C. da Costa used a dummy variable to capture the effects of oil price hike and import liberalization. But the impact of these two factors cannot be the same and hence cannot be estimated by the same dummy. Further, it is not clear why the terms of trade variable which has been taken to explain the commodity trade balance is not able to take care of the oil price hikes. There is no explicit discussion on the implications of asset markets on India's trade balance. We have already discussed the theoretical issues involved in chapter 2.

Sarkar (1999) has analysed Indian data on trade balance and BoP front since the seventies. The period of his study is divided into to sub-periods—pre-new economic policy period (January 1980 to June 1991) and new economic policy period (July 1991 to May 1996). He argues that due to the process of liberalization of the 1980's the current account deficit soared high in the 1980's for steady decline in the surplus of invisible account. And India's export performance under the post liberalization period (1991-96) is nothing but the continuation of the trend of the 1980's. However, the trade liberalization has its impact on imports; it shows a tendency to peak with the passage of time under new economic policy. As a result, the export/import ratio deviated from its trend growth path of the 1980s, and showed some sign of deceleration. He found no evidence of structural change in the trend behaviour of India's balance of trade in the 1990's.

3.8 DOES EXCHANGE RATE MATTER?

We have found some amount of literature in the 1980s and 1990s, and a few in the 1960s that tried to determine the effect of exchange rate changes on the balance of trade and or the balance of payments. This literature is neither strictly comparable, as time periods and functional forms tend to differ, nor is there necessarily any attempt to segregate the effects of other policy changes. Therefore, it is by no means obvious that an improvement in the trade balance or current account balance of payments consequent upon a devaluation or depreciation, can be ascribed to the exchange rate changes alone. Subject to these limitations, the findings of the major literature of the 1980s are summarized in Table 3.2.

TABLE 3.2
Effects of a Devaluation or Depreciation

	Study	*Balance of trade*	*Balance of payments*
1.	Mukherjee (1983)	Improvement	—
2.	Sen (1986)	No Improvement	—
3.	Singh (1986)	No Improvement	—
4.	Sundararajan and Bhole (1989)	Improvement	Improvement

Source : S.P. Gupta (1994).

Among the empirical attempts made by eminent authors cited above the Sundarajan and Bhole (1989) exercise is more sophisticated and somehow complete in that this study takes into account the policy changes other than the exchange rate changes and the results can be reproduced in some detail.

The results we reproduce are for the following: functional forms:

$$\log T = A0 + a1 \log M + a2 \log P + a3 \log G + a4 \log K$$
$$\log B = b0 + b1 \log M + b2 \log P + b3 \log G + b4 \log K$$

The estimated equations were as follows:

$$\log T = -0.06555 - 0.10435 \log M + 0.00096 \log P - 0.06414 \log G - 0.00618 \log K$$
$$\log B = 0.25597 - 0.04397 \log M + 0.01533 \log P + 0.02849 \log G + 0.07391 \log K.$$

Here, T = ratio of balance of trade to output; B = ratio of current account balance of payments to output; M = ratio of domestic portion of high power money to output relative to the rest of the world; P = ratio of domestic prices to output, relative to the ratio for the rest of the world; G = domestic growth rate in relation to a weighted average of growth rates for the rest of the world; K = units of domestic currency per unit of foreign currency.

In the balance of payment equations, all coefficients were significant. In the balance of trade equation, all co-efficients other than the one for P were significant. A1 per cent increase in money supply thus leads to a deterioration in the balance of trade (expressed as a percentage of output) by 0.10435 per cent and a deterioration in the current account balance of payments (expressed as a percentage of output) by 0.04397 per cent. A1 per cent increase in the domestic price of tradeables improves (through the real balance effect) the balance of trade by 0.00096 per cent and the balance of payments by 0.01533 per cent. A1 per cent increase in the growth rate differential leads to a deterioration in the balance of trade by 0.06414 per cent and an improvement in the balance of payments by 0.02849 per cent. A1 percent devaluation or depreciation improves the balance of trade by 0.00618 per cent and the balance of payments by 0.07391 per cent. The improvement is much more for the balance of payments. Rather interestingly, so far as the balance of trade is concerned, the most important variables in order of magnitude are money supply, growth rate, the exchange rate and prices. But so far as the balance of payments is concerned, the order of magnitude is the exchange rate, money supply, the growth rate and prices.

The result of Sundarajan and Bhole, along with other results cited in Table 3.2 points that there has been an improvement in the balance of trade following a devaluation or depreciation. But, on the whole, the findings also substantiate an improvement in the short-run. The findings also do indicate that there has been an improvement of the current account balance of payments after a devaluation.

Jayati Ghosh (1990) investigates some of issues involved in currency devaluation and depreciation for the period 1973-74 to 1985-86, using the assumption that expectations of nominal exchange rate changes are rational. Her main hypothesis is that i) each element of the current account of the BoP is affected by nominal currency devaluations in such a way as to worsen the trade balance. The argument is straightforward in that continuous devaluations of the currency operate to create an import bulge, in particular through their effect on expectations of future devaluations, and ii) the indices of SDR value of exports and the real exchange rate show no definite relationship during the period 1973-74 to 1986-87. The hypothesis is tested in the following manner:

In the first case, a two-stage least squares estimation of the change in log of import values, in SDR terms is made using an estimation of next year's nominal exchange rate, the log of the real outputs of the infrastructure and manufacturing producing sector, the log of real output on agriculture lagged by one year, lagged gross capital formation and the ratio of world prices to domestic prices as independent variable. In the second case, a least square estimation was made of changes in the log of exports in SDR terms. The independent variables are chosen as the log of world export value, log of GDP in agriculture with one year lag, log of real gross capital formation, log of the real exchange rate, and the rate of growth of SDR exports lagged by one year.

The results are as follows:

1st case:

DLMSDR = 5.58 + 1.14 DLMSDR(I) – 3.23 LGDPI + 3.10 LGDPM

(1.77) (2.26) (-5.04) (4.03)

-180 LGDPA(-1) – 0.4 LRXUPI

(-3.29) (-5.04)

Adj-R^2 = 0.83; DW = 2.63.

2nd case:

DLXSDR = -4.94 + 0.65 LVWX + 0.82 LGDPA(-1) – 0.83 LGCF

(-1.85) (5.54) (2.79) (-4.17)

– 0.38 LRERV – 0.4 LIXSDR(-1)

(-1.34) (-3.42)

Adj-R^2 = 0.91; DW = 1.71.

It may be noted that figures in the brackets in both cases are t-values of the estimated coefficients

In the first case, according to her, the result does suggest that in so far as changes in the nominal exchange rate are anticipated according to the model, they may have led to increase in import values. Changes in infrastructural output are seen to exert a negative influence on import values: if this reflects an improvement in general domestic supply positions, this would suggest that some proportion of imports are substitutes for inadequate domestic supply. This is also true for lagged agricultural output.

By another estimate over the same period, she investigates the changes in the quantum index of imports. Similar results emerge, for example, import quantities respond positively to anticipated depreciation of the nominal exchange rate, supply variables of infrastructural and lagged agriculture output are negatively related, while the demand proxy of output in the non-market sector is positively related. The ratio of import prices to the prices of non-traded goods is negatively related to the quantum of imports. In the second case, it is evident that rate of growth of world exports and the past year's agricultural output have positive and significant effects. Gross capital formation is significantly negatively related. The impact of changes in the real exchange rate appears to be in the opposite direction from the desired one. Therefore, the real exchange rate has not been an important variable influencing SDR export values during this period. Even if the estimation of change in log of SDR exports has been gone with world export value growth, changes in GDP in infrastructure and in the non-material sector, lagged export value growth and the real exchange rate, the basic conclusions are unaltered. It appears that both specifications thus suggest that the real exchange rate has played a marginal role in explaining the growth of exports in SDR terms over this period.

Hence the message of her paper runs thus: tinkering with the exchange rate instrument alone as a means of improving current account deficits is unlikely to prove successful. Depending on manipulation of one particular price—the price of the currency in terms of local currency in isolation is likely to be counter-productive both in terms of further BoP disequilibrium and internal disequilibrium through inflationary pressures. Secondly, a policy of continuous nominal devaluations creates expectations of future depreciation which in turn operate to increase current import expenditure and exert other negative influences on the current account.

R.K. Sesadri (1993) however, examines in some detail the Reserve Bank's claim that the depreciation in the exchange rate has helped India's exports during the 1980s. The following Table 3.3 summarizing the findings of the Reserve Bank of India seem to support this view.

Table 3.3
Export Growth and REER

Years	*Export Growth (per cent per annum)*	*Depreciation/Appreciation In the REER (±)*
1976 to 1979	+ 6.80	– 20
1979 to 1985	Stagnant	Appreciation
1989 to 1990	+ 10.00	– 25

Source : Sesadri (1993).

But Sesadri articulates that *prima facie* it appears to be a very strong argument in favour of devaluation, but it is not wholly true, as the spurt in trade is not entirely connected with the exchange rate. Apart from this, there had been a growth in India's exports of leather goods, garments, diamonds jewellery etc., which can be attributed only to a negligible extent to a depreciation in the exchange rate.

If one excludes the rupee trade with Russia and other countries in Eastern Europe under bilateral trade agreement, and considers only the exports to the general currency areas, one gets some interesting results. Table 3.4 will be instructive in this connection. It shows that the unit values (in rupees) of exports from India have been consistently increasing, offsetting in several years the depreciation of the rupee in terms of the US dollar. There is no close link, in other words, between a depreciation in the real exchange rate, secured by a series of devaluations and export performance. Exports may increase for other reasons, despite an increase in the unit values of the exported items. The REER (Real Effective Exchange Rate),

TABLE 3.4

Value of Indian Exports and Variations in Rupee Dollar Exchange Rates

	Exports in US ($ millions)	*Averages of monthly rates for the US $ in rupees*	*Depreciation in Re rate as compared with the previous year (%)*	*Index of unit value of exports 1968-69 =100*	*Increase % in unit values as compared with the previous year*
(1)	*(2)*	*(3)*	*(4)*	*(5)*	*(6)*
1981-82	6497.21	8.97	11.8	124	13.76
1982-83	7163.39 (10.25)	9.67	7.2	132	6.45
1983-84	7949.71 (10.98)	10.34	6.5	151	14.39
1984-85	7991.59 (0.53)	11.89	13	169	11.92
1985-86	6932.95 (-7.49)	12.25	2.8	171	1.18
1986-87	7873.24 (11.94)	12.78	4.3	179	4.68
1987-88	10092.59 (28.19)	12.97	1.5	195	8.94
1988-89	11654.01 (15.47)	14.48	10.5	228	16.92
1989-90	13420.42 (15.16)	16.65	13	NA	NA
1990-91	14877.93 (10.86)	17.94	7.2	NA	NA

Figures within brackets indicate percentage increases or decreases, as compared with the preceding year.
Source : R.K. Sesadri (1993), 'From Crisis to Convertibility', Orient Longman, Calcutta.

weighted for changes in the price levels in twenty countries, is also of no particular relevance on value, when exports of individual commodities, specially to various destinations, are concerned.

Even the validity of an econometric finding by Trivedi (1992) using the data for 1973-88 and similar results of Rangarajan (1991) (for computing the export demand, using the data from 1977 to 1990) that a one per cent depreciation in the REER will increase exports by 0.66 per cent is questioned by Sesadri on the ground that the period chosen for testing the hypothesis is too short. It is also by no means normal, as both the pound and US dollar rose to all time peak levels during this period. So the econometric findings also seem to be open to question.

Prabirjit Sarkar (1992) seeks to examine the various aspects of India's foreign trade and payments over the period 1971-90. In particular, the study seeks to examine the impact of rupee depreciation on India's exports, imports and trade balance, through a simple regression analysis. Both linear and log-linear relationships are considered but the results do not differ: so the findings from only the log-linear regression are reported. To tackle the problem of autocorrelation the Cochrane-Orcutt iterative Generalized Least Square technique has been followed in all the cases. All the results are presented in Table 3.5.

The OLS estimate shows a significant positive relationship between the exchange rate, Re per US $ and the rupee or dollar value of exports. A similar conclusion can be drawn for the rupee and the dollar values of total imports. The result holds good also for the dollar value of imports less crude petroleum over the period 1971-87. The conclusion that follows is that the value of India's exports did not rise nor did the value of imports fall due to a significant depreciation of the rupee during 1971-90. Not only in value terms, the exchange rate manipulation has no statistically significant relationship with the volume of India's exports and imports.

In another study on the same theme he shows that over the period 1971-85, the dollar value and the volume of India's manufactured exports declined as Re per US dollar rose (or as the rupee depreciated). But the relationships are not much strong. There was no significant influence of the rupee

TABLE 3.5

Exchange Rate Changes and India's Visible Trade, 1971-90: A Simple Regression

Series	*Coefficient of Rs. per US $*	*t-Ratio*	*R^2*	*D-W stat*
I. Rupee values of exports	2.63* (0.14)	8.48 (0.42)	0.79	0.3 (1.59)
Imports	2.91* (-0.26)	6.96 (-0.52)	0.71	0.29 (1.49)
Imports less crude oil	3.36* (0.35)	6.22 (0.44)	0.7	0.55 (2.09)
II. Dollar values of exports	1.71* (0.13)	5.61 (0.50)	0.62	0.22 (0.74)
	(0.60) [-0.20]	1.54 [-0.67]		[0.95] [2.87]
Imports	1.93* (-0.88)	4.78 (-1.68)	0.53	0.27 (1.52)
Imports less crude oil	2.37* (-0.38)	4.44 (-0.54)	0.54	0.44 (1.73)
III. Dollar volumes	0.94*	6.21	0.68	0.61
Exports	(0.31)	(1.07)		(2.32)
Imports	1.35* (-0.52)	6.87 (-0.95)	0.72	1.04 (1.93)

Notes : *Significant at less than 5 per cent level; all others are not significant.

1. The fitted equation is: ln Y(t) = a + b ln X(t). The figures in first brackets are estimated by the CO-GLS procedure. The estimates of the intercept are not reported.
2. The period of study is 1971-87.
3. The CO-GLS procedure could not cure the problem of autocorrelation and so a log-difference equation has been fitted: ln Y(t)—ln Y(t-l) = b [ln X(t) – ln X(t–1)]. The OLS estimates are reported in the second brackets and the CO-GLS estimates are reported in the third brackets. If an intercept is added to the equation (that is to say, if a time-trend is included), the conclusion does not change.
4. The period of study is 1971-89.
5. Dollar values are deflated by dollar unit value indices to derive dollar volumes.

Source : P. Sarkar, E.P.W., June, 1992.

depreciation on the dollar value and volume of India's manufactured imports during the same period.

Again from another study on the same theme he shows that there was no significant influence of the exchange rate on the dollar values and volumes of exports and imports of food and beverages over the period 1971-85. He also finds no statistically significant relationship between the Rupee-SDR exchange rate and the SDR values of total exports and imports as well as between the annual rate of exchange rate changes and the rate of changes in the value and volumes of exports and imports over the period 1971-89/90.

He comes to the general conclusion that the process of depreciation in the exchange rate of the rupee since 1971 had no favourable effect on the dollar value and volume of India's exports. For the most category of India's exports manufactures, it might have unfavourable effect. The process of depreciation since 1971 also failed to reduce the dollar value and volume of imports. However, the growth in the trade deficit decelerated due to a deceleration in the growth of imports valued in dollars which in turn was due to a deceleration in the growth of crude oil imports. The payments deficits mounted partly due to a deceleration in the growth of private foreign remittances which was a fall-out of declining oil prices and the consequent declining prosperity of the Gulf.

From all these he firmly concludes that one expects no influence of the exchange rate changes on India's balance of trade, irrespective of whether India's balance of trade is measured in Re US $ or SDR. As such, he mentions that a number of factor may be mentioned to challenge the effectiveness of devaluation to expand exports and control imports in a developing country like India.

According to him export expansion may not be possible through devaluation for a number of reasons:

First, devaluation of the currency of a least developed country may increase the export volume by reducing the dollar price of export goods but due to the problem of inelastic demand, the value of export may fall.

Secondly, devaluation by one country may generate a spiral of competitive devaluation by others producing and exporting similar kinds of product. This may result in over-supplies of the commodities in the international markets and price crashes. This is the 'fallacy of composition'. In fact, the structural adjustment programmes of the IMF/World Bank often suffer from this fallacy. In a recent IMF study this phenomenon of over-supplies in the 1980s and the 1990s was recognised with little recognition of the fact that their structural adjustment policies in the primary producing countries had some hand in this phenomenon. This point will be more relevant for India in future when India will enter the commodity markets in a big way to take the opportunity of agricultural trade liberalization under the GATT agreement.

Thirdly, devaluation may not reduce the export prices in dollar because of a number of factors. Due to devaluation, imported inputs required in the export sector will be more costly. Moreover, costlier imports will create an inflationary spiral in a country that depends heavily on the imports of food, fertilizers and fuels. This may result in an inflationary spiral. Moreover, there is another strong point for the rise of prices due to devaluation. The combined effect from the rise of budgetary burden of debt services and creation of money by the government following that effect may create a situation where despite devaluation of the dollar, prices of export goods do not fall. This may induce the policy-makers to devalue further leading to further inflation, as it was observed in many Latin American Countries.

Fourthly, even if dollar prices of exports fall and demand rises due to devaluation, export supply may not rise due to different structural reasons such as power shortage. Lastly, the protectionist policies of the developed countries always hinder the entry of LDCs to capture the market of the developed countries. Also, on the import side, devaluation does not have much effect on the imports of necessary goods, because imports are often made in the interests of few rich peoples of the country to produce luxury goods and inputs. Due to all these factors, devaluation may fail to control imports. Hence his study casts serious doubts on the effectiveness of the regime of LERMS (Liberalized Exchange Rate Managed Systems) followed by the convertibility of the rupee and import liberalization in solving India's trade and payments deficits. From his study it follows that exchange rate does not matter and the government can't make good to the country's BoP through effective devaluation, although substantial devaluation of Indian currency (nominal and real) twice in 1991 was one essential part of the therapy of the IMF/World Bank for curing BoP deficit of the country, and enhancing export growth and competitiveness. Not only that, before the devaluation in 1991, there was also and steady depreciation of India's rupee during 1971-91.

Is there any meaningful relationship between exchange rate and balance of trade? The same question was sought to be answered by Sarkar (1994) in another article by the application of recently developed tests of stationarity (i.e. unit root econometrics suggesting an examination of co-integrating relationship). From his co-integration analysis, he argues that there is not any meaningful relationship between nominal and real devaluation of Indian rupee during 1971-91 and India's balance of trade behaviour over the same period. Rather he articulates that India's exports and imports do not have any deterministic trends. There are random walk with an upward drift. The implication is that this trend growth in the last decades of 1970s and 1980s as observed by Sarkar (1992) followed from random events. The slowing down in the drift in the 1980s might have followed from the shock of global recession and oil prices decline in the 1980s. India's trade balance and BoP, and Forex reserves are also random walk but without any drift. That is to say, there is no fundamental force inherent in the system that created the problem of India's balance of trade and BoP deficits. There was no evidence of accentuation of India's payments deficits in the 1980s. Hence he raises the question whether India needed any structural adjustment in the 1990s for her BoP crisis. His study also speaks that India's export earnings, net receipts through private foreign remittances, import spending, etc. are highly volatile since shocks have permanent effect. Hence he argues that increased globalization of the Indian economy only increased vulnerability to international shocks.

His concluding argument is that the real (and nominal) exchange rate movements do not have any meaningful relationship with India's export performance and inflow of foreign funds by way of private remittances; nor do these have any relationship with India's balance of trade and payments behaviour. This, however, contradicts the IMF/World Bank view that exchange rate manipulation does help the balance of trade and payments equilibrium. Rather it supports his standpoint and shares the same views with that of Bagchi (*Sarkar,* 1992; *Bagchi and Sarkar,* 1993).

Sarkar (1995) in his study also shows that while there is no evidence of a co integrated relationship between exports and exchange rates in the pre-liberalization period, the trend exhibited by the growth in exports even in the post liberalization phase appears stable with an absence of structural break as between the former and latter periods. The author also reports regressions between exports and various measures of the exchange rate series for the post liberalization period, and in the absence of any significant relationships, he concludes that there is no statistical relationship between exports and the exchange rate.

However, the robustness of this result, particularly his 1994 paper is challenged by three statisticians of the Reserve Bank of India (*Nag and Upadhya* (1994), *Joshi, H.* (1996)). Nag and Upadhyay argue that Sarkar's conclusion based on co-integration analysis of the real exchange rate and a few important real variables pertaining to the external trade sector go against standard neoclassical results. *Prima facie* it appears that deregulation of the foreign exchange markets would not have the desired impact on the trade balance if the trade balance itself being an unit root process, is found to exhibit no long-term relationship (linear relationship, to be particular) with the real exchange rate. So the policy of keeping the exchange rate deliberately undervalued, by the current policy stance of the RBI may turn not to be counter-productive in so far as such undervaluation fails to correct the external trade imbalance in the long run, and on the other hand adversely affects the industrial growth process by making the cost of necessary imports prohibitive. Sarkar's results, therefore, provide empirical support to the hypothesis cherished by some that foreign exchange is a scarce resource, the optional allocation of which cannot be ensured through a deregulated market. If the empirical results obtained by Sarkar are indeed robust, serious doubts would ensure about the soundness of policy stance after 1991. They, therefore, wanted to find out how robust or fragile

Sarkar's conclusions are, and in that process discovered some interesting aspects of external trade regime of India, which has escaped the notice of Sarkar.

Since annual data exhibited by Sarkar provide a small sample for co-integration test, they suggested the use of monthly data. Their analysis on the basis of monthly data covers the period starting from January 1979 to January 1993, on the logic that the external trade regime has been undergoing rapid changes over time and unless a reasonable part of the sample comes from this period, one may fail to detect the emerging relationship if only yearly data are used. They argue that if the monthly data on real export, real import, real export by real Import (instead of trade gap) and real exchange rates are plotted, the visual inspection of the data clearly suggests that the multivariate process might have undergone certain structural changes sometimes in the mid-80s. To be fair to Sarkar, they argue that Sarkar did look for structural changes in each univariate series, using Perron's (1989) method. Since use of known break-points makes the standard Dickey-Fuller critical value suspect, they used sequential test as suggested by Banerjee *et. al.* (1992) for each individual series and like Sarkar, they could not find any structural change in anyone of them. Even they found, taking the entire sample and using Johansen's method, non-existence of any co-integrating relationships among the bivariate variables one being real exchange rate and the other one being real variables, as also obtained by Sarkar.

Only when they reduced the period of study by taking a starting date as late as July, 1985, i.e. when only the later part of the sample, i.e. from July 1985 onwards, is used for time, series balance of trade (export/import), the situation change dramatically in favour of the argument that exchange rate matters in the sense that when the distortions in the external trade sector due to non-price factor is gradually being minimised and when the exchange rate starts getting determined through the market one can expect innovations in variable reflecting trade balance to start getting correlated to the innovations in real exchange process. In other words, exchange rate matters.

In a reply to Nag and Upadhya (1994), Sarkar (1997) has analysed India's foreign trade data between January 1980-May

1996 and has shown, contrary to the claim made by them that the balance of trade deficit showed some tendency to decline under the NEP regime. Real and nominal exchanges rates of the rupee showed trends of depreciation. But the exchange rate movements had no statistically significant relationship with the dollar values of India's exports and imports. Even using the nominal effective exchange rate series instead of the real one does not talk a different story. The conclusion is negative both for exports and imports.

It is worthwhile to mention in this context that some authors maintain that devaluations can be successfully used to remedy external imbalances, correct perceived 'over-valuations' of the real exchange rate, increase international competitiveness and promote export growth. Furthermore, a large corpus of the empirical literature agrees that in most devaluation episodes the real exchange rate does indeed respond significantly to a nominal exchange rate shock thereby changing relative prices for better. A recent study by Reinhart (1995) in a cross-country context shows that relative prices do affect trade balances in developing countries and that devaluation would certainly work as an effective instrument in stabilizing the external imbalance. The following studies of the Indian authors bear testimony to these facts.

In his study, Himangshu Joshi (1996) argues that the statistical evidence produced by other studies in providing a pessimistic scenario (that exchange rate does not matter) is based on rather weak foundations as the statistical tools appear to be inappropriately applied. For instance, in Sarkar (1995) the evidence of trend stationarity is based upon Augmented Dickey Fuller (ADF) tests with arbitrary first-order lag truncation imposed on monthly data even as an agnostic approach would suggest higher order lags. Moreover, given the limited power of unit root tests and the sensitivity of results to the choice of lag lengths coupled with the violation of weak exogeneity conditions necessary for all regressors in the exports supply equation, it is essential to reiterate that care may be required in the specification of the model itself and its subsequent interpretation for achieving valid inferences. An important aspect not considered by Sarkar (1995) is the role of lags in his regression analysis and this fact is recognised so often in the context of the J-curve effect and is also highlighted by Patra and Pattnaik (1994).

To conduct the test, Joshi takes the monthly data covering a period from 1991: 6 to 1995: 7 comprising a total of 50 observations spanning essentially the post (beyond 1991: 6) liberalization regime, The variables are: (i) general index of industrial production (IIP) (base: 80-81); (ii) the nominal rupees per US dollar rate of exchange of NOMEX; and (iii) US dollar denominated exports or EXPORTS in million units. Trace and Lamda-max statistics are presented in Table 3.6.

TABLE 3.6

Test for Co-integration

Numbers of cointegrating vectors under the null	*Trace Stat*	*Lamda-max*
Post-lib 91:6 95:7		
<1	31.35*	25.46*
<2	5.89	5.89
<3	0.01	0.01

Note : * implies significance at 5%.

Source : Joshi (1996).

The result indicates the presence of a co-integrating vector in case of the post liberalization phase among EXPORTS, IIP and NOMEX implying that a long-run equilibrium relationship exists among the set of chosen variables in this period.

Also he estimated the long-run co-integrating relationship for exports for this chosen phase as: EXPORTS = + 18.273 IIP + 25.923 NOMEX, from which one can infer that the downward adjustment in the nominal exchange rate led to the improvement in the export performance in the long-run in the post-liberalization phase.

However vociferously it may be claimed by the pessimists that exchange rate is not a crucial variable for India's export performance, an earlier study by Mathew Joseph (1992) and its extension by Rajiv Kumar and Mathew Joseph (1994) put emphasis on the importance of exchange rate in export growth, brought out in econometric studies. Joseph (1992) developed a general demand and supply model for India's exports for the period 1969 to 1986, and he estimated this model for the volume of India's aggregate exports for the period 1969 to 1986 and finds that real effective exchange rate (REER), world income (WY), domestic absorption (RA), and real exchange risk (REV) significantly affect India's exports and balance of payments. Kumar and Joseph (1994) estimated this model for the volume of India's aggregate exports for the period from 1972 to 1991. They have regressed the volume of aggregate exports (QEX) against real effective exchange rate (REER), world real income (WY), real fixed capital stock (KF) and real domestic absorption (HA) and the lagged value of the ratio between rupee export price (PEX) and domestic price (HP) Table 3.7 reports the results of their estimation.

TABLE 3.7

Regression Results for Volume of Aggregate Exports (Sample Period : 1972-91)

General Equation:

In QEX = 8.304 – 0.896** In REER – 00.66 In WY – 0.492 In KF

(2.28) (-5.53)(-0.07) (-0.62)

+ 0.880 In HA + 0.003 In (PEX/HP) -1

(1.83) (0.23)

Adj-R^2= 0.949, SEE = 0.062, RSS = 0.0534, DW = 1.58.

Final Specifications:

(1) In QEX= 7.062 – 1.016** In REER + 0.413* In WY

(5.19) (-7.08) (2.81)

Adj-R^2 = 0.942, SEE = 0.066, RSS = 0.0744, DW = 108.

Test against unrestricted specification: F(3,14) = 1.84

(2) In QEX= 5.473 -1.011** In REER + 0.295** In KF

(3.12) (-7.50) (3.07)

Adj-R^2 = 0.945, SEE = 0.064, RSS = 0.0700, DW = 1.16.

Test against unrestricted specification: F(3,14) = 1.45

** Significant at one per cent level.

* Significant at five per cent level.

Note : Figures in parentheses are t-values.

Source : Rajiv Kumar and Mathew Joseph (1994).

The result from the general equation indicates that only REER is significant and other variables are insignificant and/or have perverse signs. These results are vitiated by multicollinearity problem and final equation: (1) indicate significance of REER and real world income in India's export growth and equation, (2) in addition reveals the importance of the capacity variable, fixed capital stock. The results of both the final equations are equally good and both satisfy the F-test for joint estimation.

The above empirical study on India gives the message that is clear: exchange rate is a crucial variable for India's export performance; downward adjustments in nominal exchange rate of the rupee bring about real depreciation of the rupee which in turn can strongly improve India's export growth.

Arvind Virmani (1991) has estimated aggregate export and import functions for India' with the primary focus on the former, based on data for the 1970-71 to 1985-86 period. From his estimation of the manufactured export demand function, it appears that it explains 74% of the variation in the growth rate of Indian manufactured exports, where explanatory variables are PXMD being the UVI for manufactured exports PXM, multiplied by e and the $/Rs exchange rate, PXM is the US $ based UVI for world exports, temporary and permanent effects in growth of world GDP(WY) determined by including the lagged value of the variable. From his result it appears that a 10 per cent depreciation of the rupee relative to India's trading partners will result in a 29 per cent increase in the quantity of exports and a 19 per cent increase in the volume of exports. Moreover, his results also show that as manufactured exports constituted well over 60 per cent of total exports, any depreciation has a substantial positive effect on the balance of trade.

Vijay Joshi and I.M.D. Little (1994) examine whether in India the current account balance responds to variations in the real exchange rate. They start with the causal inspection witnessing thereby that in India the decade of the 1970s and the late 1980s were marked with a period of rapid export growth associated remarkably with real exchange rate depreciation, while the whole decade of the 1960s and the early 1980s were of slow export growth associated with real exchange rate appreciation. They have examined this issue econometrically. Their hypothesis is that exports are price sensitive. They estimate both single—equation as well as simultaneous export equation model after estimating export demand and supply equations with the presumption that exports are affected by foreign demand and domestic supply, all the models are being estimated in logarithm form with annual data. The single equation estimates show the volume of exports as a function of real effective exchange rate, world income and a proxy for domestic excess demand, the demand effects proxied by monetary measures which enter with a lag. All the variables turn out to be significant. The exchange rate elasticity of exports is around 0.75 in the short run and around 2 in the long-run, and so 10 per cent of the long-run effect comes through within two years. In the estimation of the demand and supply price elasticities for exports in the simultaneous equation framework what they find is that the demand equation relates the volume of India's export to world income and the relative price of Indian and world exports. The supply equation relates to the volume of India's exports to the relative price of Indian exports on the domestic market and a domestic excess demand term.

Their empirical results show that export supply is significantly negatively related to the pressure of aggregate demand on the home market and is significantly positively related with the domestic relative price of exports. The price elasticity of supply of exports is about 0.7 in the short-run and 1.1 in the long-run, with over 80 per cent of the effect coming through within one year after the current year. On the other hand, export demand is significantly negatively related to the relative price of Indian and competitor-country exports. Export is positively related to the change in world income but that dependence is not quite significant. The price elasticity of demand for exports is about 1.1 in the short-run and 3.0 in the long run, with 80 per cent of the long-run effect coming through within two years. The pressure of domestic excess demand used here as proxy in the supply equation is significant, while the world income term in the demand equation is not.

The message of their findings is clear: The price competitiveness of exports is an important determinant of the volume of exports, and for a real depreciation to improve the current account of the balance of payments, the relevant elasticities are adequate even with a zero price elasticity of demand for imports. Their estimation also show that a real devaluation does work in India as opposed to the viewpoint of elasticity pessimists who argue that a real devaluation would not work in India.

Thus it appears that the literature regarding the question whether real exchange rate depreciation matters or is necessary or helpful to the adjustment process has always been mixed. While some finds some support in their studies, others have not found any evidence of support based on long-run time series data. But what we can argue is that there is an unmistakable correlation between the strength of the Re and the import export ratio and thus the trade deficit. Moreover, exchange rate signal comes first so that the causation runs from exchange rate to trade performance. It also brings into sharp focus the need to develop an integrated macro-econometric approach where not only the exchange rate but also other macro-variables can be used to explain the behaviour of India's trade balance over the years. This would enable us to see the relative importance of these variables in influencing trade balance over time and to assess the strength of their mutual interactions. While there is no unique way to develop such a holistic approach to balance of payments adjustments in a developing economy like India, the insights of the theoretical discussions in chapter 2 together with the empirical results of some of the major studies on India's balance of payments behaviour help us develop the basic ingredients of such a holistic approach. This has been attempted in Chapter 6.

3.9 OTHER STUDIES

Among other studies of India's balance of payments mention ought to be made of the following contributors. The study of Ashok Seth and R.N. Bharadwaj (1994) deserve attention in this context. They have examined the determinants of current account surplus and real exchange rate movements in Indian economy over the period 1960-89. In the determination of current account they have found an important role of macroeconomic policies, in particular the role of the effect of budget surplus. The budget deficits affects the current account position through influencing aggregate demand in the economy. Since external terms of trade do not seem to have contributed much to current account surplus, their suggestion is that India should diversify her export baskets towards her value-added export items. Real exchange rate adjustments are found to be positive effect on current account surplus. An important determinant of current account surplus, next to budget surplus is the expansion of the markets in industrial countries. Market shrinkage in these countries due to protection may adversely affect Indian current account balance if appropriate adjustments are not made in RER (Real Exchange Rate). So India's standpoint as market adjuster i.e., letting the foreign exchange market dictate the course of the nominal exchange rate will not prove beneficial. Hence, according to them, a more active and aggressive exchange rate management will prove beneficial, directly supporting the liberalization attempt of Government of India after the crisis in 1991. In the case of real exchange rate movements, the important determinants as according to them are: (a) Trade controls, and (b) Real GDP growth (a proxy for technological progress). This result propels them to conclude that in this world of continued technical change and technological development, technical change needs to be the focus in industrial-cum-trade policies of India.

Sunanda Sen and Hiranya Mukhopadhyay (1994) have provided a macro-model of the Indian economy based on a specification of the structural linkages among GDP, exports and imports, using data for the period 1973-89, including a period of trade regime (1973-85) characterized by controls as well as the period of liberalized regime 1985-89 and have tried to identify the repercussions of trade and exchange rate policy changes on the trade deficit and GNP. The study however, does not analyse the implications of changes in the capital account of the country's balance of payments as resulted from liberalization. Their empirical results show that one has to consider the structural linkages between different sectors including foreign trade. These structural linkages are of prime importance in determining the impact of policy changes in the economy. The other important finding of their study relates to the implications of major instruments of trade policy like devaluation for the economy. Effect of devaluation of the country's trade deficit and the GDP are determined by the interplay of a structurally interdependent system. This rules out the relevance of the simplistic exercises implicit in particular approaches. The structural linkages between the dependent variables and the relation of each to the policy instruments or other parameters are both crucial in determining the final effect of real effective exchange rate. For example, the devaluation may turn out to be contractionary by curtailing the availability of imports and hence the supply of aggregate output. This may happen when devaluation causes adverse movements in the terms of trade of the country, by reducing the volume of imports which the country can afford. Thus the possibility of a 'devaluation-led' contraction in this model arises out of supply (and not demand) adjustments.

In her study, Anindita Sengupta (1996) empirically analyses the interaction between money, output, prices, international reserves and the exchange rate in the Indian economy during the period 1980-81 to 1993-94 in a macroeconomic framework, using a small macroeconometric model. The model evaluates the impact of money and monetary disequilibrium on the behaviour of major macroeconomic variables such as prices output and the balance of payments. Even though the framework of the model is in the spirit of the monetary approach 10 balance of payments (of Polak variety) and exchange rate, the model allows for adjustment lags in output and prices. The model also includes a policy reaction function which reflects the monetary authorities' policy as regards the domestic credit component of the monetary base. The model which is short-run in nature assumes that the demand for real money balances is stable in nature and any excess supply of money over its demand stimulates output and invokes inflationary pressure simultaneously. Further, an increase in liquidity brought about by, say a rise in bank credit, adversely affects, the level of foreign reserves in the economy. An increase in the supply relative to its demand results in a deterioration of international reserves as agents switch from money to both domestic and financial assets. This in turn may also lead to a depreciation of the domestic currency. These issues have been empirically tested by making use of a macroeconometric model comprising of fifteen variables, both endogenous and exogenous. The endogenous variable includes real money supply (M3/WPI), long-run—demand for real money (MD), GDP at market prices (at 1980-81 prices) (GDPMR), net foreign exchange assets of RBI (NFEA), wholesale price index (WPI) (index 1981-82 = 100), RBI's claims on government, commercial and co-operative banks, etc. (DC), potential output (GOPMRD, (GDP at market prices at 1980-81 prices), whereas the exogenous variables include intlation rate (ROF), rupee dollar exchange rate (EAVG), world commodity price index (WCP), Net RBI credit to Central Government (RBCG), total expenditure of the Central Government (TE), Government's currency liabilities to the public (GCL), net non-monetary liabilities of the RBI (NNML), and time variable (T) (1, 2, ...14). She finds that the gap between the supply of and demand for real money balances does play a significant role in determining the change in foreign exchange reserves.

The estimation procedure she adopted was that of ordinary least squares, as the system of equations is linear in variables. The results are shown below:

1. $\log MP = -4.04 + 0.55 \log GDPMR - 0.005\, ROF_{-1} + 0.64\, 10gMP_{-1}$

   (-1.29) (1.39) (-2.39) (2.65)

   Adj-R^2 = 0.99, DW = 2.2, SEE = 0.28.

All the regression coefficients have the desired signs.

2. $\log MD = -11.12 + 1.51 \log GDPMR - 0.014\, ROF_{-1}$

The result confirms that monetary disequilibrium plays a significant role in affecting the balance of payments.

3. $\log NFEA = -5.57 + 5.88 [\log MD - \log MP]_{-1} - 2.14 \log (WPI/WCP^{*}\, EAVG)$

   (-2.95) (2.68) (–2.95)

   Adj-R^2 = 0.43, D.W. = 1.9, SEE = 0.28

From the result the policy implication is that one should ideally exercise a restraint on monetary expansion beyond its level of effective demand in order to improve the balance of payments position of the country.

4. $\Delta \log DC = 0.002 - 0.03 \Delta \log NFEA + 0.99 \Delta \log RBCG_{-1}$
$(0.09) \quad (-1.44) \qquad (8.51)$

$Adj\text{-}R^2 = 0.89$, D.W. = 2.9, SEE = 0.03

The empirical result (4) shows that the impact of a rise in RBCG is positive and significant, which implies that budget deficit exerts a strong influence on the expansion in domestic credit. An increase in RBCG thus causes an expansion in the monetary base and thus an increase in overall money supply which in turn affects the balance of payments and the price level.

5. $\log EAVG = 0.80 + 0.55 \log (WPI/WCP) + 0.66 \log EAVG_{-1}$
$(2.14) \quad (2.39) \qquad (3.75)$

$Adj\text{-}R^2 = 0.98$, D.W. = 1.9, SEE = 0.06

The result (5) shows that the exchange rate equation corroborates the purchasing power hypothesis. Also it reveals that about 55 percent of the inflation differential of India *vis-à-vis* oilier currencies is transmitted to the exchange rate within the current year. But according to her, a stabilization policy of devaluing the Indian rupee to gain competitiveness would lead to arise in prices which may be counterbalanced by a cut in the budget deficit of the Central Government. Such a fall in RBCG would lead to fall in M_3 and hence a fall in prices.

Ranjit Sau (1992) has shown that the secular decay of the total factor productivity observed in India's manufacturing industries is arguably the reason for long-term strain on its BoP. Thus, he argues that the basic challenge for the Indian economy is to reverse the downward trend in total factor productivity. Unless this is done, he argues that fiscal management, no matter how conservative, would be of little avail in the long-run. It is noteworthy that the American economy described in Chapter 1 showed the similar trend when decay of the total factor productivity caused severe strain on its BoP deficits.

Meenakshi Rishi and James K. Boyce (1990) have estimated total capital flight between India and the world economy in a sixteen-year period (1971 to 1986) since the official BoP accounts do not record a number of hidden foreign exchange flows. They showed that total capital flight during this period amounted to $ 21.1 billion dollars in 1986, and that the cumulative stock of flight capital with imported interest earnings amounted to $ 28.6 billion. These were equivalent, respectively, to 52 per cent and 71 percent of the external debt accumulated during the same period, Thuş they think that the consequences of such capital flight for the Indian economy warrant serious attention. So their suggestion is that Indian policy-makers must consider the constraints posed by the threat of 'capital strike' via large scale capital transfers abroad, and the means by which these constraints can be eased.

To check the validity of the hypothesis that exports earnings are more stable than earnings on invisible account, Dhanmanjiri Sathe (1997) has examined the coefficient of variation of the components of the current account in Table 3.8.

She has estimated for the periods 1980-81 to 1984-85 and 1985-86 to 1900-91 separately and has been put in a descending orders. The first period she calls the pre-liberlization period and the second, the post-liberalization period. She finds that the coefficient of variation has been greater for the debits (imports) than for the credits (exports). It can be also seen from her findings that the variability of merchandise credits (i.e., export) and debits (i.e., imports) has increased in the said period. For the period 1980-81 to 1984-85, the coefficient of variation for exports and imports was 0.20 and 0.14, respectively. In the period 1984-85 to 1990-91, it rose to 0.38 and 0.32 respectively. The variability in exports has been higher than that in imports for both the periods. A comparison between export and invisibles (inflows) shows that the variability of the former has always been higher than that of the latter for both the periods. Thus the exports have been less stable than the inflows of invisibles (contrary to the hypothesis) over the period. When the outflows are studied, exactly opposite results are seen, though the difference between the two has been drastically reduced. For the period from 1980-81 to 1984-85, the coefficient of variation of the imports was quite low or 0.14 as she finds. However, in the next period, it rose to 0.32. Thus she concludes that both exports and imports have become more variable in the post-liberalization period as compared to the pre-liberlization period. Comparing exports/imports, (i.e., the extent to which the

TABLE 3.8
Coefficient of Variation for the Components of Current Account

	Credits		*Debits*
	(For 1980-81 to 1984-85)		
Misc.	0.47	TP Official	0.60
Insurance	0.34	Travel	0.51
Investment Income	0.25	Investment Income	0.51
TP Official	0.23	Invisibles	0.36
Transportation	0.22	Govt. n.i.e.	0.33
Merchandise	0.20	Insurance	0.33
Govt. n.i.e.	0.16	Transportation	0.31
Invisibles	0.14	Misc.	0.25
TP Private	0.13	TP Private	0.16
Travel	0.09	Merchandise	0.14
	(For 1985-86 to 1990-91)		
Misc.	0.30	TP Official	0.60
Insurance	0.37	Travel	0.23
Investment Income	0.06	Investment Income	0.55
TP Official	0.26	Invisibles	0.43
Transportation	0.38	Govt. n.i.e.	0.31
Merchandise	0.38	Insurance	0.23
Govt. n.i.e.	0.42	Transportation	0.36
Invisibles	0.20	Misc.	0.32
TP Private	0.13	TP Private	0.29
Travel	0.24	Merchandise	0.32

Notes : TP = Transfer Payments
n.i.e. = Not Included elsewhere
Source : Sathe (1997).

exports can pay for imports) with the components of invisibles, she finds that the variability of merchandise trade usually fall somewhere in between.

Rakesh Raman's study (2003) is an attempt to test whether disequilibrium in the domestic money market exerts any influence on BoP in economy likes India where money supply has been growing at a rapid rate; but there exists severe restrictions of reserves and capital movements. In order to test the validity of the monetary approach with respect to India, his study takes the following hypotheses for empirical verification:

1. Disequilibrium in the domestic money market significantly influences BoP.
2. The budget deficit and its financing by the RBI significantly influence the monetary disequilibrium factor suggesting that monetary targeting is needed to reduce fluctuations in the BoP.
3. Domestic credit control is a better measure than development to solve BoP crisis.
4. The monetary approach to BoP (MABoP) may be successfully used to analyse the short-run problems of inflation and BoP deficits.

The hypothesis number 1 and 4 are accepted. He further finds using Granger's Causality test with Schwartz criterion for the determination of the appropriate number of lags for the explanatory variables of the two equations

$$Log\ \ D = \alpha + \sum_{i=1}^{n} \beta i\left(Log\ \ D_{t-i}\right) + \sum_{j=1}^{m} \Delta j\left(Log\ \ R_{t-j}\right) + U_{1t}.$$

and

$$Log\ \ R = \varepsilon + \sum_{i=1}^{n} \lambda i\left(Log\ \ D_{t-i}\right) + \sum_{j=1}^{m} \left(Log\ \ R_{t-j}\right) + U_{1t}.$$

that an exogenous change in domestic credit (D) cause a change in forex reserve (R) and not *vice versa*. That there is a strong causality from Log D to Log R as the F value is significant.

Later he shows that the excess supply of money has a depressing impact on exports and inflow of capital and also increases imports. Hence he concludes that the disequilibrium in the money market causes changes is the BoP of a country. Thus the hypothesis number one is accepted.

The main findings of his study is that the monetary approach to BoP is definitely a better explanation of a country.

3.10 SUM UP

Chapter 3 provides us with a comprehensive review of the empirical literature of India's balance of payments by the researchers since the First Five Year Plan (beginning in 1951) that reflect the analysis of India's export performance, the progress of import substitution, or devaluation and its impact on the Indian economy or India's economic problems associated with the BoP theories, etc. The importance of exchange rate variations in India's BoP as emphasized in the literature has also been noted; and the relative impacts of other variables are also analysed in detail.

4

India's Balance of Payments : A Historical Perspective

In our endeavour to identify the major factors that govern India's balance of payments since 1950-51, we have noted the alternative theoretical perceptions and their connection with economic development, and also a brief survey of the research on India's balance of payments as undertaken by eminent economists from time-to-time. But in order to get into the exact nuances of the problems involved and the perspective, we need to view the historical roots of the problem. A brief sketch of the history of evolution of India's balance of payments position after independence will help our understanding of the fundamental issues, and the various constraints that operate on our balance of payments and shape the various policies from time-to-time. Such a fresh look at history will enable us to identify the proximate determinants of our balance of payments over time, and the importance of alternative theoretical positions in explaining its long-run and short-run behaviours. It must be understood that the history of India's balance of payments after independence cannot be divorced from the overall pattern and the strategy of economic development pursued in this country after independence, and therefore, the inter-connection between the two will be evident from our brief account of the history of India's balance of payments, which is the subject for discussion of this chapter.

A chronology of major events in the history of India's balance of payments is given in Appendix Table A 4.1.

4.1 PRELUDE TO INDEPENDENT INDIA'S BALANCE OF PAYMENTS

The history of foreign trade and payments in colonial India is itself a fascinating area of enquiry. The intricacies of the economic interests of the British rule in the sub-continent, and the switches in trade and payments policies towards India from time-to-time, affected the Indian economy in various ways, and there are several elaborate studies on each of these sequences. Here we shall briefly note the main features of India's balance of payments prior to her political independence through partition in 1947. This is necessary for our purpose, because such an account helps us identify the initial conditions of our balance of payments that we had inherited at the stroke of independence.

Indian trade balance in the late 19th and the early 20th century showed fluctuations with the variations of both exports and imports at different rates. On an average the growth of imports was at a slightly faster rate than the growth of exports throughout the period from 1865 to 1914. Exports during the period rose by about four times, while imports went up nearly five-fold. Although Indian exports suffered a setback during the initial years of the World War I due to wartime disruptions, by 1916-17 the demand for Indian exports rose back to the pre-war levels, and expanded thereafter mainly to cater to the wartime needs. At the close of the war, Indian exports in value terms were slightly higher than the pre-1914 level, although export prices suffered a decline on an average. On the other hand, Indian imports declined much more rapidly than exports during this period, and at the close of the World War I, the value of Indian imports at pre-war prices was less than 40 per cent of the pre-war level.

The period after the World War I experienced fluctuating trends for both exports and imports both in quantity and value terms. The onset of the Great Depression, and the uncertainty in the external value of the rupee affected, to a large extent, both these figures. But on the whole, India experienced trade surplus with respect to Britain between 1928 to 1934. The outbreak of the World War II in September 1939 gave a boost to Indian exports; and imports could not be maintained due to wartime disruption in supplies. The mild surplus in the current account, however, disappeared after the conclusion of the War, as pent-up demand for imports surpassed the growth of exports and India also had a negative balance on account of invisibles. However, the overall position of India's balance of payments position during the period was also related to the policy of the British government towards the external value of the rupee, although it was true that for about a decade from 1939 to 1949 the exchange rate ceased to be a live issue. But India accumulated sterling balances during the war. The sterling balances had amounted to over £ 1,300 million at the end of the war (*Sesadri*, 1993). India was able to save them merely because of the accident that a Labour Government was in power in the U.K. and was able to resist the pressure both from the USA and from others.

The post-war history of the complete control regime over imports and foreign exchange did not last long. Rather, this policy had to be modified because of the pressure of pent-up demand for consumer goods, which was severely distorting the domestic economy. In January 1946 controls were lifted from trade in a wide range of goods from the sterling area. By September 1946 the authorities allowed free imports of many types of foodstuff and consumer goods from any source inside or outside the Sterling Area. For more than a year after the end of the World War II import policy became progressively more liberal. However, with exports lagging and large imports of foodgrains still needed to supplement the rationing system, opening India's port to foreign consumer goods had a dramatic effect on her balance of payments position. To counter this a much more restrictive regime had to be imposed in March 1947. The authorities introduced exchange controls and further import restrictions in early July 1947.

Indian import policy over the next few years was dominated by attempts to cope with the irreconcilable problems of inflation and balance of payments constraints. From July 1947 to June 1948 imports other than food were successfully chocked off by the restrictive policy regime. However, inflationary pressures were becoming severe, aggravated by the rise in the price of foodgrains following decontrol in December 1947. In response, import controls were liberalized considerably. The effect of this liberalization was a new payments crisis in the early 1949, accentuated by a fall-off in exports to the dollar area as the American economy moved into recession. Thus by May 1949 policy came full circle again with the cancellation of all Open General Licences (OGLs); Licences of imports from dollar and hard currency areas were suspended from the end of June until September 1949; when sterling devalued against the dollar by 30.5 per cent in September 1949 (i.e. from $ 4.03 to $ 2.80), India followed suit, and since Pakistan kept to the old parity Indo-Pakistan trade was brought almost to a standstill.

Thus owing mainly to the necessity to import few million tonnes of food-grains each year in the system of OGL for import, the partition of India which took away some of her export items and huge demand for import of capital goods, the balance of payments situation worsened. The deficits were of the order of Rs. 58 crore in 1946, Rs. 111 crore in 1947 and Rs. 361 crore in 1948. The deficits were covered mostly by the sterling balances. It is worth noting that at the time of India's Independence the British Raj had left behind Gold, coin and bullion worth Rs. 1810 crore in the Reserve Bank plus Rs. 1733 crore of sterling balances, Rs. 425 crore of repatriation pre-war debt and Rs. 115 crore in the *Empire Dollar Pool*—a sum of Rs. 3452 crore in all. As world prices rose in the winter of 1949--50, India's export receipts increased once more, resulting in a much smaller balance of trade deficit for the year. Licensing policy was accordingly relaxed again, and import of a wide range of raw materials and intermediate goods went back into the OGL. The Korean War boom that started from June 1950 boosted India's exports still further, and this value rose from Rs. 5.02 billion in 1949-50 to Rs. 6.34 billion in 1950-51 and further to Rs. 7.14 billion in 1951-52. With world wide supply difficulties constraining imports, India achieved a trade surplus on private account of Rs. 1.58 billion in 1950-51. In 1951-52 however, imports rose again, reducing the private trade surplus to Rs. 460 million, and producing a massive deficit on the government trading account of Rs. 2.76 billion, enough to push the whole current account heavily into deficits (*Tomlinson*, 1993).

The balance of payment difficulties are imperative and implicit in the early stages of any development planning which aims at raising the per capita income quickly and modernizing its industry and at the same time expanding its agriculture. This bold and challenging task requires, of course, a fast and vigorous growth of productive capacity in the manufacturing sector, which in turn necessitates massive imports of inputs like raw materials, heavy machinery and equipments, and use of highly capital intensive techniques. India had been no exception to this process as will be evident from our account of her balance of payments experiences during the period of her various five-year plans.

4.2 INDIA'S BALANCE OF PAYMENTS IN THE 1950s

In this section, we outline the behaviour of India's balance of payments during the period 1950-60. Tables 4.1 and 4.2 provide summary of the available evidences on India's balance of payments for the period from 1951-52 to 1960-61 i.e., almost the decade that started with great promise of the planned development under a mixed economy framework, covering almost the two Five-Year Plans. For the convenience of our analysis, we may split the period into two phases: (i) The era of planning from 1951 to 1956, that is, the First Five-Year Plan; (ii) The Nehruvian-Mahalanobis Second Five-Year Plan period (1956 to 1961). It is worth-noting that both these phases did not experience any change in the exchange rate, and in both the phases, the development strategies were primarily guided by long-term considerations. For this period, the evidences in Tables 4.1 and 4.2 exactly relate to the first two Five-Year Plan period. Hence, it would be useful to give a brief account of the balance of payments situation for each of these two plan periods.

TABLE 4.1

India's Overall Balance of Payments during First Plan (1951-52 to 1955-56)

(*Rs. Crore*)

Particulars	*1951-52*	*1952-53*	*1953-54*	*1954-55*	*1955-56*	*Total*
Total Imports	963.00	633.00	592.00	690.00	773.00	3,651.00
Exports f.o.b.	730.00	602.00	540.00	597.00	640.00	3,109.00
Trade Balance	–233.00	–31.00	–52.00	–93.00	–133.00	–542.00
Non-monetary Gold Movement	–10.00	—	—	—	—	–10.00
Net Invisibles (excluding official donations and similar official assistance)	+66.00	+81.00	+81.00	+77.00	+85.00	+390.00
Current account (Net)	–162.60	+60.20	+47.40	+6.00	+6.70	–42.30
Net capital transactions (including errors and omissions but excluding official loans)	–62.00	–79.00	–4.00	–8.00	–5.00	–158.00
Total deficit (–) or surplus (+)	–230.00	–29.00	+25.00	–18.00	–37.00	–289.00
Financed through						
1. Foreign assistance	+65.00	+46.00	+21.00	+17.00	+55.00	+204.00
2. Draft on (+) of Accretion to (–) reserves	+165.00	–17.00	–29.00	+18.00	–11.00	+126.00
3. IMF. Drawings (purchases +, Repurchases –)	—	—	–17.00	–17.00	–7.00	–41.00

Source : India's Balance of Payments, 1948-49 to 1961-62: Reserve Bank of India, Bombay.

TABLE 4.2

Balance of Payments in the Second Plan (1956-61)

(Rs. Crore)

Particulars	1951-52	1952-53	1953-54	1954-55	1955-56	Total
1. Total Exports	620	635	573	640	642	3110
2. Total Imports	903	1036	904	961	1122	4926
3. Trade Balance	-283	-401	-331	-321	-480	-1816
4. Net Invisibles	154.1	133.2	126.0	113.4	82.8	609.5
5. Net Total Current Account (merchandise + non-monetary Gold Movement + invisibles)	-312.8	-431.4	-327.0	-185.6	-392.4	-1649.2
6. Net total capital account (private + banking + official)	313.1	439.3	356.1	210.1	398.7	1717.3
7. Error and Omissions	-0.3	-7.9	-29.1	-24.5	-6.3	-68.1
8. Net reserves and Monetary gold	221.3	259.9	42.3	16.0	59.2	598.7
9. Foreign currency assets	563.34	303.46	261.16	245.10	185.85	1558.91
10. Total foreign exchange reserves (Gold + SDRs value + foreign currency)	681.10	421.22	378.92	362.86	303.61	2147.71
Total deficits (-) or surplus (+)	-389	-560	-386	-289	-464	-2088
Financed through:						
1. Foreign assistance	113	266	344	297	416	1436
2. Draft on (+) of accretion to (-) reserves	221	260	42	16	59	598
3. IMF. Drawings (Purchases +, Repurchases –)	55	34	—	-24	-11	+54

Source : H.L. Chandhok and the Policy Group (1990) India Data base: The Economy Annual Time Series Data, *Economic Survey*, Government of India.

A. The First Five Year Plan: 1951-52 to 1955-56

India did not experience any serious balance of payments difficulties during the First Plan period. When the First Five Year Plan was drafted, there was an optimistic climate for receiving foreign aid, loans, and substantial sterling balances were accumulated in favour of India in London. The Korean War boom in 1951-52 had also given a fillip towards expansion of exports to a record level of Rs. 749.5 crore during 1951-52. Besides, there were other reasons, viz., the existing excess capacities and elasticities of the productive system, shortfall of expenditure in the public sector, failure to implement fully the import-intensive parts of the plan, and a record bumper harvest in 1953-54 and almost as good as that in 1954-55 resulted in a substantial decline in foodgrains imports. Total food imports during the plan period were only three million tonnes as compared to nine million tonnes anticipated. This saved foreign exchange worth more than Rs. 300 crore. Moreover, as percentage of national income, imports along with exports constituted a relatively small element of national income of India. Over the years, India's exports of commodities and services as percentage of world exports and as percentage of her GNP had fluctuated between 1.97 per cent to 1.35 percent, and 4 to 7 percent, respectively and imports between 6 to 10 per cent of GNP. These figures, however, somewhat underestimated the importance of imports and exports and the growing gap between them. The situation is revealed in the Table 4.1

The availability of the United States Wheat Loan in 1951-52 and the large increase in domestic output thereafter, the abatement of inflationary pressures within the economy and the low levels of machinery and capital goods imports almost until the last year of the First Plan, all taken together, contributed to the unexpectedly stable balance of payments position in the First Plan period. As a result of these developments, the foreign exchange reserves declined by only Rs. 138 crore as against the expected decline of Rs. 290 crore over the plan period.

Regarding the financing of current account deficit, we can say that in most of the underdeveloped countries, the deficits in the current account were financed mainly in the following ways:

(a) Drawing on foreign exchange reserves.
(b) Purchases from the IMF.
(c) Short-term loans from Foreign Banks.
(d) Longer-term capital inflow from the World Bank, IFC, etc.[1]
(e) Private capital inflow.
(f) Inter-Governmental grants or loans.

And over the First Five Year Plan, the trade deficits which averaged a little more than 100 crore per annum, was financed largely by invisible earnings and private transfer payments. With the relatively comfortable level of sterling balances, accumulated in the pre-independence period, the First Plan was indifferent to exports and the very small deficit on current accounts less than Rs. 10 crore per annum was in turn financed by inflows of foreign aid and in the main, by a rundown of the country's stock of overseas assets. With the increase in imports outpacing that of exports, a deficit in the balance of trade of Rs. 542 crore was covered by Rs. 500 crore of earnings from invisibles leaving only a marginal deficit of Rs. 42 crore in the current account of the balance of payments.

B. The Second Five Year Plan Period (1956-57 to 1960-61)

The Second Five Year Plan adopted a strategy of import substituting industrialization in the heavy capital goods sector of the Indian economy with the explicit lead role of the public sector investment in the so-called 'commanding heights of the economy under the influence of a structural model of the Feldman-Mahalanobis variety. Since India was industrially backward at the time of initiating the Second Plan, such a programme of heavy industry-led growth inevitably resulted in the spurt in the demand for imports of machinery, equipment and other intermediate inputs during this plan period. On the other hand, Indian exports, which were predominantly primary products, could not expand much during this period to finance this upsurge in import requirements. This was mainly due to low income elasticities of consumer demand for agricultural commodities in the advanced industrialized countries of the world, and the gradual displacement of the demand for primary raw materials exported by India in the industrial uses of these countries due to technological improvements. In this way India's competitiveness as an exporter of raw materials and its share of world markets declined in the later 1950s, just as the price of essential imports (food, steel, iron and capital equipments) increased. By the late 1950s, also the sterling balances, accumulated in London during the war and available to pay for imports in the years of independence, had been used up. As a result, our balance of payments position turned for the worse and a payments crisis developed in the winter of 1956-1957. By mid-1957, the foreign exchange position was so 'pretty alarming' that Finance Minister T.T. Krishnamachari told Prime Minister J. Nehru that if immediate steps were not taken the economy could grind to a halt and India would lose its international creditworthiness. Nehru confirmed the crisis in discussion with the Cabinet, accepting the crisis. Non-essential imports were then drastically curtailed and the plan outlays were scaled down. However, the crisis was partly due to the neglect of the foreign exchange constraint in our plan formulation, and over optimism with regard to the continuance of the buoyancy in our export demands abroad. Thus, in contrast to the comfortable position in the First Five Year Plan, the balance of payments position in the Second Plan Period turned adverse, showing deficits for all the years, and we witnessed a mounting deficit in the balance of trade of Rs. 467 crore per annum on an average during the entire plan period, following the strategy of import substitution and large scale investment of the Mahalanobis variety. Only 20 per cent of the deficits was met by invisible earnings and transfer payments, the rest was financed by foreign aid inflows and foreign exchange reserves. In 1956-57, the net total current account deficit was Rs. 312.8 crore which increased to Rs. 431.4 crore in the next year. In the third year of the plan, however, the deficit came down to Rs. 327 crore, and in the fourth year it touched the lowest figures of Rs. 185.6 crore. But in the last year of the plan the deficit amounted to Rs. 392.4 crore, thus giving an aggregate deficit of Rs. 1649.2 crore over the entire plan period. Table 4.2 summarizes the picture for the Second Plan period.

The current account deficit in the Second Plan period that arose due to the requirement of heavy foreign exchange expenditure was more than thrice as compared to that of the First Plan period. The factors that contributed to this deficit were as follows:

(a) The unanticipated Suez Crisis of 1956 led to a steep rise in freight rates which raised the value of imports;
(b) The spill-over of the import license issued during the First Plan into the first two years of the Second Plan, added to strain on the balance of payments. This was partly due to the delay in deliveries of goods by foreign exporters to India and partly to the delay in the implementation of the First Plan projects in India itself due to administrative rigidities and shortage of entrepreneurial and managerial staff;
(c) A large volume of food imports was necessitated during the Second Plan owing to the failure of food production to keep pace with the increase in population and also due to the widespread crop failure in the first two years of the plan due to unfavourable weather conditions. In particular poor monsoons in the 1957-58 had a very serious adverse impact on domestic food supplies. The spurt in the quantum of imports during the first two years of the plan was also partly the result of a substantial increase in import of consumer goods. This was, however, arrested in the succeeding years by severe controls and stringent restrictions on such imports. The rising trend in imports during the remaining three years of the Plan was arrested and geared mainly to the requirements of industrial development and foodgrains. Foodgrains imports during the Second Plan were of the order of Rs. 805 crore, against that of Rs. 595 crore during the First Plan;
(d) The large investment outlay during the last two years of the Plan necessitated large imports of machinery and other capital equipments;
(e) The expanding money incomes and industrial activity in India for setting up of steel plants, heavy expansion and renovation of railways and initiation of many

modern industries led to a larger domestic absorption of the export goods, as well as made the projects foreign resource-intensive;

(f) Import substitution, particularly in basic intermediates and machine building, became a major element of our trade policy in the late fifties, while exports suffered due to relative neglect in the perception of planners and policy makers;

(g) The performance of export was also not encouraging mainly owing to adverse circumstances abroad. Roughly speaking, Indian exports of goods and services were about 7.5 per cent of her GNP in 1955-56 before development really started to accelerate, and about 6 per cent of GNP in 1959. The backlog of recession in the United States and Western Europe, followed by an increase in the bank rate in the 1950s, contributed to the slow growth in the demand for India's exportables. These short-run factors aggravated the long-run trend of stagnation in India's exports, which remained virtually stagnant during the whole decade of 1951-60, averaging Rs. 606 crore a year during the First Plan and Rs. 609 crore a year during the Second Plan;

(h) The foreign exchange reserves[2] of the country declined in the two years 1956-57 and 1957-58 by some $ 1,000 million. This sharp decline was partly due to a rise in direct plan expenditure. As against a withdrawal of about Rs. 200 crore from the foreign exchange reserves of the country envisaged in the plan, the actual withdrawal was about Rs. 600 crore over the five years of the Second Plan;

(i) Invisible earnings and private transfer payments were able to finance just about 20 per cent of the trade deficit of Rs. 467 crore per annum. Foreign aid inflows financed approximately half of the resulting current account deficit of Rs. 344 crore per annum, but more than one-third of this deficit was financed by a depletion of foreign exchange reserves which were run down at a rate of Rs. 120 crore per annum.

If one takes the two plan periods together, then one finds that India's balance of payments did not exhibit any signs of substantial improvements. This may be attributed to the following factors:

(i) The investment pattern for development had been decided on the basis of heavy import contents. Steel plants, machine building, heavy electrical and engineering equipments—all required massive imports of capital goods at the initial stage.

(ii) Continuous imports of maintenance goods were necessary to keep the previous imports of capital goods properly functioning. Thus there was increasing imports of raw materials, intermediate goods, non-ferrous metals, oil and lubricants, spare parts and components.

(iii) During all these years (1951-61), Indian exports had shown practically no response to the need for extra payment abroad. The vulnerability of our export earnings due to stagnancy of world demand and price fluctuations, added to the worries in view of surge in import bills.

(iv) With every rise in internal price the home cost of production increased and to that extent, competitive strength to sell in the foreign market got reduced. Due to low productivity and inferior technology, cost of Indian goods was already very high, and with every inflationary spiral, the position worsened.

(v) Food imports, which on an average, were over Rs. 150 crore a year had considerably widened the BoP gap. This was due to the disruption in domestic food supplies following bad monsoons, and increased demand.

(vi) The barter terms of trade, that is the volume of goods which India had to export for obtaining equivalent imports, had considerably gone against India during this period. It was estimated that the adverse impact had been as much as 20% due to this factor, which meant that even with one-fifth increase in the volume of exports, India's balance of payments position had been no better.

(vii) The amount due for repayment of our external debt was quite sizeable. In the absence of any surplus made available from the current account for the repayment of external debt, further borrowing was essential to pay off old debts, and the net effect had been a cumulative increase in the burden of our foreign indebtedness.

On an average, during the period stretching from 1951 to 1961, India had a deficit to the extent of Rs. 400 crore a year— the value of imports being near Rs. 1000 crore a year, and exports roughly Rs. 600 crore. The balance had been covered by running down forex reserves which had come down from Rs. 1,400 crore in 1951 to less that Rs. 100 crore. It was obvious that with the depletion of the reserves, our dependence on foreign loans had become greater. For ten years i.e., during the first two plan periods, exports from India remained practically stagnant at about Rs. 600 crore. As national income increased during the two plan periods and exports remained stagnant, exports as a percentage of national income declined. This was rather paradoxical. Internal saving increased from 5 per cent to 10 during the two plan periods, whereas exports as percentage of national income, began to decline. This was contrary to the experiences of countries like Germany and Japan for whom the ratio of export to national income actually rose during this period. India's share in expanding world trade actually declined from 2.2 per cent in the immediate post-war period to less than one per cent during this period.

It was true that during the 1950s, developed countries fared much better than the developing countries in an environment of expanding world trade. The developing countries' share of world trade fell from 31 percent in 1950 to 21.4 percent in 1960. At the same time, the developed countries' share of world trade rose from 60.4 percent in 1950 to 66.8 percent in 1960. Backward countries had, therefore, lagged behind in sharing prosperity through trade. Two important factors contributed to this. First, in a world of rising standard of living, demand for manufactured goods like machines, capital goods, finished consumer goods like radios, transistors, etc., rose rapidly and the LDCs could not share the benefits from rising trade in the same proportion as the advanced industrialized countries, because the LDCs produced mostly primary raw materials, i.e. the products with the most sluggish demand in world markets like Tin and Rubber (Malaysia), Cocoa (African Countries), Coffee (Brazil) and Tea (India and Sri Lanka). Also the demand for raw materials tended to fluctuate owing to new inventions, changes in fashion, and/or introduction of improved technology. As a result, India along with the other LDCs had not been able to make any improvement in her export earnings and was fast losing ground in the international market.

Moreover, as mentioned earlier, the LDCs had suffered another handicap in the form of rapid worsening of their barter terms of trade between the value of their raw materials and the finished goods offered by developed countries. The competition was highly imperfect. As a result, in some cases, trade loses had been as much as 50 per cent and in the case of India, the terms of trade had been unfavourable at least to the extent of 20 per cent. Perhaps 25 per cent of India's foreign exchange gap could have been covered if the trade pattern and the terms of trade had not been so heavily against India. On the whole, it is arguable that the volume of trade was unequally divided in the world, and for Third World exporters with a heavy dependence on the export of specific commodities the international trading system had been unfavourable for most of the post-war period. And India, as a result, gradually was finding it extremely difficult to fit herself into this rapidly changing global market with any distinct advantage. India was fighting nearly a losing battle to improve her trade position in volume and terms of trade.

4.3 INDIA'S BALANCE OF PAYMENTS IN THE 1960s

During the 1960s despite the modest growth in exports[3] at an annual rate of 4 per cent, which constituted a distinct break from the near stagnation in export during the 1950s, the position of trade balance stayed at the earlier levels and trade deficits averaged Rs. 475 crore per annum.

A. The Third Five Year Plan (1961-62 to 1965-66)

According to the plan documents, exports and imports during the Third Plan were targeted for Rs. 3,700 crore and Rs. 5,750 crore respectively, against this the actual export earnings amounted to Rs. 3,735.00 crore and thus matched the plan targets. However, the import payments totalled to Rs. 6,118.6 crore, exceeding the target of Rs. 5,750 crore by Rs. 369 crore. This was necessitated mainly due to increasing defence requirements owing to the outbreak of war with China in 1962 and with Pakistan in 1965, and partly due to large food imports to match the predicament of the worst drought that broke out in 1965. The debt servicing charges also started making their impact on India's balance of payments from this plan period. The payments on this account rose from a negligible Rs. 23.8 crore in the First Plan and Rs. 119.4 crore in the Second Plan to Rs. 542.6 crore in the Third Plan. Export-import figures for 1965-66 have been taken here at pre-devaluation rates.

After several years of stagnation at about Rs. 650 crore covering the two plan periods, export had shown a welcome increase only in the early years of the Third Plan, as may be seen from the Table 4.3. The Table also points to the increasing gap in the foreign trade. However, during the latter half of the Third Plan the progress came to an abrupt end despite an increase in the coverage of schemes for export promotion. What was more disturbing was the fact that our traditional exports of tea and jute goods required much help and there was persistent demand for increases in incentives that were being given. That was not surprising as domestic inflation had been making serious inroads into the competitive power of our exports. A stage had been reached where export subsidies had to be given practically for all export items even to maintain the exports at the existing level. In such circumstances, a formal devaluation was the only straightforward case to offset the impact of inflation on the external sector of the economy and end of era of dual exchange rates owing to the plethora of export subsidies and controls. (*Bhattacharyya,* 1966)

Imports during the first year of Third Plan amounted to Rs. 1092 crore, well below the level of Rs. 1122 crore during

TABLE 4.3

India's Balance of Payments During the Third Plan (1961-62 to 1965-66)

(*Rs. Crore*)

Particulars	*1961-62*	*1962-63*	*1963-64*	*1964-65*	*1965-66*
Total Exports	661	685	783	816	806
Total Imports	1092	1133	1223	1349	1409
Trade Balance	–431	–446	-430	–533	–603
Net Invisibles	+31.3	+61.9	+94.0	+ 151.9	+72.7
Net Total Current Account (Merchandise + Non-monetary Gold movement + Invisibles)	–306.4	–354.0	–349.4	–452.0	–510.7
Net total capital account (private + banking + official)	+298.6	+348.1	+404.0	+500.8	+523.1
Errors and Omissions	+7.8	+5.9	–54.6	–48.8	–12.4
Reserves and Monetary gold (Net)	56.3	2.3	–10.8	–56.2	–48.3
Foreign currency assets	179.55	177.34	188.05	115.05	182.09
Total foreign exchange reserves (Gold + SDRs value + foreign currency assets)	297.31	295.10	305.81	249.68	297.98
Total deficits (–) or surplus (+)	–468	+465	–554	–790	–736
Financed by :					
1. External assistance	342	+451	565	687	718
2. Drawing from IMF	119	12	—	48	65
3. Decline in reserve (–) decrease (+) increase	6	2	11	56	44

Note : Due to rounding up, the totals may not tally accurately.

Source : H.L. Chandhok and the Policy Group (1990): India Database: The Economy Annual Time Series Data. *Economic Survey*, Government of India.

1960-61. However, since then imports recorded a sustained rise and totalled to Rs. 1223 crore during 1963-64, Rs. 1349 crore during 1964-65 and Rs. 1409 crore during 1965-66. The net total current account deficit comprising merchandise plus non-monetary gold movement plus invisibles during the Third Plan came to Rs. 1972.5 crore as follows: Rs. 306.4 crore in 1961-62, Rs. 354 crore in 1962-63, Rs. 349.40 crore in 1963-64, Rs. 452.00 crore in 1964-65, and Rs. 510.70 crore in 1965-66. In spite of the modest growth in export earnings which displayed a distinct break from stagnation in exports during the 1950s, the trade deficit stayed at the earlier level.

It would be clear from the above comparative figures that an adverse balance of payments persisted throughout the Third Plan period and constituted a serious pressure on foreign exchange reserves. The most significant feature of this Plan period is that Indian exports for the first time displayed a growth of dynamism due to increase in the production base, both agricultural and industrial, and a generally favourable climate of the international trade, as well as a number of factors: institutional, fiscal and other measures adopted as part of a deliberate policy package to promote exports through setting of board of trade, export councils and trading corporation. In contrast to the stagnation that persisted during the decade 1951-60 averaging Rs. 606 crore a year during the First Plan period and Rs. 609 crore a year during the Second Plan period, the level of exports rose at an annual compound rate of 4.1 per cent from Rs. 642 crore in 1960-61 to Rs. 806 crore in 1965-66.

During the Third Plan period, home investment exceeded the domestic saving (normal *ex-ante* saving). As a result, the economy suffered from internal pressure on prices on the one hand and an external pressure on the balance of payments following the mechanism prominently worked in our country during the period: Investment – Saving = Imports – Exports[4]. Due to increased defence requirements and growing development needs, the (*ex-ante*) investment saving gap widened sharply. It was this gap, or the failure of the planners in raising the rates of saving which had caused the inflationary pressure to accentuate and thus adversely affect the balance of payments.

However, during the Third Plan period, Indian economy witnessed a significant change in the commodity composition not confined as to tea, cotton textiles and jute manufacture exports but to upward export trend in case of engineering goods, chemicals, oilcakes, fruits, and vegetables, sugar and iron ore and also a directional pattern of her exports (a rapid rise in the Indian exports to the socialist countries, viz. the erstwhile U.S.S.R. and the East European Countries.) The most striking feature in this period was that there was almost no surplus on account of invisibles and private transfers, taken together. What is more, foreign exchange reserve reached the rock bottom level. Therefore, the entire balance of payments deficit was financed by foreign aid inflows, mostly in the form of loans, although there was some grants (the net inflow of external assistance actually amounted to Rs. 2,939.8 crore including Rs. 450.6 crore from PL 480 assistance). It is worthnoting that throughout the period from 1951-52 to 1965-66, the capital account was dominated by official transactions, in particular, inflows of foreign aid and movements in reserves. Private and banking transactions were negligible. This trend had continued even in subsequent years

B. India's Balance of Payments Since 1966-67—The Crisis Management Phase during the Three Annual Plans

The economic crisis of 1965-66 was further deepened by the great drought of 1965-67, accompanied by the attack of September 1965 by Pakistan which led to further commitment to defence expenditure and reduced the flow of foreign aid. There were all-round decline in economic activities. This had severe adverse effect on balance of payments, with the necessity of large scale food imports, forming about one-third of import bill. Although the broad strategy for the management of the balance of payments remained unchanged in the 1960s, there was a growing recognition by the planners that import substitution could not provide a complete solution to India's balance of payments problems. As a result, there was increased emphasis on export promotion within the framework of overall development strategy. The need for increased export earnings became all the more urgent since the quantum of aid, particularly of non-project aid that was not large enough to enable India to import adequate quantity of raw materials needed for a full utilization of its growing industrial capacity. To meet this situation the government undertook a number of institutional and fiscal measures to re-stimulate the exports, for example, setting up of the Board of Trade, Export Promotion Councils and the Mineral and Metals Trading Corporation; announcement of import entitlements against exports of certain manufactured and processed products and extension of incentives in the form of withdrawal of import duty and refund of excise duty to a number of commodities, establishment of the Marketing Development Fund to enable the Export Promotion Council to explore and develop foreign markets for Indian commodities. There was also increased emphasis on bilateral trade and payments arrangements with the countries of Eastern Europe. Simultaneously, the system of granting indirect export subsidies through the import replenishment schemes was extended to embrace a large segment of exports of non-traditional products. Moreover, India's major creditor led by the World Bank strongly felt that tight import controls and a haphazard growth of indirect export subsidies propelled by India's strategy of import substitution would be unnecessarily wasteful and inefficient. It was in response to such pressures and reasons that the Indian rupee was devalued on June 6, 1966 to strengthen and enhance the competitive power of exports and to bring in stability as well as to provide a solution to the trade and payments problems. The par value of the rupee was reduced by 36.5 per cent involving a rise of 57.5 per cent in the price of foreign exchange in terms of the Indian rupee.

This was initiated in the expectation that a reduction in the rupee exchange rate will have two effects on the prices of the commodities in which India traded. Indian export will be cheaper in foreign currencies, and the goods and services India import will be more expensive in terms of rupees. Such a rise in imported goods prices will reduce sales, adding to improvement coming from the increased exports. The process can be seen from the Figure 4.1.

It may be noted that the underlying faith in devaluation of the currency was based on the fulfilment of the Marshall-Lerner

FIG. 4.1

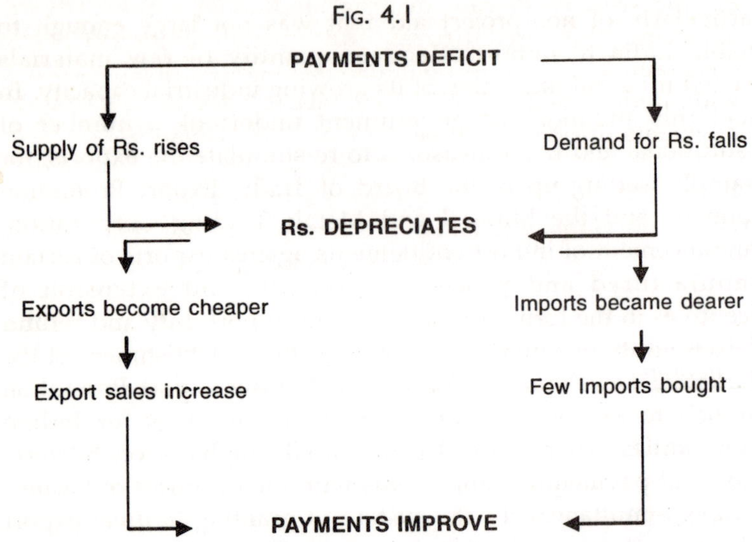

condition[5]—a contention that subsequent researchers sought to repudiate.

However, throughout these three years, the imports had a downturn trend. Compared to Rs. 1409 crore in 1965-66, this aggregated to Rs. 2078 crore in 1966-67, Rs. 2008 crore in 1967-68 and Rs. 1909 crore in 1968-69. Moreover, after devaluation, imports became more expensive and contributed to an imported inflation. Since this coincided with the great drought, the price index (general consumer price index for industrial workers: 1960 = 100) climbed from 137 in 1964 to 167 in 1967.

However, presumably because of low elasticities and non-price competitive factors, devaluation did not lead to any substantial increase in exports. The export performance was thus, not very much encouraging. Against the level of Rs. 806 crore attained in 1965-66, it slumped to Rs. 1152 crore in 1966-67. However, it partially recovered to Rs. 1199 crore in 1967-68 and regained its momentum in 1968-69, fetching Rs. 1358 crore. The total adverse trade balance during this period amounted to Rs. 2286 crore. The widespread crop failure in 1965-66, 15-20 per cent below the level of 1964-65, and also the none-too-good harvest during 1966-67, the consequent increase in cereal imports by as much as Rs. 144 crore to Rs. 651 crore during 1966-

67, the scarcity of raw material and other inputs adversely affecting the agricultural and industrial activities and constraining the export potential, on balance, contributed to this wide trade deficits. Table 4.4 summarizes the India's balance of payments during the three Annual plans (1966-69).

TABLE 4.4
India's Balance of Payments during the Annual Plans (1966-69)

(*Rs. Crore*)

Particulars	*1966-67*	*1967-68*	*1968-69*
1. Total Exports	1152.00	1199.00	1358.00
2. Total Imports	2078.00	2008.00	1909.00
3. Trade Balance	-926.00	-809.00	-551.00
4. Net Invisibles	+59.90	-8.60	+7.90
5. Net Total Current Account (merchandise + non-monetary Gold movement + invisibles)	-845.90	-801.40	-365.20
6. Net total capital account (private + banking + official)	+838.70	+881.20	+478.90
7. Error and Omissions	+7.20	+74.80	-113.70
8. Net reserves and Monetary gold	+36.50	-70.80	-38.10
9. Foreign currency assets	+295.91	+356.02	+394.17
10. Total foreign exchange reserves (Gold + SDRs value + Foreign Currency Assets)	478.44	538.55	576.70

Source : H.L. Chandhok and the Policy Group (1990).
India Database: The Economy, Annual Time Series Data.

The important feature during this period (1966-69) was that despite successive droughts and consequent food imports, payments difficulties was not as severe as it was during the second and third plan period, foreign aid flows being the principal sources of financing the payments deficits. By the end of 1966, India had received a total of 45 billion rupees of foreign aid ($ US 10 billion), according to the old official exchange rate. Only 7.5 per cent of this sum was in the form of grants; the rest consisted of loans. India's debt service after the devaluation amounted to 3.3 billion rupees in 1967 (2.1 billion rupees amortisation and 1.2 billion rupees interest). However, resorting to foreign aid as a source of financing the balance of payments deficits, had other repercussions, as the political turmoil in India and the international pressures surmounted on the Indian Government under various pretexts during this period amply demonstrate. The devaluation of the currency notwithstanding, the measures for import substitution and export subsidisation reappeared and the Indian trade regime continued with inefficient allocation mechanisms under different types of policy distortions.

4.4 INDIA'S BALANCE OF PAYMENTS IN THE 1970s

India's balance of payments remained more or less stable during the 1970s despite some major adverse incidents. Positive earnings from the current account were reported only twice during 1975-76 and 1976-77; otherwise BoP in India, whenever viewed from the national income measurement side, constitutes a very feeble position and continuous story of deficits if we take the whole period stretching from the beginning of the planned economy development upto the present time (*Chatterjee and Karmakar*, 1990).

It was for the first time since the beginning of her planned economic development that the Indian economy, in the early 1970s, almost succeeded in overcoming the chronic and persistent balance of payments difficulties that prevailed in the earlier two decades. After the devaluation and onset of industrial recession, India achieved an even balance of trade in 1970. By 1972-73 India had a small surplus of Rs. 104 crore in the balance of trade and the net aid inflow reached its lowest level in two decades. But this happy mirror soon faded out. In October 1973 and January 1974, OPEC announced dramatic increase in the price of crude oil. The price of Saudi Arabian crude oil, for instance, was raised from $ 2.69 per barrel in the middle of 1973 to $ 11.65 per barrel in early 1974. India, as one of the poor oil importing countries, was severely affected by this sudden rise in oil prices. Its direct impact was naturally felt on the balance of payments with severity in a number of ways:

(a) The massive escalation in the foreign exchange expenditure on oil imports was accompanied by a hike in the share of crude oil and petroleum products in India's import bill from 11 per cent in 1972-73 to 26 per cent in 1974-75.
(b) There were substantial increases in India's import bill on account of fertilizers and other oil-based chemicals.
(c) There was import of large quantities of foodgrains owing to successive shortfalls in agricultural production roughly during this time. A staggering sum of foreign exchange was thus required by India to import petroleum, fertilizers and foodgrains. As a result, the share of these three items in the total import bill which had been less than 25 per cent in the early 1970s, rose to more than 50 per cent in 1974-75.

Moreover, the continuation of factors like the refugee problem and the war with Pakistan in 1971, adverse agricultural seasons in 1973-74 also led to a critical situation in the balance of payments in 1974 when India had to spend almost two-third of its export revenue just to meet the import cost of crude oil.

Indeed it was hard time for the economy. But the economy, however, managed to get rid of the balance of payments crisis which surfaced in 1974-75, and within two years the trade deficit was not only covered, but for the first time since the inception of planning, India's balance of payments showed a surplus at the start of the Fifth Plan Period (1974-75 to 1978-79). During 1976 there was a large favourable swing in the merchandise trade account, from a deficit of Rs. 675 crore in 1975 to a surplus of Rs. 249 crore. This was brought about by an impressive growth of 24 per cent in export, while imports remained more or less stationary. The net surplus on invisibles, other than official transfers increased sharply from Rs. 520 crore to Rs. 930 crore, and the official transfers nearly quadrupled from Rs. 61 crore to Rs. 239 crore. As a result, the balance on net current account swung from a deficit of Rs. 644.5 crore in 1974-75 to a sizeable surplus of Rs. 294.2 crore. An overview of India's balance of payments over 1969-70 to 1979-80 is obtainable from Table 4.5. Two important features stood out: first, the deficits in the trade and current account—the trade balance was in surplus in 1972-73 and 1976-77; the current account was in surplus in 1975-76,1976-77 and 1978-79, and second, the steep rise in the trade deficits in the late seventies. The satisfactory balance of payments situation in the major part of the seventies was reflected in the substantial accretion of foreign exchange reserves of the country from Rs. 438.12 to Rs. 5219.86 crore between 1970-71 and 1978-79, that is, by almost twelve times (Table 4.5). In 1979-80 there was a further trade deficit to the tune of 2725 crore of rupees. In this year current account deficit at 234.5 crore of rupees, was still very moderate. But the slow-down in the increase in reserves in this year along with the widening trade gap in an alarming manner signalled the turning point in the history of India's balance of payments (*Da Costa,* 1990).

How did it happen that the first part of this decade had shown so impressive a performance, while the second part exhibited poor performance? To understand this phenomenon, it is necessary to find answers to the following questions: (a) How did the economy cope with the first oil shock of 1973-74, (b) What were the important factors that were responsible for the sudden transition to a comfortable position and the accumulation of unprecedented foreign exchange reserves? (c) Why did once again the payments difficulties rise so quickly in the later part of the decade?

A. Adjusting the Oil Shock of 1973-74

In so far as the direct and indirect impact of the 1973-74 oil shock was concerned, India weathered it well—at best in terms of tiding over the balance of payments difficulties. There were number of underlying factors marked with several events which, taken together, constitute an explanation.

In spite of the bottlenecks in the supply side arising out of some deflationary measures at home, particularly the cutback in real investment in infrastructure, the Indian industrial economy was on the road of ascendancy in the seventies, leaving behind the industrial stagnation and the loss-of-direction period of the mid-sixties. The economy during the decade got new avenues for export expansion as new markets in some of the LDCs were opened up, though it can be said that it could not compete successfully with some of the more dynamic exporters from the newly industrialized countries, and thereby could not make big jumps in rapidly expanding her trade regime. Though India started exporting construction services and some materials, during the period, she gained substantially in terms of foreign exchange earnings, and the gains were considerable. In contrast with the near-stagnation of the 1950s' and slow growth in the 1960s export earnings, a substantial improvement in India's export performance was noticeable during this period, and even in real terms during 1972-73 to 1976-77, her exports rose quite significantly due mainly to the conjunction of several factors such as:

(a) a substantial change in the commodity composition of her exports, (the export of the light engineering goods expanded by 470 per cent in value terms between 1970-71 and 1979-80; chemical products by 580 per cent, and certain other items like fish, handicraft, jewellery registered gains);
(b) the expansion in global trade that rose at an annual rate of 6.8 per cent in volume terms and by 15.6 per cent in US dollar terms during the decade;
(c) expansion of aid-financed exports to Bangladesh from late 1971;
(d) the boom in world prices of primary commodities of early 1970s, which continued till 1974, and finally due to the steady depreciation of the exchange value of the rupee since 1971. The export performance was unprecedented by Indian standards, though it was quite modest in terms of international comparisons;
(e) an effective devaluation of the rupee because of its link with sterling until 1975; and
(f) finally, the opening up of a large market for Indian exporters in the oil-rich Gulf countries.

The other side of the coin was a slow expansion in imports, which saved the balance of payments situation from getting worse. As regards the overall impact of the changes in the pattern of merchandise trade after 1973, there was a sharp deterioration in the terms of trade. The oil crisis and the sharp increase in the prices of India's major imports led to a marked deterioration in the terms of trade and a dramatic reduction in the purchasing power of exports. Hence, the substantial growth in exports did not increase the import capacity of the economy. The share of oil bill rose dramatically after 1973. But the rate of growth of the physical quantity of oil declined after 1973 as a result of the conservation measures adopted domestically. In terms of volume, imports of crude and petroleum products grew at the annual rate between 30 and 50 per cent before 1973; but after that they did not register any increase during the next four years. Among other things, this was attributable to an improved performance in agriculture and sluggish industrial growth. The other two factors were also important. There was an increase in the domestic production of food-grains so that, by 1977, food imports became minimal and there was no exports of foodgrains in 1978 and 1979. In fact, by the late seventies, the country accumulated about 20 million tons of foodgrains as a buffer stock. Secondly, persistent quasi-stagnation during the late 1970s in the industrial sector required a low level of imports of capital goods and intermediate goods.

The huge deficit in trade and payments prompted the Government of India into large-scale borrowings from abroad. Compared to the early 1970s external assistance, in terms of both commitments and utilization, became more than doubled in the mid-1970s. Net aid inflows, always smaller, also rose from a level of about Rs. 320 crore per annum in the period 1970-71 to 1973-74 to almost Rs. 900 crore per annum during 1974-75 to 1976-77. The aid came both from usual western donors as well as OPEC countries. In addition, India borrowed a sum of Rs. 750 crore from the IMF to finance the payments crisis that followed the oil price hike. The excessive foreign aid inflows transformed the BoP situation into a favourable one. The economy managed to generate a surplus in balance of trade in 1976-77. (Table 4.5).

Last but not the least, there was a sustained increase in private transfer payments from abroad. It should be said that remittances from Indian overseas were not entirely new and had been significant during the 1950s. We well remember the foreign exchange crisis in 1957. Following that, the regime of import restrictions and exchange controls led to a situation where remittance came to be channelled largely through unofficial

Table 4.5

India's Balance of Payments: 1969-70 to 1979-80

(Rs. Crore)

Items	1969-70	1970-71	1971-72	1972-73	1973-74	1974-75	1975-76	1976-77	1977-78	1978-79	1979-80
(1)	(2)	(3)	(4)	(5)	(6)	(7)	(8)	(9)	(10)	(11)	(12)
Total Exports	1413	1535	1608	1971	2523	3329	4036	5142	5404	5726	6418
Total Imports	1582	1634	1825	1867	2995	4519	5265	5074	6020	6811	9143
Trade Balance	–169	–99	–217	+104	–432	–1190	–1229	+68	–616	–1085	–2725
Net Invisibles	–38.6	–13.7	+36.7	–0.4	+1680.0	+332.7	+860.7	+1204.1	+1837.0	+1988.7	+3134.6
Net Total Current Account (merchandise + non-monetary Gold movement + invisibles)	–217.0	–331.4	–401.5	–251.5	–1301.4	–644.5	+294.2	+1525.8	+1734.7	+172.5	–234.5
Net total capital account (private + banking + official)	+231.4	+400.0	+490.5	+283.3	–1093.9	+940.7	+570.4	–1201.7	–1719.6	–760.9	+223.9
Foreign currency assets reserves	546.37	438.12	480.38	478.90	580.78	610.50	1491.70	2862.99	4499.75	5219.86	5163.66
Total foreign exchange reserves (old + SDRs value + foreign currency assets)	820.95	732.35	856.93	887.1 0	992.78	1021.93	1885.39	3242.75	4862.40	5820.67	5933.72

(Contd.)

Table 4.5 (Contd.)

(1)	(2)	(3)	(4)	(5)	(6)	(7)	(8)	(9)	(10)	(11)	(12)
Outstanding repurchase Obligations	153.75	—	—	—	58.80	557.30	804.00	492.10	210.00	—	—
Repurchases with IMF	125.25	153.75	—	—	—	—	—	302.80	248.60	206.90	55.10
Errors and omissions (Net)	–14.40	–78.70	–65.20	–31.80	–207.50	–296.20	–242.00	–324.10	–15.10	+588.40	+10.60
Total deficits (–) or surplus (+)	—	–942.70	–749.60	–723.80	–908.70	–1641.00	–1035.00	–178.10	+200.50	–356.80	–1250.70
Financed by:											
External assistance	—	778.6	773.1	690.4	930.5	1163.5	1657.6	1574.2	1354.5	1230.7	1493.7
Drawing from IMF	—	—	—	—	62.00	484.70	207.10	—	—	—	—
Allocation of SDRs	—	+75.4	+74.7	—	—	—	—	—	—	125.6	126.3
Decline in reserves (+) increase in reserves (–)	–237.9	+88.7	–98.5	+33.3	–83.9	–7.3	–829.7	–1396.1	–1555.2	–999.5	–369.3

Note : The period 1969-70 to 1973-74 covers the Fourth Five Year Plan period and the period 1974-75 to 1978-79 covers the Fifth Five Year Plan period, while 1979-80 was the Annual Plan prepared by the first Janata Government (1977-80). It is worthnoting that RBI data on the balance of payments do not show any trade surplus in 1972-73.

Source : Govt. of India: Economic Survey (various issues) and H.L. Chandhok and the Policy Group (1990) India Database: The Economy, Annual Time Series Data, Vol. II.

brokers who used the foreign exchange to finance smuggling. But from 1974-75, private transfers began to rise rapidly. Private transfers rose sevenfold from $ 296 million in 1974-75 to $ 2175 million in 1979-80 and in the post first oil shock period, it financed, roughly 80 per cent of the trade deficit. The trends and the possible reasons responsible for this change are discussed below.

B. The Accumulation of Foreign Exchange Reserves

As a result of the factors set out above, the massive trade deficit of 1974-75 and 1975-76 was turned into a very thin trade surplus in 1976-77: the current account was in surplus in 1976-77 and 1977-78. But this was not all. Foreign exchange reserves began to pile up at an extremely rapid rate to reach an unprecedented levels within a short span of four years. At the close of the decade, the foreign exchange reserves inclusive of SDRs stood at $ 5486.6 million providing for over seven months' imports. The data set out in Table 4.6 clearly show that, in the late 1970s, the chronic shortage of foreign exchange and the paucity of reserves was turned into a paradox of plenty. India's holdings of SDRs peaked at 529 crore of Rupees in 1979-80. The interesting feature of this period is that, on the one hand, the economy tried to tide over the payments difficulties arising out of oil crisis of 1973 and early 1974, while at the same time it began to accumulate a large level of foreign exchange reserves.

The natural question to ask is what accounted for such a build-up of reserves? In retrospect, the following factors seem important in this respect: (i) a high level of foreign aid inflow which originated in the payments crisis that surfaced in 1974-75, and its significant utilization, (ii) the dramatic increase in the net invisibles other than transfer payments constituting mostly by earnings from tourism and investment income flows, and (iii) the large increase in the number of Indians working abroad, the checking of smuggling, the narrowing down of the gap between internal and external prices of gold and the improvement in the strength of the rupee that seemed to have increased the inflow of remittance through authorised banking channels. These developments not only coincided with each other, but also with a comfortable balance of trade situation in

TABLE 4.6

India's Foreign Exchange Reserves (1950-51 to 1980-81)

Year	Foreign exchange in (Rs. Crore)	Gold in (Rs. Crore)	SDRs in (millions)	Foreign exchange inclusive of SD Rs. in (million SDRs.)	
1950-51	911.4	117.8	—	—	—
1955-56	784.6	117.8	—	—	—
1960-61	185.85	117.8	—	—	—
1965-66	182.09	115.9	—	—	—
1970-71	438.12	182.5	148.9	732.3	(3.8)
1971-72	480.38	182.5	247.7	861.0	(4.1)
1972-73	478.90	182.5	246.5	797.3	(3.9)
1973-74	580.78	182.5	244.9	837.1	(3.6)
1974-75	610.50	182.5	234.9	846.7	(2.4)
1975-76	1491.70	182.5	202.8	162.6	(4.3)
1976-77	2862.99	187.8	187.4	2962.2	(7.6)
1977-78	4499.75	196.1	161.6	4674.5	(10.1)
1978-79	5219.86	219.5	364.9	5257.9	(9.1)
1979-80	5163.66	224.7	529.1	5486.6	(7.2)
1980-81	4822.1 0	225.6	490.5	5258.2	(5.1)

Notes : (i) All foreign exchange holdings are valued at current exchange rates per 10 grams of gold.

(ii) Gold is valued at Rs. 53.58 per gram and Rs. 84.39 per 10 grams of gold thereafter until May 1966.

(iii) The increase in gold holdings during the late 1970s, are attributable to the restriction of gold by the IMF to India, and the purchase of gold by India at the IMF's gold auction.

(iv) Figures in parentheses is the number of months of imports which can be purchased with the available foreign exchange.

Source : *RBI Bulletin*, various issues.

1976-77 and 1977-78, so as to result in the accumulation of forex reserves witnessed in the late 1970s. Net invisibles mostly on account of remittances increased from a paltry Rs. 32.7 crore in 1974-75 to Rs. 3134.6 crore in 1979-80. Total remittances which were less than US $ 0.2 billion per annum until 1973-74, reached a peak level of $ 2.7 billion in 1980-81. Remittances from migrants enabled the economy to reduce the size of the current account deficit to a considerable extent. Another major impact of international labour migration from India on the balance of payments was through repatriable deposits, which financed a part of the current account deficits. Of these factors, the dramatic improvement in net invisibles primarily on account of the remittances in the form of somewhat fortuitous influx of petro-dollars from the Middle-East was perhaps the most important one in so far as they represented an entirely new factor in the payments situation.

The trends in remittances during the 1970s are outlined in Table 4.7 which confirms the sharp rise in remittances beginning in the mid-1970s. The Table also places remittances to other important components of the balance of payments, e.g., export earnings, net aid inflows, and the trade deficit, to show the growing significance of remittances as a means of financing the payments deficit in India. The macro-economic factors underlying the spurt in remittances might be attributed to the following factors:

TABLE 4.7
Trends in Remittances during the 1970s

Year	*Remittances in (Rs. Crore)*	*Remittances as a percentage of*		
		export	*net aid*	*trade*
1970-71 to 1973-74	169.9	8.9	52.5	68.7
1974-75	279.9	6.9	40.7	22.5
1975-76	541.2	10.1	46.9	74.8
1976-77	745.6	12.1	88.3	197.2
1977-78	1029.3	16.9	219.5	853.3
1978.79	1059.3	17.0	275.9	51.2
1979-80	1412.7	23.7	192.5	43.6
1980-81	2190.0	32.7	238.6	36.0

Notes : 1. The figures on remittances are the credits on account of private transfer payments in the balance of payments.

2. There was a balance of trade surplus in 1972-73 and 1976-77.

Sources : I. for remittances: RBI data on the balance of payments;

II. for export earnings and trade deficit : statistics published by DGCI and S; and

III. for net aid inflows : Ministry of Finance.

(i) The real gains to India on a large scale from OPEC countries came through the direct export of labour which increased at a phenomenal pace throughout the late 1970s, and reached their peak levels in the early 1980s. The economic boom in the Middle Eastern economies, particularly the Middle East, which followed the increase in oil prices, led to a massive temporary emigration of large number of Indian workers—both skilled and unskilled as simply labourers, skilled technicians, nurses, office assistants, etc. to the Gulf Countries. This export of labour was a principal source of foreign exchange earnings for India from oil rich Gulf countries. These workers kept sending their net earnings back home. Consequently, transfer payments to India on private account moved up from on average annual flow of Rs. 49.9 crore during the Third Plan period to Rs. 917.3 crore in 1977-78 and Rs. 2129.7 crore in 1980-81. This phenomenal rise is essentially due to the remittances from the migrant workers in the Middle East.

(ii) In 23 June, 1972, the United Kingdom allowed the pound to float. Its external value promptly began to fall in the foreign exchange market. Since the rupee continued to be linked to the pound, its external value also fell alongside that of the pound. Figure 4.2 provides confirmation.

FIG. 4.2

The Exchange Value of the Rupee

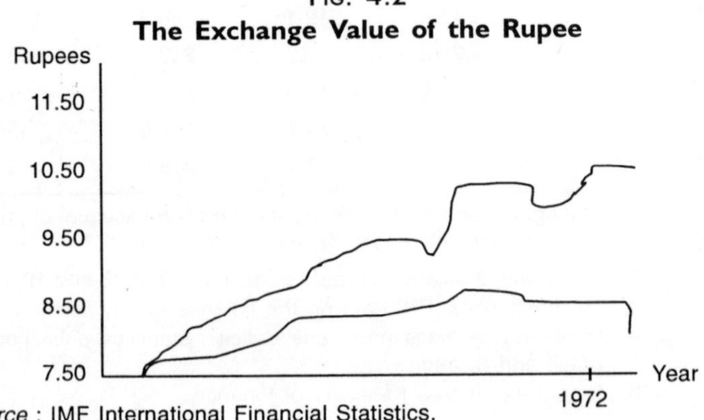

Source : IMF International Financial Statistics.

It shows that there was a steady effective depreciation in the exchange value of the rupee *vis-a-vis* the SDR basket of currencies, until 1975 and the US Dollars, until 1976. This depreciation of the rupee, in conjunction with the exchange control regime, seemed to have directed a very large proportion of inflows of remittances through official channels.

(iii) In addition to the earnings from the direct export of labour and to that of earnings of reserves from the fall in the external value of the rupee, there was another reason behind the improvements in the balance of payments position in the 1970s, although it is difficult to make precise estimates regarding the contributions made by this factor. Following the crisis in the international monetary system during the early 1970s, the international market price of gold shot up dramatically in the mid-1970s. There was even periods when the domestic price of gold (at the official exchange rate) was lower than the international price. As is well known, the enormous financial attraction of moving gold illegally into India has been an important basis for the substantial smuggling activities across the Indian borders. Hence after a long time, elimination of the large price-gap between the international price of gold and the domestic price of gold in India, led to a significant dampening influence on the smugglers' trade and their demand for foreign exchange, resulting in a better showing in the receipts and payments statistics of the Reserve Bank of India. At the same time, there emerged the disparity in price between the price of silver in India and the world price of silver-while the former price did not keep pace with the increase in the price of the latter. This also led once again in the fall of smugglers' demand for foreign exchange.

(iv) The policy that made simplification of banking procedures for remittances, an extension of banking services overseas and most importantly, liberalization of foreign exchange regulations for non-resident

Indians on the one hand, and Government's extensive use of Conservation of Foreign Exchange and Prevention of Smuggling Act (COFEPOSA) and Maintenance of Internal Security Act. (MISA) against smugglers during the period of Internal Emergency between 1975 and 1976, enhanced the inflow of remittances through official channels.

All these factors taken together contributed for the first time in three decades a net surplus in the current account of India's balance of payments. The net surplus was Rs. 1525.8 crore in 1976-77 and Rs. 1734.7 crore in 1977-78, that is confirmed by Table 4.5. However, these few years can be hailed as the golden years for India's balance of payments situation. The gold and the exchange reserves held by India in 1978-79 was well above Rs. 5000 crore. Equivalent to about seven months imports. The increase in foreign assets led to a substantial acceleration in the growth of money supply during the period (about 20 per cent per annum). However, the rate of inflation was surprisingly low. Excluding the drought year of 1979-80, the rate of inflation was barely 5 per cent per annum during this decade. Fiscal deficits, as a percent of the GDP, were also moderate (about 7 per cent on an average). During the same period the country had merely 20 million tonnes of foodgrains as a buffer stock against all possible future domestic harvest failure. It may be mentioned that harvest failures in India not only generate poverty and hunger for poorer people in rural areas, but also put pressure on the price levels and on the balance of payments.

This period (1976-77 to 1979-80) also saw the beginning of a slow process of industrial and import liberalization. The most important change in the import policy was introduced in 1978-79 when all items were listed under the open general license (OGL) category and could be freely imported for domestic production. There were also some changes in the industrial licensing system which facilitated expansion of output in important sectors.

4.5 INDIA'S BALANCE OF PAYMENTS DURING THE 1980s

As we have witnessed at the end of 1970s, the scenario on the external front changed dramatically. The trade gap had widened dangerously and the stock of foreign exchange reserves which was ten times what it was at the beginning of the decade had been reduced to a considerable extent and continued over the entire decade. Now it is obviously important to examine these changes in the BoP situation and to analyse the underlying situations that persisted in the 1980s.

A. The Return to Difficulties—BoP upto 1981-82

The BoP adjustment process, which was unexpectedly smooth in India in response to the first round of oil price increase during the mid-1970s, had turned out to be much more difficult in the early 1980s, following the second oil price hike in 1979. What was more, the factors that had a favourable influence in India's BoP waned in their impact and this oil price hike queered the pitch once more. For one thing, there was a substantial squeeze on foreign aid programmes which led to an increasing reliance on expansive commercial borrowing in international capital markets. For another, there was a sharp and continuous decline in net invisibles (excluding transfer payments) and there was a significant deceleration in the growth of remittances.

The main factor underlying the balance of payments crisis during the second-half of 1970s was the slowdown of exports[6] and dramatic escalation of import bill, which accelerated the foreign exchange expenditure on imports—the imports of crude oil and petroleum products on the one hand and the imports of edible oils, fertilizers, iron and steel, paper and cement and intermediate inputs on the other. There was as much as 33 per cent of the increase of imports of edible oils, fertilizers, iron and steel, paper and cement, while crude oil and petroleum products (which dominated the import bill in 1980-81) accounted for 54 per cent of the total increment. This aspect was extremely important because this signified the high import intensity of India's domestic industry. Table 4.8 shows the trends in selected imports (1976-77 to 1980-81).

TABLE 4.8

Trends in Selected Imports : 1976-77 to 1980-81

(In Rupee Crore at the then exchange rates)

Particulars	*1976-77*	*1977-78*	*1978-79*	*1979-80*	*1980-81*
Crude Oil and Petroleum Products	1413	1552	1667	3146	5215
Fertilizers	261	338	449	546	938
Iron and Steel	220	260	472	872	—
Edible Oils	101	712	532	442	805
Newsprints	47	61	80	120	133
Total Imports	5072	6020	6814	8908	12106

Sources : Statistics Published by DGCI and S, Calcutta.

The BoP situation deteriorated sharply in 1980-81. The doubling of OPEC oil prices from December, 1978 to January, 1980 had inflated the import bill in 1979-80, but its full impact was felt only in 1980-81. Exports remained sluggish partly reflecting continued domestic supply constraints, and partly also due to unfavourable world market conditions. This resulted in a massive drawdown of forex reserves. There was a cry for external assistance.

Foreign exchange reserves which had peaked at 5219.9 crore of rupees at the end of 1978-79, and had stood at 5163.7 crore of rupees in 1979-80, plunged to 3354.5 crore of rupees at the end of 1981-82. Foreign currency assets of the RBI had declined by Rs. 313 crore at the end of January, 1981.

To a considerable extent, the payments crisis of 1979-80 was the outcome of the increase in oil crisis and deterioration in India's international terms of trade. After the price hike in 1973, price of crude oil increased only from $ 11.65 per barrel in 1974 to $ 13 per barrel in 1978, but was almost trebled to $ 35 per barrel in 1979. This second oil price hike together with worst drought in 1979-80, the historical coincidence within the economy, had an unfavourable impact on India's BoP which spilled over into the 1980s, and the mounting trade deficits reappeared in 1980-81. Following the second oil price hike of 1979-80, foreign trade deficit widened sharply to about 4.4 per cent of GDP in 1980-81. Trade deficit increased from Rs. 1816 crore in 1978-79 to Rs. 3369 crore in 1979 and further to Rs. 5967 crore in 1980-81 and Rs. 6121 crore in 1981-82. India's imports of Petroleum, Oil and Lubricants (POL) rose from Rs. 1677 crore in 1978-79 to Rs. 3146 crore in 1979-80 and Rs. 5215 crore in 1980-81. The increase in POL imports accounted for a little over half of the increase in the overall imports. This was followed by the second round effect on non-POL imports. The full impact of the price increase was felt in the fiscal year 1980-81, when POL imports absorbed nearly 75 per cent of the export earnings and accounted for 46 per cent of the import bill. Thus the increase in world prices of oil was a major factor underlying India's massive import bill for oil in 1980-81. Moreover, there was also a substantial reduction in the domestic production of crude oil on account of the violent agitation in Assam to the tune of 3.5 million tonnes.

Export performance during the period recorded a volume growth of just a little over 3 per cent. Net invisibles receipts continued to provide support to the balance of payments, largely in the forms of earnings from tourism and the sustained buoyancy of private transfers. However, the sharp widening in the merchandise trade deficit resulted in a turn around in the current account balance from a surplus in 1977-78 to a deficit in 1981-82 of the order of US $3.166 million i.e., the order of 1.8 per cent of GDP and foreign exchange reserves declined to a considerable extent. The trade deficit shot up to Rs. 5967 crore in 1980-81 and further to Rs. 6120 crore in 1981-82 (Table 4.9, Part I).

As a result, the current account deficit rose seven-fold. The ratio of current account to GDP went up significantly from-0.2 percent in 1979-80 to 1.2 per cent in 1980-81 and further to 1.5 per cent in 1981-82 (Table 4.12). In order to safeguard the development plan process and the growth process of the economy, there were some efforts to improve domestic production of crude petroleum as a response to step up the pace of import substitution. The country achieved a spectacular success in this field. The Sixth Plan allocated Rs. 2864 crore for the exploration and production of crude oil and envisaged a cumulative production of domestic crude oil during the plan period of 93.4 million tonnes. The implementation of Oil &

TABLE 4.9 (PART I)

India's Balance of Trade and Current Account Balance (1980-81 to 1989-90)

(*Rs. Crore*)

Year	*Exports f.o.b.*	*Imports c.i.f.*	*Balance of trade*	*Net Invisibles*	*Current Account balance*
1980-81	6576.4	12543.6	–5967.2	4310.6	–1656.6
1981-82	7765.5	13886.5	–6121.0	3803.7	–2317.3
1982-83	9137.1	14913.2	–5776.1	3479.7	–2296.4
1983-84	10168.5	16039.3	–5870.8	3608.4	–2262.4
1984-85	11959.2	18680.3	–6721.1	3848.5	–2872.6
1985-86	11577.6	21163.6	–9586.0	3630.2	–5955.8
1986-87	13315.0	22668.9	–9353.9	3523.9	–5830.0
1987-88	16396.4	25692.5	–9296.1	3003.5	–6292.6
1988-89	20646.7	34202.3	–13555.6	1975.5	–11580.1
1989-90	28229.0	40642.4	–12413.4	1024.8	–11388.6

Note : Balance of Trade and Current Account Balance, inclusive of net non-monetary gold. It is worthnoting that BoP data relating to merchandise trade compiled and published by RBI are different from those compiled and published by the DGCI & S. The differences are greater in the case of imports and have been rising over years. The differences arise on account of coverage, valuation and timing factors. Annual Report of RBI for 1988-89 explains the sources of difference. Briefly, export data differ because of exclusion of a part of exports by parcel post in the DGCI & S data, different valuation procedures adopted and different data sources; import data differ because the RBI data are on a payments basis which the DGCI & S data are based on arrival of goods at the customs.

Source : Economic Survey, GOI (various issues).

Natural Gas Commission's (ONGC) programme has gone ahead with remarkable speed. As a result, the production of crude oil in the country moved from 10.5 million tonnes in 1980-81 to 16.2 million tonnes in 1981-82, to 21.1 million tonnes in 1982-83. So far as the issue of import substitution in the fields of nitrogenous fertilizers and non-ferrous metal and edible oils were concerned, the outputs of the above three items had increased over time—the output of nitrogenous fertilizer had gone up by an estimated 41 per cent between 1979-80 and 1981-

82, the coal production went up by about 25 per cent during the first three years of the Sixth Plan with a declining trend after that, due to problems like industrial relations and of managerial and technical nature; with regard to non-ferrous metals and edible oils, there were also significant gains up to 1981-82 (in the field of import substitution), though the bad harvest of 1982 adversely affected the production of oil-seeds and the shortage of electric power led to a shortfall in the production of non-ferrous metals subsequently.

The main cause for worry on the balance of payments fronts seemed to be flattening out of the flows of workers remittances from the Middle East and repatriable deposits. This was reflected to some extent in the stagnation and decline in the dollar value of total remittances. The drop in oil prices and the consequent economic slow-down in the Middle East squeezed the labour outflows to and remittances from that region.

Faced by the prospect of prolonged balance of payments difficulties, the Government of India entered into an arrangement with the International Monetary Fund (IMF) under the Extended Fund Facility (EFF) which enabled India to draw up to SDR 5 billion record breaking loan over a period of four fiscal years from 1980-81 to 1984-85 for amelioration of BoP difficulties. India, however, drew only SDR 3.9 billion and the arrangement was terminated in May 1984 on India's request because of the improvements in the BoP in 1983-84. The IMF helped India to maintain reserves at comfortable level in the first half of 1980s even though the current account deficit had increased after 1979-80 (*Jalan*, 1992)

B. 1982-83 to 1984-85: Easing of Pressure on BoP

A reprieve came during the period 1982-83 to 1984-85 almost coincident with the Sixth Five Year Plan with the easing of pressure on the BoP mainly due to the decline in the overall growth of imports from an average rate of 11.0 per cent during 1978-82 to little over 2 per cent during 1982-85. Net oil imports (net of crude oil exports which commenced in 1981-82 after the discovery of crude oil in Bombay High), declined substantially as domestic production of crude oil rose from around 10.5 million tonnes in 1980-81 to 30.2 million tonnes in 1984-85. As a result, the share of domestic production in meeting consumption requirements rose from a little over 50 per cent in 1981-82 to 75 per cent in 1984-85. This indeed was the main cause of the easing of the balance of payments. (*Rangarajan*, 1993). Non-oil imports rose at an average rate of 3.6 per cent in dollar terms. Export, however, was sluggish, and grew only at an average rate of 3.2 per cent in volume terms, due to a combination of adverse internal and external conditions. During the years, the major component to reduce or limit deficits was net invisibles. Net invisibles declined from Rs. 4310.6 crore in 1980-81 to Rs. 3848.5 crore in 1984-85, as the interest payments to service external borrowing acquired a steady rising trend (Table 4.9 Part I).

Private transfers stagnated with the arrest in the labour migration boom. As a result, with a sharp rise in trade deficit, the contribution of net invisibles in financing the deficit declined. This led to greater dependence on inflows of external capital, for which invisibles including private transfers and other surpluses which had earlier financed 89 per cent of the trade deficit, could meet only 57 per cent of the trade deficit in 1984-85. The current account deficit fell to US $ 2416 million or 1.2 per cent of GNP in 1984-85 and reserves, which were US $ 5952 million at the end of the year, stood to cover a little over five months of imports (Table 4.12). However, external assistance remained to be the major component of foreign capital inflows, accounting for 39 per cent of the financing requirement. By 1983, debt service had increased to 8.7 billion rupees (5.7 billion amortisation and 3 billion interest). In 1985, total debt service amounted enormously to 13 billion rupees. At the close of 1984-85, the external debt to GNP ratio was more than 17 per cent (Table 4.12). Compared to the crushing burden of debt service of other Third World countries, India was still much better off and had an excellent credit rating. In this way, India was able to go in for more commercial credit, as the prospects of aid became dim.

In the years of growing foreign debt service, India was able to accumulate foreign exchange reserves in an unprecedented manner owing to the remittances of Indian working abroad. The manpower exports to the oil-exporting countries proved to the very lucrative as far as the Indian BoP was concerned. In order to encourage remittances, Indian working abroad were permitted to open special accounts in Indian Banks. The remittances so deposited were freely convertible. In actual fact Indian citizens were prohibited from maintaining accounts in foreign countries after returning home, but this prohibition could be easily circumvented; therefore, it was prudent to introduce this new scheme. The net transfer of these remittances increased. This bonanza continued for some time; by 1982 private net transfer reached almost 30 billion rupees from 21 billion rupees in 1980. By the end of 1985, non-resident external rupee had deposits amounted to 31 billion rupees; in addition, the non-residents deposited foreign currency worth 18 billion rupees in India. Total non-resident deposits thus were worth 49 billion rupees. The special favours shown to the non-residents were somewhat resented by Indian capitalists at home, but this policy certainly contributed to India's credit rating abroad and to a fairly comfortable position as far as the national BoP was concerned (*Rothermund,* 1991)

C. The Build-Up to The Crisis: BoP during the Seventh Plan (1985-90)

Though the BoP issue during the Sixth Plan was satisfactorily settled mainly on account of restrictions of POL import, the trade deficit had widened since 1984-85, despite deep depreciation of the exchange rate.

However, the second half of the 1980s i.e., during the entire seventh plan period (1985-86 to 1989-90) witnessed the building up of tremendous strain on BoP, in spite of the robust export growth (only the exports of manufactured goods jumped from 63 billion rupees to 237 billion rupees from 1985 to 1991). They increased the share in total exports from 58 to 73 per cent. The problem was rooted in the continuing high average trade deficits because of a sharp decline in the import bill and a large loan repayment to the IMF to the tune of Rs. 1749 crore (Rs. 1547 crore under the EFF and Rs. 202 crore in respect of the IMF Trust Fund Loan) and a sharp decline in the role of the invisibles in financing these deficits [*Economic Survey,* 1989-90]. To an extent the spillover of essential imports necessitated by the 1987-89 drought, a rise in the international prices of certain commodities and large imports of capital goods had contributed to the rise in import bill. The increase in the import bill was also attributable to liberal imports permitted by the government to encourage exports to improve efficiency and upgrade technology standards, and generally to create competitive conditions for the domestic manufacturing firms. Non-oil imports had grown at a rate of 19.3 per cent per annum in rupee terms and at 14.7 per cent per annum in US dollar terms during the first four years of the Seventh Plan, with the income elasticity of non-oil imports nearing 2.0 during the period. Because of a tremendous increase in domestic demand, the volume of net POL imports continued to rise from 12.4 million tonnes in 1984-85 to 23.5 million tonnes in 1989-90 (the share of import of petroleum items in total imports was 25 per cent in 1985 as well as in 1990). While the production of crude oil had remained stagnant at around 30-32 million tonnes during 1985-86 to 1989-90, the consumption of POL products had been rising at an annual rate of 6.7 per cent. Imports of capital goods rose by an average of 16.2 per cent during the period. Export-related imports as well as other miscellaneous imports also rose significantly. The category of non-DGCI & S imports, comprising defence import and imports of ships and aircrafts, etc. also rose significantly from about US $ 12 billion in 1985-86 to US $ 31 billion by 1989-90. The support from invisibles receipts fell in the face of steadily growing interest payments and the outgo on account of profits, dividends, and royalty, technical and professional fees.

As for exports, we can say that recovering from the stagnation in 1985-86, the volume growth of exports in the succeeding four years ranged between 10 to 12 per cent per annum on an average. The share of manufacturing exports rose from 56 per cent in 1980-81 to 75 per cent in 1989-90. Moreover, the various policy initiatives, fiscal relief including complete exemption of export profits from income or corporation tax, rate of interest, and other monetary concessions, relaxation in industrial controls, liberal access to industrial raw materials and capital goods for export-oriented industries, and appropriate exchange rate for the rupee had been put in place so as to make India's exports truly competitive.

But overall, the picture was dismal. Partly as a result of the faster growth of imports (the period when the trade regime had comparatively more liberalized) and partly due to rising debt service burden (during the Seventh Plan SDR 2752 million was repaid to the IMF on account of EFF drawals), the current account deficit averaged $ 5.8 billion or 2.4 per cent of GDP during the Seventh Plan period (*Da Costa,* 1988). It is worth noting that the current account deficit as a percentage of GDP exhibited an average of 1.2 per cent in the Sixth Plan. The period also marked a deterioration in fiscal imbalances as the ratio of fiscal deficit to GDP rose from 6.3 per cent in the first-half of the Eighties to 8.2 per cent during the 1985-90. The widening investment-savings gap which reflected the steady deterioration in the budgetary position had its expected cumulative impact on the trade balance and overall balance of payments. The successive import liberalization measures since 1978-79 contributed to the emergence of the trade gap.

Net invisible earnings that had a positive balance of Rs. 3630 crore in 1985-86 in financing trade deficit lost their buoyancy largely on account of rising interest payments on foreign debt. The share of net invisibles declined from 62.6 per cent during the Sixth Plan to 29.6 per cent during the Seventh Plan; correspondingly net inflows on the capital account of the BoP played a growing role in financing the trade deficit.

Table 4.9 Part II puts down the net balance of the different components of the capital account. It needs to be noted that total capital account has been defined as total capital account + repurchase of rupees from IMF+ SDRs allocation. It can be seen that the net positive balance in 1985-86 was due to large inflows of funds in the official loans account (this included drawings on loans from international institutions such as the World Bank and International Development Association (IDA) and from other countries and private (long-term) account). Thus, while the first item accounted for 78.89 per cent of net capital account surplus, the second item accounted for 44.81 per cent. For the same year outflows could be observed for official amortisation to the tune of 24.67 per cent (*Sathe* 1996).

The share of miscellaneous inflows increased from 2.43 per ent in 1985-86 to 19.59 per cent in 1989-90. All these informations are captured in Table 4.9 Part II.

Moreover, there was substantial build-up in external debt and a rise in debt service ratio, from 13.6 per cent in 1984 to 30.9

TABLE 4.9 (PART II)

Net Inflow of Capital in India (1980-81 to 1989-90)

(*Rs. Crores*)

Items	*1980-81*	*1981-82*	*1982-83*	*1983-84*	*1984-85*	*1985-86*	*1986-87*	*1987-88*	*1988-89*	*1989-90*
(1)	*(2)*	*(3)*	*(4)*	*(5)*	*(6)*	*(7)*	*(8)*	*(9)*	*(10)*	*(11)*
1. **Private**										
Long-term	77.10	118.40	208.10	696.70	192.70	292.70	2257.50	2238.30	4414.00	4768.20
Short-term	0.50	-17.20	9.30	0.20	-0.90	-1.10	9.40	10.10	6.20	-59.80
Total	77.60	101.20	217.40	696.90	1091.80	2091.60	266.90	2248.40	4420.20	4708.40
2. **Banking Capital**	-12.70	-12.60	68.40	181.60	-193.40	186.10	-70.10	74.80	-256.20	+59.20
3. **Official**										
Loans	1664.50	1257.40	1689.30	1782.40	3034.00	3683.40	6462.40	6831.60	8437.40	8427.90
Amortisation	-611.20	-575.60	-611.40	-693.50	-726.50	-1152.10	-2587.90	-2833.60	-3066.80	-2990.10
Misc.	-227.20	-278.20	+538.8	-219.4	184.40	85.10	-171.90	1171.90	1949.10	2130.40
4. Total capital account (1+2+3)	916.40	492.20	824.90	2186.80	3390.30	4922.20	5899.40	7493.10	11474.70	12335.80
5. Repurchase of rupees from IMF	-9.50	-34.50	—	-72.00	-152.40	-253.00	-672.30	-1209.00	-1547.30	1459.60
6. Allocation of SDRs	120.50	—	—	—	—	—	—	—	—	—
Total capital account (4+5+6) surplus	1027.40	457.70	824.90	2114.80	3237.90	4669.20	5227.10	6284.10	9927.40	10876.20
Percentage increase over preceding year	—	-55.45	80.23	156.37	53.11	44.21	11.95	20.22	57.98	9.56

Source : *Economic Survey*, Govt. of India 1987-88 and 1992-93).

percent in 1989-90, along with a sharp decline in foreign exchange reserves. India's foreign exchange reserves (comprising foreign currency assets of the RBI, gold holdings of the RBI and SDRs holding of the Government, declined by Rs. 647 crore to 7040 crore during 1988-89 (*Economic Survey*, 1989-90), altogether showing the intensification of BoP strains. On the IMF account (which includes the transactions related to purchases and re-purchases by India from the IMF) also capital outflows increased from Rs. 253 crore in 1985 to Rs. 1460 crore in 1989-90 (Table 4.9 Part III).

TABLE 4.9 (PART-III)

Other Items in India's Balance of Payments 1980-81 to 1989-90

(*Rs. Crore*)

Year	*Net IMF drawings*	*SDR allocations*	*E & O*	*Reserves and Monetary gold*
1970-71	-154.00	75.40	-66.90	88.70
1980-81	2617.00	120.50	-158.00	516.00
1981-82	602.30	0.00	-395.50	1618.30
1982-83	1892.90	0.00	-203.10	-624.50
1983-84	1338.50	0.00	-490.00	-772.90
1984-85	64.40	0.00	+323.60	-925.90
1985-86	-253.00	0.00	+580.10	706.50
1986-87	-672.30	0.00	-129.30	732.20
1987-88	-1209.00	0.00	-947.70	956.20
1988-89	-1547.30	0.00	-203.40	1449.30
1989-90	-1460.00	0.00	-720.00	1232.40

Note : E & O: Error and Omissions.

Source : *Economic Survey*, Government of India (various issues).

At the end of March 1989, outstanding debt to the IMF under the EFF[7] (Extended Financing Facility) and the Trust Fund aggregated SDR 1829 million and SDR 162 million respectively, and they were equivalent to Rs. 3697 crore and Rs. 326 crore, respectively.

The huge current account deficit had to be financed by substantial inflows of capital in the form of loans from multilateral and bilateral sources, commercial borrowings, inflows of funds from non-resident Indians under the Non-Resident External Rupee Accounts (NRERA) and the Foreign Currency Non-Resident Account (FCNRA). This increased India's external debt from 36,000 crore at the end of 1985 to Rs. 84,000 crore at the end of March 1990. Financing pattern of current account deficit was more limited in the Seventh Plan as compared to the Sixth Plan period. In the Sixth Plan, the current account deficit was financed to the extent of 55 per cent by external assistance and 28 per cent by IMF resources. Non-Resident deposits formed 17 per cent of the total financing. In the Seventh Plan loan under external assistance from multilateral and bilateral sources was 29 per cent, commercial borrowings provided 25 per cent, non-resident deposits 23 per cent and other capital transactions 13 percent. The remaining 10 per cent was financed from the country's reserves. Table 4.10 shows the pattern of financing needs and the sources of financing for the period 1985-90.

In retrospect, the 1980s was characterized by the emergence of severe political as well as macro-economic imbalances, which made the old economic order unsustainable. In spite of Rajiv Gandhi's attempt since the mid-eighties towards reform at a relatively quicker pace than Smt. Indira Gandhi in the early 1980s, particularly after her return to power in 1980, towards industrial deregulation, exchange rate flexibility and partial lifting of import controls, the major issue of the emerging macroeconomic imbalances, calling for a stabilization of the fiscal and BoP deficits, was left unattended. Reforms of the financial and labour markets and the public sector also essentially remained untouched. Even some piecemeal attempts at reforms made by Rajiv Gandhi got abandoned after some time mainly due to the political crisis centred around the Bofors allegations and the desertions of V.P. Singh and others. The causes generally cited for the unprecedented crisis might be grouped under two major aspects, the first relating to the overall plan strategy, and the second to the macro-economic mismanagement of the economy during the Sixth and Seventh Plans. The factors that contributed

TABLE 4.10
Financing Need and Sources of Financing : 1985-90

(*Rs. crore*)

Particulars	*1985-86*	*1986-87*	*1987-88*	*1988-89*	*1989-90*	*1990-91*
Current account deficit including errors	5347	5959	7240	10207	10113	13088
Repayment to IMF	253	672	1209	1547	1460	-2178
Financing need	5600	6631	8449	11754	11573	10910
Financed by						
(a) External assistance	1676 (30.00)	1808 (27.30)	2928 (34.70)	3210 (27.30)	3054 (26.40)	3241 (29.70)
(b) Commercial borrowings	1166 (20.80)	2513 (37.90)	1283 (15.20)	2740 (23.20)	2886 (24.90)	1244 (11.40)
(c) Non-residents	1767 (31.60)	1650 (24.90)	1840 (21.80)	2465 (21.00)	2175 (18.80)	209 (1.90)
(d) Other capital	285 (5.10)	-7.1 (-1.10)	1442 (17.10)	1887 (16.10)	2247 (19.40)	3923 (36.00)
(e) Use of reserves	706 (12.50)	732 (11.00)	956 (11.30)	1449 (12.30)	1231 (10.60)	2293 (21.00)
Total	5600 (100)	6631 (100)	8449 (100)	11754 (100)	11573 (100)	10910 (100)

Figures in brackets are the shares in total financing.
Source : RBI Annual Report, 1990-91.

to the first aspect were excessive regulation and quantitative controls on investment, imports and credits, an inward-looking trade strategy, and large-scale investment in the public sector at the expense of the private sector. In the 1980s the Government initiated several measures of import and industrial liberalization for which imports had increased rather sharply in the second half of the 1980s in rupee terms (Table 4.11), and there was a decline in the rate of public investment during the Seventh Plan. But these, especially the rise in imports alone could not be held responsible for the disturbing developments of the 1980s, because as far as the external balance was concerned, demand-led growth, no doubt, raised imports of capital and intermediate goods, especially during the Seventh

TABLE 4.11
Growth Rates in Imports

(in per cent)

Years	*Net Oil Imports*		*Non-oil Imports*		*Total Imports*	
	In Rs.	*In SDRs*	*In Rs.*	*In SDRs*	*In Rs.*	*In SDRs*
1985-86	21.00	11.70	25.10	15.50	14.70	5.90
1986-87	-44.80	-53.80	17.80	-1.40	2.20	-14.50
1987-88	43.80	29.70	-6.00	-4.40	11.50	0.60
1988-89	7.90	-4.10	28.50	14.10	23.90	10.20
1989-90	49.60	34.90	24.30	12.00	27.90	15.30
1990-91	77.70	52.80	11.10	-4.50	21.90	4.80
Annual average growth 1985-86 to 1990-91	25.90	11.90	18.80	5.20	17.00	3.70

Source : DGCI and S data published in Annual Reports of Reserve Bank of India.

Plan, but this rise was however neutralized by the buoyancy of export earnings, partly due to the low rate of domestic inflation, but mostly to the steady devaluation of the rupee and the plethora of various exports subsidies. To understand what went wrong during the last two plans, other than overall plan strategy, it appears to look for the most important factors like:

(i) poor performance of the public sector in respect of savings;
(ii) the rapid rise in the foreign debt due to a fairly steep rise in the investment saving gap;
(iii) a sharp rise in the fiscal deficits as a ratio of GDP, leading to a continuous dose of money creation and consequent inflation to be contributing towards the current account deficits in BoP.[8] Thus persistence of high fiscal deficits averaging 8.7 percent of GDP (Centre and States) in the later half of 1980s, which could be only partially financed by the private sector surpluses, became a major cause of deteriorating current account deficit in BoP.

(iv) an increase in the monetized deficit; and
(v) financial repression.

An increase in both the fiscal and monetized deficits, raised inflationary pressure, reduced private investment and growth, and widened the current account deficit. While the rise in prices was due to the generation of excess demand, the problem on the balance of payments front was created through (i) the spill over of part of additional domestic absorption into imports and exports; and (ii) the switching of expenditure, both at home and abroad, as the real exchange rate rose with inflation. What was of greater significance in the medium term, was that under a regime of financial repression and preferred allocation of credit to the government and 'priority sectors' the crowding out of private investment due to the increase in the fiscal deficit tended to raise the overall capital-output ratio and to reduce private savings. This had an adverse effect on economic growth (*Rakshit*, 1994). Table 4.12 indicates the major developments in the external sectors before the payments crisis of 1991, and brings into the contrasting picture of foreign indebtedness during the 1970s and 1991s.

It may be noted that one important feature of the period (1980-81 to 1989-90) was that there was a gradual decline in the flows of concessional assistance to India, principally from the World Bank group. The invisibles account also deteriorated as the interest payments to service external borrowing acquired a rising trend. Private transfers stagnated with the arrest in the labour migration boom. As a result, with sharp rise in trade deficit, the contribution of net invisibles in financing the deficit declined leading to greater dependence on inflows of external capital. Net invisibles which financed nearly half of the trade deficit during 1981-82 to 1984-85 contributed only 8 per cent towards financing the BoP deficit in 1990-91, while on the other hand, the credits from the International Development Association (IDA) on soft terms declined. The loan from the World Bank on market terms increased sharply. The debt service payments on multilateral loans increased sharply from US $ 371 million in 1984 to US $1347 million in 1990.

Several interesting observations follow from our analysis of India's trade balance. In the Seventies, we observe high

TABLE 4.12

Some Indicators of India's External Imbalance

(*Per cent*)

Items	*1970*	*1978*	*1980*	*1981*	*1982*	*1983*	*1984*	*1985*	*1986*	*1987*	*1988*	*1989*	*1990*
(1)	*(2)*	*(3)*	*(4)*	*(5)*	*(6)*	*(7)*	*(8)*	*(9)*	*(10)*	*(11)*	*(12)*	*(13)*	*(14)*
Current account deficit to GNP	0.80	-0.20	1.20	1.50	1.30	1.10	1.20	2.30	2.00	1.90	2.60	2.20	2.50
Debt stock to GNP	14.90	13.80	11.90	14.40	14.90	16.10	17.70	19.30	21.30	22.00	21.70	24.50	25.00
Debt Stock to Exports	357.50	164.80	136.00	144.30	179.80	207.90	209.50	265.20	294.80	288.20	276.20	265.10	262.70
Interest to Exports	8.70	3.80	4.20	3.00	4.20	9.40	10.70	12.60	14.20	14.10	14.90	14.40	14.80
Debt serving to Exports	22.80	10.50	9.30	8.10	10.60	16.90	18.20	22.70	32.00	29.40	29.80	26.60	26.80
Foreign Exchange Reserves to Imports (Months)	4.40	9.60	7.90	5.40	5.80	5.90	5.40	5.40	5.80	5.30	3.60	4.30	1.90

Source : World Bank, World Debt Tables, various issues.

growth of the volume of exports, coupled with moderate increases in the volume of imports. Because of the helpful trends in respect of exports and imports, the country's trade balance retained its healthy character, in spite of the sharp fall in the terms of trade from the peak of 116.6 in 1972-73 to the low of 72.3 in 1979-80. By contrast, in the Eighties due to the high growth of the Indian economy and to the lower relative price of imports, but largely in response to the more liberal import policy, export growth fell tremendously, but imports rose sharply. The foreign exchange reserve position deteriorated due to this slowdown in exports and surge in imports while its position was exceptionally favourable in the 1970s.

It may be noted that the 1970s were characterized by a phenomenal growth in nationalised banking, a sharp rise in the allocation of credit to priority sector and a large public investment, as part of the strategy of import substitution. During this period, the country was able to take the oil shocks in its stride and ended the decade by a fairly comfortable position regarding foreign-exchange reserves and with a significantly reduced burden of foreign debt and debt servicing as ratio of both GNP and exports. By the end of the 1970s, India's external commercial debt was US $ 15 billion, amounting to a debt service ratio of less than 15 per cent. By contrast, all the indices relating to debt burden rose steeply during the 1980s, pointing clearly to an impending BoP crisis. The ratio went up to 18 per cent in 1980-81 and 38 per cent in 1987-88 and came down slightly to 34 per cent in 1988-89. Total external debt including the IMF credit increased from US $ 22 billion in 1980-81 to US $ 34 billion in 1984 and then to US $ 53 billion and US $ 70.1 billion in 1988-89 and 1990, respectively, or from about 11.9 percent of the GNP in 1980 to 25 percent in 1990 (Table 4.12). Debt servicing, as a percentage of exports of goods and services increased from 9.3 per cent in 1980 to 22.7 percent in 1985 and further to 26.8 per cent in 1990 (Table 4.12). This represented a more than 500 per cent increase in ten years. Suddenly, within a span of a decade, India had been transformed from one of the credit-worthiest economies to a highly indebted country. Moreover, 'other' capital flows and errors and omissions went from being a large negative in the first decade of 1980s to a positive in the second half, likely indicating an increase in the short-term borrowing. As a result, the external debt to GNP ratio rose from 17.70 percent in 1984 to 24.50 percent in 1989 and 25 percent in 1990.

Consequently the large current account deficit, particularly after 1984-85, have had to be financed, by substantial inflows of capital by way of large commercial borrowing and non-resident Indian's (NRIs) deposits both of which carried high interest rates. And in the 1980s as a whole almost the entire incremental deficit (in dollar terms) was financed through non-concessional loans on market-related terms. By contrast, almost the entire deficits were financed in the 1970s (particularly in the period 1970-71 to 1976-77) largely through inflows of concessional assistance, which kept the debt servicing burden low. Thus, as regards the source of financing there was a major difference in the nature of balance between the 1970s and the 1980s.

Another important difference is that, in contrast to the 1970s period, the macroeconomic policy in the 1980s was highly expansionary. Fiscal deficits mounted. The combined fiscal deficits of the Central and States, which averaged 8.0 percent of GDP in the first-half of the 1980s, went up 10.10 percent of GDP in the second-half, while this was less than 6 percent of GDP in the 1970s. These burgeoning deficits represented a breakdown in the financial discipline of the government and a dominance of populist policies. Continued large deficits led to a build-up of a very substantial public debt with interest payments accounting for a large proportion of the government revenues. They also invariably led into current account deficits, which kept rising steadily until it reached 3.5 percent of GDP in 1990-91.

In the 1970s, the smooth adjustment in the external sector following the oil price hike was attributable not only to remittances, but also to larger inflow of external resources, a dramatic increase in the net invisibles, other than transfer payments and above all, to the management of the balance of trade which transformed a large deficit into a modest surplus. For another, there was a discernible shift in the industrialization strategy which diluted the emphasis on import substitution and perceived a more active role for foreign trade in the national economy. In the 1980s, however, the balance of payments factor was not even permissive. Import liberalization was substantially sustained in spite of the difficult payments situation. The stagnation and decline in remittances was compensated for by the large net inflows in the form of repatriable deposits during the second half of the 1980s. Thus, it was possible that capital flows from migrants helped sustain the import liberalization which gathered momentum in the mid-1980s, just as remittances from migrants helped sustain the import liberalization which began in the late 1970s.

The whole decade of 1980s was, however, marked with significant acceleration in economic growth, particularly industrial growth. During the 1980s, the Indian economy apparently broke through the low growth syndrome in which it had been trapped for the previous decades. India's GNP, as measured at factor cost, grew at a rate of 5.6 per cent annually over the decade. This higher rate of growth yielded an unprecedented rise of nearly 3 per cent in per capita income per annum. To a large extent the improvement was a result of the sustained growth in industrial output, which increased to 7.71 per cent during the 1980s and at the beginning of 1990, value-added in the manufacturing sector grew at 9.42 per cent during this time. The share of industry and services in national output remained unchanged throughout the decade. Finally, higher growth could not reverse the decline of India's shares in global exports. Moreover, the share of exports in manufacturing output dropped further during the 1980s.

In the context of the balance of payments the financial flows arising out of international labour migration: remittance inflows (which constituted unrequited transfers) and in the form of repatriable deposits were large and acquired significant dimensions from the mid-1970s onwards. The significance of remittances declined in the second half of the 1980s as compared to the 1970s and this decline in magnitude of these financial flows was quite pronounced by the end of the 1980s' decade as it is evident from Table 4.13.

By the end of the 1980s, remittances had fallen to one-eighth of the export earnings and less than one eighth of the import bill. Yet, even these remittances were to finance a large part of the balance of trade deficits (30 per cent) and more than 50 per cent of the burden of debt servicing. The decline in the remittances contributed in the worst form not only on the

TABLE 4.13
The Significance of Remittances *vis-a-vis* Selected Components of India's Balance of Payments

Year	*Remittances as a percentage of*				
	Exports	*Imports*	*Balance of trade deficit*	*Current accounts receipts*	*Interest on foreign loans plus amortization*
1970-71	5.70	4.70	19.10	4.20	18.50
1971-72	7.20	5.60	25.50	5.30	24.90
1972-73	5.50	4.80	41.50	4.30	20.60
1973-74	6.10	5.20	37.60	3.10	26.40
1974-75	6.90	5.30	22.50	5.40	45.30
1975-76	10.10	8.90	74.80	7.30	81.60
1976-77	12.10	12.90	197.20	8.60	107.80
1977-78	16.90	16.60	853.30	11.10	122.70
1978-79	17.00	12.80	51.20	10.80	128.90
1979-80	23.70	15.40	43.60	13.70	180.60
1980-81	32.70	17.10	36.00	17.20	220.70
1981-82	26.80	15.00	34.00	15.30	205.20
1982-83	26.60	16.30	42.10	16.00	183.10
1983-84	26.00	16.50	45.10	15.50	158.10
1984-85	24.90	16.00	44.40	14.70	134.50
1985-86	23.50	12.80	28.30	13.90	95.70
1986-87	22.50	13.20	32.00	13.90	65.40
1987-88	21.50	13.70	38.00	13.80	63.50
1988-89	18.70	11.30	28.50	12.20	59.60
1989-90	13.50	9.40	30.80	9.40	52.30
1990-91	11.00	7.60	24.20	7.90	42.90

Note : There was a surplus in the balance of trade in 1972-73 and 1976-77, while there was a deficit in all the other years.

Source : (a) For data on exports, imports, balance of trade deficit and current account receipts, Reserve Bank of India, Balance of Payments Statistics Published in the Report on *Currency and Finance Annual Issues.*

(b) For data on interest on foreign loans plus amortization, Ministry of Finance, *Economic Survey*, data on Balance of Payments (adjusted), various issues.

(c) For data on remittances, see Table 4.7.

balance of payments scenario but also through it on the economy as a whole.

There was a dramatic increase in capital flows from migrants in the form of repatriable deposits during the 1980s. The total amount outstanding in such repatriable deposits from migrants rose from US $ 1.3 billion at the end of 1980-81 to 10.4 billion at the end of 1989-90. These capital inflows continued to be as important as net aid inflows in financing a part of the current account deficits during the second half of the 1980s.

Table 4.14 presents evidence on the significance of repatriable deposits in relation to selected components of the balance of payments. It shows that during the first half of the

TABLE 4.14

The Significance of Deposits made by Non-Resident Indians in Relation to Selected Items in India's Balance of Payments

Year	*Net inflows into external accounts of NRIs as a percentage of*		
	Current account deficit	*Capital account receipts*	*Net aid inflows*
1980-81	10.70	5.30	13.10
1981-82	8.90	7.90	19.80
1982-83	16.70	10.30	29.80
1983-84	31.30	14.30	57.40
1984-85	30.80	14.90	74.60
1985-86	29.80	22.00	112.60
1986-87	28.30	13.80	104.70
1987-88	29.20	10.70	75.80
1988-89	23.70	11.60	104.50
1989-90	22.10	7.80	102.80
1990-91	3.10	n.a.	17.00

Sources : (a) For data on the current account deficit and capital account receipts (excluding transactions with the IMF), Reserve Bank of India, balance of payments statistics published in Report on *Currency and Finance*, annual issues.

(b) For data on net aid inflows, Ministry of Finance, *Economic Survey*, various issues.

(c) For data on net inflows into external accounts of non-resident Indians see Table 4.12 for non-resident external rupee accounts.

1980s there was a dramatic increase in the relative importance of net inflows into external accounts maintained in India by non-resident Indians. This significance was sustained through the second half of the 1980s, but almost vanished in 1990-91. Such capital inflows were sufficient to finance only one-tenth of the current account deficit in 1980-81 but as much as three tenths of the current account deficit in 1985-86. Inflows in the form of repatriable deposits continued to be as important as net aid inflows in financing the current account deficit during the second half of 1980s. The evidence suggests that the financial flows associated with international labour migration for India were significant in the context of BoP. The remittance inflows made a macroeconomic contribution by financing a large proportion of the balance of trade deficit and thus reducing the current account deficit to manageable proportions (*Nayyar*, 1995)

4.6 THE CRISIS IN 1990-92

The fact that India's BoP problem has assumed the nature of a 'crisis of an unmanageable proportion' became well-established by the close of the eighties itself. Various powerful external pressures from the IMF and the World Bank to adjust the real economy as the incident like the disintegration of the former Soviet Union, in the aftermath of the revolutions in Eastern Europe of late 1989 predominated. India's old development strategy not only had recognizable similarities with the Soviet model of development, but also relied on the Soviet Union both for barter-based trade and as a political counter-weight to United States influence. The crumbling of a major international ally was a blow to India. The third oil shock and the Gulf-crisis of the second half of 1990-91 added fuel to the fire. The immediate impact was the rise in the oil import bill. It also resulted in virtual stoppage in workers' remittances to the tune of about 25 billion rupees from April to July 1991 as well as additional burden on repatriating and rehabilitating about 150,000 non-resident Indians from the affected zones in West Asia. The loss of Indian exports to West Asia was estimated to amount to 5 billion rupees while the rise of oil price enhanced the cost of imports. As a consequence of the rise in the price of oil as well as certain other oil-related imports, the trade deficit amounted to a hefty 106 billion rupees by March 1991. As this could no longer be matched by 'invisibles, India was on the verge of bankruptcy. Since there was a deterioration in invisible account also, the overall net current account deficit in 1990-91 was $ 9680 million. The process of liberalization seemed to be doomed, but on the other hand the situation also did not permit any attempt at turning the clock back to protectionism.

Apart from various external pressures, there were some internal pressures. Some of the internal indicators of India's BoP crises were:

- During the 1980's, control of the public finances were allowed to become lax. These allowed a resurgence of inflation, which apart from a brief episode in 1974-75 had otherwise been kept low levels by LDC standard. Accelerating inflation from 4.4 percent in 1985 to 13.7 percent in 1991-92 eroded the country's trade competitiveness.
- Between 1988-89 and 1989-90, exports rose by 36.72 per cent, which was a very high rate for the Indian economy, and imports rose by 18.83 per cent only. Between 1989-90 and 1990-91 the rate of growth of exports abruptly decreased to 17.44 per cent and the import growth rate increased to 23.24 per cent. The sudden fall in the export growth rate was due to the Gulf crisis, contraction in world trade, recessionary conditions in the U.S.A. and the UK and the political uncertainty in the rupee payments areas [*Report on Currency & Finance,* 1990-91, Vol. I]. As a result in 1990-91, balance of trade deficit (one of the highest) increased by, as much as 38 per cent over the respective figure for 1989-90.
- The accrual of surpluses in invisible account had become increasingly insufficient for covering the trade gap. During the Sixth Plan period (1980-81 to 1984-85), invisibles financed on an average—62.6 per cent of the trade gap. The respective figure for the Seventh Plan

period (1985-86 to 1989-90) stood as merely 29.5 per cent.

- The prospects of obtaining external assistance—another option for financing balance of trade gap—had became bleak, thereby accentuating the problem of financing balance of trade and the current account gap. Moreover, the grant component of the overall external assistance had witnessed a declining trend across the years. During the later half of the seventies and the earlier half of the eighties, the grant component accounted, on an average, 21.05 and 16.46 per cent respectively of the overall external assistance. Thereafter i.e. during 1985-86 to 1990-91, it declined further to 11.19 per cent.
- The deceleration in the rate of growth of indigenous oil production, protectionist tendencies in the international trade, the bunching of repayments obligations to the IMF, the unfavourable climate for the external assistance and the decline in India's credit rating in the international financial markets had gripped the economy into a kind of vicious circle. These problems had played a mutually supportive role in aggravating India's external payments position. To these medium-term pressures on BoP, in 1987-88, was added the problem of severe country-wide drought, which entailed substantial additional imports of essential commodities, such as edible oils and pulses.
- In the event of a gloomy scenario of obtaining official loans and grants, the prospects of augmenting the level of commercial borrowings had been impaired during the period. Due to the decline in the credit rating of the Indian economy, inflow of finance even on commercial terms had been chocked up. In fact, in 1990-91, the commercial borrowings fell by 38 per cent over the 1989-90 figure (*Trivedi,* 1992).
- Debt-accumulation proceeded at a compound rate of 20 per cent per annum in rupee terms. As a result, the external debt-GDP ratio (excluding NRI deposits) recorded at the end of the eighties was around 18 per cent. Inclusion of NRI deposits as an item of external

debt raised the debt-GDP ratio by another 4 per cent. As a consequence of rapid debt accumulation, the debt service ratio—a measure of the percentage of current account receipts spent on servicing debt had been on a rapid rise. The debt-service ratio increased from 9.4 per cent in 1980-81 to 21 per cent in 1990-91, after attaining a peak of 23.3 per cent in 1987-88.

- There was a decline in the ratio of foreign exchange reserves to import payments. Forex reserve declined from a level of Rs. 5480 crore ($ 3.11 billion) at the end of August 1990 to Rs. 1666 crore ($ 896 million) on 16 January 1991. By 1990-91, the forex reserve just worth Rs. 11416 crore (US $ 5831 million) (Table 4.15) could barely finance even 1 or 2 months of imports. This was undoubtedly the worst face of India's BoP. Nevertheless, the decline in reserves continued unabated. The situation had become more critical in 1991-92. Moreover, the purchase from the IMF in January 1991 amounted to Rs. 3334 crore ($ 1814 billion). Meanwhile, to deal with the situation and bring the economy back from the brink of default, the 'lame duck' government of Chandra Shekhar leased 20 tonnes of gold out of its stock to the State Bank of India to enable it to sell the gold abroad with the option to repurchase it at the end of six months. This export took place in May 1991. In addition, the government allowed RBI to ship 47 tonnes of gold to the Bank of England in July. This helped to raise about $ 600 million. The exchange rate of the Rupee was also adjusted in July 1991 to bring it to a credible level which could be defended (*Economic Survey*, 1990-91). These incidents bore testimony to the fact of an unprecedented and acute shortage of forex reserves not only for financing imports but also for timely meeting of interest payments and amortization schedules.
- The years 1989 and 1990 had witnessed severe political instability in the country, with a hung parliament and a minority government in power. Political uncertainty and the sharp deterioration in the balance of trade in the second half of 1990 (Table 4.9) led to a outflow of

foreign currency deposits held by NRIs. The outflow of Foreign Currency Non-Resident (FCNR) deposits had accelerated from $ 59 million a month in October-December 1990 to $ 76 million in January-March 1991 and $ 310 million in April-June, 1991. The ratio of FCNR deposits to forex reserve which was around 14 percent in 1984-85, had shot up to 327.3 per cent in 1990-91. There was also evidence that expectations of default, and, therefore, of devaluation, were creating a longer leads in payments for imports and lags in the realization of export proceeds which had the effect of exacerbating the foreign exchange shortage. By June 1991, other adverse developments in the capital account had become over-whelmingly a crisis of confidence in the government's ability to manage the BoP. The loss of confidence had itself undermined the government's ability to deal with the crisis by closing its all recourse to external credit. A default on payments had become a serious possibility in June 1991 for the first time in India's history.

4.7 ECONOMIC REFORMS AND ADJUSTMENT PROCESS IN THE BoP

In what follows the unique conjunction of increasing balance-of-trade deficits, governmental financial profligacy and break-down of financial discipline, sharp increase in external debt, an environment of extremely political instability and uncertainty, and adverse international events like the Iraq's invasion of Kuwait in August 1990 as well as the uncompetitive economic structures that had evolved over the previous four decades precipitated a financial and payments crisis in May-June 1991. While taking steps to avert a state of immediate bankruptcy, enamoured with an attempt to integrate Indian economy more fully, and on a competitive basis with the world economy through trade and capital flows, the Rao government which came in power in June 1991 following the elections, (with the then, Finance Minister and now, Prime Minister Manmohan Singh), undertook emergency measures of far-reaching importance and launched a two-part package of stabilization programme and a programme of structural adjustment, involving trade, industrial and foreign investment policy reforms to redress the fundamental cause, endorsed by the multilateral financial institutions, who stepped in with nearly $ 3 billion credits to tide over the crisis. The reform that was designed to handle properly the BoP problem and ensure longer-term budgetary viability consisted of an 17-19 per cent devaluation of the rupee *vis-a-vis* five major currencies in two successive steps in July 1991 as a part of the stabilization package, reduction in fiscal deficits through expenditure compression, tax reforms, partial privatization drive and signals to public sector undertakings to operate on commercial principles, granting a large measure of autonomy to the RBI for maintaining full employment and BoP equilibrium. These measures were supplemented by (a) transition to a system of market-driven exchange rate system with current account convertibility of rupee; (b) permitting select Indian corporates to raise funds from international capital market; and (c) encouragement of capital flow by way of foreign institutional investments, foreign direct investments and Non-Residents Indian deposits. This time India witnessed a general shift (more or less full-fledged) from the inefficient macroeconomic trade and investment policies grounded on inward-looking substitution philosophy justified by the objectives of self-sufficiency towards exports-orientation and liberalization of trade regime. Negotiating stances *vis-a-vis* the IMF and the World Bank as well as in the other multilateral fora, like the GATT, were changed to correspond more closely to the new set of domestic policy perceptions and imperatives. Although these reforms had been sequential and somewhat incremental, their overall coverage and scope marked a turning point in Indian history (*Kumar*, 1993).

Following the reform measures, the economy responded quickly and positively to the changes and GDP growth crossed 1.3 per cent level in 1991-92 to more than 5.2 per cent on average in the next two years. The loss of reserves was stemmed and from October 1991 onwards there was a steady build-up. With the sharp decline in absolute levels of imports, 1991-92 ended with an improvement in the trade balance as well as current account balance—the former being less than one per cent of GDP.

Between 1991-92 and 1992-93, the first year under the new economic policy (NEP) the net current account deficit has fluctuated widely—it increased from Rs. 2237.3 crore to Rs. 12763.40 crore i.e., a rise by three times. However in the next period, the deficit had fallen. The reason for these fluctuations seemed to be rooted in the trade deficit that had fluctuated widely. In 1991-92, the trade balance was Rs. 6495 crore and it increased to Rs. 14100.9 crore in 1992-93 (an increase by three times). However, by 1993-94 the deficit had decreased to Rs. 7484.3 crore (Table 4.15).

An important reversal that can be observed from Table 4.15 was that the net invisibles, which had turned negative in 1990, became positive in 1991-92. According to the *Economic Survey*, 1993-94, the surplus on invisible account was generated through a two-fold increase in net private transfer and 50 per cent increase in the surplus on travel account. The increase in net private transfers was achieved through different kinds of no-question asked schemes through which black money that smuggled out of India through hawala market was turned into white dollar deposits. Table 4.15 shows that the trade balances as well as current account balances have improved considerably since 1991-92, resulting in the ascend of the certain components of the BoP in the post-liberalization period.

The improvement might be attributed partly to the depreciation of rupee, almost 100 percent against US dollar since 1991. But several other factors also contributed to this. First, the domestic industrial recession had curbed the import demand and encouraged exports. Second, eight consecutive normal/good monsoons had minimised the imports of agricultural commodities, especially foodgrains. Third, the international oil price had very much subdued after the Gulf War. As a result, imports of petroleum and oil products, which used to account for nearly 40 per cent of total imports during the second half of the eighties, accounted for only 20 per cent. However, in spite of the improvement, the current account balance continued to be negative even now.

There was a big surge in the foreign capital inflows after liberalization of the external sector. The portfolio capital inflows

TABLE 4.15

India's Overall Balance of Payments : Key Indicators

Items 1990-91	1991-92		1992-93		1993-94	
	Rs. Crores	US $ Million	Rs. Crores	US $ Million	Rs. Crores	US $ Million
(1)	(2)	(3)	(4)	(5)	(6)	(7)
1. Current Account						
Exports (f.o.b.)	33152.60	18477.00	44922.50	18266.00	54762.00	18869.00
Imports (c.i.f.)	50086.20	27915.00	51417.50	21064.00	68862.90	23237.00
Trade Balance	16933.60	9438.00	6495.00	2798.00	14100.90	4368.00
Net Invisibles	434.90	242.00	4257.70	1620.00	1337.40	842.00
Current Account (Net)	17368.50	9680.00	2237.30	1178.00	12763.40	3526.00
2. Total Capital Account	12897.60	7188.00	10005.20	3968.00	11963.30	2966.00
3. Overall Balance	4470.90	2492.00	7767.90	2790.00	800.20	560.00
4. Monetaly Movements (a+b+c)	4470.90	2492.00	7767.90	2790.00	800.20	560.00
(a) Net IMP Transactions	2177.80	1214.00	2077.30	786.00	3363.40	1288.00
(b) SDR Allocation	—	—	—	—	—	—
(c) Reserves and Monetary gold, increase (-)/decrease (+)	2293.10	1278.00	9845.20	3576.00	2563.20	728.00
Memo Items			**As per cent of GDP**			
Exports	6.20		7.30		7.80	
Imports	9.40		8.30		9.80	
Trade balance	3.20		1.10		2.00	
Invisible balance	0.10		0.70		0.20	
Current account balance	3.20		0.40		1.80	

(Contd.)

TABLE 4.15 (Contd.)

Items	1993-94		1994-95	
	Rs. Crores	US $ Million	Rs. Crores	US $ Million
(1)	(8)	(9)	(10)	(11)
1. Current Account	71146.00	22683.00	84326.00	26857.00
Exports (f.o.b.)	78630.30	25069.00	99973.00	31840.00
Imports (c.i.f.)	7484.30	2386.00	15647.00	4983.00
Trade Balance	3848.50	1228.00	7165.00	2282.00
Net Invisibles	3635.80	1158.00	8482.00	2701.00
Current Account (Net)	30852.00	9835.00	27634.00	8806.00
2. Total Capital Account	27216.20	8677.00	19152.00	6105.00
3. Overall Balance	27216.20	8677.00	19152.00	6105.00
4. Monetaly Movements (a+b+c)	587.20	187.00	3588.00	1146.00
(a) Net IMP Transactions	—	—	—	—
(b) SDR Allocation	27803.40	8864.00	15564.00	4959.00
(c) Reserves and Monetary gold, increase (-)/decrease (+)				
Exports	8.80		8.80	
Imports	9.70		10.50	
Trade balance	0.90		1.60	
Invisible balance	0.50		0.80	
Current account balance	0.50		0.90	

Source : *RBI Annual Report*, 1994-95, 1995-96, and *Economic Survey*, 1996-97.

might have been attracted by relatively higher financial return in the Indian stock market, higher interest rates in India *vis-a-vis* the Euro-Dollar Market and exchange rate stability. (*Bhattacharya,* 1995).

We are now reviewing the performance of the India's Post-Reform BoP scenario in terms of certain broad macro-economic indicators. Section 4.8 gives post-reform developments in India's BoP upto the mid-nineties. Section 4.9 gives an overall picture of BoP development since the reform process to the present.

4.8 POST REFORM DEVELOPMENTS IN INDIA'S BoP UPTO THE MID-1990s

During 1992-93 overall export performance subdued with a growth rate of 3.1 per cent in US dollar terms over the year. Exports to the General Currency Area, however, exhibited resilence in the face of recession in industrial countries and social disturbances, which affected transport activities in Bombay. The exports rose by 10.4 per cent during 1992-93. Exports to the Rupee Payments Area, mainly to the erstwhile USSR, fell by 62 per cent in dollar terms and acted as a drag on the overall exports. The invisibles account recorded a deterioration as travel receipts continued to suffer from a decline in tourist arrivals. Private transfers remained broadly stable. On the other hand, there was a rise in the outgo on interest payments. As a result, current account deficit which had shrunk to $ 2.1 billion in 1991-92 rose to $ 4.9 billion or 2.1 per cent of GDP in 1992-93. It is worthnoting that a current account deficit of more than 2 percent of the gross domestic product (GDP) is considered to be unsustainable (*Economic Survey*, 1994-95, p. 84). The deficits on current account were financed through a combination of traditional financing sources and exceptional financing.

During 1993-94, a distinctive improvement in the BoP occurred. A robust export growth of 20 per cent in dollar terms, fall in international prices of crude oil and the continuing slack in non-POL imports had resulted in a sharp contraction in the merchandise trade deficit. The decline in international interest rates had also provided a measure of savings in invisibles account. Strong growth in remittances in response to the introduction of the market determined exchange rate had helped to counteract the deceleration in earning from tourism. At the same time, significant developments in the capital account had taken place. There was clearly a perceptible shift in the financing pattern in favour of non-debt creating foreign investment flows. Non-resident deposits had yielded net inflows. As a result there had been a build up of foreign currency assets of the RBI. The foreign currency assets had risen about 7 times during 1991-92 to 1993-94 from US $ 2.4 billion at the end of 1990-91 to US $ 15.07 billion at the end of 1993-94. Those rose further to US $ 20.81 billion at the end of 1994-95.

During 1994-95, India's external sector acquired a distinct resilience and it was the strength of the current account that underpinned the health of the BoP. During the year, the demand for imports rose significantly to record growth of 21.7 per cent in US dollar turns as per data of the Ministry of Commerce. The non-POL imports also surged. The large increase in imports was comfortably accommodated by the robust performance of current earnings, both on merchandise and services. Exports of merchandise, in particular, continued to build upon the high growth witnessed in 1993-94 and rose by 18.22 per cent during 1994-95, to US $ 26.2 billion. As regards the direction of exports, while West Asia and North America remained important destination for Indian exports, exports to Russia and Africa have indicated higher growth. A significant improvement also occurred with regard to the performance of invisibles, after the introduction of a market determined exchange rate regime. During 1994-95, there was a larger inflows of remittances from Indians working abroad. The performance of exports and invisibles earnings enabled the financing of the surge in imports. Although the current account deficit widened from US $ 315 million in 1993-94 to about US $ 1700 million in 1994-95, it remained comfortable at only about 0.6 per cent of GDP.

There was also a continued accumulation of reserves. By the end of March 1995, the foreign exchange reserves including gold reached an unprecedented level of US $ 25.2 billion, equivalent to around 10 months of imports, reflecting thereby a sustained improvement in the current account balance and strong capital flows. The export performance of 1994-95 benefited from the recovery in world trade, a conducive policy environment and a stable exchange rate. Unlike in the preceding year when the improvement in external accounts was essentially brought about by the lack of domestic demand and a surge in capital flows, the balance of payments in 1994-95 was underpinned by the strength of current account which occurred in the face of a resurgence of economic activity. The improvement in the current account is amply reflected in the indicator presented in Table 4.15. The satisfactory growth of current receipts has brought the debt service ratio down from 35.3 per cent in 1990-91 to around 27.5 per cent in 1994-95. The debt servicing cover of reserves has also improved significantly from 8.0 months in 1990-91 to 27.2 months in 1994-95.

During 1995-96, the level of foreign currency assets of the RBI at US 17.04 billion was equivalent to 4.9 months of imports of goods and the cover of foreign currency assets to total payments in the current account of BoP was 3.8 months, while the later was only 0.8 months in 1990-91. Total forex reserve rose from and abnormally low level of US $ 9.22 billion at the end of 1991-92 to a historical peak of US $ 25.19 billion at the end of 1994-95, something which was not seen for many years. Although the level of reserves was comfortable, there was a need for a further build-up in reserves to have greater flexibility in exchange rate management, to absorb any unanticipated external shocks, to facilitate India's move towards full capital account convertibility, and to impart confidence in the international investor community about the soundness of India's balance of payments. By end-March 1996, the country's external balance sheet was strong enough to withstand considerable shock. This along with the cautious policy concerning capital account convertibility stood the country in good stead in weathering the Asian financial crisis well during 1997-99. It is noteworthy that all the movements in India's total forex reserves are mostly governed by the movements in foreign currency assets components of forex reserves since changes in other two components, viz. gold and SDRs are few and far between. Table 4.16 gives the trends in foreign currency assets and some critical indicator of reserve management.

TABLE 4.16

Foreign Exchange Reserves[1] : Historical Perspective

(US $ million)

Years	Foreign Reserves[2]	Import Cover (No. of Months)[3]	Current Payments Cover[4] (Number of Months)[3]
1950-51	1914.00	16.80	14.60
1955-56	1648.00	12.20	10.60
1960-61	390.00	2.00	1.70
1965-66	383.00	1.60	1.30
1970-71	584.00	2.90	2.20
1975-76	1657.00	3.20	2.80
1980-81	5850.00	4.30	3.80
1985-86	5972.00	4.10	3.50
1990-91	2236.00	1.00	0.80
1991-92	5631.00	3.20	2.30
1992-93	6434.00	3.30	2.50
1993-94	15068.00	7.20	5.40
1994-95	20809.00	7.80	5.80
1995-96	17044.00[5]	4.90	3.80
1996-97[6]	19847.00	5.50	4.00

Notes : 1. Excluding Gold and SDRs.

2. Year-end level.
3. Based on foreign exchange reserves of respective year-end levels.
4. Current payments represent sum of merchandise imports and invisible payments.
5. Here total Forex Reserve includes Gold holding of the RBI + SDRs + Foreign currency assets.
6. Reserve level at end-January 1997.

Source : *Economic Survey*, 1996-97.

4.8.1 The Merchandise Trade Balance—What Lies Ahead?

The successful completion of Uruguay Round provides greater opportunities for exports for LDCs, including India. The tariff reduction offered from developed countries cover US $ 464 billion of the industrial imports. The share of duty-free merchandise imports to the developed countries from LDCs, are expected to rise. The progressive dismantling of the multi-fibre agreement may strengthen India's exports in areas where it has a strong comparative advantage. However, the emergence of regional trading blocks turn out to be unfriendly coalition, is something that future alone can tell. India's share in the world exports stands at 0.60 per cent as compared to 0.42 per cent and 0.52 per cent of exports of world trade in 1980 and 1990, respectively (Table 4.17). If global exports rise by 5 per cent annually, India's share in world export would be below 1 per cent (*Rangarajan*, 1993).

TABLE 4.17
India: Share in World Trade

(in per cent)

Year	*Exports*	*Imports*	*Trade*
1980	0.42	0.72	0.57
1990	0.52	0.66	0.59
1991	0.50	0.56	0.53
1992	0.53	0.61	0.57
1993	0.58	0.60	0.59
1994	0.60	0.63	0.61

Source : UNCTAD Handbook of International Trade and Development Statistics, 1994, United Nations, 1995.

In the above circumstances it appears that the performance of exports is the most significant aspect of the development in the external sector in the upcoming years. The provisional data of the Directorate General of Commercial Intelligence and Statistics (DGCI & S) indicate that export growth in US dollar terms was 18.4 per cent in 1994-95. Exports rose from US $ 22,683 million in 1993-94 to US $ 26,857 million in 1994-95. The export performance was enabled by ongoing structural changes in the policy regime. The exchange rate provided a competitive edge to exports. As a result, export activity proved to be attractive relative to sales in the domestic market. This is indicative of an outward-orientation in the export sector and a receding of the vent-for-surplus approach which characterized export activity in past years before the reforms (*Rangarajan*, 1993).

Imports rose sharply as the progressive elimination of quantitative restrictions and reduction in tariff allowed for import demand. According to DGCI & S, imports at US $ 31,840 million rose by 22.9 per cent during 1994-95 as against a modest rise of 6.5 per cent in the preceding year. During 1995-96, imports at $ 36,370 million rose by 26.9 per cent and the Import bill on account of petroleum and oil products (POL) had a large impact on the balance of trade, the balance of payments and on the general health of the economy. In 1995-96, the POL import bill registered a rise of 27.3 per cent to US $ 7526 million from US $ 5928 million in the previous year following the hardening of international prices for petroleum and petroleum products, fall in domestic product of crude oil as well as the increase in the demand for hydrocarbons. During 1994-95 non-POL imports, however, recorded a massive increase of 29.5 per cent in US dollar terms. But during 1995-96, non-oil imports rose by 26.8 per cent. Thus both 'oil' and 'non-oil' imports contributed to the high import growth.

Consequently, the trade deficit in 1995-96 nearly doubled to US $ 4539 million as compared US $ 2324 million in 1994-95 primarily due to sharp surge in imports. As a ratio of GDP, the current account deficit rose from 0.5 per cent in 1993-94 to 0.9 percent in 1994-95 and further to 1.7 per cent in 1995-96.

4.8.2 Invisibles

The earnings of invisible accounts had been one of the major factors reducing the impact of net merchandise trade deficit in India. The receipts on invisible account went on increasing. However, invisible trades did not figure prominently during early years of the 1960's and 70's, but it gained prominent in the year 1980-81 financing as much of 73 percent of the total trade deficits but this momentum was not maintained and during 1986-89, it has brought to a level of almost 38 percent, which was almost half of the levels achieved in the year 1980-81. The net surplus under the invisible account rose from US $ 1228 million or 0.4 per cent of GDP in 1993-94 to US $ 2282 million or 0.6 per cent of GDP in 1994-95 (Table 4.18). During 1995-96 this was estimated at US $ 3451 million. The invisibles account has assumed importance in view of the growing role in services in world trade, spurred also by a revival of tourist interest in India and supported by a buoyant private transfer receipts that stood at US $ 7.5 billion in 1995-96. From our elaborate discussion, it appears that for India, invisibles trade that played a crucial role in the 1970s waned in importance during the 1980s. They have re-emerged as a strong source of support in the balance of payments offsetting the deficit in the merchandise trade account.

TABLE 4.18
Net Invisibles After Reform

(US $ million)

Particulars	*1990-91 (P)*	*1991-92 (P)*	*1992-93 (P)*	*1993-94 (P)*	*1994-95 (P)*	*1995-96 (Q.E.)*
Net Invisibles	-242.00	1620.00	842.00	1228.00	2282.00	3451.00
Invisible Receipts	7463.00	9502.00	8241.00	9649.00	13372.00	16109.00
Payments	7706.00	7882.00	7399.00	8421.00	11090.00	12658.00

Note : (P): Preliminary Actuals.
Source : *RBI Annual Report*, 1995-96.
(Q.E.) : Quick estimates.

4.8.3 Current Account

Given these developments, with the merchandise trade deficit being only partly offset by net invisibles earnings in 1995-96, the current account deficit widened to an estimated US $ 5487 million or about 1.7 per cent of GDP in 1995-96 as against US $ 2701 million or 0.9 percent of GDP in 1994-95 and that of US $ 1158 million (0.5 per cent GDP) in 1993-94. The criterion of sustainability of the current account, recommended by the High Level Committee on Balance of Payments as Chaired by Chakravarty Rangarajan viz. that the current account deficit must be limited to a level that could be sustained by normal capital flows, has been to some extent satisfied.

4.8.4 Capital Account

India had experienced surges in capital flows since 1992-93, except during 1995-96. The inflows of capital had eased the external constraint and helped pursue liberalization in trade, foreign investment and industrial policies. By freeing restrictions on current account transactions, and by accepting obligations under Article VIII of the IMF Articles of Agreement from August 20, 1994, international confidence in the Indian economy had been built up, providing a basis for capital flows to be durable in character. The capital flows had helped further to build up the foreign currency assets by US $19,847 at end January 1997. In relation to capital account, there are some major elements on which some observations may be appropriate:

4.8.5 External Assistance

Over the last two decades, there have been significant composition shifts in the pattern of external financing. External assistance as one of the sources of external capital other than commercial borrowing and non-resident foreign currencies deposits for support of India's external payments played a dominant role in financing current account payments deficits during the 1970s. Almost the whole source of external capital in the 1970s was external assistance. This even enabled building up of the reserves. However, during the 1980s, the share in external assistance fell. It fell from 61 percent in 1980-81 to 31 percent in 1990-91. It went up sharply in 1991-92. Thereafter during the first half of the 1990's, the share had gone down. Drawals under the EEF contributed 29 per cent, while commercial borrowings accounted for 20 per cent. NRI deposits provided for 15 per cent of the financing need. During the second half of the 1980s, the share of the commercial borrowings and NR deposits rose, each meeting 23 to 24 per cent of the financing need. External assistance declined to 29 per cent, reflecting poor utilization of concessional loans, while the reserves met 12 per cent of the financing and the rest came by way of other capital flows.

During 1995-96, the share of India's external assistance in total capital inflows had declined following the emphasis on capital account restructuring. External assistance which

TABLE 4.19

External Assistance during 1991-92 to 1995-96

Particulars	Rupees crores					US $ million				
	1995-96 P	1994-95 P	1993-94	1992-93	1991-92	1995-96 P	1994-95 R	1993-94	1992-93	1991-92
(1)	(2)	(3)	(4)	(5)	(6)	(7)	(8)	(9)	(10)	(11)
1. Loans	9,959.00	10,024.00	10,895.00	10,102.00	10,696.00	2,978.00	3,192.00	3,486.00	3,302.00	4,318.00
2. Grants	1,064.00	1,167.00	886.00	880.00	919.00	318.00	372.00	283.00	287.00	371.00
3. Gross Utillisation	111,023.00	11,191.00	11,781.00	10,982.00	11,615.00	3,296.00	3,564.00	3,769.00	3,589.00	4,689.00
4. Repayments	7,569.00	5,773.00	5,363.00	4,788.00	3,650.00	2,263.00	1,839.00	1,710.00	1,562.00	1,492.00
5. Interest Payment	5,080.00	4,635.00	4,211.00	4,314.00	3,006.00	1,519.00	1,476.00	1,343.00	1,408.00	1,228.00
6. Net (3-4-5)	-1,626.00	783.00	2,207.00	1,880.00	4,959.00	-486.00	249.00	716.00	619.00	1,969.00

P: Provisional. R: Revised.

Notes : 1. Loans are inclusive of non-government loans but exclusive of suppliers credits and commercial borrowings.

2. Grants are exclusive of PL 480-II grants.
3. Figures in US dollar are converted from the Rupees crore data based on the respective annual average Rupee-US dollar rates.
4. Repayments include amortisation of civilian debt owed to Russia.

Source : Controller of Aid, Accounts and Audit, Government of India.

comprises loans and grants net of repayments of principal declined from US $ 1725 million in 1994-95 to US $ 1033 million in 1995-96 as a result of a fall in gross disbursements to US $ 3296 million and a rise in repayments with US $ 424 million in repayments to US $ 2263 million. It might be noted that the disbursement had been falling since 1991-92 due to slower utilisation. Moreover, this period witnessed a transfer of resources of US $ 486 million to various donor countries which eventually made net of amortisation and interest payments and aid utilisation negative. The trends in external assistance in the crisis year 1990-91 as well as the aftermath of reform period upto 1995-96 is exhibited in the Table 4.19.

4.8.6 External Commercial Borrowings (ECBs)

External Commercial Borrowings (ECB) constituted an important source of finance for Indian firms for the expansion of existing capacity and also for new investments as permitted by the Government. Recourse to ECBs in the form of loans from international banks, bond placements, trade-related credits and institutional lines was essentially a phenomenon of the 1980s. In the face of a deterioration in the utilization of external assistance and persistent larger deficits in the current account, ECB emerged as an effective source of external finance. During 1985-90, ECB provided 24 per cent of the financing need, almost equal in importance to external assistance. During the late 1980s, the cost of commercial borrowings was on favourable terms to the country with average maturity of 7 years. Gross disbursements of commercial borrowings averaged $ 2.0 billion per annum over the second half of the 1980s, rising to a peak of $ 2.8 billion in 1988-89. In 1989-90, the year immediately preceding the payments crisis of 1990-92, gross disbursements of commercial borrowing amounted to $ 2.5 billion, comprising mainly trade-related credits and syndicate bank loans. Borrowings in the form of securities instruments, especially in the Japanese bond market also entered the portfolio of India's commercial exposure.

Bank loans and bond placements virtually stopped during the years of the payment crisis, as India's credit rating was downgraded. Exports credits supported by official export credit agencies emerged as the single source of commercial borrowings. Net of repayments, commercial borrowings yielded an outflow of $ 0.5 billion in 1992-93.

In the year 1993-94, even though the credit rating continued to be low preventing access to international financial markets, there were encouraging results. While trade related credits continued to be the major source of disbursements, there had been a modest increase in access to bank loans. Borrowings in the form of loans, including trade credits, accounted for 50 per cent of disbursements. During 1994-95, after a sharp drop from US $ 425 million in 1990-91 to US $ 117 million in 1992-93, gross disbursements of ECB rose markedly to US $ 3841 million; after that total drawals under ECB registered a marginal increase to US $ 3876 million in 1995-96, while repayments increased from US $ 2812 million to US $ 3349 million (Table 4.20). As a result, ECB (net) at US $ 527 million in 1995-96 were sharply lower than that of US $ 1029 million in 1994-95. Net drawals under short-term credit were US $ 160 million during 1995-96 as compared with US $ 330 million in the previous year. Placement of convertible bonds in the Euro-market had emerged as an important source of commercial borrowing.

In the years to come, disbursement of commercial borrowings could be even higher than the levels reached in the late 1980s reflecting the international perception of strengthening of the fundamentals of the economy. Euro issues would remain an important avenue of accessing commercial markets. Thus, even though amortisation of commercial borrowing would be in the range of $ 2.3 billion per annum over the next few years, with a peak of $ 5 billion in 1996-97, as the India Development Bonds matured in net terms, Commercial Borrowing could well yield inflows of $ 1 billion per annum over the medium term.

4.8.7 Non-Resident Foreign Currency Deposits

During 1985-90, non-resident deposits accounted for 23 per cent of the financing need. In a large measure, the inflows of funds under these deposits was a response to conscious policy incentives in the form of attractive interest rate differentials, exchange risk guarantees to banks and fiscal concessions. However, the experience of the crisis of 1991-92 clearly revealed that excessive dependence on non-resident deposits must have to be avoided. Mobilization of deposits under the FCNRA was also not cost effective. In pursuance of the recommendation of the High Level Committee on Balance of payments a restructuring of the FCNRA Scheme was effected during 1993-94. Deposit maturities upto two years have been discontinued and interest rate differentials narrowed. Simultaneously, two new schemes viz. the Foreign Currency non-resident (Bank) FCNR(B) Scheme and the Non-Resident Non-Repatriable Rupee Deposit NR(NR)D Scheme have been introduced. The introduction of the two schemes proved to be fruitful as there were positive inflows. While carrying all the feature of the FCNRA Scheme, exchange guarantees are no longer borne by the RBI under these schemes. Incentives have also been offered to banks to encourage them to mobilize deposits. Under the NR (NR) RD Scheme, banks are even free to fix interest rate corresponding to various maturities.

The response to these policy initiatives has been encouraging so far. Outflows for the FCNRA Scheme have been more than compensated for by inflows under the new scheme. Indeed, if all the non-resident deposit schemes are taken together, there has been a net inflow of US $ 1365 million (inclusive of accrued interest) in 1995-96 as compared to US $ 854 million in the preceding year. This healthy trend is expected to continue but it is necessary to ensure that these deposit come out of the genuine savings of NRIs.

4.8.8 Foreign Investment

The Capital account was dominated by foreign investment inflows which met more than half of the financing need. The response of foreign investment flows to the liberalization measures has been highly encouraging. Total investment flows, direct and portfolio, rose sharply to US $ 4.23 billion in 1993-94, with a further increase to US $ 4.89 billion in 1994-95. However, foreign investment inflows were of the order of US $ 4.34 billion during 1995-96. The trend in Foreign Direct Investments (FDI) flows has been encouraging. From US $ 586 million in 1993-94,

FDIs more than doubled to US $ 1314 million in 1994-95. During 1995-96, FDIs were US $ 2133 million. The ratios of foreign investment to exports and to GDP show that there has been a growing integration of the Indian economy with the global economy over time.

4.8.9 Overall Balance

While the improvement in the current account and the continuing strength of capital flows yielded an overall balance of surplus of US $ 6105 million during 1994-95 (Table 4.15), it appears that during 1995-96, net capital inflows which amounted to US $ 4278 million fell short of the current account deficit. As a result, the balance of payments recorded an overall deficit amounting to US $ 12 of million in 1995-96. Repurchases from the IMF peaked at US $ 1710 million during 1995-96. The foreign exchange reserves were drawn to the tune US $ 2919 million (Table 4.15)

4.8.10 External Debt

A country's external indebtedness is a mirror image of the behaviour of the current account in the balance of payments. In this sense, the outstanding volume of India's external debts represents the accumulation of deficits in the current account over the past years. India's external debts with high share of multilateral and bilateral debt as at the end of March 1996 amounted to US $ 92199 (P) million. Bulk of this debt was accumulated in the 1980s. Although India was the fourth largest debtor among developing countries, in terms of the nominal volume of debt (according to World Bank, World Debt Tables, 1996), the volume of debt came down when measured in terms of present value method. The share of concessional debts at around 35 per cent was quite high as compared with other developing countries.

India's external debt as proportion of GNP was less than 12 per cent in 1980. In 1985, the Debt GNP ratio at 19.3 per cent was still one of the lowest. In 1992, the Debt-GNP ratio jumped to 32.3 per cent. It had marginally exceeded the ratio for Brazil though it was lower by 3 percentage points than that of Mexico.

TABLE 4.20
India's External Debt (1990-95)

Items	1989-90		1990-91		1991-92		1992-93	
	Rs. Crore	US $ Million	Rs. Crore	US $ Million	Rs. Crore	US $ Million	Rs. Crore	US $ Million
(1)	(2)	(3)	(4)	(5)	(6)	(7)	(8)	(9)
I. Multilateral	32886.00	19164.00	40366.00	20900.00	68262.00	23090.00	77758.00	25008.00
II. Bilateral	22993.00	13564.00	27378.00	14168.00	47603.00	15466.00	50258.00	16154.00
III. IMF 2572.00	1493.00	5132.00	2623.00	8934.00	3451.00	14985.00	4799.00	
IV. Export Credit	8002.00	4655.00	8374.00	4301.00	12418.00	3990.00	13484.00	4322.00
V. Commercial borrowing	15988.00	9335.00	19727.00	10209.00	35711.00	11715.00	36367.00	11643.00
VI. NRI and FC (B and O) deposits	15719.00	9124.00	20030.00	10209.00	27384.00	10083.00	34941.00	11141.00
VII. Rupee Debt*	19075.00	11021.00	25199.00	12847.00	31956.00	10420.00	33149.00	10616.00
VIII. Total long-term Debt (I-VII)	117235.00	68356.00	146226.00	75257.00	232268.00	78215.00	260942.00	83683.00
IX. Short term DEBT	12964.00	7501.00	16775.00	8544.00	20642.00	7070.00	19804.00	6340.00
X. Total DEBT	130199.00	75857.00	163001.00	83801.00	252910.00	85285.00	280746.00	90023.00
XI. Total DEBT service of which:		7598.00		8982.00		8250.00		7658.00
(a) Principal	—		5628.00		4705.00		4181.00	
(b) Interest			3954.00		3545.00		3477.00	
XII. Debt indicators in percent								
(a) Debt-GDP ratio	28.50		30.40		41.00		38.90	
(b) Debt-Service ratio	30.90		35.30		30.20		28.60	

TABLE 4.20 (Contd.)

Items 1993-94	1994-95		1995-96			
	Rs. Crore	US $ Million	Rs. Crore	US $ Million	Rs. Crore	US $ Million
(1)	(10)	(11)	(12)	(13)	(14)	(15)
I. Multilateral	82199.00	26263.00	89819.00	28542.00	98020.00	28571.00
II. Bilateral	54580,00	17450.00	83761.00	20270.00	63991.00	18705.00
III. IMF	15812.00	5040.00	13545.00	4300.00	8152.00	2374.00
IV. Export Credit	16307.00	5203.00	20876.00	6629.00	18940.00	5523.00
V. Commercial borrowing	38782.00	12363.00	40915.00	12991.00	43742.00	12748.0
VI. NRI & FC (B and O) deposits	39729.00	12665.00	39006.00	12383.00	37802.00	11011.00
VII. Rupee Debt*	31634.00	10084.00	30315.00	9624.00	28150.00	8233.00
VIII. Total long-term Debt (I-VII)	279043.00	89068.00	298237.00	94739.00	298798.00	87165.00
IX. Short-term Debt	11375.00	3627.00	13448.00	4269.00	16637.00	5034.00
X. Total Debt	290418.00	92625.00	311685.00	99008.00	315435.00	92199.00
XI. Total Debt service	12378.00					
of which:						
(a) Principal		4783.00		6825.00		8063.00
(b) Interest		3818.00		4099.00		4315.00
XII. Debt indicators in percent						
(a) Debt-GDP ratio		35.90		32.70		28.00
(b) Debt-Service ratio		26.90		27.50		25.70

Notes : *Debt owed to Russia denominated in Rupees converted in current exchange rates and payable in exports.

1. The data on NRI deposits are inclusive of accrued interest credited and the accounts under Foreign currency (Non-Resident) accounts (FCNRA), Foreign Currency (Non-Resident) accounts (Banks) scheme (FCNR(B)) and non-resident (External) rupee account (NR(E)RA) schemes.
2. Multi-lateral loans do not include revaluation of IBRD pooled loans and exchange rate adjustment under IDA loans for pre-1971 credits.

India's debt-GNP ratio of 34.2 per cent remained lower in 1994 than that of Philippines (59.3 per cent), Indonesia (57.4 per cent) and Thailand (43.1 per cent) (*Economic Survey,* 1996-97). In recent times, both the debt-GDP ratio as well as debt-service ratio have come down (Table 4.27).

4.8.11 Concluding Remarks

From our overall assessment on India's balance of payments position in the post-independence period we find that right from the very beginning after Independence India has faced with severe balance of payments problems of varying intensity, irrespective of the changes in strategy and policy that have occurred in India's plan development strategy. Though the magnitude of the problems was meagre in the First Five Year Plan, the Second Five Year Plan however, witnessed severe balance of payments troubles, for which India relied heavily on the rescue operation performed by the World Bank. Balance of payments concern also shaped the formulation and implementation of the Third and the Fourth Plan. Only the Fifth Plan could be hailed as golden years for balance of payments situation because of dramatic improvement in net invisibles primarily on accounts of the remittances in the form of somewhat fortuitous influx of petro-dollars from the Middle-East. During the Sixth Plan Period, the external sector became critical following several incidents for which the Plan had to be supported by a massive loan from the IMF. This increased the debt-servicing burden and further widened the deficits in the upcoming years. And the Seventh Plan was entwined with a heavy pressure arising out of commercial debt. The balance of payments situation became unmanageable at the end of the Seventh Plan, but the economic reform package launched in 1991 tried to improve the balance of payments. At the beginning of the Eighth Plan period, India for another time looked for rescue operation to revive the economy.

A simple analysis of available data has shown us that during Eighth Five Year Plan the balance of payments position constitutes a large improvement over five years earlier. Exports are growing at a much faster rate than imports and the capital account are showing buoyancy. The current account deficit is about 1.5 per cent of GDP. The external debt position has improved quantitatively and qualitatively. The debt/GDP has come down from 41 per cent in March 1992 to 28.7 per cent in March 1996. Similarly the debt service ratio has come from 35.3 per cent in March 1991 to 25.7 per cent during 1995-96. (Table 4.20) Over the same period, short-term debt has fallen 10 per cent of GDP to 4 per cent and foreign exchange reserves have increased from $ 2 billion to $ 17 billion. There has been significant progress towards current account convertibility for everyone, and capital account convertibility for foreign investors and Non-Resident Indian's for undertaking direct and portfolio investment in India. This is not to say that balance of payments position is completely secured and the crisis has been managed. But it can be said that India has been creditworthy enough to survive a short-term worsening of the current account. Oil imports are expected to increase rapidly. There is a possibility of a sizeable hump in debt repayments over the next few years. Non-resident deposits that exhibit high volatility still constitutes 15 per cent of total external debt of $ 92 billion. Even so, the fundamental position in the balance of payments scenario might prove to be healthy provided the rate of export growth stays robust and much higher than the ratio of growth of consumption and investment. This will require an appropriate macroeconomic/exchange rate policy, continuation of trade reforms and easing of institutional and infrastructural constraints, which are severe in nature.

4.9 INTERNATIONAL SCENARIO CHANGES AND POST REFORM INDIA'S BALANCE OF PAYMENTS : HOW WELL INDIA IS DOING ?

Economic policies meanwhile throughout the world have converged around three basic principles. First, there is emphasis on using market mechanisms to achieve objectives, with resort to state intervention on a highly selective and targeted basis. Secondly, macroeconomic policy has been oriented towards ensuring a stable economic framework. Thirdly, national policies have become more outward-looking, as evidenced by the steadily increasing membership of the World Trade Organization (WTO), the relaxation of controls on capital mobility and the globally more benign stance towards foreign investment. The economic policy consensus has evolved because over time we have learned to what have to be done in future course of action.

The first pillar of the consensus concerns the role of the market system and competition in ensuring that the economy operates effectively. This embraces pro-competitive policies, labour market flexibility, privatization, deregulation and enterprise-friendly environment. This consensus springs from that basic philosophy which emphasizes absolute freedom to market to determine prices and production and distribution pattern and views government interventions as processes that create distortions and bring inefficiencies. Thus public enterprises have to be privatized through disinvestments and sales; sectors and activities hitherto reserved for the public sector would have to be opened to the private sector. This logic extends to the social services like education and health. Employment and wages would have to be governed by free play of market forces, as any measure to regulate them can discourage investment and also create inefficiency in production.

In macroeconomic policy there has also been a marked shift in organization. Since the 1990s, price stability has been identified as key objective. Together with prioritising price stability, another key element in a macro-stability package is a commitment to low budget deficits. Besides, in line with the overall philosophy of reduction in the role of state, there has been an emphasis on stabilization and structural adjustment programme which has incorporated fiscal balance as a key objective. In other words, fiscal reforms would have to be taken on domestic front to have generally low levels of taxation and government expenditure should be kept to the minimum to abide by the principle of fiscal prudence. A central tenet of the current consensus is that better control of government finances will stimulate private investment and help to reduce unemployment. Thus macro-stability has become an effective means of achieving sustained growth.

The liberalization of international transactions, that is, the removal of barriers to international trade and investments and thus promotion of free flow of goods, finance and technologies across the countries, is the third pillar of the new policy consensus. The catchword globalization has been coined to describe these processes that are leading to broader and deeper integration between countries and peoples. The three elements of the policy package are interdependent. Professor Jeffery Sachs has succinctly described the logic of the package saying that basic goal is to move from a situation of extreme shortage and hyperinflation to one of supply and demand balance and stable prices. For this a country needs tight macroeconomic policies with the decontrol of price. To have a working price system, that country needs competition. To have competition it needs free international trade. To have free trade it needs not only low-tariffs, but also the convertibility of currency. To have convertibility of currency at a stable exchange rate, it needs monetary discipline and a realistic exchange rate.

In what follows is that globalization has been the most frequently used term mostly in the economic discourse. It has been projected by international financial institutions (World Bank and International Monetary Fund) and globally dominant economic entities (multinational and transnational corporations) and supported by national governments and governing elites of the developed as well as developing countries, not only as inevitable, but also necessary and desirable for bringing prosperity and well-being around the world. In fact, globalization as a tactic for development has been propelled by them. Most of them by now seem to have been convinced that globalization will bring prosperity to their countries, though they do not have control over the processes and mechanisms that can ensure such result.

Having tried import-substitution policies, many countries concluded that they are of limited value and that openness was a superior policy. Since the 1990s, a virtual revolution in trade policy has taken place, as one country after another liberalized trade regime. Over 150 countries (151 countries as on 11 January, 2007) have signed up to membership of the World Trade Organization (WTO) and 95 per cent of the global trade is now governed by the rules and regulations of the WTO. Developing countries are now active participants in the movement towards a more liberal world trading system. Although wedded to the idea of self-sufficiency, China becoming a member of the WTO has indicated its readiness to abide by the liberal trade rules of that organization and surprisingly, her share in the world export has doubled during 1995-05, which made her possible to become the fourth largest exporter in the world, and even, the United States and Germany export less than twice as much. The dramatic entry of China onto the world's economic stage has been one of the last acts of China's economic reform. Further liberalization of international transactions has been through regional integration initiated in Asia, Latin America and tentatively in Africa. Most countries have abandoned the idea of development through intensive cultivation of the domestic market and have replaced it with the ambition of penetrating foreign markets and of achieving growth through exports.

In the early 1990s, India too abandoned its *dirigiste* policies and replaced them with trade liberalization and a more open-door policy to foreign investment as it was found in the Indian case that interventionist economic regime, with indiscriminate import-substitution public sector-driven industrialization, and self-defeating complex administrations of economic behaviour as well as self-sufficiency as its objective followed since the 1960s, is largely responsible for the India's poor economic performance. Following international scenario changes, India's BoP has faced major challenges in the 1990s and beyond.

4.9.1 Reform Process and the Foreign Trade Scenario

The reform process in India has led to the growth of exports, but simultaneously it has also led a larger growth of imports fuelled by liberalization of imports (most of which are by multinational corporations) through a hurried withdrawal of quantity restrictions and repeated reduction in custom duties, even without giving adequate time for ·preparation to the domestic producers. Exports, as a proportion of GDP, on BoP basis, have grown from 5.8 per cent in 1990-91 to 12.2 percent in 2004-05 and it grew further to 13.1 per cent in 2005-06. The corresponding rise in imports was from 8.8 per cent in 1990-91 to 17.1 per cent in 2004-05 and further to 19.5 per cent in 2005-06. Trade deficit as a proportion of GDP, which have actually declined from 3.0 per cent in 1990-91 to 2.1 per cent in 2002-03, widened to 4.9 per cent in 2004-05 and further to 6.4 per cent in 2005-06. The trade deficit widened very sharply, particularly in 2004-05 and 2005-06. As a result of following this policy of import liberalization with undue haste, which in turn has effectively increased the monopoly powers in the structure of trade, the domestic producers have been continuously placed at a position of relative disadvantage—a position of unequal competition. As an overall effect of this policy, in 2004-05, growth in India's merchandise imports is at 40 per cent in dollar terms, the highest since 1980-81. In 2005-06 merchandise imports grew by 33.8 percent. This high growth in imports are in value terms was primarily due to high POL prices. Even this DGCIS data excludes defence imports, while the rate growth in merchandise exports is 26.2 per cent (*Economic Survey,* GoI, 2005-06). As a result, the critical trade gap between imports and exports, which was Rs. 3.8 thousand crore in 1991 has increased alarmingly by 46 times and reached a staggering figure of Rs. 1.76 lakh crore in 2005-06 (*Ministry of Commerce and Industry,* GoI, 2006) or a record high of US 446 billion (as per custom data) in 2005-06. This implies that the economy spent more on final goods and services than it produced. Hence, its imports exceeded its exports to the tune of the excess domestic expenditures. The higher is domestic absorption relative to GDP, the bigger the trade gap, as domestic absorption is the total of GDP plus trade gap. This also implies that the gulf of difference exists between the foreign exchange flowing into the country from its exports of goods and services and the foreign exchange needed to pay for its imports of good and services. In other words, the domestic entrepreneurs, every year, are losing, in the net sense, this large share of their market which is about 12 per cent of the total annual production (Rs. 15.1 lakh crore) in agriculture and industry in the country (*Economic Survey,* GoI 2005-06, Table 4.21). It is apprehended, on the basis of the latest data for the current year (2006-07), that if this trend continues, then even within this year, the domestic manufacturers may lose 15 per cent of their market, with possibility of a more severe loss in future. As a result of loss of this significant share of the market year after year, farmers have been adversely affected, and industrial sickness has also increased. It is for this reason also that there has been shrinkage of the opportunity of growth

-liberalization period. The growth of employment (at 1.07 percent per year) has been systematically lower than the rate of growth of labour force (at 1.31 per cent per year) causing a widespread incidence of unemployment in the entire country.

4.9.2 India's Export Performance

Trade reforms were an essential part of economic reforms. Trade reforms included rationalization of exchange rate policy, liberalization of imports, incentives to promote exports and introducing administrative flexibility. These reforms marked a distinct shift in the trade strategy: from import substitution to export promotion. There is no denying the fact that the health of India's balance of payments crucially depends on export performance. Success in sustaining a strong export growth will depend on the maintenance of a competitive exchange rate, overall macroeconomic stability, steps to enhance the relative profitability of exports, as compared to the domestic market and growing competitiveness of India's industry, agriculture, and services.

In the 1990s and beyond a number of exports promotion schemes were put in place with the genuine intention of promoting exports from the country. Export promotion zones, export-oriented units and export houses were given a number of incentives. Easy availability of inputs, including export credit and imported raw materials, was ensured. The response to the policy reforms implemented in the midst of the crisis of 1991 was quick and the economy was already in recovery made by 1992-93, thereafter experiencing quite satisfactory growth by historical standards. Higher export growth, helped by better export prices, raised the exports to GDP ratio from 5.8 percent in 1990-91 to 8.9 percent in 1996-97, despite the loss of East European markets. Growth of exports was nearly 20 percent during 1993-94 to 1995-96. Thereafter the export growth slowed in 1996 (partly due to lower prices), and the trade deficit widened. The East Asian crisis in the summer of 1997 was a prime mover towards the slow-down in the growth of exports. Following East Asian Crisis, Indian exports demand in the affected countries was shrunk, also its international competitiveness due to sharp depreciation of East Asian currencies. India's competitiveness was also affected due to the appreciation of the Rupee in real terms in the mid-1990s, following its switchover to the market determined exchange rate management launched in March, 1993. . But exports (i.e. the value of all goods and services sold to firms, households and governments in other countries) picked up since 1999-2000. Exports as percentage of GDP at market prices raised from 8.3 percent in 1999-2000 to 11.8 percent in 2004-05 and grew further to 13.1 per cent in 2005-06. In 2004-05, export growth was a record of 26.2 per cent. During 2005-06, while volume of exports increased by a record 45.4 per cent (mainly in items like petroleum products, chemicals and related products and machinery and transport equipment), the unit value increased by 20.4 per cent (mainly in petroleum products, mineral and ores, footwear etc.). Exports had nearly tripled between 2001-02 and 2006-07. Indian merchandise exports (in US dollar terms and on custom basis) posted 22.6 per cent growth in 2006-07. Exports during 2006-07 reached US $89.5 billion in April-December 2006 with growth of 36.3 per cent, the highest since 1975-76. A host of favourable external developments and domestic policy initiatives (like availability of adequate export credit at competitive rates) have contributed to the satisfactory performance of exports. This significant growth of exports was also aided by improved global growth and recovery in world trade along with the earnest effort of domestic manufacturers for better export orientation. This and India's exports growing at more than double the rate of growth of world exports have enhanced India's share in world merchandise exports to reach at 1 per cent in 2005-06 after a prolonged period at 0.8 per cent.

In the Indian economy services growth in the post-reforms period had been more stable and impressive as compared with the growth of agriculture and industry. Services sector emerged as the dominant sector and main driver of GDP growth. In 1950-51 services accounted for a little less than 30 percent of GDP while the share of agriculture and industry were about 57 per cent respectively. Since then both services and industry gained at the expense of agriculture and by 1990-91 services become the leading sector with a share of 41 percent. However, it was in the post-reforms period, especially from the mid of 1990s that there occurred a major divergence between the performance of the tertiary and the secondary sectors and the economy has been characterized by what World Bank (2004) called "India's Services Revolution". It took forty years, from 1950-51 to 1990-91, for services' share in GDP to rise by 11 percentage points; an increase in the same magnitude came about in the post-reforms era in only 14 years, from 1990-91 to 2004-05. Services sectors' growth thus had shown an upward trend, growing faster than merchandise trade and the share of services in total external trade has increased to 27.1 per cent in 2005-06. and it grew, since the 1990s at an average annual rate of 9 per cent, contributing to nearly 60 per cent of the overall growth rate of the economy. (*World Bank*, 2004). It now exceeded that of industries by more than 2.5 percentage points during 1995-05. After the post-liberalization period, exports of services from India exhibited one of the fastest rates of growth in the world—over 17 per cent per year in the 1990s. In fact, growth of services' exports had been much more spectacular, especially from the mid 1990s. While in the 70s and the 80s services accounted for 48 per cent and 49 per cent of GDP growth respectively, the figure shot up to more than 66 per cent during 1995-05. The increasing dominance of services' GDP had gone hand in hand with emergence of India as a major exporter of services, especially in IT and IT enabled products such as call centers, back-office operations, transcriptions payroll accounting services, etc. The reasons as to why the services sector has performed better in the 1990s and beyond versus the 1980s, unlike agriculture and industry are not far to seek. First, the governmental intervention was less in this predominantly unorganized sector. Second, the absence of a structured tax system for this sector makes services more lucrative. Third, economic reforms covering banking, insurance, ports and road operations have greatly helped to give a further boost to growth in the service sector and helped spread efficiency gains. Lastly, a new demand for skills and application of processes has gone hand in hand with the emergence of vibrant IT, telecommunications, bio-technology and electronics sectors. This has in fact given a further boost to the economy. It is pertinent to speak in this connection that India's booming software exports do not feature in balance of trade figures. Instead they feature in "Invisibles" under the head Private Transfers. Since the early 1990s both merchandise and services exports of India had grown at a higher rate than GDP as well as world exports. With an average growth of 17.05 per cent the country's services exports as a proportion of world exports of services rose from 0.53 to 2.32 percent between 1992 and 2005. Indeed, during 1995-2005, the growth of India's services exports (at 21.5 percent) was almost two times that of world exports. Nay, in 2005-06, with a growth of 42 per cent, services exports reached US $61.4 billion, constituting almost 60 per cent of merchandise exports during that period. In fact, services exports-captured by net non-factor services, including software and IT-enabled services—has emerged as another key component of invisibles trade. Growth had been particularly rapid in the miscellaneous services category, which comprised of said software services, business services, financial services and commercial services. Both demand and supply side factors are the contributory factors behind this phenomenal growth. The most important demand side factors driving services growth are sources of change in aggregate demand and income elasticity of demand for services. There are varieties of routes through which supply side factors affect both the overall growth and its sectoral composition. First of all, there has been an easing of capacity constraints. Secondly, with the expansion of industrial production it becomes economical for producers to outsource advertisement, consultancy, marketing, transport, security, etc. from firms specializing in provision of these services. The implication is that over time growing final demand for industrial products will tend to raise the share of services' GDP at the expense of industres. Thirdly, technological progress, the main driver of long-run growth, can have substantial impact on sectoral shares. While the overall growth due to technical improvements takes place through an increase in total factor productivity, their growth will not generally be uniform. Fourthly, an important constituent of supply-side factors is the country's tax-*cum*-regulatory system. Changes in the regulatory framework can have a far reaching impact on growth of aggregate GDP as well as its sectoral composition. But the irony is that in spite of the sharp rise in services exports, their net contribution toward imports was no more than 2.0 per cent of GDP in 2004-05. Thus financing even 10 per cent of domestic absorption of goods through services exports over the next decade appears next to impossible (*Rakshit,* 2007). Add to that volatility of export demand, highly imperfect international market for food grains and other agricultural products, and the consequent problem of ensuring food security (*Storm,* 1997), and it is not very difficult to ascertain why enhancing productivity of primary and secondary sectors has to be the most important role of services in a poor country like India . However, sustainability in growth of Indian exports of goods and services, which is central to the long-term health and viability of the external sector should have to be maintained and framed in tune with the ongoing world of increasingly integrated global environment by an enlargement of productivity and competitiveness.

Since 2002-03, while improved global growth and recovery in world trade aided in strengthening of Indian exports, firming up of domestic economic activity, especially in the manufacturing sector, as well as effort to fine-tune the export promotion schemes launched during the 1990s, providing also a supporting base for strong sector specific exports. Various policy initiatives for export promotion and market diversification seem to have contributed as well. Some of the important trade policy changes were affected to make them WTO-compliant, for example, the removal of QRs. For other policy changes, such as phase-out of tax exemption on export income, it is hard to fathom whether the motivation was fiscal imperative or WTO compliance: probably, both motivations were present. A few export promotion programmes are still in vogue. Some programmes that qualify as subsidies have invited Countervailing Duties (CDVs) exports from India invited the maximum number of CVDs as at 31 December 2002. The government in its Foreign Trade Policy 2004-09, had announced a medium-term export strategy to increase the share of country exports in world exports from 0.75 per cent to 1.5 per cent by 2009 and is endeavouring to use trade policy as an effective instrument of economic growth with a thrust on employment generations.

The products and the markets where the country enjoyed competitive advantage were also identified. There were other schemes such as the "Export Promotion Capital Goods" scheme that allowed for import of capital goods to be used in export production on concessional terms. A new scheme to accelerate growth of exports called "Target Plus" had been introduced. Another new scheme called *"Vishesh Krishi Upaj Yojana"* had been introduced to boost exports of fruits, vegetables, flowers etc. and their value added products. To take the benefits of foreign trade further to much areas and to meet the objective of employment generation in rural and semi-urban areas, export of village and cottage industry products were included in the above *yojana* and it was therefore renamed as *Vishesh Krishi and Gram Udyog Yojana*. The earlier duty free export credit scheme for services had been revamped and re-cast into the *"Service from India"* scheme. To make India into a global trading-hub, a new scheme to establish "Free Trade and Warehousing zone" had been introduced to create trade-related infrastructure to facilitate the imports and exports of goods and services with freedom to carry out trade transactions in convertible currencies. The SEZ Act, 2005, supported by SEZ rules, came into effect on February 10, 2006 to generate additional economic activity, promotion of goods and services, promotion of investment from domestic and foreign sources, creation of employment opportunities and development of infrastructure facilities. During 2005-06, exports from functioning SEZs (Special Economic Zones), which were mainly the former EPZs (Export Processing Zones) were around US $ 5 billion. On the basis of the latest data for the current year 2006-07, 1,016 units are in operation in these SEZs providing direct employment to over 179 lakh persons (about 40 per cent of whom are women).

4.9.3 The Terms of Trade and the Purchasing Power of Exports

For countries which engage in foreign trade on a large scale, movements in the Terms of trade (ToT) are important. When the volume of trade and exports are large, quite small changes in the ToT can make a large impact on BoP. For example, in 2004-05, India's imports were Rs. 5,32,969 crore. So even, a 1% fall in import prices would have meant a saving of Rs. 5329 crore in foreign currency, or alternatively the existing level of exports could have bought additional imports of Rs. 5329 crore.

Now we may pertinently ask the question as to what has happened to India's net terms of trade (ToT) during this reform period, that, is the general ratio of exports to import prices. The picture is that net ToT, which has increased on an average by 1.5 per cent per annum in the 1990's has witnessed a continuous decline since 1999-00, except in 2003-2004, reflecting a growing competitiveness of India's export. In 2004-05 and 2005-06, there was a sharp deterioration in both net and income ToT (Table 4.21), indicating that India was receiving less and less for its exports relative to the prices of its imports. A decline in the ToT implies that a country needs to export progressively more in volume terms just to be able to afford the same volume of imports. But the fundamental concern of macroeconomic policy makers seeking economic development is not export volume but the purchasing power of exports: what amount of imports the exports will buy from abroad. While export volume is a measure of production effort, the purchasing power of exports is a measure of the reward for production effort, assessed in terms of imports which the exports earning can buy, that which is measured by the volume exported, multiplied by ToT.

The ToT, which measures the terms of exchange between a unit of exports and a unit of imports, have been improving in the post-reform period. Two common ways of measuring the ToT are net ToT and income ToT. The net ToT (with the base of 1978-79=100),which is an index of export of prices divided by an index of import prices, improved from 109.3 in 1990-91 to 152.4 in 1994-95 but declined to 137.9 in 1995-96. After a rising tendency between 2002-03 to 2004-05, it deteriorated as the unit value index of imports rose by 49 per cent (mainly due to a sharp rise in the price of crude petroleum by over 40 per cent, and of gold and other metals). The income ToT, which indicates the purchasing power of exports, improved from 212.2 in 1990-91 to 530.7 in 1995-96 and jumped to 991 in 2004-05. It may be noted that India's purchasing power of exports as reflected through income ToT has been improving continuously since 1990-91 with the exception of the period 1996-97 and 2005-06. It also implies, in terms of volume that the indices of exports is relatively higher in comparison to that of imports. Thus there is a hope. for better price of exports.

TABLE 4.21
Index Numbers of Foreign Trade (Base 1978-79=100)

Year	*Terms of Trade (ToT)*		
	Gross	*Net*	*Income*
1990-91	122.5	109.3	212.2
1991-92	109.3	119.5	249.3
1992-93	126.5	127.3	283.8
1993-94	127.8	144.9	373.1
1994-95	139.5	152.4	446.0
1995-96	134.0	137.9	530.0
1996-97	124.3	126.2	519.7
1997-98	145.6	145.8	562.8
1998-99	161.4	150.0	598.8
1999-00	152.9	134.2	618.7
2000-01	122.1	128.1	732.0
2001-02	123.6	125.4	743.2
2002-03	111.2	113.6	819.7
2003-04	126.9	123.4	943.5
2004-05	110.0	124.0	991.0
2005-06	67.0	90.0	662.0

Notes : 1. Gross ToT implies Volume Index of Imports expressed as a percentage of Volume Index of Exports.

2. Net ToT implies unit value of Exports expressed as a percentage of Unit value Index of Imports.

3. Income ToT implies the product of Net ToT and Volume index of Exports expressed as a percentage.

Source : *Economic Survey*, Government of India, 2006-07.

Does the ToT matter at all in terms of people's livelihood? Yes. If we insert imprudent policy like putting less attention to agricultural growth and its exports into a context of falling ToT, in that case it can constitute a potent force extracting more work from people including many of the poorest people living in this country without a commensurate gain at their incomes and standard of living. This is what is happening. At one hand India is taking serious measures to get ready to operate in a new globalized liberal trade framework, at the same time its process of economic reform has virtually neglected agriculture. Nay, using agriculture as an export promotion area via multinationals and Indian big business, there was gross neglect of agriculture to enlarge irrigation, to ensure credit and fertilizers in adequate measures so as to give a further boast to agriculture. This decelerated growth rate in agriculture during the 90's and beyond has caused trouble to the of rural India, in spite of the high growth of overall GDP and per capita income after the launching of economic reforms in 1991.

Since agriculture continues to be the largest sector of the economy in terms of employment, and export potential, deceleration of growth of this sector has serious implications for the living standard of agricultural workers—both farmers and agricultural labourers. Incidence of rural poverty and unemployment will increase. All evidence now suggests that both have increased in the post-liberalization period.

A large majority of India's population still relies and will continue to rely on agriculture and on export agriculture, to secure their livelihoods. Agriculture matters because the income-generated from broad-based growth in agricultural production is an important stimulus to rural diversification, including rural industrialization. It is indeed hard to conceive of a viable strategy of development without poverty reduction that would not address the importance of agriculture, its present predicament and its potential to generate broad-based rural development, through both on and off-farm activities.

4.9.4 Current Account Position

Current account is that part of BoP accounts that records payments and receipts arising from trade in goods and services and from interest and dividends that are earned by capital owned in one country and invested in another. When the reforms began in 1991 there was a hefty current account deficit (3.2 per cent of GDP) and its reduction was the main focus of policy. Thereafter the current account position was comfortable. After a prolonged period of deficits in the current account since 1990-91, there was a surplus in the current account during the period from 2001-02 to 2003-04 and during these short periods, the net invisibles always overcame the trade deficit to maintain the current account in surplus. The trend was however, reversed in 2004-05 and 2005-06. At present, India exhibits a fairly large current account deficit (US$ 9186 million in 2005-06), the difference between current receipts from exports and invisible earnings and current spending on imports, dividends, interests and other invisibles.

In other words, the current account deficit is the sum of capital account surplus plus drawing down of reserves. This means that if a country has a deficit on its current account, the country has spent more abroad than it has earned during the specified period. This can be settled by international borrowing, or by seeking capital flows in the form of direct or portfolio investment or by depleting forex reserves that have built up over the years. Now any changes in the capital account of the BoP, brought about particularly by autonomous capital flow, get reflected through changes either in the current account position or the reserve position.

The growing strength of India's BoP observed in the post-reform period since the crisis of 1991 continued despite the total current account deficit from US$ 2.5 billion (0.4% of GDP) in 2004-05 (Table 4.22) to US$ 9.7 billion, equivalent to 1.1 per cent of GDP, in 2006-07. With a burgeoning merchandise trade deficit, primarily on account of imports fuelled by high global crude oil prices and sustained demand for non-oil imports from a buoyant domestic industry, the reversal from current account surpluses witnessed between 2001-02 and 2003-04, to a current deficit in 2004-05 appears to be continuing into 2006-07 so far.. The widening trade deficit could be compensated by surpluses in net invisibles. The deficit in the current account has moderated the accumulation of forex reserves. Another consequence may likely to happen, as the literature shows that with large current account deficits, a country would in any time be put to highly vulnerable to speculative attacks.

4.9.5 Invisibles Trade

A noteworthy development in the country's balance of payments had been the improvement in the invisibles trade account since 1991. The deficit in the invisible account in 1990-91 was converted into surplus of about $ 1.6 billion in 1991-92

TABLE 4.22

Some Macroeconomic and External Sector Indicators

% to GDP	1990-91	1991-92	1992-93	1993-94	1994-95	1995-96	1996-97	1997-98	1998-99	1999-2000	2000-01	2001-02	2002-03	2003-04	2004-05
(1)	(2)	(3)	(4)	(5)	(6)	(7)	(8)	(9)	(10)	(11)	(12)	(13)	(14)	(15)	(16)
Total Investment	26.30	22.55	23.61	23.09	26.00	26.90	24.28	24.60	22.57	26.29	24.36	22.95	25.79	27.25	30.10
Private Corporate Investment	4.13	5.66	6.46	5.61	6.91	9.58	8.05	7.79	6.39	7.23	5.74	5.59	5.75	6.84	8.25
Current Account Balance	-3.05	-0.34	-1.71	-0.42	-1.05	-1.65	-1.19	-1.37	-0.96	-1.05	-0.6	0.7	1.3	2.3	-0.4
Capital Account Balance	2.27	1.46	1.59	3.54	2.84	1.31	2.96	2.47	2.01	2.48	2.11	1.80	2.13	3.43	4.62
FDI and FPI of Which :	0.03	0.05	0.23	1.52	1.59	1.38	1.59	1.31	0.58	1.16	1.48	1.70	1.18	2.67	2.09
FDI	0.03	0.05	0.13	0.21	0.41	0.60	0.73	0.87	0.59	0.48	0.88	1.28	0.99	0.78	0.80
FPI	0.00	0.00	0.10	1.30	1.19	0.77	0.86	0.44	-0.01	0.68	0.60	0.42	0.19	1.89	1.29
Reserve (increase +/ decrease -)	-0.40	1.43	0.33	3.18	1.44	-0.82	1.52	0.94	0.95	1.38	1.32	2.48	3.33	5.22	3.73
Net foreign exchange assets of RBI	1.40	2.88	3.03	5.98	7.38	6.24	6.93	7.61	7.92	8.56	9.44	11.57	14.50	17.55	19.73

Source : *RBI Hand Book of Statistics on Indian Economy*; 2003-04, GOI, *Economic Survey*, 2005-06.

and the invisibles amount remained in surplus in subsequent years. And this surplus from invisibles not only wiped out deficit in balance of trade, but also created a positive balance on current account. For example, in 2003-04, trade deficit was of the order US $ 13718 million, but the surplus from invisibles shot up to US $ 27801 million. As a result the BoP on current account became positive to the extent of US $ 14083 million (*Economic Survey*, 2006-07, p. S-71). The net invisibles comprising of non-factor services (like travel, transportation, software services, business services), investment income, and transfers, insurance and government transaction, have traditionally compensated to a large extent the trade deficit, and this trend continued in 2005-06 with a moderate current account deficit at 1.1 percent of GDP. As a proportion of GDP, invisibles (receipts) at 11.5 per cent of GDP in 2005-06 exhibited steady growth from a modest level of 2.4 per cent of GDP in 1990-91.

Within invisibles the contribution of different categories to overall invisible earnings has changed significantly since the early 1990s. Traditionally, private transfers, comprising mainly remittances from Indians working abroad, have been the main source of invisible earnings. Remittances are currently the second most important source of development finance at the global level after FDI. Also they are more stable than private capital flows such as portfolio investment and bank credit. The sustainability over time of remittances as a source of income, of course, depends on the cycle of migration and the expected flows of migration. They are also a source of foreign exchange: they support the consumption levels of low to middle income families and constitute a direct source for funding a small, community-oriented investment projects through the migrant's associations that send donations home in support of these projects. From a social point of view remittances can have a positive poverty-reducing effect. The properly mobilized remittances can contribute to increase investment in basic infrastructure such as water, roads, low-income housing, school-buildings, investment in human capital (education), and help to finance micro and small-scale firms. The pick in international tourism, another element of invisibles, observed in 2003-04, 2004-05 continued in 2005-06 and resulted in a net inflow of US$ 1.4 billion in 2005-06. Transportation (net) yielded modest sign with insurance receipts and payments more or less balancing each other and Government account yielding a modest outflow of US $ 197 million, the total net invisibles amounted to US $23.9 billion in 2005-06 for non-factor services. Net investment income continued to be negative since 1990-91, reflecting the servicing of cost of capital flows. Indeed, beginning from 1991-92 till 2001-02 (except 1999-2000), net private transfers always exceeded invisibles (net). However, since 2002-03, overall invisibles have been higher than private transfers, mainly due to rising contribution of non-factor services. As a proportion of total invisibles, the share of private transfers has declined from 121 percent in 1996-97 to around 65 percent in 2004-05, while that of non-factor services has improved from 7 percent to 45.5 percent during this period.

In a world of volatile capital flows, remittances are now a stabilizing component of external resources transfers to the developing world. Remittances to the developing countries have increased steadily from around US$ 15 billion in 1980 to US$ 80 billion in 2000. India continues to remain the highest remittance receiving country in the world, followed by China (US$ 21.3 billion), Mexico (US$ 18.1 billion), France (US$ 12.7 billion) and Philippines (US$ 11.6 billion). India's share in total global remittances of US$ 225.8 billion in 2004 was almost 10 percent (*Global Economic Prospects* 2006). Buoyant software services and private transfers in the form of remittance from Indians abroad have provided the highest contribution to receipts, apart from moderate contribution by travel, transportation, investment income and miscellaneous items had imparted strength and stability to net invisibles receipt in the Indian economy. Economic Survey rightly pointed out, "The main driver behind the current account surpluses, buoyant invisible flows, particularly private transfers comprising remittances, along with software services exports, have been instrumental in creating and sustaining current account surplus for India". As a consequence, invisible balance as a proportion of GDP increased from 3.1 percent in 2001-02 to 5.3 percent of GDP in 2005-06. Between 1991 and 2003-04, private transfers increased every year except in 1997-98 and 1998-99. In 2004-05, however, private transfer declined by 6.3 percent.

Invisible receipts and payments both rose sharply during 2005-06 and 2006-07 but the worrisome fact is that net invisible receipts are not large enough to offset the rising trade deficit (US$ 35.1 billion). Consequently India was back to its proverbial current deficit which widened from US $ 7.2 billion in 2005 to US $ 11.7 billion in 2006.

4.9.6 Capital Account

Capital account is that part of the BoP accounts that records payments and receipts arising from the import and export of long-term and short-term financial capital. Since 1990-91, India's capital account had experienced several interesting changes in terms of the relative roles played by different varieties of capital flows in augmenting the overall balance. Rising simultaneously with current account deficit barring some exceptions, there had been a widening of capital account surplus from US$ 8.401 billion in 1990-91 to US$ 19.458 billion in April-September 2005. Between 1998-99 and 2001-02, the share of foreign investment in the overall capital account balance had increased steadily from 29 per cent to 80 per cent. Since 2002-03, much of the strengthening of India's capital account had emanated from augmentation from non-debt creating foreign investment (net) inflows, particularly Foreign Institutional Investor (FII) inflows. Moreover, there had been an increase in inflows of commercial borrowings (CBs) and short-term credits. This debt-creating flow comprising external assistance, CBs and non-resident deposits were 19 percent of capital surplus. The cumulative impact of higher debt and non-debt creating flows was a notable cause to the expansion in the size of the capital account surplus. The expansion succeeded in retaining an overall surplus in the BoP and resulted in a net reserve accretion of US$ 6.5 billion during April-September 2005. This is the bright side of the picture. But the dark side is that foreign traders in the capital market may behave in an unpredictable way. For instance, if some foreign institutional investors turn hostile and take out a part of their financial investments from the Indian market, it would dramatically bring down the stock market and the external value of the rupee. Even worse, it might trigger of a panic among ordinary investors who would follow them to turn it into a full-fledged financial crisis.

4.9.7 Movement of Foreign Capital Towards India

The inflow of foreign capital has played a significant role in the development of the developing countries as well as developing developed East Asian countries. The foreign capital is sought for not only because it provides access to closely held technology and to global marketing linkage, but also as a preferred means of financing BoP deficits compared to external borrowing. The inflow of foreign capital to finance current account deficits can be beneficial to a country, if borrowing from abroad is used to finance capital formation in productive assets rather than consumption. Foreign capital can also be used to enhance export earnings in excess of debt-servicing requirements, or even for productive investment that does not generate foreign exchange. The reforms process, especially its emphasis of globalization, was intended to help the acceleration of the growth process by attracting larger doses of foreign capital. In that sense, globalization represented deeper integration in that international interactions became qualitatively transformed from exchange transactions to long term, multidimensional links. At the heart of this deeper integration is foreign direct investment (FDI). The other aspect of foreign capital in the form of buying shares (equity), with only motive of investment for relatively short-term gains, is foreign portfolio investment (FPI), consisting of foreign institutional investment (FII) flows, resources mobilized by Indian Companies through ADRs (American Depository Receipts) and GDRs (Global Depository Receipts) as well as offshore funds. Such type of flows into India mirror the robustness of capital markets and overall macroeconomic conditions.

Since portfolio investment displays and creates volatility in the domestic stock markets, and tends to be pro-cyclical, in the sense that it comes in when BoP position is seen to be strong and goes out when the BoP position is expected to weaken, thus accentuating the direction of movement of the BoP, both type of countries, developing as well as developing developed, often prefer FDI for its elements of stability. Other advantage of such investment is that its returns are closely linked to the performance of the real economy and is less volatile than FPI. Moreover, the orthodox and the most widespread view is that FDI triggers technological spillovers through the transfer of technology to a local affiliate or through technological spillover, assists human capital formation, contributes to international trade integration, and consequent specialization according to comparative advantage, helps create a more competitive business environment and enhances enterprise development. These are the indirect effects of FDI or spillovers from the MNCs that developing host countries, and especially their domestic firms, might benefit.from and which could encourage them to export more. One such spillover effect is where local firms can learn how to succeed in foreign markets simply by imitating the activities of local MNC affiliates. Moreover, local firms may also benefit indirectly from the pressures exercised by local MNC affiliates on the liberalization of trade. The local firms may therefore enjoy reduced trade barriers between their country and the developing world. There is also likely to be diffusion of skills by ex-MNCs employees. Employees who have been trained in export management by MNCs might decide to move to local companies and automatically take the acquired skills with them. Beyond this macroeconomic stimulus FDI influences growth by increasing total factor productivity, and more generally, the efficiency of resource use in the recipient country. That is why policy-makers have eased restrictions on inward FDI, and in many instances provided special incentives for inward investment. They hope that MNCs will bring in capital which will be available for local firms to borrow and realize their investment projects, and this will lead to strong and sustained growth. Moreover, the ability to exploit increasing returns to scale and the benefit the consumers of increased competition are also cited. But the critics argue that it is possible that MNCs can cause substantial current account deficits by importing more than exporting, and that since most developing countries already run such deficits, inward FDI can further worsen the host country's balance of trade. For example, transfer prices manipulated by MNCs for their foreign affiliates' exports and imports are a major reason for the constant increase in trade deficits of foreign firms. Foreign-owned firms import the majority of their raw materials, spare parts and components.

In the 1980s India warmed to market-opening policies. Until 1991 it counted heavily upon inward-looking and regulation-focused policies to spur economic development. A maze of restrictions shackled most private capital transactions, including FDI, portfolio equity investment, borrowing from foreign sources, non-resident deposits, short-term credit and investment in foreign countries. India, under the approving eye of the IMF, liberalized capital flows to fix balance of payment problems on the logic that initial inflow of capital would be recorded as a credit in the country's capital account, as it would bring in foreign exchange. Second, if the FDI inflows replace imports, for example an MNC decides to undertake FDI in a country to which it exported previously, this would certainly benefit the country's current account. Third, the FDI would be motivated by a lower cost of production in the country ('export-oriented affiliates'), which will improve the country's current account.

Prior to 1991, foreign investment had played a very limited and somewhat timid role in India's economy. It was permitted in industries where foreign technology was deemed necessary for economic growth. Foreign equity participation was tightly regulated to a limit of 40 per cent total equity capital. The restrictions on equity participation, the technology requirement and the existing industrial licensing regime tended to dampen the climate for FDI. In fact, India lacked any interest in welcoming foreigners. Jagdish Bhagwati described India's policies from the 1960s to the 1980s as "three decades of illiberal and autarkic policies" in other words, the government sat hard on the market and did its best to prevent trade and investment flows, without being encouraged by, and some would say pressurized by, institutions such as the IMF, the World Bank and the WTO, as well as not following the China's plan to create "special economic zones", where the normal rules of the economy would not apply to foreign investors. Historically speaking, the United States, the United Kingdom, France, Germany, Japan, Korea and Taiwan did not use liberal FDI policies before they became rich. In fact, the policies followed by a number of East Asian economies were strategic rather than liberal. This means that they followed liberal policies for some sectors but highly protective ones for others. So a cautious approach should be followed because globalization, in the sense of integrating with the world commodity and capital markets, in general, and FDI in particular, could not be useful to developing countries in their effort to develop and they are therefore advised by many to adopt a strategic approach in formulating policies regarding international trade and FDI.

The Government policy on FDI since 1991 had aimed at encouraging foreign investment, particularly in the core and infrastructure sector on the firm conviction that FDI would make up not only for deficiencies in the availability of saving and foreign exchange—which is true of all external flows-but also for weaknesses in domestic entrepreneurial capacity. In July 1991, providing a window of automatic approval of FDI, India consented to 51 percent direct foreign investment equity in 34 priority industries, which had latter extended to 48 sectors. India also opened equity markets such as stock and shares to foreign portfolio investment (FPI). Cases requiring prior Government approval were considered by the Foreign Investment Approval Board (FIPB) which was set-up to process applications for cases not covered by automatic approval in a time bound and transparent manner. Several additional measures were undertaken during 1992-93 to encourage investment flows including FDI, portfolio investment, NRI investment and deposits and investment in Global Depository Receipts (GDRs). A KPMG study states that Canadian executive see India emerging as a land of opportunities. A recent Confidence Survey by global Consultancy A.T. Kearney rated India as second most favored FDI destination, next only to China and USA. FDI inflow in China, mainly through joint ventures with partners from western economies reached a record $52.7 billion in 2002, followed by $53.5 billion in 2003. Inward FDI stock had rapidly risen from virtually nil in 1980 to 35.6 per cent of GDP in 2003. FDI into China (and many other East Asian countries) was driven by capital-intensive manufacturing. According to World Investment Report of 2004 of UNTACD, net FDI inflow to India had shown a rise to reach US $4.7 billion particularly in 2005-06 after a decline in the period from 1990-91 to 2004-05, except the year 2001-02

(Table 4.23). Both inward and outward investment showed signs of a pick up. India's share in global FDI was 5.9 per cent in 2004. Sector wise FDI inflows from August 1991 until Nov 2004 indicates that the highest share of FDI inflows had gone to the data-processing software and consultancy services, followed by pharmaceutical and automobile industry.

Regarding FDI approvals what we can say is that total approvals for FDI have increased from $ 527 million in 1991-92 to $ 1475 million in 2004-05, reaching the peak in 1996-97 to the tune of $ 11,484 million. Actual inflows were of course much lower. This continued upto 2000-01, reflecting the lag between approvals and inflows, but thereafter upto 2004-05 inflows were little higher than the total approvals. The total actual inflows had increased from a negligible level oh $ 165 million in 1991-92 to $ 2549 million in 2004-05. As per the latest available figures, the cumulative amount of FDI approvals accorded till November 2005 was US $ 69,001 million. This change in foreign investment environment in India was reflected in the fact that a large number of Indian companies had sought foreign joint venture partners while major foreign investors had focused on India for the first time. Investors are now showing their growing confidence in the prospects of the Indian economy. Government has put a liberal and investor-friendly FDI policy, wherein FDI upto hundred percent is now allowed under automatic route for most of the sectors/activities, where the investor does not require any prior approval. Only notification of the RBI within 30 days of inward remittance or issue of shares to non residence is required.

The Indian economy was also opened to foreign portfolio investment (FPI) in two ways. In 1993 foreign institutional investments (FIIs) meeting certain minimum standards were allowed to invest in India's equity and also in debt instrument s through secondary market purchases in the stock markets. Between 1993-94 and 2004-05, the number of FIIs registered in India increased from 3 to 685. And the number of FIIs registered with the Securities and Exchange Board of India (SEBI) increased from 685 at the end of financial year 2005 to a record high of 823 by October 2006. FIIs registered with SEBI are of two types: regular FIIs and Debt Fund FIIs, the latter was permitted to invest only in debt instruments. Indian companies meanwhile

TABLE 4.23
Foreign Investment Inflows in India

(in Million US $)

Items	*1990-91*	*1998-99*	*1999-00*	*2000-01*	*2001-02*	*2002-03*	*2003-04*	*2004-05*	*2005-06*	*2006-07*
(1)	*(2)*	*(3)*	*(4)*	*(5)*	*(6)*	*(7)*	*(8)*	*(9)*	*(10)*	*(11)*
Net Foreign Investment of which :	103	2312	5117	5862	6686	4161	13744	13000	15528	15541
FDI (Net)	97	2380	2093	3272	4734	3217	2388	3713	3034	8479
FIIs	0	-390	2135	1847	1505	377	10918	8662	9926	4529
FPI (Net)	6	-68	3024	2590	1952	944	11356	9287	12494	7062
Euro Equities and others	6	322	889	743	447	567	438	625	2568	3800

Source : *Economic Survey*, 2007-08.

Fig. 4.3
Trade Openness Since 1991-92

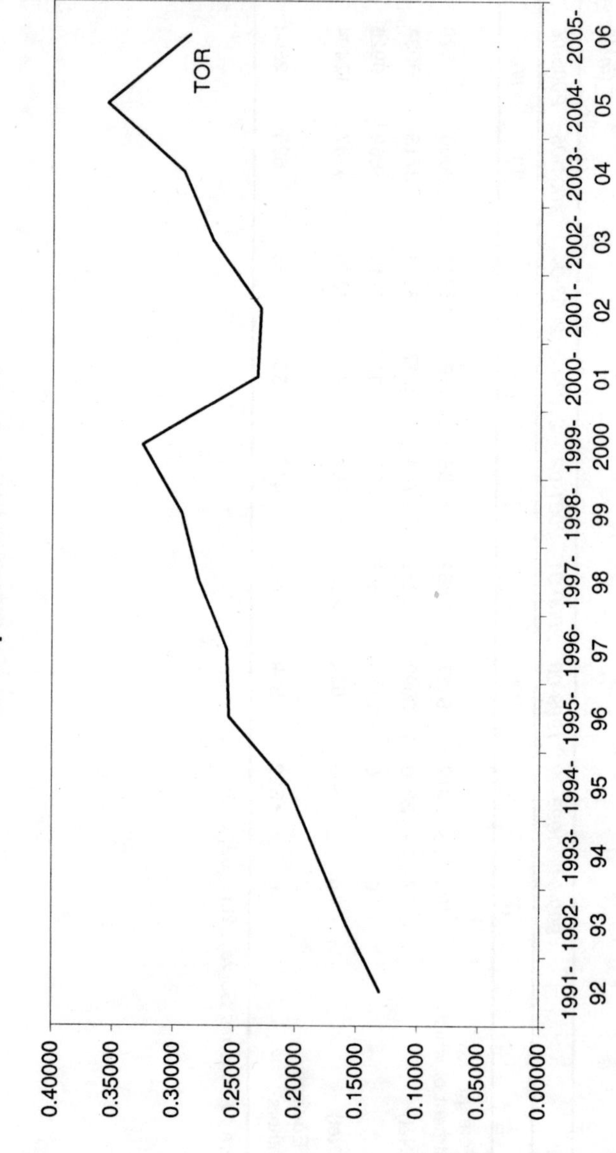

were permitted to raise equity capital from overseas capital market through the mechanism of Global Depository Receipts (GDRs) and Foreign Currency Convertible Bonds (FCCBs). They were also permitted to invest overseas through the ODI (Overseas Direct Investment) except in real estate or banking. This enabled Indian companies to raise resources from passive investors in world markets. However, FPI, with NRI deposits being an important source of such funds had expanded rapidly in the post reform period. From a level of $ 4 million in 1991-92, the inflow on the account of FII flows and GDRS taken together quickly increased to $ 3567 million, and fluctuated hereafter. It declined to $ 1828 million in 1997-98 reflecting the effect of the Asian Currency Crisis on capital flows to emerging markets. It is interesting to note that inflows of portfolio capital had fluctuated since the reform period till 1997-98, but they did not turn negative even in 1997-98 during the East Asian Crisis. They turned negative during 1998-99; thereafter net portfolio inflows increased from $ 3026 million in 1999-00 to a record high of $ 12,492 million in 2005-06 with inflows at US $ 68.1 billion and outflows at US $ 55.6 billion. GDRs/ADRs and others, which are a part of the portfolio flows rose. The impressive performance of FPI in 2005-06 was on the account of rapid influx of FIIs inflows driven by a healthy bullish sentiments prevailing in the Indian stock markets. Inflows under various deposits schemes for NRI played a significant role in bolstering overall banking capital and capital surplus since 2001-02.

In 1992 India's company obtained permission to issue equity abroad. Control on external borrowing lightened up without going away. Within the ranks of developing countries India, even after these reforms, stood low on the ladder of economic openness according to mid-1990s data. *(Karl Habermeier,* 2000). Moreover, while the magnitudes of foreign capital inflows in India have recorded impressive growth, they are still at a low level compared to the country's potential. China alone had been absorbing more than $30 billion of FDI every year. In 2005, China and Hong Kong managed to attract over 40 per cent of all the FDI into the world's developing countries. India, being the other Asian giant, attracted a little over 2 per cent. However, the policy reforms had enabled the country to widen the sectoral as well as the source country composition of FDI inflows. The bulk of the new inflows had come in the energy and service sectors. To attract export-oriented policy, liberalization policies aided by active negotiations and bargaining with MNEs would yield fruitful results on this front. Total foreign investment in the BoP including portfolio investment increased from $101 million in 1990-91 to $7411 million in 2005-06 (April-September), peaking at $ 13744 in 2003-04. Table 4.23 shows the pattern of these flows. Net FDI flows, after reaching a peak of $4,734 million, in 2001-02, declined to $2304 million in 2005-06 (April-September). Between1991 to 1996, FDI increased at nearly 100 per cent per year.

Foreign Institutional Investment (FII) inflows increased form a mere of $2135 million in 1999-00, reached their peak of $10918 million in 2003-04 and declined to $9926 million in 2005-06. The year 1998-99 witnessed FII flows to record a negative of $390 million. Since FIIs are still subject to a number of regulations and controls, the government appointed a committee in 2002 and an Expert Group in 2004 in order to suggest measures for liberalizing FII without making the capital market vulnerable. But the Expert Group views on the investment enhancing the role of FII are imbibed with limitations. They do not consider the linkages of the capital inflows and domestic economic activities and on the expansion of infrastructural facilities. Their suggestions are however based on piecemeal basis, not on sound macro-economic perspectives.

Permission to access the international market enabled Indian companies to raise Euro Equities and others from merely $5 million in 1990-91 to $880 million in 2005-06 (April-September) through GDRs and Foreign Currency Convertible Bonds (FCCBs). All forms of capital flows excluding portfolio flows and short-term credits still accounted for around 6 per cent of total capital flows in 2004-05.

To sum up, since 1991, the regulatory framework for capital inflows in India has been significantly liberalized particularly for FDI and FPIs (mostly FIIs). Excepting six prohibited sectors, the government has permitted access to the automatic route for FDI in most sectors. In certain sectors like insurance, banking, telecom, oil refining, the FDI limit is below 50 per cent. Between 1990-91 and 2005-06, cumulative FDI in India amounted to US $42519 million.

Indonesia, Korea, Thailand and Malaysia liberalized capital flows before India and scored livelier growth. Based upon 1994-98 data, a small country Malaysia was one of the most open economies in the world. Exports plus imports added up to over 175 percent of Malaysian GDP. Running a distant second by this measure went the Philippines, where exports plus imports equaled 90 percent of GDP. This trade orientation ratio (TOR) as widely used indicator of openness being the proportion of import and export of goods and services to GDP fell below 25 percent for the United States. India, Japan, Argentina and Brazil. Figure 4.3 shows that since 1991-92, there seems to be an accelerating tendency for the TOR for India, thus reflecting the response of the growth process of the economy to regime shifts in trade and payments policies towards greater globalization and liberalization, although there is some periodic fluctuation in the trend.

Tariff levels are other indicators of trade openness. Prior to 1991, India's import tariff structure was among the highest in the world, with duty rates above 200 percent being fairly common. Significant progress, though is still incomplete has been made in reducing tariff rates since then, to create a more open economy and for congenial atmosphere for Indian firms as Indian firms in that case will be pushed to restructure their operations to become more competitive. The Chelliah Committee (1992) proposed that import-weighted average duty rate should go down from 87 percent in 1989-90 to 45 percent in 1995-95 and further to 25 percent by 1998-99 [(GoI), *Tax Reforms Committee,* 1991 and 1993)]. India has lowered its average applied tariff rate from 125 percent in 1990-91 to 71 percent in 1993-94, 41 percent in 1995-96 and to 35 percent in 1997-98.

The corresponding reduction in the import weighted average tariff rate for all products has gone down from 87 percent in 1990-91 to 47 percent in 1993-94, 25.9 percent in 1995-96 and 25.4 percent in 1997-98, 29.2 in 1989-99 and 35.1 percent in 2001-02, thus moving ahead of Chellaih Committee's recommendations. The pick rate of custom tariff has declined from 300 percent in 1990-91 to 40 per cent in 1997-98 and to 35 percent in 2001-02. The peak rate of custom tariff was brought down to 20 per cent in January 2004 and further down to 15 per cent in February 2005. As a commitment, India is supposed to bring the tariff level between 12 per cent to 7 percent in the years to come. In fact, Indian industry has been able to adjust large tariff reductions and successful to survive foreign competition. Reduced tariff on inputs obviously helped domestic industry to become more competitive.

Table 4.24 shows the progressive decline in the average tariff rates. Besides India has also undertaken a major commitment to liberalize its trade regime under WTO Agreement. Tariff rates on most of the commodities have been brought well below the bound rates by 1998-99 except for 40 commodities. As tariff increase is not permissible; India has been using NTBs permissible under the WTO framework to

Table 4.24

Custom Tariff Structure of India

	Maximum Tariff Rate (%)	*Average Weighted Tariff rate (weighted by 1992/93 import values)*
1990-91	300.0	87.0
1991-92	150.0	72.5
1992-93	170.0	60.6
1993-94	85.0	47.0
1994-95	65.0	38.2
1995-96	50.0	25.9
1997-98	40.0	25.4
1998-99	45.0	29.2
1999-2000	40.0	31.4
2000-01	38.5	—
2001-02	35.0	35.7
January 04	20.0	35.1
February 05	15.0	30.0
2007-08	10.0	27.0

Note : Tariff averages consider only those tariff lines with *ad-valorem.*

Source : *Trade Policy Review: India* (various issues).

protect the domestic producers. The non-tariff barriers (NTBs) on the remaining items are being phased out by March 2001. India has unilaterally removed all quantitative restriction on imports of around 2300 items from SAARC countries in August, 1998 in order to give a boost to trade liberalization in the region.

In what follows, while India's weighted mean tariff has come down substantially, but they are much higher than the other developing developed countries, where tariff rates typically range between 5 to 15 percent. Though the government vociferously gave a broad indication that tariff rates would be reduced to bring them in line with East Asian Countries within few years, it is three times still high compared with many other countries like Japan, EU, Singapore, Hong Kong and the economy continued to remain protected by quantitative restrictions (QRs) on consumer goods. This created incentives for misuse of export subsidies since rent seeking behavior continues to be an attractive option. India does not provide direct subsidies to exporters but relies on a wide range of indirect subsidies, including duty and tax concessions, export finance, export promotion and marketing assistance. Thus the process of reducing tariff levels clearly leads to continue to complete the reform process in this area.

4.9.8 Foreign Exchange Reserves

Most of the countries have adopted the definition of foreign exchange reserves as suggested by the IMF (*BoP Manual and Guidelines on Foreign Exchange Reserve Management,* 2001), which defines reserves as external assets that are readily available to and controlled by monetary authorities for direct financing of external payments imbalances, for indirectly regulating the magnitude of such imbalances through intervention in exchange markets to affect the currency exchange rate, and/or for other purposes.

The foreign exchange reserve of any country acts, in fact, as a cushion to withstand any jolt to a sudden rise of imports or fall in exports. In the absence of adequate reserves, payments for imports or on other counts, as and when they become due, may become difficult. The country may thus be starved of timely imports, which can cause serious disruptions in the domestic economy. Even in a flexible exchange rate regime, there arises the need for holding reserves so that the central bank can prevent sharp, short-term changes in the rate. It also provides the country with the necessary international liquidity, often creates confidence to the policy-makers to initiate any long-run decisions. A country is in need of it in order to install confidence in the international community, meet debt servicing obligations as well as to handle the short term capital flows, also to smoothen the seasonal volatility in the foreign exchange transaction and to counter speculative attacks on the currency. An important means of promoting investors' confidence and averting currency turmoils is the holding of large foreign exchange reserves by the central bank: not only can it then repel sporadic, probing forays by speculators to test the currency's strength, but also the knowledge of such reserves itself acts as a deterrent to attacks.

The movements in foreign exchange reserves is, in fact is the net result of all external transactions. They therefore, provide a summary statement of the state of the country's BoP. A developing country like India has already accumulated a hefty amount of forex reserve in the post-reform period. A question that is now uppermost in the minds of observers of the Indian scene is whether India would be able to handle this large amount of reserves properly in its onward march to strengthen the economy without any adverse effects on it. It needs to be explained in the present context. The explanation is divided into two sub-sections. First of all, we highlight a prudent policy for managements of forex reserves. Thereafter, the question like whether the expanding forex reserves in India represent improvement in its economic strength, or the present level of reserve is consistent with the overall macroeconomic management of the country, is addressed.

A. A Brief History of India's Foreign Exchange Reserves

Foreign exchange reserve positions change dramatically after the launch of the structural program. The Table 4.25 clearly shows the stupendous rate at which the foreign exchange reserves of the country have increased. From US $ 5831 million in 1990-91 it has gone up to US $ 42281 million in 2000-01 at the compound annual growth rate of 33%. The foreign currency assets have increased from US$ 2236 million in 1990-91 to US $ 160,669 million in 2006-07 (upto October). The country is now sitting pretty with sufficient foreign exchange reserves on stock basis (worth US $ 290.9 billion at the end of February 8, 2008) to finance more than 13 months of import bills compared to a horrifying import cover ratio of one month at the time of BoP crisis in 1990-91. All the criteria for defining a given reserve as sufficient are being achieved despite umpteen elections, coalitions, hung parliaments and governments. A number of factors explain this rapid increase in the foreign exchange reserves of the country.

- Impressive performance of exports and buoyancy in invisible receipts have become the driving force towards building of reserves of this order. Correspondingly to the increase in reserves, the import cover by foreign currency assets has arisen from 1.0 month of imports in 1990-91 to a very comfortable level of mostly 14 months of imports in 2005-06. Forex reserves on February 2, 2007 provided an import cover of about 11 months (*Economic Survey,* 2006-07).
- The institution of market determined exchange reserves system has led to a massive inflow. In the absence of demand for foreign exchange market, the RBI to build reserves has bought the surplus inflows.
- There has been a surge in non-debt creating foreign investment inflows especially inflow through FDI. Before the reform measure FDI in the country was almost non-existent but the facilities provided to the foreign capital and the investment climate in the country have attracted FDI thereby adding to the foreign exchange reserves of the country. Thus foreign investment inflows become instrumental behind such a good build-up.
- The country has also received foreign exchange through increased flow (in absolute terms) of debt-creating inflows like external commercial borrowing, external assistance and short-term credit. Table 4.27 on

BoP for the country between 1990-92 and 2004-05 clearly reveals this.

B. *Policy for Management of Foreign Exchange Reserves in India*

The unprecedented high level of reserves, with the prospect of continued growth and accretion, has raised issues relating to the management of foreign exchange reserves. In the light of the volatility induced by capital flows, there is now a growing consensus for emerging developing countries to maintain adequate foreign exchange reserves. How much to be preserved and adequate is still an open question. India's approach to reserve management, until the BoP crisis in 1991 was essentially based on the traditional approach for maintaining an appropriate level of imports equivalent to reserves. The emphasis on import cover constituted the primary concern till 1993-94. The approach to reserve management, as part of the exchange rate management underwent a paradigm shift with the recommendation of the High Level Committee on BoP (Chairman Dr. C. Rangarajan). It is now increasingly being felt that reserves should be adequate to cover likely variations in capital flows.

In India, the adequacy of foreign exchange reserves has to be viewed in the context of many factors, including trade and payments regime, the type of short-term debt and various type of capital flows imbibed with latter's size, composition and risk profiles as well as types of external shocks to which the economy is vulnerable—as also the currency in circulation and the extent of current and capital account liberalization. The High Level Committee on BoP suggested that while determining the adequacy of reserves, due attention should be paid to the payments obligations in addition to the traditional measure of import cover of three to four months. The Committee recommended that the foreign exchange reserves targets be fixed in such a way that they are generally in a position to accommodate imports of three months (Paragraph 6.3). In view of the Committee, the factors that are to be taken into consideration in determining the desirable level of reserves are the need to ensure a reasonable level of confidence in the international financial and trading communities about the capacity of the country to honour its obligations and maintain trade and financial flows; the need to take care of the seasonal factors in any BoP transactions with respect to the possible uncertainties in the monsoon conditions of India; the amount of foreign currency reserves required to counter speculative tendencies or anticipatory actions amongst players in the forex exchange market; and the capacity to maintain the reserves so that the cost of carrying liquidity is minimal (Paragraph 6.4). In 1997, the Report of Committee on Capital Account Convertibility under the Chairmanship of S.S. Tarapore also suggested four alternative measures of reserve adequacy which in addition to traditional trade-based indicators, viz. import cover of reserves, also included money-based and debt-based.

It is true that India cannot go forward with a mere frugal measure of US $ 5-8 billion in 1990-91. The things are now altogether changed. India has stepped into the globalization era and has come a long way from the situation prevailing upto 1991. It should act, act in the living present. Before India, now there are large debt service payments and leads and lags, short-term debt and there is the existence of relatively large portfolio flows and, therefore, it is essential to hold larger reserves; otherwise, if short-term liabilities like debt and portfolio stock anyhow flow out of India, the country would lose 70 percent of its reserves. And then this inadequate balance of reserve would be of no use to meet other needs and requirements. Given the extent of short-term debt and portfolio flows, India's present level of reserves comprising foreign currency assets, gold, SDRs and the reserve position with the IMF of US $180.0 billion as on February 2, 2007 is not usually high as compared with those of other countries like China, Taiwan, Hong Kong, Singapore, South Korea, Brazil, Mexico and Argentina.

One way of assessing of reserve adequacy is based on a 'Liquidity at Risk' rule that takes into account the foreseeable risks that a country could face. This approach requires that a country's foreign exchange liquidity position could be calculated under a range of possible outcomes for relevant financial variables, such as exchange rates, commodity prices, credit spreads, etc.

The other one of assessing adequacy of reserves is to track the net-foreign exchange assets-currency ratio (NFA-C ratio).

TABLE 4.25
India's Foreign Exchange Reserves

(US $ million)

Years	*Gold Holding of the RBI*	*RTP*	*SDRs*	*Foreign Currency assets held by the RBI in major convertible currencies*	*Forex Reserves*	*Import Cover (No. of months)*
1990-91	3496		102	2236	5834	0.8
1991-92	3499		90	5631	9220	2.3
1992-93	3380		18	6434	9832	2.5
1993-94	4078		108	15068	19254	5.4
1994-95	4370		7	20809	25186	5.7
1995-96	4561		82	17044	21687	6
1996-97	4054		2	22367	26423	6.5
1997-98	3391		1	25975	29367	6.9
1998-99	2960		8	29522	32490	8.2
1999-2000	2974		4	35058	38036	8.2
2000-01	2725		2	39554	42281	8.6
2001-02	3047		10	51049	54106	9.6
2002-03	3534	672	4	71890	75428*	12
2003-04	4198	1311	2	107448	112959*	12.2
2004-05	4500	1438	5	135571	141514*	13
2005-06	5755	756	3	145108	151622*	13.2
2006-07	6784	469	2	191924	199179*	13.6

*Includes Reserve Tranche Position (RTP) in IMF.

Source : *Economic Survey*, Government of India, Various Issues.

The present NFA-C ratio is 87 percent. That implies that forex reserve are now sizeable in relation to the currency with the public and this ratio has been rising steadily over the past several years, indicating thereby that this gives a great degree of comfort to the foreign portfolio investors and the authorities. Obviously if there happens currency expansion, this ratio would start falling and a sharp falling ratio would eventually transmit a warning signal to the foreign investors. Experts articulate that if this ratio falls below 40 percent, which is a Plimsoll line, it would be wise decisions for foreign investors to exit. Now the time has come for RBI to look into this ratio, hitherto neglected, into its monitoring systems.

Another way of assessing adequacy of reserves is to observe the reserve-liabilities ratio and to follow Guidotti Rule. The rule recommends that reserves should be adequate to cover one year's imports and capital flow requirement, that is to say, the reserve, as according to Pablo Guidotti, the former Deputy Minister of Argentina, should be sufficient for the country to live without additional foreign borrowing for one year. Taking a similar view, Alan Greenspan (1990) proposed short-term debt by remaining maturity of one year as the yardstick to measure reserve adequacy. He further extended Guidotti Rule in terms of two aspects: (i) average maturity of external debt should be three years and above; and (ii) countries must maintain liquidity at risk. Thus, the reserve should not only be able to finance the difference between the expected imports and exports but also to be sufficient to meet with the external amortization due in the next one year. On the basis of Guidotti and Greenspan Rule, India would probably need somewhat more reserves to maintain the foreign exchange rate at the desired level as well as to face volatile flows like net portfolio, non-resident repatriable deposits as well as requirements of debt servicing and the threat of impending capital flight, if any. It is a hope that India's net international investment position, that is the stock of external assets net of external liabilities, due to its hefty stock of international reserves, now the fifth largest stock of reserves in the world, which can finance about 14 months of imports, has improved.

C. Foreign Exchange Reserves and Its Implications to the Present Context

India's total foreign exchange reserves (including gold, SDRs and Reserve Tranche position (RTP) in IMF and foreign currency assets) have increased from US $5.834 billion (excluding RTP) during 1990-91 to US $ 151.6 billion during 2005-06 and to US $ 199.17 billion during 2006-07. The stock of forex reserve has reached US $ 273.5 billion at the end of

November, 2007 providing an import cover of over 13 months. Since 1991-92, India has also made significant progress in all the reserve adequacy indicators, like import adequacy (measured in terms of number of months of imports that can be financed by the reserves held by the country), debt adequacy (measured by the ratio of reserves to total external debt and short-term debt, that is, it is the ability of reserves to cover particularly short-term debt liabilities,) and monetary adequacy measured by the ratio of reserves to broad money (M3) and reserve money (Mo) For example, the import cover of reserves has increased from 2.3 months in 1991-92 to almost 14 months in 2006-07.

The fast accumulation of reserves in the Indian economy has drawn attention to the sources of reserve accretion. A recent study conducted by the RBI identifies capital flows as the largest contributor to growth of reserves during the period 1991-92 to end December 2003-04. Current account surplus during the period 2001-02 to 2003-04 as well as valuation gains arising from a steady appreciation of the Euro and Pound Sterling against US dollar, have also contributed significantly to growth of reserves, though during 2005-06, with the US dollar appreciating *vis-a-vis* other major currencies, there is a valuation loss of US 5.0 billion on the existing stock of India's forex reserves, with a simultaneous valuation gain of US $ 5.1 billion on the existing stock in the first half of 2006-07 with other major currencies appreciating *vis-a-vis* the US dollar.

Now the question crops up whether these expanding forex reserves always represent improvement in the economic strength of the country like India or they help in its economic development. The answer is that expanding forex reserve always do not represent improvement in economic strength nor do always stand for macroeconomic stability as is exemplified in the case of Indian economy.

There is as yet no room for complacency as the bulk (i.e., 61 per cent) of these reserves comprise of short-term debt and portfolio investments (such as FIIs investments driven by the heavily bullish sentiments prevailing in the Indian stock market). The East Asian crisis of mid-1997 portrayed these resources as highly volatile in nature.

The high growth of reserves has raised now the questions of an "optimum" level of reserves and the possible implications of the reserve built-up on an overall macroeconomic management. Earlier it was thought that the reserve must approximate about three month's equivalent of imports. This is because imports may be essential while exports depend not only on the country's ability to export but also on the demand for them from the rest of the world, which can hardly be assured. The impact of reserves on macroeconomic management deserves serious attention. First of all, high reserve can lead to rising domestic prices and inflationary pressures in the economy. *(Rakshit, 2005)*. On the other, there is a cost to them as well. These reserves are practically income barren, but they have high opportunity cost (defined as the marginal product of the available alternative investment) for they could be used to repay costly external debts and/or to upgrade infrastructure etc. All available evidence suggests that these high opportunity costs have exceeded the gains from reserve accretion, especially since 1998. Further, critics argue that huge accumulation of reserves has additional macro-economic cost arising out of a sterilization of capital flows. Also, accumulating of large volume of reserves creates moral hazards and reflects insurance against weak domestic fundamentals and political uncertainty. For this reason, many economists are already complaining of "excess reserves". For example, the forex reserves stood at $ 80.9 billion in June 2003. Of this, $29.8 billion were held in foreign securities, $36.9 billion as deposits with other central banks and the remaining $14.2 billion as deposits with foreign commercial banks. Obviously the average returns on these must have been less than the average cost of our external borrowings.

If we look at the various aspects of international transactions which result in increase/decrease in forex reserve particularly since 2000-01 (Table 4.26), we find that on trade account, India is facing a regular deficit during this period. It had also faced regular deficit since the 1990s. This indicates that the Indian importers of commodities have spent more than Indian exporters have earned. So far as service exports and imports are concerned, India is on better footing. If the current account deficit is considered, it is seen that expenditure has always been more than earnings, except during 2001-02 to 2003-04. Therefore, it is clear that India's forex reserves are not expanding on the strength of India's forex earnings. In what

TABLE 4.26
India's External Payments Position

(US $ Billion)

Items	*2004-05*	*2003-04*	*2002-03*	*2001-02*	*2000-01*
Merchandise Exports	45.5	44.7	53.8	64.7	80.8
Merchandise Imports	57.9	56.2	64.5	80.2	119.0
Trade Balance	-12.4	-11.5	-10.7	-15.5	-38.2
Net Invisibles Trade	31.7	26.0	17.0	15.0	9.8
Current Account Balance	-6.4	10.6	6.3	3.4	-2.7
Capital Account Balance	32.2	20.5	10.8	8.6	8.8
Foreign Investment (Net)	11.9	14.8	4.2	6.7	5.9
Banking Capital (Net)	4.0	6.2	10.4	2.9	-2.0
Short-term Credit (Net)	3.8	1.4	1.0	0.8	0.6
External Assistance (Net)	1.9	-2.7	-3.1	1.1	0.4
External Commercial Borrowings (Net)	5.9	-1.5	-1.7	-1.6	4.3
Other items in capital Account (Net)	4.6	2.4	0.1	0.3	-0.3
Foreign Exchange Reserves	141.5	113.0	76.1	54.1	42.3

Source : Reserve Bank of India.

follows, India at one hand, is facing large deficit on trade as well as on current account; on the other hand, her forex reserves are increasing. The answer lies in the capital account of India's BoP, consisting of foreign investment, borrowing, debt servicing and IMF transactions. The foreign investment inflows have increased India's forex reserves but it may result in steady outflow by means of remittance of profits, fees, royalty, etc. Due to foreign assistance, commercial loans and net banking transactions to foreign currency to India, forex reserves are also going up. These have also increased additional liability on the Indian economy.

While the high level of forex reserves held by India at present termed by RBI and experts as comfortable in terms of all the commonly applied adequacy indicators pointed out at the outset, it is also important to reflect upon the cost of holding reserves, though it is true that sufficient stock of forex reserve is preventive from fortuitous speculative attacks mainly from the private traders. It is also equally true that the high levels of reserve management indicators reflect to some extent, the slack in capacity of the economy to absorb foreign savings. In other words, the import and investments absorption capacity of the economy has not expanded to make use of foreign currency assets. Two issues are significant in this respect. There are the returns earned from deploying the reserves in various securities *vis-a-vis* the interest paid on external debt and the costs of building-up reserves through sustained open market operations. While the first issue entails the direct economic costs of holding reserves, the second, apart from involving costs of intermediation for the banking system, includes the consequences of prolonged sterilization on domestic money supply and price levels. It may be through that Central Bank intervention to maintain a stable exchange rate by holding reserves such as is happening in India, can solve the problem. Actually it is not. As a matter of fact, forex reserve with the central Bank typically earns very little interest, no more than 1 to 2 per cent, for instance, in the case of India. On the other hand, the finance capital which comes into the country earns rates of return (including capital gains) which are quite hefty (which after all is the reason for its flowing in). India in other words is borrowing from abroad at high rates and using the funds to earn low rates, which is indefensible. The maintenance of large forex reserves therefore entails a loss for the country. *(Patnaik, 2003).*

We must not forget that today the volume of private trade in foreign exchange is a staggering daily volume of some 1.2 trillion (i.e. 10^{12}) dollars. The daily volume of private trade in foreign exchange can easily overwhelm the forex reserve of any central bank. This predominance of private finance capital has become by far the single defining characteristic of the modern phase of globalization *(Bhaduri, 2005).*

Therefore fear now looms large in that a sudden bout of speculative capital inflow may perpetuate de-industrialization on an economy like India. Since the purpose of economics is to bring about an improvement in the lives of the people, voices must be raised to re-activation of public investment, together with some capital control.

It is true that India has accumulated the fifth largest stock of international reserves in the world. And India is now heading towards capital account convertibility. It is noteworthy that for the first time in the current year 2005-06, capital inflows are not augmenting RBI's holding of forex reserves, but they have been fully utilized for financing the investment-saving gap. These developments have no doubt raised the possibility of productive use of forex reserves. It is also noteworthy that, judged by the amount of reserves in relation to imports, short-term debt and non-debt liabilities, and by other usual criteria mentioned, India's external shock absorptive capacity has improved dramatically in recent years and the country now ranks among the top group of developing economies in terms of her ability to counter speculative attacks on her currency.

The objectives of reserve management in India should be to preserve the long-term value of the reserves in terms of purchasing power and to minimize risk and volatility in returns.

4.9.9 External Debt

Indian Economy in the 1990s and beyond is a queer blend of successes as well as failures. On the one hand, the economy since the economic reforms in 1991 has been successfully launched onto a high growth trajectory and has registered an improvement in a number of macroeconomic indicators, while at the same time it brought to the fore a number of challenges relating to sustainable trade position, the strategies to promote capital flows in line with internal and external balance, keeping in view their implications for exchange rate and sustainability of external debt[9]. Here we shall focus only on the magnitude of India's external debt and its evolve over the 1990s and beyond.

There is no denying the fact the gap between the investment and savings as well as the import-export gap may be well managed by the inflow of sufficient amount of external assistance and foreign borrowings, conducive to the process of development by properly utilizing borrowed funds to have a desired rate of growth of output and the warranted rate of investment in the borrowing country.[10] For that, development process must be well-knitted to service the past loans in such an efficient manner so that in due course indebtedness begins to subside and after some time it disappears. As ill luck would have it, in many cases it is usually found in a large number of countries that the administrative machinery of the borrowed country is too weak to handle properly with the borrowed funds, resulting in heavy borrowing to service past loans. This increases the debt burden further impinging on the very process of development (*Sharan, 1998*). It is well known that the thrust of the external sector reform in India in the 1990s and beyond had been mainly on reducing this debt burden.

This on the above backdrop endeavours to identify the factors that led to the growth in India's external indebtedness during the late 1980s, 1990s, and beyond and to mention dispassionately what had been done meanwhile to arrest the growth in the quantum of external debt by different policy prescriptions taken by its government, also to find an answer to the question : are we out of the danger from the clutches external debt yet ?

A. India's External Debt Burden

One of the underlying causes of the 1991 balance of payments (BoP) crisis was the rapid growth in external indebtedness in the latter half of the 1980s and the associated deterioration in the key external debt indicators. In terms of indebtedness classification, the situation was so worse in the early 1990s that Global Development Finance, 2001, World Bank did not hesitate to say that India was close to severely indebted category. In terms of the absolute level of debt, India's position was third as largest indebtor after Brazil and Mexico in 1991. At that time, India's total external debt was US $ 83.8 billion. The reasons for increasing external indebtedness were : governmental resort to large scale borrowing from abroad to cover the high level of fiscal deficits during the 1980s, thus causing greater indebtedness, the growing size of the current account deficit after the second and third oil shock that forced the government also into external borrowing, less inflow of concessional loans, even in case of multilateral loans, the increased share of non-concessional loans. The flow of both the concessional and non-concessional loans from outside government sources was also, however, not sufficiently available. Besides, over the years there was a tremendous increase in commercial borrowings which inflected very high rate of interest as well as shorter maturity. They greatly added to external indebtedness. Harder-term loans led to bigger servicing payments. Consequently, India's external indebtedness was on the ascend. The magnitude of external debt moved up from US $ 20.6 billion in 1980-81 to US $ 75.85 billion in 1989-90 (Table 4.20). The accumulation was specially rapid during the second half of the 1980s with long-term borrowing (*Joshi and Little, 1996*). Moreover, 'other' capital flows and errors and omissions went from being a large negative in the first half of 1980s to a positive in the second half, indicating an increase in short-term borrowing. As a result, the external-debt-to-GDP ratio that shows the magnitude of external debt in relation to domestic output rose during 1985-90. In fact, share of external debt in GDP ratio had risen to a peak of 41 per cent in 1991-92, short-term debt as a proportion of total debt (with maturity up to one year) had also attained a peak of 10.2 per cent by March 1991, debt-service ratio,[11] that measures the ability to serve debt obligations (repayment of principal and interest payment), it also being the most important indicator of the burden of debt, had risen above 35 per cent of current receipts in 1990-91 and the ratio of short-term debt to foreign currency assets had soared to a perilous high of 382.1 per cent at end March 1991. The share of concessional loan was steady around 45 percent during the first half of the 1990s. Thus a vicious circle of external indebtedness was very much apparent during the early 1990s. Since huge pile-up of external debt hampered the very process of developments, its management became an important agendum for the macro economic reforms in the country.

B. Policy Reform Endeavours to Cure External Indebtedness

To cure external indebtedness, government policy from the very beginning tried to keep the Indian economic environment congenial for foreign investors—FDI (Foreign Direct Investment) and FPI (Foreign Portfolio Investment)—so that the above two inflows could act as substitute for foreign borrowings. The Rangarajan Committee, constituted for BoP reform, submitted its report on June 4, 1993 and proclaimed in its report to shorten the size of the service payments of external debts. For that the report suggested some essential measures. First, external commercial borrowings (ECBs) for less than five years of maturity were not to be encouraged. Second, NRI deposits for more than one-year maturity were to be encouraged. Third, short-term borrowings were to be made only for trade-related purposes. Fourth, recourse to external debt for BoP support would have to be discouraged unless it is on concessional terms or with vary long maturity. Following the recommendation of the above High Level Committee, with regard to ECBs, there were certain important policy changes during the 1990s and beyond that had a profound positive impact on the external debt situation of the country. It is a fact that ECBs, being the medium and long-term loans has been guided by the overall consideration of prudent external debt management. Over the years, ECB policies having been gradually liberalized in view of the larger objective of enabling Indian corporates' greater access to international capital markets and providing corporates more flexibility in managing their exposure on ECBs, have been framed with the broad objectives of keeping cost of debt low, avoiding quick depletion of forex reserves by ensuring high debt maturities and encouraging channelization of ECBs into high priority sector like infrastructure and exports. Following the policy imperatives, gross disbursement of ECB [excluding India Development Bonds (IDBs), Resurgent India Bonds (RIBs) and India Millennium Deposits (IMDs)] declined, reflecting reduced reliance on debt financing.

Significant changes have also been made in the policy framework for Non-Resident Indians (NRI) deposits held by the Indian banking system, which constitute a major portion of external debt for India. The BoP crisis of 1990-91 pinpointed to the fact that the excessive dependence on non-resident Indian's (NRI) deposits must be avoided, considering its volatility nature. Mobilization of deposits under the FCNR[A] (Foreign Currency Non-resident [Accounts]) was also not cost effective as there are fiscal costs involved in terms of the interest outgo on these deposits. Despite constituting an important source of external finance, NRIs are liability to the banking system. Since 1990s therefore the policy towards NRI deposits has been aimed to achieve the twin objectives of retaining the attraction of the stable deposits, while simultaneously reducing their effective costs. This has been achieved through the following steps :

> In pursuance of the recommendations of the High Level Committee on BoP, a restructuring of the FCNR (A) (Foreign Currency Non-Resident [Accounts]) scheme was effected during 1993-94. Deposit maturities up to two years have been discontinued and interest rate differential narrowed. Simultaneously, two new schemes viz. the FCNR (B) [Foreign Currency Non-Resident (Banks) and the Non-Resident (Non-Repatriable) Rupee Deposits [NR (NR) RD] have been introduced. Under these schemes, incentives have been offered to banks to encourage them to mobilize deposits. These deposits have been made free of reserve requirements. However, from April 1, 2002, the second one discontinued. Other forms of current NRI deposits, viz. NR (E) RA (Non-Resident (External) Rupee Accounts and FCNR (B) remained. To prevent arbitrage-driven inflows on rupee-denominated NRI deposits, short-term flows (less than one year) have been discontinued and there has been the rationalization of interest rates on the various non-resident deposit schemes through, thinning of spreads and eventual linkage with LIBOR/SWAP rates. This has led to a perceptible reduction in fresh NR (E) RA inflows. The FCNR (B) and NR (E) RA flows together resulted in the total flows of US $2.7 billion during 2005-06. Meanwhile, the exchange rate guarantees on various deposits was already withdrawn.

Against this background, it was quite remarkable that India was able to avoid a full-blown debt crisis as well as the contagion effect from East Asian Crisis in mid-1997 because the multi-pronged cautious external debt management policy of the Government since the late1990s and after, continued to focus on (i) raising funds on concessional terms and from least expensive sources with longer maturities; (ii) monitoring and maintaining a strict control on short-term debts; (iii) encouraging long-term debts; (iv) avoiding the bunching of repayments liberalizing the debt inflows for their utilization to productive investments; (v) providing necessary flexibility to borrowers for their risk management of their debt portfolios; (vi) keeping the maturity structure as well as total amount of commercial debt under manageable limits; (vii) restricting end-use and enforcing limits on ECBs and option to convert external commercial borrowing into equity; (viii) restriction on trade credits; (ix) encouraging non-debt creating capital flows, notably FDI and FPI; and accelerating the growth rate of exports. Besides, a number of new initiatives had been undertaken. This included coverage and computerization of external debt data, better co-ordination among agencies' reporting debt statistics, pre-payments/ refinancing of more expensive external debt and other measures to actively manage sovereign external debt of the country. This had helped in containing the accumulation of external debt and maintaining external debt within manageable limit. In the Report of the Tarapore Committee II on Fuller Capital Account Convertibility (2006), there were also several recommendations on external debt management:

- Overall ECB ceiling as also the ceiling for automatic approval should be gradually raised. Rupee denominated ECB (payable in foreign currency) should be outside the ECB ceiling.
- Adequate coverage of trade credit figures as well as volume of trade credit should be a matter of concern, as in the latter's case there could be sudden changes in the availability of such credit. Import-linked short-term loans should be monitored in a comprehensive manner. And suppliers' credit up to 180 days should be included in short-term debt data.
- Since the banks' borrowing facilities are at present restrictive, the limits for borrowing overseas should be linked to paid-up capital and free reserves, and not to unimpaired Tier-1 capital as at present. Ultimately, all types of external liabilities of banks should be within an overall limit.
- Non-residents (other than NRIs) should be allowed access to FCNR (B) and NR (E)RA deposit schemes. Since NRIs enjoy tax concessions on FCNR (B) and NR (E) RA deposits, it would be necessary to provide those deposit facilities as separate and distinct schemes for

non-residents (other than NRIs) without tax benefits. This should be done in diferrent Phase-wise. The present tax regulations on those deposits for NRIs should be reviewed by Government.

- The present ceiling of FII should be raised and calibrated as a percentage of annual gross issuance rather than an *ad hoc* fixation of ceiling.
- The limit for FII investment could be raised from 6 per cent of total gross issuances by the Centre and States to 10 per cent between 2006-07 and 2010-11. Moreover, the allocation by SEBI of the limits between 100 per cent debt funds and other FIIs should be discontinued.

C. *Impact of Reforms Process on External Debt Situation in India*

Overall the prudent external debt management policy adopted so far has had a far-reaching positive consequence onto the improvement in the debt sustainability indicators like debt-to GDP, debt servicing, short-term debt to total debt etc. By the end of March, 2006 the total external debt to GDP ratio (that shows the magnitude of external debt in relation to domestic output) had fallen to 15.8 per cent, the ratio of short term debt to total external debt was down to 7.7 per cent at end of September, 2006. The external debt service payments as a ratio of gross external current receipts had fallen from over 35.3 per cent in 1990-91 to 10.2 per cent in 2005-06, though it was 6.1 percent in 2004-05. In what follows while external debt has increased in absolute terms, as a proportion of GDP it has dropped. The share of concessional debt declined to 35.8 percent at end-March 2002 and 29.3 percent at end-March 2006. Much more significant, due to tight control on short-term debt, was the fall in short-term debt, it being the villain of the piece in many a currency crisis in the past and recent decades, from US $8544 million in end-March 1991 (10.2 percent of total debt) to US $ 4431 million in end-March 2004 (3.10 per cent of total debt). This is so because huge accumulation of short-term debt had assumed the aspect of a villain in the countries like Thailand, Indonesia, Malaysia, the Philippines, Korea and

Russia. A high level of short-term debt always tends to inflate the servicing burden. Nonetheless, it can make a country any time vulnerable because of the continuous need of rollovers, which becomes extremely difficult at times of crisis. However, the short-term debt as a proportion of current assets has declined from 382.1 per cent in end-March 1991 to 6.7 per cent at end-September 2006.

Now at the end of March 2007 and September 2007, India's total external debt stood at US $ 169.6 billion (Rs. 7,40,099 crore) and US$ 190.5 billion (Rs. 7,57,967 crore) respectively *(Economic Survey, 2007-08)*,while it was US $ 123.2 billion (Rs. 539,389 crore) at the end of March 2005. The rise in external debt during this period was brought about by a rise in ECBs, NRI deposits (both bearing a relatively higher interest rate and imposing a higher service burden) and short-term debt. Imports and import-related trade credit was the main driver behind the huge pile-up of short-term debt, both as a proportion of total debt as well as a proportion of foreign currency assets. It is worth mentioning that external assistance accounted for about 38.2 percent of the total debt burden in 2005-06-(Rs. 215,775 crore). Out of this multi-lateral assistance was of the order of 25.8 percent and bilateral assistance of the order of 12.4 percent. After reaching a net inflow from US $22.5 billion in 1990-91 to more than US $4.3 billion in 2000-01, ECBs had become larger and larger net outflows in the three year period to the tune of US $ 1.58 billion in 2001-02, US $1.69 billion in 2002-03 and US $ 2.92 billion in 2003-04. Higher levels of repayments, *vis-a-vis* widening differential between disbursements, on the one hand and amortization payments on the other have resulted in these net outflows. However, such ECBs turned back into net inflows in the capital account in 2004-05 and 2005-06 to a record level US $ 5.1 billion and US $2.7 billion respectively. Thus India witnessed net outflows only in four out of last sixteen years ending in 2005-06. On the other, export credits have continued to be around 4-7 percent between 1990-91 to 2006-07. The share of NRI and Foreign currency deposits has risen in absolute terms during 1990-91 to end of March 2006. Following the significant policy-induced shift in the composition of NRI deposits to ensure their stability, outstanding NRI deposits grew steadily from US $ 14.0 billion at end-March, 1991 (constituting 16.7 percent of total external debt) to US $ 35 billion at end-March 2006 (*Hand Book of Statistics on the Indian Economy, RBI,* 2005-06). There is a decline in Rupee debt in relative terms from 15.5 percent in 1990-91 to 1.6 percent in 2005-06. Taking all this components together, it may be stated that long-term debt has indicated a tendency to rise from US $ 75.2 billion in 1991 to 116.39 billion in 2006. This implies a tendency of the short-term debt to declining during the period of intensive economic reform (1991 to 2002) (Table 4.27). It is also worth mentioning, whereas India's external debt rose by 2.8 percent in dollar terms between 1990-91 and 2005-06, it rose by 8.6 percent in rupee terms during the same period, following the deterioration of the exchange rate between US dollar and Rupee from Rupees 17.94 in 1990-91 to Rupees 44.3 in 2005-06. The position relating to India's outstanding external debt is given in Table 4.27.

With comparatively comfortable external debt indicators, India ranked fifth in position among the top ten debtor countries of the world in 2006 after China, Russian Federation, Turkey, and Brazil according to the Global Development Finance 2006, (World Bank) while it was the third largest debtor country in the world in 1991. In terms of the indebtedness classification, India has improved its position from close to 'severely indebted category' in 1991 to 'less indebted benchmark'. Another crucial feature of India's external debt management is a history of strong commitment towards making no compromise on honouring debt service obligations. The country has never been a defaulter on any external obligations (*Jadhav, 2005*). The improvements in India's external indebtedness in recent years has been through not by 'default but by design'.

In what follows from the above discussion is the fact that India has been able to manage its external debt within reasonable limits as the key external debt sustainability indicators exhibits to GDP ratio and debt service to current receipts ratio, etc. It is quite remarkable that India was able to

TABLE 4.27
India's External Debt

(end March US $ million)

Item	1991	1992	1995	1999	2000	2001	2002	2003	2004	2005	2006
(1)	(2)	(3)	(4)	(5)	(6)	(7)	(8)	(9)	(10)	(11)	(12)
Long-term Debt	75257	78215	94739	92612	94327	97698	96098	100289	107284	115680	116393
Short-term Debt	8544	7070	4269	4274	3936	3628	2745	4669	4431	7524	8788
Total External Debt	83801	85285	99008	96886	98263	101326	98843	104958	111715	123204	125181
Concessional Debt as % of total debt	45.9	44.8	45.3	38.5	38.9	35.4	35.9	36.8	36.1	33.3	31.5
Short-term debt as % of total debt	10.2	8.3	4.3	4.4	4.0	3.6	2.8	4.5	4.0	6.1	7.0
Debt Indicators :											
Debt stock-GDP ratio (%)	28.7	38.7	30.8	23.6	22.1	22.4	21.1	20.0	17.8	17.3	15.8
Debt-Service Ratio (%)											

(Contd.)

TABLE 2.27 (Contd.)

(1)	(2)	(3)	(4)	(5)	(6)	(7)	(8)	(9)	(10)	(11)	(12)
(For fiscal year)											
(including debt servicing on non-civilian credits)	35.3	30.2	25.9	18.7	17.1	16.6	13.4	16.4	16.5	6.1	10.2

Note : Debt service ratio from the year 1994-95 includes the revised private transfer contra-entry on account of gold and silver imports.

The figures about the magnitude of external debt provided by the official Economic Surveys of Govt. of India varied significantly from the figures provided by the World Bank Debt Tables, OECD, BIS, IMF and IIF, even for the RBI. To rationalize the external debt statistics, the RBI appointed a Task Force on External Debt Statistics of India. The RBI Bulletin Supplement of November 1992 published the Report of the Policy Group and Task Force on External Debt Statistics. The Economic Survey of 1992-93 and later years, therefore, published data on external debt on the basis of RBI methodology and thus streamlined the data on a scientific basis.

Long-term debt includes external assistance consisting of multi-lateral borrowing (Govt.+Non-Govt. borrowing including concessional and non-concessional loans), bi-lateral borrowing, borrowing from IMF, Trade Credit, Commercial Borrowing, NRI & Foreign Currency (Bank & Other) deposits, Rupee debt (i.e., debt owed to Russia denominated in Rupees and converted at current exchange rates, payable in exports).

Short-term debt is the sum total of NRI deposits (upto one year maturity) + Foreign Currency (Bank & Other) FC (B & O) deposits (upto one year maturity) + Others trade-related debt excluding supplier's credit of up to 180 days.

Source : External Debt Management Unit,, Ministry of Finance and RBI.

avoid a full-blown debt crisis as well as contagion effect from East Asian Currency Crisis in mid-1997. The reason for India for not facing turbulence at that time was that it followed a multi-prolonged cautions debt management policy along with a sensible exchange rate policy and that its key external parameters were sound with significant reductions, as compared with the position at the time of the crisis of 1990-91, in the current account, the external debt service ratio and the proportion of short-run debt to total external debt. Furthermore, in the capital flows there was a shift from exclusive debt financing to a blend of debt-equity financing with a significant liberalization of FDI and FPI flows. The government deserves a word of appreciation for this achievement.

Despite the success story there arises several disturbing elements in the Indian economic situation, which needs to be addressed in this context. First, the share of the private creditors has begun to rise after March 1995. Moreover the proportion of non-concessional debt in total debt has a rising tendency. The share of commercial debt increased after 1995-96. These types of developments will definitely increase interest burden in the coming years. Secondly, two more debt indicators viz., debt to exports ratio and the ratio of short-term capital to forex reserves, as opined by C.P. Chandrasekhar and Jayati Ghosh (1999), should be taken into account, since the use of debt to current receipts conceals certain deep-seated and endemic weaknesses. For example, the inflows of the remittances reflecting as transfer payments from Indians abroad may not be sustained. In view of the uncertainty of maintaining high level of current receipts, the authors have argued for preferring debt to exports ratio as a more appropriate indicator. Nonetheless, since the ratio of foreign capital to forex reserves had shown a tendency to fluctuate over time, government should take care on the components of liquid foreign capital, which are of a similar nature as short-term debt : otherwise the Indian economy can become vulnerable at any time.

Thirdly, one of the key indicators, which should be closely monitored, is the ratio of short-run debt (defined as upto one year) plus portfolio stock as a percentage the forex reserves. The

Capital Account Convertibility Committee (Tarapore Committee II) had recommended that this ratio should preferably not exceed 60 percent. Now its is a fact that India's external debt burden has reduced during the later years of economic reforms. Both the position relating to external debt is not wholly secure. Though there has been an improvement in the debt service indicators and others, India still continues to be among the top ten indebted countries. Hence we need to pursue to more rational debt management policy, prioritizing the use of commercial credit and encouraging foreign investment. Despite the fact that the short-term debt management is well within limits, caution need to be exercised to see that it is kept low.

Notes and References

1. Since India's problem was not once of short period seasonal and cyclical savings in it exports and imports but of long period growth-reliance IMF 'credits' were not likely to be of much help except in periods of acute strain due to temporary, self-correcting, unforseen disturbances. Aid from foreign, private banks, similarly were short-term in character and the interest rates, particularly in Great Britain, were too high. Obviously the foreign capital needed for long-term economic growth must be long term and preferably stable in character. Long-term foreign capital could be obtained (a) from international organization like IBRD, Asian Development Bank, etc. (b) foreign government, and (c) in the form of private capital inflow.
2. Foreign exchange reserves can be conceived here in the narrow sense of official holdings of gold and convertible currencies or in the wider sense including all holdings—official and non-official—of gold, foreign exchange of all types, short term foreign securities and even readily marketable long-term foreign assets.
3. Factors which constrained export growth during the 1960's included both external factors (such as slow growth in world demand for jute manufactures, cotton textiles, tea, tobacco, manganese ore and mica) as well as doméstic factors (i) sharp rise in costs and prices due to shortage of raw jute and cotton, relatively high prices of intermediates and inputs largely as a consequence of import substitution policies, (ii) rising domestic absorption of exportable due to increase in population and high income elasticity of demand for exportables, (iii) Supply bottlenecks such as lack of infrastructural facilities for exports, stagnant or inelastic domestic production, shortages of imported intermediates and inputs.
4. The resource-imbalance mechanism of the external deficit may be seen by considering national income accounts identities. 'Gross national product (GNP) may be considered either from the product side (demand) or the factor payments side (supply). On the product side, we have:

Y=C+I+G+X-M (i)

where Y is GNP, C is consumption, I is investment, G is government purchases, X is exports, and M is imports. All elements on the right-hand side contribute to domestic demand except imports, which enter negatively because imports are an alternative to demand for domestic production.

On the factor payments side, we have

Y = C + Sp + T (ii)

where C is again consumption, Sp is private saving, and T is tax revenue. Here the right-hand side shows that payments received by factors of production are exhausted by their alternative uses for consumption for saving, or in tax payments to the government.

We may subtract equation (ii) from equation (i) to obtain:

0 = [I—Sp] + [G—T] + [X—M] (iii)

Rearranging, we may identify the resource gap as :

M—X = [I—Sp] + [G—T] (iv)

Thus, the excess of imports over exports must equal the excess of investment over private saving plus the excess of government purchases over tax revenue. Considering that the government's fiscal balance is tax revenue minus government spending, or [T—G], and that this balance may be thought of as government's saving, we may write the fiscal balance as : T—G = *Sg*. We may therefore rewrite the resource gap as :

M—X = I—Sp—Sg = I-S (v)

where S is the total of all saving, government plus private. Thus the need for external resources, and therefore the trade gap, equals the excess of domestic investment over total domestic saving, government plus private.

5. According to Marshall—Lerner conditions depreciation of currency against another currency will improve the balance of trade of that country whose currency depreciates provided the absolute values of the demand elasticities for exports and imports add up to more than unity. Strictly speaking, the Marshall-Lerner conditions only hold if the supplies are perfectly elastic and the country whose currency has depreciated is initially in a balance of trade equilibrium; the elasticity conditions, are the nevertheless, a reasonable guide for other situations, If, as seems likely, both the volumes exported by India to rest of the world (ROW) and the quantities imported by India from the ROW take some time to change, then the J-curve effect will operate. The India-ROW trade balance will improve in India's favour until the volume changes have taken some time. For depreciation of a currency have a volume and a value effect. The volume effect will change the quantities exported and imported while the value effect will alter the revenue resulting from exports and the expenditure incurred in importing, expressed in domestic currency, that is, the currency of the country effected by currency depreciation.
6. The petering out of the commodity boom in 1975, the onset of the recession in developed countries and slow recovery of economic activity, the slowdown of exports to Bangladesh with the reduction in aid flow led to a slow down of the growth of exports in the latter half of the 1970's.

7. The 1980s, and marked by the 1990s, many developing countries had changed their policy stance to favour free-market operations, price liberalization and deregulation and an export orientation, even if all had not made equal progress in those directions. This change of stance was most likely the result of developments in the world economy in the 1980s. The combined impact of the world-wide recession, the debt crisis and the scarcity and high cost of international capital flows to developing countries created crisis conditions in many countries. A number of them came to the IMF and the World Bank for financial assistance. The IMF, which was essentially a provider of stabilization assistance to take care of short-term BoP problems, shifted its emphasis in lending towards structural adjustment assistance through the Structural Adjustment Facility (SAF), Extended Structural Adjustment Facility (ESAF), and Extended Financing Facility (EEF) windows. The World Bank which primarily lent for development projects also started providing substantial structural adjustment loans (SALs) to national governments. These structural adjustment finances were frequently made conditional on market-oriented reforms.
8. That large current account deficits may cause problems has achieved acceptance. Large current account imbalances were associated with currency attacks in Chile in the early 1980s, in the UK and Nordic countries (late 1980s), in Mexico and Argentina (mid-1990s) and in several Asian countries including India and Russia in 1997 and thereafter. As the current account deficit worsens, more capital inflows would be needed. This would then lead to an appreciation of the real exchange rate. In a globalized world in which export promotion is an integral part of the development strategy , such appreciation would lead to a drop in growth rates and, therefore, potential tax revenue. Agosin (1994) finds that large swings in the real exchange rate because of temporary capital flows significantly depress capital investment, and thus long-run growth, leading to lower tax revenues. Moreover, much evidence shows that sustained, large fiscal deficits are deleterious to economic performance (*Fischer, 1993 : Easterly, Rodrigues and Schmidt-Hebbel, 1994)*.The three methods of financing deficits all have drawbacks: internal finance raises domestic interest rates , external financing can be unsustainable and money creation causes inflation.

   There is no simple formula for determining the optimum level of the budget deficit. The optimum deficit-or the range of sustainable deficit—depends on circumstances, including the cyclical state of the economy, prospects for growth, the uses of government spending, the depth of financial markets and the levels of national savings and national investment.
9. Jha (2000) develops an aljebra of external debt sustainability. He shows that a positive trade balance would reduce a country's external indebtedness whereas an increase in the world interest rate would worsen it. And external debt is sustainable only when it is financed by future trade surpluses. In the existing literature, this requirement has been interpreted to imply stationarity of the current account deficit or the co-integration of exports and imports inclusive of net interest payments.

10. A current account deficit can be financed by an increase in net foreign debt, DD (capital balance surplus), and/or by a decrease in international reserves (balance of payments deficit). If the international reserves of the debtor country remain unchanged, we have:

DD	=	Im-X	+	rD	(i)
←→		←→		←→	
capital balance surplus		trade balance surplus		net factor payments deficit	
		←——— current account balance deficit ———→			

In the absence of any further increase in net foreign debt [DD = 0 in equation (i)], the interest payments to foreigners (rD) have to be financed by a corresponding trade balance surplus (X—1m), which means a net transfer of resources from the debtor country to the creditor countries. The above situation in the balance of payments also means that the national product (GNP) is lower than the domestic product (GDP) by the amount of net factor payments abroad. Since the current account deficit (/rn—X + rD) of equation (i) is also equal to the savings gap (investment minus national savings), the evolution of investment and savings will determine the time path of foreign indebtedness. Thus, the current account deficit must be equal to the domestic savings gap (in private and public sectors) :

$\Delta D = 1m—X + rD = I—S_n$

or

$\Delta D/Y = I/Y—S_n /Y$

S_n has to be interpreted as national savings.

Thus, a 'young country', which has high investment requirements and very low saving resources, will borrow heavily abroad. If the investment requirements are very high relative to the domestic saving resources, indebtedness will rise, and over a certain time, the growth rate of debt will exceed the growth rate of income. With efficient investments, the growth rate of the domestic product will rise, involving an increasingly higher volume of domestic savings, and thus eventually closing the savings gap. The rise in foreign debt will then reach a maximum and decline if savings exceed investment. As soon as it has repaid all its outstanding (net) debt, the country will become a 'mature country' acting as a net lender to foreign countries.

11. When DSR—the ratio of debt service to export earnings is high (say, over 25 percent), it indicates that a country is vulnerable to adverse changes in its foreign trade for the level of international interest rates. Because a country's primary obligation is to service foreign loans, domestic interest rates may have to be raised and vital imports may have to be cut with economic performance suffering.

The DSR can be written as DSR = DS/X where DS is debt service and X is export earnings—both expressed in a foreign currency. It follows that dDSR/DSR = dDS/DS—dX/X . . . (i) The DSR increases it debt service grows at a faster rate than export revenue.

The absolute increase in debt service (dDS) depends on four factors: this year's trade deficits (with a positive sign), the interest rate paid on this increment to foreign debt outstanding, the change in the rate of interest (if any) paid on debt outstanding at the beginning of the years and the change in repayments of principal (known as amortization). The annual absolute rupee increase in *debt service obligations* is given by:

dDS = iTD + diD + dA

where iTD is the interest paid on the current year's trade deficit (i is the interest rate and TD the trade deficit); diD is the change in the amount of interest paid on debt outstanding at the beginning of the year (di is the change in the rate of interest) and dA is the change is annual repayment (or amortization) of principal).

Dividing the above equation through by DS and substituting into equation (i) yields

dDSR/DSR = iTD/DS + diD/DS + dA/DS—dX/X

Thus, the DSR rises if the trade deficit, the interest rate or annual amortization rises or if the export growth rate falls. Most debt rescheduling agreements push current amortization off into the future thereby reducing the present level of A (dA/dDS is negative). But the success of this tactic depends rather on the ability to reduce the trade deficit or to raise the rate of export growth.

APPENDIX

TABLE A 4.1

Major Events in the History of Balance of Payments in India

Period	*Major Events*
1951-52 to 1955-56	During this First Plan period there was no serious payments difficulties. A moderate deficit in balance of trade (Rs. 542 crores) was financed largely by invisible earnings and private transfer payments. A very small deficit on current account was financed by inflows of foreign aid and depletion of foreign exchange reserves. The overall picture was satisfactory.
1956-57 to 1960-61	During this Second Plan period there happened a dramatic change in the payments scenario as import substitution policy and high level of ambitious investment strategy guided by Mahalanobis model brought into a severe BoP crisis in the winter of 1956 57. It was the dismal export performance along with the rising import costs, especially of food, iron and steel and capital equipment, which led to persistent current account deficits (2.3 percent of GDP). Import cover of reserves (or foreign currency assets) plunged to barely two months' by the terminal year of the Second Plan. Invisible earnings, private transfer, foreign aid inflows and forex reserves contributed 20%, 50% and 30% respectively in financing the current account deficit.
1961-62 to 1965-66	In 1965 war with Pakistan and drought in several states of the country brought about a crisis. During this Third Plan period exports grew moderately from 1960 to 1963, stagnated in 1964 and collapsed in 1965. There was no surplus on account of invisibles and private transfer. Hence the entire BoP deficit was financed by foreign aid inflows, mostly in the form of some grants and loans from the World Bank and withdrawals from the IMF and by loans from foreign countries, PL 480 and PL 665. In spite of these efforts, there was some depletion of forex reserves of the country.
1966-67 to 1970-71	There occurred large nominal devaluation of the rupee (36.5 per cent) in June 1966 (undertaken under foreign pressure which was ultimately proved to be failure to reduce trade deficits). This was only a period of high

(*Contd.*)

TABLE A 4.1 (*Contd.*)

Period	*Major Events*
	inflation Export volume fell in 1967 due to economic recession. Heavy imports of foodgrains to overcome famine conditions and internal shortage of foodgrains on the other played a significant role in creating a weak BoP situation. For the first time, positive net invisibles used to reduce the trade deficit became negative. There was hardly any sign of improvement in the BoP situation during the Annual Plans (1966-69). In fact, current account deficit-GDP ratio widened to 2 percent during the Annual Plans. Foreign aid inflows remained the principal source of financing the payments deficit. The country thus faced the threat of falling into a financial assistance trap.
1971-72 to 1975-76	First oil shock came in 1973 and there were severe droughts in 1972 and 1974, leading to high inflation and the country saw a record level of trade deficit in the year 1974-75. The behaviour of the Real Exchange Rate helped exports to grow rapidly in spite of the high domestic inflation. In 1975 there was improvement in the forex position (due to growth of exports and private remittances).
1976-77 to 1979-80	This period was characterized as Golden years on the BoP front exhibiting a substantial improvement in the BoP and forex reserve position. The latter one's position was so strong enough to finance 9.5 months of imports in 1978-79. Net receipts from invisibles provided valuable support. This was achieved because of a strong export boom, large food stock, high demand for Indian labour in Gulf countries and increase in domestic crude oil production. The main source of financing the current account deficits were official loans on concessional terms
1980 to 1981	BoP situation turned out to be difficult in the early 1980s, following the second oil price hike in 1979. There was a substantial squeeze on aid programmes as well as decline in net invisib1es and international terms of trade. India drew SDR 3.9 billion record-breaking loan from IMF.
1981-82 to 1984-85	The Sixth Plan Period (1980-81 to 1984-85) showed a consistent increase in current account deficit. During this period, due to the decline in the overall growth of

(*Contd.*)

TABLE A 4.1 (*Contd.*)

Period	*Major Events*
	imports a reprieve came, although by 1983, debt service had increased. Export was sluggish and stagnant in 1985. During this period net invisibles financed nearly half of the trade deficits. And the 51 per cent of current account deficit was met by way of foreign loans, 40 per cent through use of fund resources (including loans from IMF Trust Fund) and the rest was met by deposits from NRIs.
1985-86 to 1989-90	During this Seventh Plan period, there were severe strains on BoP. Huge trade deficits emerged due to sharp increase in import bill and a large repayment to the IMF. Debt service burden rose along with marked deterioration in fiscal imbalances. Net invisib1es lost their buoyancy. Official loans and proportion of concessional loans declined to a great extent. The continuing strain on BoP is reflected in steep depletion of forex reserves. Net inflows of capital from abroad have accordingly played a growing role in financing the trade deficit. So financing becomes very much difficult.
1990 to 1992	During the first half of 1991, India's BoP problem had assumed the nature of a crisis of an unmanageable proportion. Due to declaration of independence by the Soviet satellites in Central and Eastern Europe in 1989 and the collapse of Soviet Union itself, India's trade with the Eastern Block and the aid from the Soviet to India were highly disrupted. Rise in oil import bill due to the third oil shock that erupted in January 1991 and the Gulf crisis, fall in export volumes, decline in 130,000 Indian workers' remittances, high debt accumulation were the main reasons for the crisis. A default on payments had become a serious possibility in June 1991 for the first time in Indian history.
1992-93 to 1996-97	During this Eighth Plan period, trade deficit had reached a record level. For the entire plan period, invisibles neutralized the trade deficit to the extent of about 58 percent—a really commendable achievement. Despite this, BoP has shown continuously a deficit in all the years.
1997-98 to 2001-02	During this Ninth Plan Period, India's BoP position remained mostly comfortable. The current account deficit narrowed down, following positive current account balance in 2001-02 and on the average it was

(*Contd.*)

TABLE A 4.1 (*Contd.*)

Period	*Major Events*
	0.8 percent of GDP. The growth of exports and imports in dollar terms had been 5.6 percent and 3.3 percent respectively. The country could escape the East Asian Crisis of 1997-98. Invisible receipts had been buoyant though event of September 11, 2001 following the attack of Trade Centre of America by terrorist, reduced the flow of remittances during 2001-02. Foreign exchange reserves had increased significantly to $ 54.106 billion by the end of March 2002. FDI flows had increased while FIIs had gone down. The external value of the rupee seen in terms of REER had appreciated slightly. The key indicators of external debt had improved considerably as a result of better management of external debt.
2002-03 to 2006-07	During this Tenth Plan period, India's BoP was less comfortable than the earlier Plan Period. In July, 2002 the country faced one of the worst droughts. July rainfall was a record low in the past hundred years. This adversely affected the GDP growth rate and BoP position. The year 2004-05 marked a significant departure in the structural composition of India's BoP, with current account, after three consecutive years of surplus in 2001-02, 2002-03, 2003-04, turned into deficit. But exports have nearly tripled between 2001-02 and 2006-07. India's share in world merchandise exports reached 1 per cent in 2005 and 2006. It recorded high growth in the export of services during the plan. Export of services grew faster than merchandise exports. Invisible and strong capital flows—particularly of the non-debt variety financed current account deficits. There was a drawdown of forex reserves by US $ 26.2 billions.

5

Trade and Payments Policies in India—A Critical Evaluation

In Chapter 4 we reviewed India's record in the balance of payments front which commenced from some earlier years of its First Five Year Plan (1951-52), particularly since Independence and which had persisted over the past five decades and beyond, with varying degrees of intensity. These records coupled with her trade and payments policies had actually shaped its course over the period. A proper understanding of India's balance of payments requires the examination of the trade and payments policy regimes which virtually dominated the history of balance of payment of India like in other Asian, African and Latin American countries. It is now clearly recognised that there is a clear nexus between trade policies, industrial policies and other domestic policies in the monetary and fiscal spheres which determined the nature and pace of industrialization. In this chapter, an attempt is made to bring out the policy details of the Indian trade and payments system as it moved away from the policy of 'orthodox' economic orientation of import-substitution at the cost of export-expansion for the development of industrial sector in her economies to a more open liberalized regime backed by outward-looking export-orientation drive under the mixed economic framework.

A chronology of major events in the evolution of trade and payments policy regimes in India since Independence is given in Appendix Table A5.1.

5.1 AN OVERVIEW OF TRADE AND PAYMENTS POLICY REGIMES DURING 1950s

In many of the most developing countries, paucity of foreign exchange constitutes a major constraint on the pace of economic development. This may be due to (a) inelastic demands for many of their exportables, (b) structural and institutional rigidities and imbalances in these economies, and (c) non-diversification of their exports. At the same time, import requirements remain high to meet the needs of speedy development. The only way out to enable the developing nation to finance its growing import bills is to expand its export of goods and services and diversify the production base of the economy over the medium run, thus gradually relaxing the above-mentioned constraints.

If economic development is usually be viewed as the transformation of a low-income country using traditional technologies and producing mainly primary products into a high-income country using modern technologies to produce both primary products and a variety of industrial goods in its stride towards industrialization, then voluntary participation in the world economy can only augment a country's production possibilities. Exporting a part of a country's production in exchange for what is produced elsewhere, is nothing more or less than adding a technique of transforming domestic resources into desired goods and services, in addition to those available at home. Participation in the world capital markets enables a country to augment its investment opportunities. It is also a fact that by efficiently exploiting the trading and investment opportunities available in the world market a country can achieve high levels of real income[1] and possibly a faster rate of growth as well. The efficiency and exploitation no doubt will depend largely on the trade and payments policies successfully pursued and at the same time, on the quality of the economic management as a whole. Since there is an intimate relationship between trade policy and trade performance, and between trade performance and overall economic development, foreign trade policy[2] and the formulation of trade and payments strategy are important in the development process.

There are a variety of means such as institutional innovation, organisational reform and policy initiatives which may be deployed individually, or in concert, to attain the desired long-run objectives relating to foreign trade. But among these, trade and payments policies have a certain primacy. For, if policy and payment levers are not properly weilded, wrong signals could be transmitted through a totally inappropriate set of incentives or disincentives, and much of the institutional or organisational effort may turn out to be futile exercise[3]. By now, there are extensive evidences from many developing and least developed countries of the failure of choosing the 1950s' orthodox prescription of the most *dirigistic* and inward-oriented autarkic development strategy with import substituting industrialization[4] at its core, which these countries initiated for their economic development. Such a strategy will not necessarily minimise the present value of resource cost of meeting present and future final demands. Apart from this analytical argument, competitive pressure from imports in the domestic markets and from rival exporters in the foreign market will not generate production efficiency. It is in this setting that a brief critical evaluation of the trade policies of India as have been evolved over various Five Year Plans in India with regard to the various constituents of her external payments are portrayed. We see that the country has come a long way in her attitude towards international trade and payments policy since Independence.

It was in 1950 that the Government of India set up the Planning Commission. At that time, the Indian planners led by Jawaharlal Nehru, were faced with a difficult situation. On the one hand, the country strived to bring about structural transformation of a backward society within the framework of a political democracy; at the same time it was apprehended that, even though the free play of market forces could also achieve structural transformation, such a process might result in inequitable distribution of income and assets. As a result, India opted for the path of planned economic development within the framework of a *mixed* economy. And right from the beginning, Indian planners recognised that planning of foreign trade and payments policy had got to be an integral part of the national development effort. However, ever since 1950, they had tended to view the problem of foreign trade planning largely in terms of the management of the balance of payments. The role of foreign trade in improving the efficiency of resource allocation and in securing greater return from internal resources had not received adequate attention in the official documents on Indian Planning. The strategy/policies for the management of the balance of payments had also undergone significant changes over time. To manage the balance of payments, these policies had combined adjustment and financing. Long-term capital at concessional terms had been sought for and at the time of crisis new sources of capital had sometimes been tapped. Adjustment had consisted of policies of export promotion, import substitution programmes for important commodities which accounted for large share of the import bill, and control of import of non-essentials. When there had been crises these policies had sometimes been supplemented by demand management and more stringent import controls[5].

India's economic development since its Independence in 1947 had been planned in accordance with a series of five-year plans. India entered its **First Five Year Plan** in 1951 with a relatively comfortable currency reserves (sterling balances) accumulated during World War II, and with the modest size and import requirements of First Plan (1951-56). The Plan focused on raising savings by means of fiscal policy to accommodate projected investment levels. The building of infrastructure was accorded first priority and the plan was largely indifferent to exports although the official document of India's Five Year Plan laid almost equal emphasis on export promotion and import substitution and the trade gap was financed, in the main, by drawing upon foreign exchange reserves. During the first decade after Independence, India's trade regime was relatively free of restrictions. Some QRs (Quantitative Restrictions) that were left over from World War II remained in place as well as the machinery to administer them but their scope was tightly circumscribed. India's share of world exports fell from 2.6

percent in 1948 to 1.0 percent at the end of 1965 (Table 5.1) remaining relatively stagnant in absolute value after the Korean War Peak, to those of her competitors because of increasing price uncompetitiveness, rather than being subjected to a 'Prebisch' effect, and import demand balanced this off to result in a roughly equilibrated exchange rate which put pressure on the QR-framework that had been inherited from the World War II. The foreign exchange reserves position, however, remained comfortable and official reserves remained close to $1.9 million through this period (1950-56). The favourable position of forex reserves immediately after the Korean War Boom did not instigate the Indian policy-makers to prescribe any strategy during the First Plan. Rather the policy-makers to start with were indifferent to exports. There was no evidence of high import premia, systematic allocation of imports and industrial licenses and associated economic policies of the kind that were to spring up in the next period. The decline in export performance did not, however, bring about change in policy during the period of the Second Plan.

By contrast, the **Second Five-Year Plan** (1956-61) emphasized the determination and control of the pattern of investments. Within a year of launching of the substantially large Second Plan in 1956, with its emphasis on foreign exchange intensive investment in the manufacturing and heavy industries, a foreign exchange crisis of major proportion developed. Thus in early 1957, in response to a severe balance of payments and foreign exchange crisis caused largely by the previous over-expansion of investment, heavy foreign exchange expenditure on account of machineries and industrial raw materials, imports of food grains and defence equipment, and the decline in exports earnings, the Indian authorities introduced strict import and investment licensing schemes that shifted the investment pattern towards inward-oriented, capital-intensive manufacturing industries centred on import substitution as a means of stimulating industrialization, intent on attaining the objective of self-reliance but did not alleviate the shortage of foreign exchange. The Second Plan did not envisage a significant increase in export earnings. This bearishness with regard to exports was apparently attributable to two specific perceptions. Exports of primary products or of

TABLE 5.1

India's Exports and Shares of Total Value of World Exports (1948-70)

Calendar Year	*World Exports (US $ millions)*	*Indian Exports (US $ million)*	*Indian Exports as percentage of World Exports*
1948	53,000	1,363	2.6
1949	53,900	1,309	2.4
1950	55,200	1,146	2.1
1951	74,800	1,611	2.2
1952	72,400	1,295	1.8
1953	73,400	1,116	1.5
1954	76,400	1,182	1.5
1955	83,200	1,276	1.5
1956	92,600	1,300	1.4
1957	99,300	1,379	1.4
1958	94,800	1,221	1.3
1959	100,600	1,308	1.4
1960	113,400	1,331	1.2
1961	118,600	1,387	1.2
1962	124,700	1 ,403	1.1
1963	136,700	1,631	1.2
1964	152,600	1,749	1.2
1965	165,400	1,686	1.0
1966	181,400	1,606	0.89
1967	191,200	1,612	.084
1968	213,700	1,766	0.82
1969	244,900	1,835	0.75
1970	280,500	2,026	0.72

Source : International Financial Statistics, Supplement to 1966-67 issues, March 1968, October 1973, International Monetary Fund.

traditional manufacturers based on them were seen as facing poor demand prospects in the world market. At the same time, it was felt that other newer manufacturers had little likelihood of securing a sizeable export market until industrialization itself was well under way. The natural consequence of such export pessimism was a conviction that, in the long-run, industrialization could lead to a viable balance of payments only if it was based on a programme which minimized imports. Influenced by the structuralist school, much of the then policy was dominated by a feeling of export pessimism which lasted upto 1972-73. Following the writings of Prebisch, Singer and Nurkse, Indian Planners felt that there was very little scope for expansion of exports in view of the limitations on the size of the foreign markets. It was also believed that the international terms of trade of developing countries were destined to deteriorate over time regardless of the policies of developing countries. This was a crucial assumption as it firmly established a case for discouragement of exports and for policies, which encouraged production for the domestic market. Furthermore, the prices of primary commodities were inherently more unstable than prices of manufactures. Because India often depended on a comparatively small number of basic commodities for export earnings, dependence on trade would mean greater fluctuations in the level of economic activity and these fluctuations were assumed to be harmful to long-run growth. So the aim of trade policy in India was to foster import substitution in order both to conserve scarce foreign exchange and to promote the development of indigenous manufacturing industries. Agriculture was regarded as being much less important in the development process than the establishment of new manufacturing industries. Import substitution policies aimed at fostering the growth of consumer goods industries through a policy of high tariffs or quotas. Once successful, the emphasis was to switch to promoting the development of local intermediate and capital goods industries by the same means. In addition to tariffs and quotas, reliance was placed on exchange controls to ration the use of scarce foreign currency. Further, to hold down the cost of imported raw materials and intermediaries products needed for industrial expansion, the exchange rate for these purposes were kept artificially high.

Inflows of capital from abroad, including direct investment by multinational companies attracted by the need to jump high import barriers, were supposed to make good of any deficiency in local savings.

Thus the state-backed import substitution, particularly in basic intermediates and machine building became the key thrust of the trade policy in the late fifties as a long-term solution to India's balance of payments difficulties. The short-term problems were sought to be taken care of by a tight system of import controls as well as by arranging for a large-scale inflow of assistance. Protection to promote domestic industries through high tariff barriers, multiple exchange rates, import licensing arrangements and subsidies was not seen as detrimental to trade and development.

It may be of interest to speculate on the reasons for the adoption of an import substituting policy in India. First, such a policy may have been considered a means towards the achievement of a faster rate of economic growth. For example, following Hirschman, the government officials might have felt that the principal constraint on India's development was the inability of potential domestic investors to decide where to invest, with the consequence that they preferred to consume rather than to invest. As imports are proof of a domestic market, import substitution policy might induce people to make an investment decision and ultimately, according to the argument, people would be willing to invest in other areas, including potential exports.

A second reason for pursuing an import substitution policy stems from the belief that the country's potential exports would face a dismal future regardless of what policies the country adopts and so the country is forced to economise on its future use of foreign exchange as a 'second-best' policy. Moreover, there was general recognition that import substitution is an entirely natural process in the course of economic growth and provides the key to easing the structural constraints which expanding imports otherwise are likely to place on growth. The logic of import substitution derives as much from the fact of a high import propensity during the phase of development and equally, from the lack of international incentives to the exports from developing countries.

In any case, much of the import-substituting and inward-looking nature of the industrialization was the almost inevitable result of the political situation. The struggle for independence had been intimately mixed up with protection against the imports from industrial countries destroying local and traditional industries. The linkage between national independence and inward-looking industrialization was also due to the political perception that national independence and sovereignty would be meaningless without a measure of industrialization and self-sufficiency. This perception was to be repeated in the 1960s in the newly independent African countries with economically even more unsatisfactory results, because of the absence of many preconditions for successful industrialization compared with Asia or Latin America. Thus the desire for economic 'independence' was particularly another reason for import substitution policies in India. Shortages of certain commodities in world markets during the Korean War, the danger on being dependent on foreign suppliers in case of a possible World War III and the difficulty of some types of economic planning in an 'open' economy, all combined in India with the emotional desire to be independent economically as well as politically, after 1947. Thus import substitution became an objective *per se*.

The fourth reason for having followed an import substitution strategy stemmed from the existence of global uncertainty and the asymmetrical rewards and penalties to those officials associated with the success and failure of policies.[6]

A final reason was that the challenge to free trade came from the fear of the income distributional effects of trade with the South. During the 1950s and the 1960s, much of the South regarded trade with the North as a threat, not as an opportunity. It was argued that without protection it could not industrialize and turned to import substitution while the North was opening to the South (as to itself) through extensive liberalization.[7]

However, some of the observations that had generated from the introduction of import substitution policies in the late

1950s and from then on, can be summarized in the following arguments:

(a) Exports were discouraged relative to production of import substitutes. In fact, the strategy did not really substitute for imports. Due to lack of vertical integration, it shifted imports from finished products to inputs of intermediate and capital goods, saving very little foreign exchange in the process.

(b) As the developmental projects depended heavily on the imports of foreign capital goods and machinery, there was soon a shortage of foreign exchange, which was to be compounded in later years with large imports of food-grains and petroleum. Thus the policy failed in its aims of conserving scarce foreign exchange. The attempt to promote the development of local consumer goods industries in the first stage of the policy resulted in the import of more intermediate goods and raw materials to supply those industries. So the total volume of imports rose and the trade balance deteriorated. The second stage, which was supposed to result in the establishment of local capital goods firms and producers of intermediate products, was often never reached. At the same time, moreover the neglect of agriculture which such policies often entailed necessitated increased food imports to feed an expanding population.

(c) The policy had a harmful effect on those industries in which India hoped to enjoy a comparative advantage and therefore, earn the country's precious foreign exchange through exporting. By favouring the development of essentially import-competing industries producing largely for the local market, a bias was created against industries belonging to the export sector which were those in which the country was best able to compete internationally. The export sector faced a double jeopardy from the overvalued exchange rate: a low price received for units sold abroad and more costly raw materials and intermediate supplies to the extent that these had to be imported from abroad.

(d) The emphasis placed on increasing capital investment in manufacturing ran into the problem of inadequate domestic savings which was only partly overcome by importing capital from the developed world. Moreover, reliance on attracting large inflows of foreign capital was merely to create another kind of dependence.

(e) The high levels of protection afforded to manufacturing industry raised the price of manufactures relative to agriculture and so created discrimination against the farming sector. Long-term investment in farming was thereby discouraged and because agricultural output did not increase sufficiently the need to import food was increased.

(f) Development strategy was perhaps the most fundamental internal distortion. For years, India like other key Latin American and African countries had pursued the model of import substitution industrialization (ISI), which sought rapid industrial development behind high protective barriers against imports. This model eventually fostered domestic monopoly and created a fertile ground for bribery and corruption of state officials. It had a serious side effect of discouraging export development. Firms could sell in the domestic market at the world price plus a high import tariff [(Pd =Pw (1. + t)] but only at the world price in the export market (Pw). It was no accident that Korea and other East Asian countries, which had followed export-oriented development strategies, did much better than India and other African and Latin American countries in withstanding the debt crisis.

(g) Import licensing led to excessively capital-intensive import licenses. One finds that between 1957 and 1965 India's industrial output rose at an annual rate of 7.9 per cent and employment by 6.3 per cent per year.

(h) The import control and foreign exchange allocation regime have governed the external transactions of the Indian economy since then.

(i) The available foreign exchange from exports and foreign aid after deducting the cost of essential imports such as food, fertilizers, crude oil and defence needs, was allocated through licenses issued on a strict priority basis to different categories of importers.

(j) Imports were not allowed if a domestic substitute was available. Direct imports of non-essential food, consumer goods were discouraged.

(k) Transferability between licenses and categories of imports and licenses were restricted which eventually brought about a lot of bureaucratic problems leading to delays, administrative expenses and a lack of co-ordination among different categories of workforce.

(l) The strict licensing procedure, as argued by Bhagwati and Srinivasan (BS 1976),[8] for setting up domestic production capacity eliminated free entry and efficiency-induced capacity expansion. One further consequence of such a high cost-inefficient production was a bias against exports. Such a situation prevailed up to May, 1966.

(m) India persisted with her import substitution policies, which encouraged high cost of industrial production which in turn prevented India from being able to benefit from the world export boom.

(n) The bias against exports in the exchange control regime led to a continuous decline in India's share in world exports further increasing the severity of the foreign exchange constraint. This led to the introduction of a policy of export subsidization through the grant of exporters of: (a) import entitlements (twice the import content of exports subject to a maximum of 75 per cent of the f.o.b. value), and (b) fiscal concessions such as exemptions from, and/or refund of certain direct and indirect taxes, like sales tax, custom duties, etc.

(o) The concentration of investment in import-saving sectors did not, however, produce the desired result. The process of import substitution in the machine building and basic intermediate goods sector not only involved a difficult, yet necessary, learning by doing but also absorbed imports of goods not yet readily available within the economy. Thus, the step-up of investment in the capital goods sector compounded import needs rapidly. As a consequence, notwithstanding export pessimism, there was a growing realisation that if the Indian economy was ever to attain its objective of self-reliance, it would become unavoidable to finance an increasing proportion for maintenance and developmental imports from export earnings. From being a side issue, export growth, thus came to acquire importance in planning.

(p) From 1956 to 1966, the import regime and the exchange control policy were aimed at comprehensive and direct control over foreign exchange utilization. The control system resulted in rigidity and inflexibility in the pattern of the utilization of imports and in administrative red-tapism. Also, due to the high premium on foreign exchange and import licenses, a black-market emerged for illegal transferability of imports and import licenses. As a result there was a discrimination against exports because: (a) the effective export exchange rate, on an average, was less than the effective import exchange rate (BS (1975).[9] Table 2.1, pp. 46-48) illustrated that the Purchasing Power Parity Effective Exchange Rate (PPP-EER) for imports was higher than exports on an average by about 20% from 1950 to 1971; (b) exports found it difficult to compete internationally when the 'import substitution' inputs were inferior; (c) they could not expand quickly in response to foreign market signals. Until export initiatives started which was not before 1964, the trade policy with its inward-looking bias remained unfavourable especially to manufactured exports. All this brought about export stagnation, both as a proportion of GDP as well as of world exports.

5.2 FIRST TRANSITION PERIOD: 1961-66

The **Third Five-Year Plan** (1961-66) accordingly showed a distinct change in the perception about the role of exports. There had been a growing concern that if the Indian economy was ever to attain its objective of self-reliance, it was necessary that an increasing proportion of the external reserves required to finance economic development be met out of forex receipts derived from exports (*Nayyar,* 1982). Hence equal emphasis was given to both export promotion and import substitution. And a more liberal view of self-reliance evolved over the Third Plan with a shift in stress from "import substitution" to policy emphasis on "efficient substitution of imports". Within the framework of overall development strategy, exports, specially of non-traditional manufactured products were accorded high priority in the Plan and this shift in policy approach was followed by the introduction of a number of active export promotion measures, including export subsidization (that began in earnest around 1962 and intensified through the period on a whole range of exports) and import entitlement schemes[10] and a planned use of aid to expand domestic production of imported goods although this did not, however, represent a change in the strategy of industrialization or development. These measures were implemented by the authorities to reduce the impact of the import substitution policies, so that the policy should be directed towards controlling import through restraints mostly of fiscal nature and the profits made by the importers find its diversion to the exchequer, while the economy was under the pressure with the depletion of foreign exchange reserves : These and other measures had resulted in a degree of improvement in the BoP position when we witnessed a welcome increase in the export earnings only in 1963-64. And the current account deficit caused mainly by a large trade gap was financed initially by drawing down of the accumulated sterling balances, but later through a large inflow of foreign aid.

Reserve position continued to be 'thin'; aid flows were stabilized up to nearly 1964-65; QRs remained severe (the premia on imports, however, rose to unprecedented levels around late 1965 and early 1966 with the suspension of aid following the Indo-Pakistan War in late 1965); and export performance registered a significant improvement (until 1965 when major drought affected the traditional exports adversely). Industrial licensing also continued to be severe but, towards the end of the period, efforts were made to loosen it up. Towards the end, the Government also steadily deployed import duties to mop up the import premia.

This period from 1961 to 1966 can be broadly characterized as on involving "partial liberalization" in view of the export subsidization and growing resort to import duties, both of these policies involving, therefore, a growing, selective, *de facto* devaluation of the Rupee because the Indian Rupee become increasingly over-valued in terms of foreign exchange leading to a large proportion of exports being supported by subsidies at high rates by the government which urgently needed foreign exchange in order to import capital goods required for India's industrialization. Exporters were tempted to manipulate their invoices with the connivance of their foreign partners in order to get higher subsidies or compensatory import licenses. A drastic devaluation seemed to be the only measure that would help to cut this Gordian knot of black-market rates (of the Indian rupee deviated to a large extent from the official exchange rate), spurious invoices and rampant corruption. At the same time, one could hope to promote exports and liberalize imports by means of this devaluation. A devalued rupee would make export cheaper and more competitive, and import more expensive, so as to reduce the necessity of protective measures. But there were also weighty arguments that could be adduced against devaluation. For most Indian export items such as spices, tea, jute products etc., there was a very low elasticity of demand in the world market. India's industrial products were not yet of a sufficient quality to compete with the world market, even if they would be cheaply available after the devaluation. On the other hand, India still depended on import of capital goods, which would be much more expensive after a devaluation. Moreover, India had a foreign debt, for which the debt service would increase. The World Bank brushed aside all these arguments and forced India to devalue the rupee by 57.5 per cent in June 1966 computed as the increase from Rs. 4.76 to Rs. 7.50 in the official rate on the dollar and simultaneously the rigour of import controls was relaxed. Under the new arrangements, 59 priority industries, whose output covered about 70 percent of the organised industrial sector, were assured of liberal supplies of imported raw materials, spare parts, and to meet these import requirements, donor countries agreed to make available to India significant amounts of non-project aid to India. Simultaneously the import entitlement schemes were also abolished because it was considered that devaluation would be an adequate and more effective incentive for exports. However, on account of strong inflationary pressures in the economy in 1966 and 1967, it was considered necessary to grant fresh incentive for exports of selected non-traditional products. Thus, a new scheme of compensatory cash assistance was devised for providing cash subsidies varying from 5 to 30 per cent of f.o.b. value for exports of selected product groups, and other incentives such as supply of indigenous material at international prices (which were cheaper) were made available to the exporters. Export processing zones were developed as a part of special export promotion programmes. On the other hand, export duties were also introduced partly as countervailing duties to offset the devaluation on traditional exports and partly to offset the significant reduction in import duties. Also, export incentives were made much higher for non-traditional exports and the export duties were structured to encourage processing and value-added in exports.

These moves towards the rationalisation of the trade and payments regime culminated in the Liberalisation Episode, the June 1966 devaluation and the accompanying import liberalisation. Most of the policy measures that intensified and expanded the import substitution policy continued until the mid-seventies with the exception of a short-lived phase (1961-66) when there had been an attempt to liberalize the economy. We may call this phase (1961-66) as the **First Transition Period** that occured in the trade and payments regime.

But this phase was not without problems. There were some political and economic effects of devaluation. Devaluation can increase export earnings either by a reduction in domestic expenditure on exportables or by inducing an increase in the supply of exportables, which would exceed the normal increase in the supply of exportables, which, in turn exceed the normal increase in consumption, associated with increased output. There is no assurance that devaluation not accompanied by a successful control of domestic expenditure, can by itself bring about the desired increase in exports. The greater the inelasticity of the supply of exportables, the greater must be the reduction in domestic expenditure for a devaluation to succeed. And the greater must also be the political difficulties in enforcing these cuts in domestic expenditure.

It would appear that the conditions for successful devaluation did not exist in India in the summer of 1966. The country was in the midst of a severe inflationary pressure. It had still to recover from the dislocation caused by the Indo-Pakistan War of September 1965. There was a drastic fall in agricultural output and the availability of basic wage goods like food as well as the supply of some important agricultural raw materials to industry had been highly affected.[11] In these circumstances, the prospect for controlling of inflationary pressures or for any further cut in domestic consumption were indeed very dim. There was considerable excess capacity in the industrial system which could be used for increasing exports. However, the utilization of this excess capacity was dependent on a prior analysis in the supply of imported inputs, so that the balance of payments would have to deteriorate before it could improve. In such an environment, the incentives to increased exports offered by a devaluation were bound to waste themselves.

Bhagwati and Srinivasan (1976, p. 146), segregating the drought effects and devaluation, argued that the Indian decision to devalue in 1966, in so far as it replaced the earlier *ad hoc* and selective subsidies on exports, represented primarily an attempt to rationalise the then prevailing system of export subsidies and import restrictions which had grown to be extremely cumbersome, chaotic and cost-unconscious as a process of automatic protection for import substitution and that only a marginal increase in exports was expected in the short run. Subsequent events did not justify these. As a result of the inflationary increases in domestic costs and prices, a system of export subsidies had to be re-introduced for a number of products soon after the devaluation. There was a liberalisation of imports made possible by the resumption of the flow of foreign aid as well as by the recession in the industrial sector induced by the poor agricultural performance of 1965-66 and 1966-67. Exports in fiscal year 1966-67 and 1967-68 were lower than in 1964-65 and 1965-66. In 1968-69 they increased by about 9 per cent, but even then they were not much higher than the 1964-65 and 1965-66 levels. Items like engineering goods and iron and steel made an important contribution to the growth of exports in 1968-69. It appears that the growth of these exports in 1968-69 was due at least partly to temporary favourable factors such as slack domestic demand on account of the industrial recession as well as the favourable competitive situation created for India in the market in and around the Indian Ocean by the closure of the Suez Canal since 1967.

By 1968, the liberalization efforts had been largely reversed and import protection had been further intensified: QR protection was enhanced while import premia reached over 50 per cent of import values on an average. Export subsidies had been reinstituted and went up to high levels, industrial de-licensing had amounted to little. In this sense, the liberalization episode had failed.

Three important factors influenced this policy reversal. The first was the disastrous drought in 1966-67 that led to inflation and economy-wide recession. To control inflation, the authorities implemented contractionary monetary and fiscal policies and diverted public expenditure away form investment to consumption.

Second, although the 1966 devaluation was intended mainly to encourage export expansion, the magnitude was too small to reduce significantly the over-valuation of the effective exchange rate (mentioned earlier). In addition, the withdrawal of export subsidies more than offset the effects of the devaluation on most exports. The net effects, therefore, was to increase the bias against exports in comparison to the situation before the reforms.

Finally, a massive adverse political reaction to the devaluation developed because of the circumstances under which it was implemented. The Aid-India Consortium had made the resumption of aid (following the cessation during the Indo-Pakistan War in late 1965) conditional upon the implementation of liberalizing reforms that included a devaluation.

In addition to the damaging effects of drought, the weak commitment to change and the mistaken judgement on the part of the authorities with respect to the pace and sequencing of policies contributed to the reversal of the very brief liberalization attempt (based on enlarged aid flows). Given the initial conditions of a highly restricted economy, the pace of adjustment called for was too slow, as evidenced by the insufficient devaluation and the widespread distrust of the government's intentions, while the sequencing of reforms resulted in policy inconsistency—inconsistency between the stabilization and liberalization policies as well as between the policies affecting the export sector that, in fact, reinforced the inward-orientation of the economy.

By the late sixties, the domestic consequences of India's trade isolation and loss of competitiveness were also becoming apparent. Domestic industrial production was stagnating, costs were rising, employment growth was slow, and industrial sickness was spreading. Unfortunately, an overhaul of trade policy was not possible as India, by then, was trapped in a low-level equilibrium characterized by low growth, periodic external and domestic shocks (e.g., wars, poor harvest and successive droughts of the mid-sixties) and persistent balance of payments problems with little room for manoeuvre. Ultimately, these shocks, when domestic resources available for development shrank greatly, led to an interregnum of three years of Annual Planning (1966-69). Dependence on foreign aid inevitably increased. By then, a powerful domestic industrial lobby had also emerged. Among domestic industrial interests which were opposed to trade liberalization, there were hundreds and thousands of small scale units in all parts of the country. These provided substantial employment, and enjoyed total protection from competition from large domestic units or imports. Thus both practical considerations (e.g. shortages of foreign exchange) and political economy compulsions (e.g., labour and industrial interests) propelled the policy-makers and planners to the continued pursuit of inward-looking and anti-trade policies,[12] geared only to short-term crisis management rather than to longer-term exports, or foreign trade development strategies. Policy response showed excessive concern with the containment of the payments deficits in the short-run. To be fair to the planners, however, it should be recalled that trade policy during 1966-69, like other types of intervention, was intended primarily to step up readjustment and to put the economy back on the normal growth path. The large current account deficit caused mainly from the excessive rise of import volumes index from about 60 during 1961-64 to about 77 during 1965-69 (Table 5.2) was financed mainly by inflows of medium and long-term official capital and by some drawdown of reserves.

Unlike the export pessimism of the earlier plans, the **Fourth Five Year Plan** (1969-1974) visualized an aggressive approach to export growth for achieving self-reliance. As a consequence, trade policy became the primary instrument for achieving a more dynamic concept of self-reliance than what was prevalent in earlier decades. It was only in the Fourth Plan (1969-74) that a detailed programme of exports was incorporated in the plan and the Government took various institutional and other promotional measures also for encouraging exports. As a result, there was a phenomenal growth in India's export during this period, when exports increased by an average of almost 8 per cent a year.

TABLE 5.2

Export and Import Volumes (1960-69)

Year	*Volume of*		*Share in constant Price GDP (%) (In constant prices)*	
	Exports	*Imports*	*Exports*	*Imports*
1960	54	55	5.7	10.1
1961	57	57	5.8	10.1
1962	60	61	6.0	10.5
1963	68	60	6.4	9.8
1964	73	64	6.4	9.7
1965	67	77	6.1	12.2
1966	70	77	6.3	12.2
1967	66	78	5.5	11.3
1968	76	75	6.2	10.6
1969	74	75	5.7	8.2

Source : IMF, International Financial Statistics, and Government of India, *Economic Survey.*

And for the first time in the early seventies, the chronic trade gap disappeared and in 1972-73, the economy generated a surplus on its balance of trade accounts with its net aid inflows reaching its lowest. Export increased by 23 per cent during the first eighth months of 1972-1973. Though the Fourth Plan, however, renewed the emphasis on exports, but again it was as a means of financing imports and progressively eliminating the dependence on foreign aid. In fact, the fervour with which the import substitution had earlier been advocated regardless of costs now shifted to export planning and promotion, once again with little attention being paid to costs, including economies of specialization and scale. For example, a report of a study group (NCAER,1969)[13] argued that while efforts should be made to reduce inefficient high costs of domestic production, "exports cannot wait for cost reduction". Since the volume of exports depends basically on the profitability, it further argued that "we should match our prices with the international prices, irrespective of our cost of production" (*NCAER* 1969; 128,130, Also *Parliament's Export Policy Resolution 1970; the Report of the Committee on Export Strategy, 1980s; and the Report of the Import and Export Policies*, 1978). On the whole, during this plan period, as per import substitution, the gestation lag of import replacement projects and fuller utilization of existing productive capacity were the main concerns.

Meanwhile, the first petroleum price hike that thrust upon in 1973-74 resulted in acute foreign exchange shortage and worsened the trade deficit for India which was financed by increasing remittances from expatriates working in the Gulf countries and aid flows which made both trade deficit and foreign exchange position more comfortable. The resulting evolution has increased imports and led to a much bigger gap in the trade balance and consequently more and more emphasis was given on increasing exports. Moreover, the linking of the Indian rupee with the depreciating pound-sterling soon after the collapse of the Bretton Woods system of the fixed exchange rates in 1973 (and subsequently to a busket of foreign currencies) brought, in effect, a further mild but not insignificant devaluation[14] which helped exports. Apparently, however, export promotion appears to have been pushed regardless of considerable private and social costs involved. Such a strategy was clearly a prescription for economic trouble.

By the mid-1970s the constraints on the relatively unproductive sector on growth had been acknowledged by the authorities and in the Fifth Plan (1974-79) export projections did explicitly take into consideration the expanding market potential for the new and dynamic exports such as engineering goods, garments, leather manufactures, and marine products. On the other hand, during this plan invisibles surfaced as an important element of the current account with policy attention on tourism and shipping. Notwithstanding, remittances from Indian workers came as a new source of meeting the growing financing needs. So the period witnessed new confidence in external sector and prepared the groundwork for take-off to the exchange rate regime based on a busket arrangement initiated since 1975. But on the whole there was no discernible shift in foreign trade policy, except for broad indications of preference for exports not needing a subsidy and use of imports to build buffer stocks of mass consumption goods as a contra-inflationary measures.

However, during this decade there was a proliferation of export incentives; many of them concentrated on a few industries and not all of them conducive to economic efficiency. Most of the export taxes were reduced or eliminated. One new feature introduced in the seventies was the special export obligations imposed on the industries at various stages of licensing. Apart from the complicated administration and overlapping of many of the policies, one major handicap was the uncertainty regarding the value of the incentives, as well as the length of their operations due to their being subjected to frequent changes.[15]

5.3 PROGRESS OF IMPORT SUBSTITUTION

Right from the beginning of the planning era, Indian Planners have recognised that planning of foreign trade is an integral part of the national development effort. However, ever since 1950, they had tended to view the problem of foreign trade planning, largely in terms of the management of the balance of payments. The role of foreign trade in improving the efficiency of resource allocation and in securing great return from internal resources had not received adequate attention in the official documents on Indian planning. The strategy for the management of the balance of payments had also undergone significant changes during the period. While the official document of India's First Five Year Plan laid almost equal emphasis on export promotion and import substitution, the outlook of the Planners had undergone a major change by the time of Second Five Year Plan was formulated. The Planners took an extremely pessimistic view of India's export prospects. Thus, by 1956, official thinking came to rely heavily on import substitution as a *long-term solution* to India's balance of payments difficulties. The short-term problems were sought to be taken care of by a tight system of import controls as well as by arranging for a large-inflow of external assistance, prospects for which seemed to improve considerably with the formation, in 1958, of Aid-India Consortium under the leadership of the World Bank. India became increasingly dependent on external aid both for food and for plan financing. Aid as a percentage of total plan outlay more than trebled in the course of the Second Plan compared with the First. By 1960-61 America was the largest single donor to India providing nearly 348 million dollars. The Congress President Dhebar wrote Nehru a secret letter pointing out the dangers of becoming dependent on aid just for survival.

Meanwhile, there was a growing recognition by the Planners that import substitution could not provide a complete solution to India's balance of payments problems. As a result, there was an increased emphasis on export promotion within the framework of overall development strategy. The need for increased export earnings became all the more urgent since the quantum of aid was not large enough to enable India to import adequate quantity of raw materials needed for a full utilization of its growing industrial capacity.

To meet this situation, the government undertook a number of measures, of which devaluation of 1966 was one such major attempt along with other measures like the relaxation of import control and increased emphasis on bilateral trade and payments arrangements with the countries of Eastern Europe. From then on the import- substitution policies (that were put in place in 1957) were gradually intensified and expanded until the mid-1970s in accordance with the broad objective of self-reliant development with the exception of this short-lived attempt to liberalize the economy during the period 1962-66. While these policies succeeded in creating basic heavy industries and a highly diversified industrial structure with a high degree of self-sufficiency in a wide range of producers' goods, in making India a major industrial country of the world, they also entailed a considerable cost to the economy in terms of economic efficiency, technological competitiveness, and export performance, raising thereby the cost structure of Indian industry, distorting allocative efficiency in the economy, and severely blunting the edge of export competitiveness.[16] The efficacy of various policy instruments that had been adopted from time-to-time for dealing with India's balance of payments problem as well as the extent and efficacy of import-substitution-based development strategy that had taken place in India since 1957 had been criticised by a number of economists. They had shown that, except for the most striking success, in this regard, in the oil sector and in the Indian automobile industry, import substitution in industry nurtured a host of industries with sub-optimal efficiency behind the sheltered market conditions leading to high domestic resource costs. As in the case of production for exports so also in respect of import substitution, the high cost structure derived not only from the trade regimes but also from the imperative of domestic industrial policy especially in relation to unit capacities. In a well-presented and cogently argued book on Industrial Stagnation in India, Isher Judge Ahluwalia[17] (1985) had shown how, though the strategy of import substitution was developed on the basis of protecting infant industries, the manner in which policy evolved protected not only infants but in her expressive phrase, 'elderly incompetents' also. She also pointed out how, as the process of import substitution was carried deeper and deeper, industries were set up in which the economy became less and less competitive. In this process as J. Bhagwati and T. N. Srinivasan (1975) had shown that there had been considerable misallocation of scarce investment resources, the emergence of a high-cost industrial structure, strengthening the forces of cost-push inflation and weakening both the price and quality competitiveness of exports. The effective exchange rate for imports was consistently higher than for exports and there was a built-in-bias against exports which the various export incentive schemes had not been able to correct fully. The Tandon

Committee on Exports also made the same point when they referred to the way in which high effective protection for imports contrasted with negative effective protection for exports. The import substitution model had led to development of domestic production at cost above international levels when perhaps the imports so substituted could have been obtained by exporting items which might have been produced at less international cost.

Examining the evidence and analysis presented in the studies of Bhagwati and Desai (1970) and Bhagwati and Srinivasan (1975), Kelkar[18] (1977, p. 997) comes to the conclusion that most of the criticism of India's trade policies based on arguments derived from the excessive 'economic costs' due to such policies, have a rather weak empirical foundation. He points out the various inadequacies in the estimates of Domestic Resource Cost used in the studies of Bhagwati, Srinivasan and Desai, and argues that taking these estimates as an indicator of the long-run marginal cost can be quite misleading. Kelkar also notes that there is little evidence to suggest that import substitution industrialization strategy has led to the absence to technological adaptation and innovation. On the other hand, he is in sympathy with the argument that trade policies along with industrialization policies have led to fragmentation of industrial plants, and this has in turn led to high costs. However, whatever may be the Kelkar's criticism in this respect of the need for the empirical studies on the effects of India's foreign trade regime on industrial efficiency, one could argue that protectionist policies at best had created administrative delays in the implementation of projects and at the same time resulted in inefficient production and waste of resources arising out of granting protection to whichever industry set-up indigenous capacity, without calculating the relative costs of foreign and domestic production or for quality.

However, the hypothesis that import substitution will lead to industrial efficiency by providing greater access to imported inputs and by creating a situation of greater competition is far from adequate as it appears from the further empirical evidence made by Bokil, Chitre and Murthi (1981) Wolf (1982), Sandesara (1979), Golder (1986).

In this context, Manmohon Singh's (1976)[19] arguments deserve serious attention when he articulated that while in the process of import substitution a number of industries had come into existence whose contribution to the future growth of the economy was not likely to be insignificant, the fault quite often lay in a faulty programming of import substitution. For example, balance of payments difficulties often led to the imposition of severe restrictions on the import of non-essential consumer goods. But due care was not taken to discourage their domestic production. Very often, import controls rather than tariffs had been the principal instrument of protection. These controls created a protective wall which could not be crossed of foreign competitors regardless of the degree of inefficiency of local producers. Hence the latter's incentive to reduce their cost of production through innovation was greatly reduced. It was no doubt true that import substitution in intermediate products and capital goods that constituted inputs of manufactured exports raised the cost of production of exportables and to that extent, in the absence of special remedial measures, hampered the growth of exports.

Later on, the same point was made by Balasubramanyam and Basu (1990) who argued[20] that India's export incentive schemes appeared to have been not only expensive relatively to what they had achieved but many of the schemes also appeared to lack any sort of economic rationale. The root cause of India's export problem was the indiscriminate import substitution policy the country had pursued. Symptomatic of the problem were the existence of 'cost plus' protection together with public enterprise inefficiency, highly profitable domestic markets, lack of imported inputs, high costs of production, high capital intensity of exports and poor quality of products exported—all of which had in effect constrained exports, . . . the import substituting industrialization policies have imparted a bias against exports. Sunanda Sen[21] (1982), however, argued that the growth and distributional implications of export-oriented strategies launched after Fourth Plan were not satisfactory. The possible loss in employment as might result from the dismantling of controls, especially on import or from the difficulty of pushing exports in an otherwise stagnant world market were the considerations which had little appeal to the policy-makers.

Overall, it is now widely agreed that prolonged application of ISI is a mistake. Although ISI did encourage industrialization but the balance of payments did not improve because the capital intensive components needed to produce the finished products increased import costs, and the reallocation of resources in favour of the manufacturing sector reduced traditional agricultural exports and curtailed efforts to foster export-oriented industrialization. Moreover, capital-intensive technologies had a negative impact on employment and shifted income in favour of capital. In addition, the concentration on domestic industry shifted the internal terms of trade against agriculture. Declining profits in agriculture led to reduced investment in the agricultural sector, further increasing the income inequalities between agriculture and industry. Industrialization through import substitution required the creation of an institutional framework conducive to capital accumulation and the efficient allocation of resources, but these conditions were not met. Inefficient economic management by the companies established to promote ISI and the inability of the state to create regulatory frameworks that limited waste and corruption increased the costliness of the ISI experiment. In spite of the above shortcomings of the ISI strategy, we can say that this strategy had no doubt gave the Indian economy a certain depth and spread, increased its bargaining power and independence, and lent the Indian economy and society the dignity it did not possess after the colonial experience. But, over time, certain negative features developed. That, and the response to the changed world conditions, required a shift in strategy for the achievement of the same goals of self-reliance and rapid growth (*Reddy*, 2006b).

5.4 SECOND TRANSITION PERIOD: LATE 1970s TO 1985

During the late 1970s, there was the reversal of the trend of increasing export volumes and the move towards a more liberal import policy which meant more liberal access to imported raw materials, spares, components and to a lesser extent, capital goods and technology, was initiated, when the policy-makers and planners felt that India's foreign exchange situation permitted such a move towards liberalization and was designed to give a fillip to growth and investment. This resulted in increased non-petroleum imports. Concessional aid financed most of the current account deficit during this period. Despite the severe shocks administered to balance of payments as a result of the second oil price increase in 1979 (also coincided with a severe drought which cut-back agricultural output, depressed GDP and set off inflationary pressures), the accompanying sharp deterioration in the terms of trade of the order of nearly 38 per cent between 1978 and 1980 (leading to a net annual transfer of income abroad of over 2 percent of India's GDP) and the weakening of export market and price, the planners and the policy-makers held fast to this programme of import liberalization. It could, in fact, be argued that the desire to keep up with import liberalization was a factor in the approach to the Fund. The imports was not liberalized because of the Fund. The country went to the Fund because it desired to keep import policy liberal. The programme of import liberalization itself was built into the investment and growth strategy of the **Sixth Plan** (1980-85) that began in the shadow of this external shock, especially in areas where direct import saving was both possible and could be efficient and equally in areas which would strengthen the export capability in essential component of the structural adjustment effort was the acceleration of the investment in the oil sector which was made possible by the availability of resources and foreign exchange cushion represented by the Fund Programme. The availability of IMF credit enabled the economy to keep both the maintenance and developmental imports at a sufficiently high level and at the same time eased the adjustment problems of the Indian economy as far as the balance of payments difficulties were concerned. But it also imposed debt-service obligations.

The crisis in the international economy which in a sense had disrupted the structure of India's external payments and at the same time, from the mid-seventies the negative effects on growth resulting from the technological obsolence of many industries and the related poor export performance called for a far-reaching re-examination of trade and payments policies and related aspects of domestic policies. Thus trade policy reform became a consistent theme in official reports and various policy statements. In effect, three high powered official committees (Alexander, Abid Hussain and the Narasimham) were appointed by the government in quick succession between 1978 and 1980, primarily to look into the various aspects of trade and payments policies. Recommendations of the Committee set-up in the late seventies brought alongside the winds of change in trade and payments policy. Two areas for reform had been consistently stressed: making exports more profitable (less costly) and moving away from the highly discretionary import licensing system towards one based on more unified tariffs. However, neither the concept of a neutral trade regime nor the idea of import competition from domestic industries had been emphasized in public discussion of trade policy issues. The official export policy of 1978-79 implemented the recommendations of the Alexander Committee (1978)[22] for (a) achieving efficiency in the system through a rationalization of the structure of subsidies, and (b) increasing facilities for export services. The changing attitudes of the government to the question of export promotion was reflected in the consensus arrived at in the Dagli Committee (1979) and Tandon Committee (1980) Reports. "*The term export subsidy*", according to the former, "*is a misnomer (since) ... it consists, in many ways, of bare compensation to offset indirect taxes and (thus) the taxes and subsidies cancel out*." The Tandon Report on export strategy (1980), however, was more explicit regarding the desirability of the export-promotion devices. The recommendations included a blanket approval of the prevailing preferential treatment of the export sector in regard to licensing facilities, duty exemptions, the MRTP regulations, technological imports, rules relating to royalty rates and dilution of equities in MNCs/foreign companies and all concessional facilities to the availability and pricing of input" (*Tandon Committee on Export Strategy*, Government of India, 1980, p. 52).

Accordingly, during the Sixth Plan period (1980-85) there had been renewed thinking regarding liberalization of the industrial and trade regimes. The period emphasized the strengthening of the impulses of modernization for achievement of both economic and technological self-reliance. Committees set-up by the government (notably the Abid Hussain Committee and the Narasimham Committee) made a number of recommendations to give greater impetus to the ongoing process of trade liberalization (*Report of the Committee on Trade Policies, Ministry of Commerce*, 1984, publicly released in August 1985). The most important of these included the suggestion for a change from quantitative restrictions of imports to regulations through higher tariffs, to suitably, compensate the existing bias against exports by modernizing protection in the domestic market, adequate export incentives, and a real effective exchange rate at a level which would maintain the competitiveness of exports.

In sum, export incentives had been strengthened and expanded particularly since the early 1980s. They had consisted mainly of import entitlement schemes and fiscal measures for selected industries. Because of the strong bias towards domestic production, however, the authorities had surrounded the export incentives with complex and onerous controls to prevent the diversion of imported raw materials, equipment and credit intended for exports to domestic production or direct resale. They had not modified, however, the regulations that obstructed the entry and exit of firm.

With respect to the escalation of tariff, the primary motivation of the authorities was not to offset the effects of the relaxed QRs, but to increase government revenues. The actions of the Indirect Taxation Enquiry Committee bears testimony to this fact. The long-term fiscal policy had clearly emphasized on the necessity and urgency of custom tariff in regulating the BoP situation and also promoting built-in-revenue raising capacity. Tariff escalation had been accompanied by a trend away from uniformity, as pressures from user industries for special exemptions had increased in tandem with the tariff increases. The net effect of the increased tariffs and exemptions had been increased variability of protection and increased inefficiency of the tariff system with respect to the allocation of resources, making it more difficult to move to a more uniform system.

Estimates of the level of effective protection afforded by the export incentives revealed that the most protected industries (about two-fifths of the total) were highly capital- and energy-intensive, largely owned by the public sector, and paid an average wage nearly double that of the industries receiving low protection. Nearly 80 per cent of employment was concentrated in the low protection industries (three-fifths of the total).

Despite the considerable incentives directed to exporting, the superior profitability and security of producing for the domestic market ensured that exporting remained a marginal activity for Indian firms.

5.5 THE THIRD TRANSITION PERIOD TOWARDS A MORE DYNAMIC ECONOMY: 1985-91 AND BEYOND

Keeping in view that imports of state-of-the-art capital goods would provide the faster route to modernizing the Indian economy and improving efficiency and exports must grow to provide the foreign exchange for imports and the markets for increased production of labour and skill-intensive goods, also at the same time foreign trade could, over time, be used to expose Indian producers to foreign competition, thereby complementing the Government's efforts to enhance domestic competition, in 12 th April 1985, for the first time, a three-year import export policy covering the period, April 1985 through March 1988 was announced by the Government of the then Commerce Minister, Mr. Vishwanath Pratap Singh with a view to improving export incentives and rationalizing import restrictions, injecting confidence also among the trading communities to take a long-term investment decisions. It is noteworthy that before 1985-86, the annual export-import policy was announced at the beginning of the financial year. However, the liberalization was within the parameters of a system of controls and focused on rationalization and removal of some recognized distortions; it by no means implied a delicensed regime. The direction of policy was best expressed in the Seventh Plan (1985-90). It conceptualized self-reliance not only in terms of reduced dependence on aid but also in terms of building up domestic capabilities and reducing import dependence in strategic materials. Achievement of technological competence through liberal imports of technology was also envisaged.

The Seventh Plan also stressed the necessity of reducing the ever-increasing gulf of difference between exports and imports, with the full recognition that the pull of domestic demand and the high cost of production had become the persistent onslaught to high export growth potentiality. It stated explicitly that a whole array of policy instruments, will need to be deployed to attain the BoP objectives (GOI, *Seventh Five Year Plan*, p. 75). The Seventh Plan recognised the fact that quantitative restrictions had over-protected the domestic market and without a well-conceived sectors package for sales abroad, they had discriminated against export, and import substitutes had been produced at a higher domestic resource cost. This situation required correction. Further, the Seventh Plan stated that tariff rather than import restrictions to restrain the demand for imports should be the priority concern and also, there should be less variability in the overall tariff structure. Finally, the 1987/88 Budget unified tariffs on many capital goods. Despite these changes, numerous additional reforms were needed to increase the competitiveness of Indian exports and, over time, to rationalize and reduce the level of import protection.

On the expiry of import-export policy (1985-88), new import-export policy (April 1988 to March 1991) was announced, that tried at best to provide a stable framework so as to minimise year-to-year uncertainties and enable entrepreneurs to plan their activities in a longer-term perspectives. Besides, they provided a framework for a flexible and liberal response to the growing needs of the economy for increasing production and exports, while the import-export policy 1985-88 reflected the second liberalization trend with considerable relaxation of import controls and lowering of import duties on capital goods, the tariff structure being simplified by reducing the previous eleven auxiliary custom duty rates to three rates of nil, 25 percent and 40 percent with an attempt to reinforce the policy of canalising agencies, though this export-import policy had been under attack with the blame of 'tinkering' with the problem only (not repayment of debts and restoration of balance of payments equilibrium).

The Import-Export Policy, 1988-91 reinforced the process of trade liberalization. 745 new items had been brought under OGL. The benefits of import replenishment had also been enlarged, based on the net value-added element in the export products, and for the first time, the imports up to certain financial limits could be made without indigenous clearance. The policy also made a conscious effort to reduce the control on exports 'to the barest minimum, both in their coverage and nature of restrictions'. Twenty-six items of exports had been decanalized and some of the earlier licensing had been abolished. However this policy laid grater emphasis on promotion of exports which had been more facilitated by import liberalization. The result was, in the last three years of the seventh plan, export promotion had been quite satisfactory.

In retrospect, between 1985 and 1990 the pattern of reform in India was one of moving toward a more neutral trading regime[23] with much less progress towards liberality. Some selective reduction in QRs took place, as well as rationalization of the tariff structure and some small reduction in tariff. Despite these changes, both tariffs and QRs remained significant impediments to trade. And the luxury consumption-led growth motivation behind liberalization had been anti-egalitarian, with production and consumption of durable consumer goods for the rich and upper middle classes.

The crisis at the end of the decade of the eighties had many facets of which sharp worsening of balance of payments appeared to be critical. The crisis that compelled the policy makers to institute widespread reform was mostly macro-economic in origin. In the year 1990-91, inflation exceeded 10 per cent, a rate to be considered high. The debt to GNP ratio was around 60 per cent, a near doubling of the ratio in 1980, fiscal deficit increased to 10 per cent of GDP from 8 per cent in 1985. The deficit on the current account of the balance of payments, arising out of the decline in the average rate of growth of exports substantially after 1989-90 and increase of the import bill as well as volume of imports from three billion dollars in the mid-eighties to more than seven billion dollars, was 3.1 per cent of GDP; the gap between domestic investments and savings grew between 1.5 per cent of GDP in 1980 to around 3.3 per cent by the end of 1990 and this was reflected in the current account deficit. The severity of the BoP crisis in the later half of the 1980's could also be judged from the fact that India's foreign currency assets depleted rapidly from US $ 3.1 billion in April 1990 to US $ 975 million on July 1991. Credit rating of the country was lowered, restricting the country's access to commercial borrowings and unwillingness on the part of the normal banking channels to provide renewal of short-term credit to Indian banks abroad. As forex reserves kept on falling on expectations of an impending depreciation of rupee, there was a temporary loss of confidence leading to a flight of non-resident Indian (NRI) deposits. The current account deficit was financed partially through reduction in official reserves as a consequence of which foreign currency reserves of about $ 1 billion could finance no more than two weeks' imports in June 1991. The weaknesses of the Indian economy were exposed.

This state of affairs was not entirely due to the current account deficit, it was also in part due to the Gulf War, which not only pushed up oil prices but also led to the loss of several million dollars of workers' remittances from the Middle East. This was compounded by the trend towards withdrawal of deposits by non-resident Indians[24] during the first half of 1991, stated just now.

The crisis at the end of the eighties served to highlight the fragility of an economy subject to recurring crises which could be just about contained with foreign borrowing and inflows of remittances. Such borrowing and remittances could be relied upon only because of fiscal prudence and low inflation rates exhibited in the past; but once the grip of public finances was loosened, the fragility of the economy, weakened by years of interventionist policies, was exposed. And in the vastly changed international economic environment, India could no longer rely on external assistance and short-term fire-fighting tactics to cope with the crisis. The immediate cause of the crisis was no doubt macroeconomic in nature, but the growth in the gap between savings and investment was a consequence of low growth over the years which in turn had its origin in the inefficient macroeconomic trade and investment policies grounded in the inward-looking import substitution philosophy justified by the objective of self-sufficiency.[25] Both the magnitude of the crisis and the realization that in the absence of reforms India could not hope to attract external capital, appeared to have convinced the policy-makers of the need for reform.

5.6 RECENT DEVELOPMENTS: THE REFORM OF THE TRADING SYSTEM OVER THE 1990s AND BEYOND

Only after June-July 1991, the Central Government had started initiating a series of measures to revive the economy out of shambles and tackle the chronic balance of payments deficits. The measures included taking loans from the IMF and initiating structural adjustment reforms of various kinds with explicit objectives of correcting payments imbalances, stimulate exports, curtail imports and contain domestic fiscal deficits and inflationary trends, including controls on domestic investment, exchange rate and tariff reforms, measures relating to foreign direct investment.

The set of measures initiated by the government of India might be divided into two groups, one pertaining to short-term temporary financing of current account deficit through loans, another relating to the trading regimes including competitive exchange rate through downward adjustment in the par value of the rupee' which is nothing but devaluation.[26] The concommittant reform measures with respect to export-import policies of the country belonged to the second set of measures. Among the measures belonging to the first set, the most significant had been the mortgaging of 30% of the gold reserves of the RBI in the foreign banks to obtain foreign exchange with the provision of releasing the mortgage after six months by paying a rate of interest lower than the London inter-bank offer rate (LIBOR). As a temporary measure to tide over the foreign exchange crisis, this measure was likely to have a cushioning effect. Second, the IMF had been approached to grant $ 7 billion credit to India on a medium term basis from the upper 'tranche' arrangement and under the Extended Fund Facility and the stand-by-arrangement'.[27] Here we note only the major measures of reform and their consequences on the Indian economy with greater emphasis on exchange rate evolution and reforms since Independence, in particular.

5.6.1 Controls

India's industrial policy structure with its extensive controls, which required entrepreneurs to obtain licenses from the government for almost each and every aspect of their business including establishment of enterprises, expansion of investment and access to foreign exchange, raw materials and imported technology, familiarly known "as the permit raj," had been mostly dismantled. Industrial licensing was abolished for all except a list of environmentally sensitive industries. Large and dominant firms were no longer required to obtain permission to expand their investments. The number of industries reserved for the public sector was reduced from 17 to 6 and the private sector was allowed participation in the reserved list. Access to technology was much freer than before. These domestic delicensing reforms, which removed stifling restrictions on entrepreneurship and more importantly remove opportunities for bribery and corruption, should count as a significant departure from the interventionist regime. The easing of licensing policies and quantitative restrictions on import of capital goods and raw materials led to a rapid growth in the manufacturing sector.

5.6.2 Tariffs And Controls on Trade

Prior to 1991, tariff rates in India were very high and the tariff system was also quite complicated. Thus reforms were necessary because the custom tariff had become, over the years, very complicated in terms of multiple rates, innumerable exemptions, excessive controls, and elaborate procedures. These infirmities of the custom tariff often led to delays, harassment, corruption, and litigation. Moreover, rationalization and simplification of the custom duties was needed to move towards a market economy, freedom of trade, and opening up the Indian economy to the outside world.

Reforms in this category included thus reduction of tariffs and liberalization of import licensing requirements. Tariffs had been lowered using mainly a 'tops down' approach; peak applied tariffs had drastically been reduced, although not sufficiently to remove the cascading structure of protection. The effective tariff rate (actual tariff rates which takes into account tariff exemptions) on manufacturing was reduced from 126 per cent in 1990-91 to 26 per cent by the end of the fiscal year 1997-98; on agriculture the average tariff rate was lowered from 113 per cent to 26 per cent and on mining from 100 to 25 per cent. The reform package also allowed for tariff concessions on imports of capital goods by user industries, especially exporters. The scheme permitted imports of both new and second hand capital goods at a concessional rate of 15 per cent, with the proviso that the manufacturer should increase direct exports above the average level in the preceding three years, by an amount equivalent to four times the value of capital goods imported.

Another significant trade policy reform was the liberalization of the import-licensing system. Until 1991 imports were subject to a complex licensing system consisting of 26 commodity lists covering all merchandise. The export and import policy reform of 1992 replaced the 'positive' list with a consolidated 'negative' list of goods subject to licensing; all items not on the list could be imported without licence. The negative list consisted of all consumer goods including consumer electronic goods, drugs and pharmaceuticals, chemicals and allied items, and items relating to the small-scale sector. Items in the negative list are subject to import licences and the actual user condition, which requires the approved importer of the goods also to be the end user of the goods.[28]

Yet another move towards liberalization related to the reduction in the number of the so-called canalised items or items which could only be imported by state-trading agencies. The rationale for the grant of this monopoly to the state-trading agencies was that they could obtain improved terms of trade through handling of bulk transactions. Available evidence suggests that the measure only served to restrict competition and any benefits in terms of scale economies the system provided were outweighed by bureaucratic inefficiencies.[29]

In retrospect, the trade and payments regime as it existed prior to the reform was more or less complex. In order to remove the complexity, the thrust of the major reforms in trade policy and procedures since the announcement in March 31, 1992 of the EXIM Policy for 1992-97, coinciding with the period of **Eighth Five Year Plan** was on accelerating the transition of the Indian economy to an internationally-oriented economy to reap the benefits of international trade by stimulating exports and facilitating imports of essential inputs as well as capital goods. The trade liberalization process had progressed in two directions/phases. The first phase was one of removing the obstacles to exports, which typically involved unifying and devaluating the exchange rate and removing quantitative restrictions on imports of intermediate and capital goods. In-addition, during this phase, direct inducements to exporting were generally provided in the form of duty drawback schemes and preferential export financing. The second phase, during which remaining quantitative restrictions were virtually eleminated and tariff began to be gradually reduced, generally commenced only after balance of payments were strengthened. The progress in eliminating quantitative import restriction in India is shown in Table 5.3.

It appears that in 1990-91 the unweighted average nominal tariff was 128 per cent, with a peak rate of 355 per cent. Following the recommendations of the Tax Reform Committee the process of effecting a reduction of peak tariff rate commenced with the Union Budget 1991-92. With a view to improving competitive efficiency of domestic industries, the peak tariff rate was slashed to 65 percent in 1994-95 from 170 per cent in 1992-93 and 85 per cent in 1993-94. Encouraged by the dynamism displayed by the industrial sector as evidenced by the strong growth of the Indian industry, especially the manufacturing sector, the Central Budget for 1995-96 had effected a further reduction in peak tariffs to 50 per cent, together with reductions in almost all other rates. With a view to avoiding the cascading effects and to curbing inflation, substantial reduction in Customs duty on critical raw materials and on simplification and rationalization of tariff structure in critical sectors had been effected. Thereafter, the maximum tariff rate again fell, while the average import weighted tariffs also fell drastically, the details of which were discussed in chapter 4.

5.6.3 India's Trade Policy in the Reform Era

Meanwhile India became a Founder Member of the World Trade Organization (WTO) on 1st January 1995 by ratifying the WTO Agreement on 30 December 1995. In line with the WTO Agreements, India's Trade and Payments Policy had undergone several major changes from time to time in regard to import liberalization, export promotion and liberalization and tariff reduction.

TABLE 5.3

India: Average Nominal Tariff Rates[a]

In percent, unless otherwise specified

Prior to Reform Period	*Crisis Period*	*Post-Liberalization Reform Period*			
Year 1986 (without exemption)	*1990-1991*	*1992-93*	*1993-94*	*1994-95*	*1995-96*
137 (300)[b] {50}	128 (355) {87[c]}	94 (110) {64}	71 (85) {47}	50-55(65) {33}	50-55 (50) {27}

Note : (a) Unweighted, rounded off to nearest integer.

(b) Figures in parentheses indicate the peak tariff rate

(c) Figures in second bracketed part indicate average tariff, import weighed.

RBI Annual Reports, 1994-95, *Economic Survey*, 1996-97. World Bank SINTIAL File Published in "*India—An Industrializing Economy in Transition* (1989)", World Bank, Washington.

Source : GATT (1993), *Trade Policy Review*, India.

Modifications to the Exim Policy 1992-97 announced, coinciding with the period of 8th Five Year Plan on March 31, 1995 and subsequently on May 2, 1995, giving a new thrust to exports of agricultural and allied sectors and services reflected the continued commitment of the Government to dismantle QRs. The policy made a conscious effort to dismantle various protections regulating policies and accelerate India's transition towards a globally-oriented economy. Substantial concessions had been announced to boost agricultural exports. The Government had also announced a Centrally sponsored scheme to set-up industrial parks in different states. The Chief Controller of Imports and Exports was redesignated as Directorate General of Foreign Trade (DGFT). The salient features of the Modified Exim Policy were: (i) further pruning of negative list of imports and a simultaneous expansion of items importable under the OGL, and Special Imports Licence (SIL);

(ii) allowing exporters to import on zero duty basis capital goods, (iii) widening the scope of deemed exports, (iv) introduction of a new trade finance instrument for exporters, and (v) allowing a large number of consumer goods to be imported under OGL and SIL.

The Export and Import Policy, 1997-2002 (coinciding with the period of **Ninth Five Year Plan**) sought to consolidate the gains of the previous policy and further carry forward the process of liberalization by deregulating and simplifying procedures and removing QRs in a phased manner. It had an ambitious target of achieving 1 per cent share in world trade.

The revised Exim Policy (1997-98) contained many changes to enhance export competition by simplifying procedures, minimizing transaction costs, delays and improving the attractiveness of various schemes. The measures inter alia included:

- The threshold limit for Export Promotion of Capital Goods (EPCG) zero duty scheme was brought down massively.
- DEPB (Duty Entitlement Pass Book Scheme) was modified to neutralize both the basic custom duty as well as special custom duty.
- Permission was given to set up private warehouses for exports and imports.
- Exports of oil seeds for consumption purpose and vegetables were made free without any quantitative and licensing requirements.
- Changes in threshold limit for export houses, SIL entitlement were made to provide impetus to exports.

In April 1998, the WTO Disputes Settlement Panel ruled that India's QRs were contrary to the WTO rules. In August 1999, an appellate body of the WTO upheld the early ruling. India had to phase out the QRs on 2300 tariff lines. The items in the Restricted List were reduced to 667.

On 31st March 1999 the following trade policy changes were announced:

- Discontinuation of the convention of publishing negative lists for exports and imports.

- New schemes to boost service exports.
- Special status to manufacturing and merchant exporters.
- Special benefits to direct exports by small scale, tiny and cottage industries.
- Extension of additional incentives to the export of products from sectors such as biotechnology, textiles, engineering and chemicals.

In April 1999 the DGFT set up a fast track counter to cater to the requirements of exports houses and various trading houses in the context of Advance License and DEPB schemes. The Ministry of Commerce took the initiative to strengthen the infrastructure for Electronic Data Interchange and electronic commerce. Thus the interface between government authorities and importers and exporters was reduced.

Moreover, in order to promote trade among SAARC countries, India unilaterally removed all QRs on imports of 2300 items from SAARC countries with effect from 1 August 1998. This move gave a boost to the establishment of a South Asia Free Trade Area (SAFTA). (*The Economic Times,* 12 August 1999, p. 3)

The important measures announced in the Budget of 1999-2000 were:

- Rationalization of customs duty structures,
- Reduction in duty rates for capital inputs in the information technology sector,
- Revamping of the scheme of export credit in foreign currency to revitalize exports and to bring about major simplification of procedures, and
- Setting up of a High Powered Committee to investigate the issue of high transaction costs for exporters and to make concrete recommendations for reduction of such costs.

Some important announcements during the 1999-2000 were :

- Import of 894 items were made license free and another 414 items could be imported under SIL.

- Duty exemption scheme had been made more flexible.
- Green cards for exporters exporting 50 per cent of their production.
- Golden Status Certificate for Export and Trading Houses, which means that an exporter who has been a status holder for three terms will acquire the status permanently.

On 28 December, 1999 India and the USA reached a bilateral agreement to remove QRs in 18 months from the adoption of the panel reports in September 1999. QRs on 714 items were to be removed by 1 April 2000 and the remaining 715 items by 1 April 2000.

The Union Commerce and Industries Minister announced major policy changes in Exim Policy 2000-01 on 31 March 2000 with a view to achieve an export growth target of 20 per cent in dollar terms in 2000-01. This Exim Policy brought about a major rationalization in export promotion schemes and launched a series of sector-specific initiations. Emulating the Chinese model, Special Economic Zones (SEZs) to promote exports from India were being undertaken. These SEZs would operate free of all rules and regulations governing import and export units subject to the condition that what they produce would be exported. The only laws which will operate within the SEZs will be those related to labour and banking. The objective was to involve the states in export promotion. For providing impetus to exports Rs. 250 crore was made to the states. Procedural simplification was announced. A policy to attract 100 percent FDI in the SEZs had also been announced.

It is noteworthy that presently China derived 40% of its exports from such SEZs. However, Chinese SEZs were based on contract labour system (hire and fire policy). The Commerce Minister of India categorically ruled out any changes in labour laws, still applying the existing labour laws to the units in the SEZs. Still further, there are various infrastructure bottlenecks. Hence in view of India's BoP difficulties success of SEZs in India is a moot question.

India was unable to remove QRs on its imports fully with respect to consumer products and certain other agricultural products. The US Government lodged a complaint with the

WTO and the appellate body upheld the US position. India was then requested to speedily remove QRs. Exim Policy (2000), as expected, therefore, removed QRs on 714 commonly used items (agricultural products and consumer durables) out of 1429 items (nearly 50 per cent items). Thus items like meat, milk powder, cigars, cigarettes, televisions, tape recorders, umbrellas, etc. could be imported freely. However, most of these items would attract peak rate of basic import duty of 35 percent which when increased with surcharge and special custom duty would add up to a total of 44% in import duties. Furthermore, the 44% would be enhanced by countervailing duty equivalent to domestic excise duty on the product being imported.

It is important to note in this connection that import restrictions were being phased out since 1996 but no extraordinary growth had occurred from the import of freed items. Removal of licensing and quota restrictions would lead to surge in imports of these items, hurting and causing serious injury to the domestic industry. Reports of desperation among weavers and farmers committing suicides were mounting in evidence of the backlash of removal of QRs. So anti-dumping and anti-subsidy tariffs and other safeguards should be used in case of sudden surge in imports.

Our analysis so far pinpoints the fact that India has taken major steps towards trade liberalization since 1991, partly on its own initiative and partly from its commitments to WTO. In particular trade policy over the last decade have provided an export-friendly environment with simplified procedure conducive to enhancing export performance. The focus have been on liberalization, transparency and globalization with basic thrust on outward orientation focusing on export promotion activity moving away from QRs and improving competitiveness of Indian industry to meet the global market requirements. Over the years, significant changes in the Exim Policy have helped strengthen the export production base, remove procedural irritants, facilitate input availability besides focusing on quality and technological upgradation and improving competitiveness. Steps have also been taken to promote exports through bi-lateral and multi-lateral initiatives, identification of thrust areas and focus regions. Still there remains many obstacles affecting the export prospects of Indian exporters due to non-flexibility of labour laws, ill-conceived policy regarding reservation of items for the small scale sector and complicated port procedures.

At the stroke of the New Millennium, India's Exim policy (2001-02) announced by the Commerce Minister, decided to dismantle quantitative restrictions on the remaining 1429 items at one stroke, warning thereby the domestic producers to face competition with international players. The salient features of the Exim Policy were :

- Import restrictions of the remaining 715 items were removed.
- Imports of second hand vehicles, poultry products and primary agricultural products and textile articles were allowed.
- Imports of farm products, petrol, diesel, urea, etc. had been permitted only through designated state trading agencies.
- EPCG scheme and Duty Exemption Scheme (DES) was extended to agricultural exports as well.
- Agri-economic Zones would be formed for promotion of agricultural exports.

In early 2002 the Government presented a Medium Term Export Strategy for 2002-07, coinciding with the period of **Tenth Five Year period**, providing a vision for creating a stable policy environment with indicative sector-wise targets, with a mission to achieve 1 percent of global trade by 2007. The Exim Policy (2002-07) sought to usher in an environment free of restrictions and controls.

The salient feature of this Exim Policy (2002-07) were as under :

- Indian Banks were allowed to set up offshore banking units in SEZs.
- The policy gave a major thrust to agricultural exports by removing QRs on all agricultural products except a few sensitive items like jute and onions.

- The policy for improving the productivity and export competitiveness of small-scale cottage and handicrafts sector, provided a package of incentives including exemption from maintaining the average export obligations under the EPCG scheme, permission to achieve lower threshold level for achieving the Export House status, preferential access to Market Access Initiative funds and duty free access to trimming and embellishment for achieving value-added exports.
- In view of the phasing out of all restrictions on textile products by 2005 under the Agreement on Textile and Clothing (ATC), the Exim Policy has focused on measure to encourage value-added exports in the garment sector.
- Procedural simplification have been made in the Exim Policy to further reduce transaction costs covering Directorate General of Foreign Trade, Customs and Banks.
- Market Access Initiative Scheme was widened to include activities considered necessary for a focused market promotion of exports, setting up of "Business Centre" in India missions abroad for visiting Indian exporters/businessmen for ensuring a facilitory environment for exporters.
- Focus Africa was launched in April 2002 for a gain in trade for India with Sub-Saharan African region. During 2001-02, Indian exports-imports statistics accounted for US $ 108 billion and $ 1.5 billion respectively.

The Foreign Trade Policy (2004-05) announced on August 2004 had the twin objectives of doubling India's share in global merchandise trade from 0.7 percent in 2002-03 to 1.5 percent in 2009 and of acting as an effective instrument for generation of employment opportunities. It endeavoured to develop India as a global hub for manufacturing, trading and services. The Annual Supplement to the Foreign Trade Policy 2004-09 announced on April 2005 by the Union Commerce and Industry Minister, Mr. Kamal Nath incorporated additional policy initiatives and further simplified the procedures. State

Governments would be actively involved in providing an enabling environment for boosting international trade. The Supplement provided renewed thrust to agricultural exports by the extension of Vishesh Krish Upaj Yojna to poultry and dairy products.

The SEZ Bill was passed by Parliament in June 2005. Implement the provisions of this SEZ Act, 2005, the SEZ Rules had been framed and notified.

India has perusing for negotiations on non-tariff barriers (NTMs) in WTO. Use of contingent protective measures allowed under the WTO Agreements like anti-dumping subsidies and countervailing duties has increased over time.

5.6.4 Reforms Relating to Foreign Direct Investment

India is not a major recipient of foreign direct investment (FDI). Both controls over trade and the complex set of regulations governing inward investment and technology flows have deterred foreign investors from investing in India. During the period 1985-87 FDI in India amounted to a meagre 0.2 per cent of capital formation, compared to 25.5 per cent in Singapore, 15.2 per cent in Hong Kong, 14.4 per cent in Indonesia, 8.7 per cent in Malaysia and 1.4 per cent in South Korea. The liberalization of rules and regulations relating to FDI counted as a significant move towards integrating India with the world economy—the primary objective of reforms. Significant departure from the earlier restrictive regime included the abolition of the requirement that FDI inflows should be accompanied by technology transfers, automatic approval of FDI up to foreign equity participation of 51 per cent in a range of industries in 34 sectors, and automatic approval of technology transfer agreements subject to limits on royalty and lump-sum fee payments. Accordingly, policies with regard to FDI have been liberalized substantially since 1991. Measures adopted ranged from opening new areas to FDI and raising participation limits across a wide spectrum of activities to bringing several sectors under the automatic route of the Reserve Bank of India. This was done in order to strengthen the development of export houses as well as trading houses as an instrument for promoting exports, to have a viable BoP situation.

5.6.5 Exchange Rate Management and Reforms in India: An Evaluation

Since exchange rate influences the prices of tradables vis-a-vis non-tradables and thereby induces shifts in consumption and production patterns and also the profitability of the export industry, the exchange rate adjustment in conjunction with other macro-economic policies is a necessary part of the balance of payments strategy of the less developed nations. These countries face an uphill task of defending the existing level of traditional exports in the context of adverse technological developments aboard and domestic inflation, output and employment, (i) promoting the exports of new manufactured products which are initially handicapped on account of an un-competitive cost-price structure, arising in part out of an inadequate exploitation of economies of large scale; and (ii) reducing the excess domestic demand for imports and thereby facilitating a more orderly administration of import controls. It is precisely because of the need for support of other macro-economic policies that the role of the exchange rates in imparting sustainability to the current account has often been subjected to sharp criticism. In a large measure, the critics have ascribed the failure of exchange rate to correct trade and current account imbalances to restrictive and unrealistic initial assumptions and to the pressure of trade and price controls which have often effectively prevented the smooth functioning of the exchange rate mechanism.

The Indian experience with the exchange rate mechanism as one of the arms of trade policy has been the subject of a theoretical as well as empirical enquiry. But there are a number of issues that need to be addressed if exchange rate policies should be fashioned in co-ordination with other policies for higher growth and stability. In order to give a pointed focus to the issues, there is a need to have a brief look at the way the policy in regard to the exchange rate of the rupee has evolved over time.[30]

With special emphasis of how LDCs have tackled the issue of the choice of exchange rate regime, we examine below the developments in the exchange rate regime of India down from the Bretton Woods par value system (1944-71) (Adjustable Pegged Rates) upto the New Economic Policy enunciated in July 1991 and afterwards.

A. External Value of the Rupee in the Bretton Woods System

The establishment of the Bretton Woods System at the close of the War in 1944 in which India was a founder member, logically implied that India should break her ties with the sterling area. This is so because, the sterling area with exchange controls operating around it, was definitely incompatible with the IMF objective of *"the establishment of a multi-lateral system of payments in respect of current transactions between members and ... the elimination of foreign exchange restrictions which hamper growth of world trade"*. (Article I(iv) of the IMF). Nevertheless, the immediate post-war period did not involve any significant change in the working of the sterling area arrangement and, India's continued membership in that association in turn meant no substantial change in her exchange rate arrangement.

Under the Articles of the Fund, the members were to align their respective exchange rates in terms of either gold or the US dollar. India complied with that provision in December 1946 by declaring the value of the rupee in terms of gold but the par value was so fixed as not to disturb the rupees then prevailing parity with sterling of 1s. 6d (i.e. 1 = Rs. 13.33). As a result, the immediate post-war period saw India adopting the Bretton Woods par value system only *de jure* as her exchange rate system remained on a *de facto* sterling peg. Meanwhile, the UK devalued sterling from $4.03 to $2.80 (30.5 percent) in September, 1949. The question then arose as to whether India should follow suit. Ultimately, it was decided to maintain the parity with sterling by devaluing the rupee against the dollar by an identical extent. This decision to follow sterling was dictated by the fact that India's trade was concentrated in sterling area countries. Hence when the Scandinavian countries and every sterling area countries except Pakistan devalue *vis-a-vis* Sterling, India followed the same line keeping the rupee-sterling rate intact at £ 1 = Rs. 13.33 (*Joseph,* 1992).

Thereafter we noted a shift in India's external transactions from the mid-fifties towards the non-sterling countries. This was so because by the beginning of the 1960s (February, 1961), the phenomenon that sterling gradually became an informal and voluntary association with the restoration of total full current account convertibility to sterling and the dollar pool arrangement within the sterling area dismantled, gave a big push in India to her drive for diversification of transactions away from the U.K. and the rest of the sterling area, a drive which at first started after the 1949 sterling devaluation, particularly with regard to India's export. The share of India's current spending (imports plus invisible payments) in the sterling area declined from nearly a half of the total in the mid-Fifties to just under a fifth by the end of the Sixties. Similarly, the share of India's current receipts (exports plus invisible receipts) from the region declined by more than half from 54 percent of the total to 26 percent over the same 15 year period. This altogether reflects the intensity of the trade and exchange controls erected against the non-sterling world. Sterling continued to be the intervention currency of the system, the authorities kept parity with sterling and kept the bulk of foreign balances in sterling. This situation would have continued but for two developments: first, the deterioration of India's BoP by early 1966-67 and second, the devaluation of the pound in November 1967 from $2.80 to $2.40 (14.3 percent) (rupee-sterling parity changes to £ 1 = Rs. 18), which gave a significant jolt to the sterling area.

B. A Rupee Devaluation in 1966 and Exchange Rate Regime Prior to 1975

India's BoP that remained in difficulty throughout the decade after the mid-1950s became critical by early 1966-67. The government's measures in the form of export subsidies, import restriction and incentives for foreign remittance proved inadequate and, with the situation worsening, the government took the radical decision of devaluation of the rupee by 36.5 percent on June 6, 1966; rupee-sterling parity changes to £ 1 = Rs. 21.

There were other major events happened subsequently in India's Exchange rate regime.

They were:

(a) Britain entered into agreement with India to restrict the drawing down of sterling reserves from September, 1968. This, to some extent, revives the formal nature of the sterling area arrangement.

(b) Rupee pegged to the US dollar on August 22, 1971. That is, India adopted a dollar peg in August 22, 1971, for the rupee and this development is significant. It could have been interpreted as the first official recognition of the reality of the predominance of the US dollar in India's external transactions. But this official act turned out to be quite different, and did not in any way represent the beginning of a consistent policy giving larger importance to the dollar in India's exchange rate system. Because, it was known that the dollar was greatly over-valued and, therefore, would depreciate against other major currencies. Therefore, the Indian authorities might have seen this as an opportunity to bring out a gradual devaluation of the rupee by linking its value with the weak dollar and this, in effect, was the result. The rupee depreciated 5.1 percent against the pound and by similar amounts against other major currencies depending on the rate of depreciation of the dollar against them.

(c) Rupee re-pegged to sterling on December 19, 1971 at the Central rate of £1 = 18.9677. This arrangement meant a comeback to the sterling peg, although with broader margins, after a brief spell (August 22 to December 19, 1971) of the dollar peg. The sterling, during the short spell, continued to be the currency of intervention.

(d) Pound floated on June 23, 1972 consequent upon the worsening BoP situation in the U.K.; India's maintenance of the parity with the sterling remained unchanged. This repeated the events of 1931 when the pound floated with the departure from gold standard by Britain.

The authorities' policy of a sterling peg during 1972-75 resulted in large depreciation of the rupee against other major currencies: 10 percent against the dollar, 13 percent against the yen, 34 percent against the deutsche mark and 18 percent against the French franc other than sterling: the effective exchange rate of sterling declined by 22 percent during June 1972- June 1975; the large nominal depreciation of the rupee by about 20 percent during the sterling peg (1972-75) had been beneficial from the view point that it helped in improving the competitive position of India's exports: the volume of India's exports recorded a remarkable growth by an annual rate of 8 percent during that period. The share of India's exports to OPEC nations rose sharply from 5 percent in 1973-74 to 15 percent in 1975-76, in spite of the relatively higher inflation (the index of wholesale prices rose by 10 percent, 20 percent and 25 percent in 1972-73, 1974, 1974-75 respectively), oil shock with two consecutive bad harvests in 1971-72 and 1972-73 which were followed by an industrial recession in 1973-74. Although this arrangement of the sterling peg had been beneficial, it could at best be a transitional arrangement applicable during a period of considerable uncertainty at home and abroad.[31]

In brief, the following account demonstrates the fact that prior to 1975, the external value of the rupee was determined by its historical link with the pound sterling which also enabled the rupee to participate in the par value Bretton Woods system. With the collapse of the Bretton Woods system[32] in 1973, as a result of growing financial strains and external imbalances, the world moved to what is now known as a system of generalized floating. This implied that no numeraire or anchor existed for the system as a whole, a role played by gold. Individual countries were free to peg their currencies to any other currencies, or basket currencies, such as the IMF's Special Drawing Rights (SDRs) or to allow the exchange rate to vary according to market forces or some other type of adjustment mechanism. The generalized floating experience of the early Seventies imposed severe downward pressure on the Pound sterling against other major international currencies, resulting in a misalignment of the rupee *vis-a-vis* the other currencies. The link system, besides importing volatility also rendered the exchange rate regime passive, subjecting it to policy changes in the U.K. economy, rather than to domestic policy initiatives. On 25 September, 1975, therefore, the Indian authorities introduced a basket peg and the rupee was delinked from the Pound sterling and its external value was determined with reference to a basket of a selected number of currencies of India's major trading partners with the Pound Sterling as the intervention currency. The rationale behind this decision has been exchange rate stability which is clear from the statement given in the Government's Economic Survey for 1975-76 presented to Parliament in February 1976. It said: ". . . in order to impart greater stability to the effective exchange rate in a world where the major currencies are floating and in the wake of the continuing depreciation in the exchange value of the pound in recent months, a new arrangement was instituted whereby the exchange value of the rupee is changed periodically with reference to a suitable weighted average of the exchange rate movements of the currencies of India's major trading partners" (p. 41) .

C. *Shift to A Basket Peg: India Adopts a Basket Peg on September 25, 1975*

It would not be out of place here to examine the conditions of the Indian economy during that period which was essentially characterized by a decline in the inflation rate especially from the second half of 1974-75 and also in the index of wholesale prices in the second quarter of 1975-76 as compared to the previous year. The agricultural situation and industrial production somehow registered buoyancy with signs of an exceptional harvest in 1975-76, and with improvement in production. On the external front, import prices continued to rise faster than export prices resulting in further deterioration of India's terms of trade. In this situation, there were sharp increase in the import prices particularly of oil, fertilizers and food. The rupee's continuing link with the pound was considered to be an aggravating factor in this regard, as the Annual Report of the RBI, 1975-76, stated that:

> 'The effect of this change (from the sterling peg to the basket peg) has been to stabilize the value of the Indian rupee *vis-a-vis* currencies other than sterling and to

increase the purchasing power of the rupee in terms of sterling. This has contributed to some extent to the stabilization of prices, by preventing an increase in the prices of imported commodities and services' (p. 4).

The developments which significantly influenced India's decision to shift out of the sterling peg to basket peg on the ground that it is more able to stabilize the effective exchange rate, prices and output can be summarized as under:

- For the satisfactory operation of a floating exchange rate system, there was minimum institutional back-up. India at this stage could hardly afford the scrapping of controls on trade and capital flows on the reason that floating always pre-supposes the existence of a well-knit domestic financial market, often integrated with international financial market with extensive freedom of movement of capital flows externally. Free capital mobility in turn implies the virtually absence of any trade and exchange controls.
- From early 1973, developing countries were gradually shifting from single currency pegs to multi-currency pegs.
- The IMF's decision to introduce a basket valuation for the SDR, the internationally created reserve asset, from July 1974 attracted countries like Burma (January 1975). Iran (February 1975), Jordan (February 1975), Saudi Arabia (March 1975), and Qater (March 1975) to switch over to an SDR peg by the middle of 1975, There were at least nine developing countries following a currency basket peg and another seven on a SDR peg.
- By December 1974, the India's foreign exchange guarantee agreement with Britain expired and, therefore, the sterling balances were subject to fluctuations in the value of pound that was still weak in the market. This prompted India to accelerate the diversification of foreign exchange reserves away from sterling from early 1975 which culminated in the

scrapping of the rupee's tie with sterling on September 25, 1975.

D. *India's Move to a More Flexible System*

Initially, the Indian basket system had a band of 4.5 percent, i.e., 2.25 percent margin above and below the value of the basket. Since January 30, 1979, the band had been widened to 10 percent. The broadening of the basket margins which took place on January 30, 1979 for maintaining the basket-determined value of rupee to ± 5 percent to be allowed by the IMF to chose any exchange rate regime as one of the members in line with the Second Amendment to the IMF's Articles which came into effect from April 1978, is a quite significant event in the evolution of the Indian exchange rate regime. Here the exchange rate acted as an important instrument for achieving alternative macro-objectives other than stability including the BoP adjustment without in any way violating the basic basket rule [by 'fixing a more appropriate exchange rate for the rupee' (RBI Statement)].

The experience of the managed float regime under a basket arrangement was favourable at the outset with the rupee appreciation by 7.16 percent against the US dollar during 1975-81. This exchange rate variability of the rupee did not have an adverse impact on export growth, on an aggregate, due in large measure, to the fortuitous combination of an oil boom in the Gulf and the consequent surge in demand for goods and labour and favourable inflation differential of around 13.6 percent between India and her major trading partners. However, the exchange rate risk, as reported by its variability, had significant impact on the prices of exports. Increased remittances from the Gulf coupled with the healthy growth in India's exports eased the pressure on the BoP and the current account recorded a surplus in 1976-77 and 1977-78 by an amount of Rs. 1525.8 crore and Rs. 1734.7 crore respectively.

The second oil shock in 1979 was not however, accompanied by the favourable factors which occurred after the first oil shock. Moreover, excess demand effects generated by the stance of liberal domestic fiscal policies were superimposed upon the exogenous terms of the trade shock. The revenue balance of the Centre turned into deficit in 1979-80 and with the imperative move to a higher growth path that followed, fiscal deficits became large and persistent. The monetization of a sizeable portion of the fiscal deficit led to monetary expansion and thereby created an inflationary situation which had its spillover effects in terms of an increase in the demand for imports as well as a rise in the domestic production costs of exports. Compensatory policy action was necessitated and this required for external sector policies to take on a distinct export bias since 1978-79. This exchange rate policy had to subserve the promotional environment created for exports. As a result the regime of managed float came under considerable pressure, and the rupee, which, had been appreciating upto 1980-81 took a turn for the worse and started to decline since 1981-82.

E. Developing Countries' Experience with Exchange Rate Policy in the 1980s

The 1980s saw major changes in exchange rate regimes in most developing countries, including India, the significance of which can now be assessed. In addition, there had been, since 1978, and especially during the period 1980-90, some fascinating experiments in the use of exchange rate policy for inflation stabilization.

For India, the 1980s was characterized by a general turbulence in the international foreign exchange markets. A steep appreciation of the US dollar against the major international currencies during the first half of the decade led to an erosion in the value of the rupee by 24.6 percent against the dollar between 1981-82 and 1984-85. The rupee, however, appreciated against the Pound Sterling and the French Franc by 15.09 percent and 20.71 percent, respectively. The dollar revised its trend in the second half of the Eighties when it plunged into the international exchange markets. Although the US dollar depreciated during the second half, a widening negative inflation rate differential between India and her competitors, and the deliberate devaluation undertaken by the competitors themselves necessitated a faster depreciation of the rupee *vis-a-vis* the dollar in order to enable Indian goods to compete in the global markets. This resulted in adjustments of the rupee-sterling rate on a step-by-step basis to reflect a 31.81 percent depreciation of the rupee against the dollar during 1985-91. The cumulative depreciation of the rupee *vis-a-vis* the dollar was 50.02 percent between 1981-82 and 1990-91. The governments' objective in effecting the small, step-by-step devaluation were to offset the higher rates of inflation in India relative to those of trade partners.

The evolution of the India's exchange rate reform is at variance with general experiences of other developing countries. Under the impetus of the world recession and debt crisis, under the pressure or guidance of the international institutions like the IMF and the World Bank etc., and from a realization in many cases of the failure of earlier import-substitution policies, most of the fixed-rate countries switched regimes in the early Eighties, moving to flexible (though not floating) exchange rates, either allowing their exchange rates to crawl or at least making frequent adjustments.[33] Many countries devalued their currencies from 1980 to 1982 and brought about further real devaluation later. Fuller details are in Table 5.4 and Table 5.5.

It is generally agreed that the maintenance of fixed exchange rates implies subordination of domestic economic policy to balance of payments considerations. In the face of payments deficits, it would not be possible for a country to maintain fixed exchange rates and at the same time follow an independent course of monetary and fiscal action to foster full employment and economic growth. Because such a course of action would allow payments deficits to persist, the country would suffer losses of foreign exchange reserves and a weakening of its currency in international markets. Correcting balance of payments would either require deflationary monetary and fiscal policies, with some measures of unemployment, or devaluation or a combination of both or some form of direct and indirect control over international transactions.

Under flexible exchange rate arrangements, balance of payments adjustments are effected through exchange rate changes. Since the shocks generated by the adjustment process are absorbed by exchange rate changes, the adjustment process does not affect domestic income and employment. An increase in the demand for foreign exchange generated, by say, an increase in the demand for imports, would cause the exchange

TABLE 5.4

Devaluations, Exchange Rate Regime Changes, and Inflation Rates of Some Selective Developing Countries

Devaluations and Regime Changes

	GDP 1990 $ US m rates ended	Regimes, dates when fixed rates ended	Dates of devaluations 1974-83	Real depreciation	Inflation rates 1970-72 %	1988-90 %
(1)	(2)	(3)	(4)	(5)	(6)	(7)
Argentina	93,260	Varying	Frequent	23	36	3079
Brazil	414,060	Crawling peg, mostly	1979, 1983	9.5	19	**1287
Cameroon	11,130	+ Fixed to French Frank	—	(23) B	7	4
Chile	27,790	Varying, 1982	1974, 1982	5.7	74	16
Columbia	41,120	Crawling peg	—	67	10	27
Costa Rica	5,700	+ 1981	1974, 1981	33	4 II	19
Cote d'Ivoire	7,610	+ Fixed French Franc	—	(22) B	3	7
India	254,540	+ September, 1975	—	30	5 II	8
Indonesia	107,290	+ (1986)	1978, 1983	55	8 II	7

(*Contd.*)

TABLE 5.4 (Contd.)

(1)	(2)	(3)	(4)	(5)	(6)	(7)
Kenya	7,540	+ 1982	1974, 1984	44	4 ‖	9
Korea	236,000	Fixed 1974-80	1974, 1980	26	14	6
Mexico	237,750	+ 1982	1976, 1982	79	5	**20
Morocco	25,220	+ 1984	—	14	3 ‖	3
Nigeria	34,760	+ 1985	—	461	11 ‖	40
Pakistan	35,500	+ 1982	1982	52	6 ‖	8
Sri Lanka	7,250	+ 1977	1977	37	5 ‖	13
Thailand	80,170	+ 1984	1981	42	2 ‖	5
Turkey	96,500	+ 1980	1980	28	12 ‖	69

Sources: 1. Column 1 : World Development Report, 1992, Washington, DC: The World Bank.

2. Column 2 and 3: Little, M.D., Cooper, Richard, Cordon, W. Max and Rajapatirana, Sarath (1993), *Boom, Crisis and Adjustment: The Macro Economic Experience of Developing Countries*, New York: OUP for the World Bank.

3. Column 5 and 6: World Bank Data. Note that the dates and figures in column 2-4 are subject to numerous qualifications, set out in Little. (1993)

* Average of annual CPI inflation rates.

** 1989 only

\+ Exchange rate fixed in 1973, and before.

B Real appreciation

‖ Ten countries whose regime shifted from fixed to flexible.

rate to rise. The rise in the exchange rate, in turn, would promote exports. It follows that, under a flexible exchange rate arrangement, the authorities can pursue an independent course of monetary and fiscal policies and leave the operation of free-market forces to take care of balances, imbalances by letting the exchange rate find its own equilibrium position in the foreign exchange market.

In the backdrop of the above, we find that the developing countries have undergone a thoroughgoing change in the exchange rate regimes, especially for adjusting the BoP constraints. From the tabulation of exchange rate arrangements published by the IMF it is evident, as Table 5.5 shows, that there has been a clear tendency for the number of developing countries pegged to single currency to fall since the late 1970s. The number pegged to a composite currency has also fallen since the early 1980s. The number of developing countries adopting a form of crawl rose significantly during the 1980s, with the majority using a discretionary version (Table 5.5). Table 5.5 also indicates that the number of countries operating a form of floating[34] increased considerably during the 1980s, with as many as 27 developing countries listed as having a market determined floating system (independent floating) in 1993. Of course, recent experience with floating system has been mixed.

In sum, 1980s began as the high noon of freely floating exchange rates. Individual countries pursued domestic macro economic objectives and allowed foreign exchange markets to assess the consequences for the right price of different national currencies. Also the decade saw the continual movement from countries pegging their exchange rates, to greater flexibility, to floating, and then back to pegging and returned again to flexible rates in 1989-91. And in general, during the decade the developing countries preferred to use import restrictions to deal with BoP problems. The exceptions were the four South American countries and Korea, all of whom had inflation rates far above normal for developing countries. It is interesting to compare average inflation rates for ten countries (the ten countries are marked with a cross in the second column of Table 5.4) between two periods, 1970-72 and 1988-89. In all cases there bad been a regime switch between the two periods. In the first period the ten countries had fixed rates and in the second case,

TABLE 5.5

Developing Countries' Exchange Rate Arrangements from Mid—1970 to Early 1990s

Number of Countries	*1976*	*1982*	*1987*	*1993*
Pegged to single currency of which	67	56	53	41
US $	46	38	34	22
Fr. Franc	13	13	14	14
Sterling	3	1	—	—
Other	5	4	5	5
Pegged to a composite of which:	25	34	37	25
SDR	11	15	10	4
Other[a]	14	19	27	21
Flexible arrangements of which:	15	35	42	55
Limited flexibility against a single currency[b]	2	10	4	4
Adjusted according to a set of indicators[c]	6	4	4	3
Managed floating[d]	4	16	22	21
Independent floating[e]	3	5	12	27
Total	107	125	132	121

(a) Corresponds to tailor-made basket.

(b) Currently covers only four Middle Eastern countries which are in effect pegged to US dollar.

(c) Corresponds to rule-based crawl.

(d) Corresponds to a discretionary crawling peg.

(e) Covers both floats and auctions.

Notes:

Peg: Single Currency : The country links its exchange rate to the value of a major currency, usually the US dollar or the French frank, but does not change the rate frequently. This arrangement exists in about one-half of all developing countries.

Peg : Currency Composite : A composite or basket, is usually formed by the currencies of major trading partners to make the pegged currency more stable than if a single-currency peg were used. Currency weights may be based on trade, services, or major capital flows. Composite pegs exists in about one-fourth of all developing countries.

Flexibility Limited vis-a-vis single currency : The value of the currency is maintained within certain margins of the peg. This system exists in some Middle Eastern Countries.

Flexibility Limited : Co-operative arrangements : This applies to countries in the exchange rate mechanism (ERM) of the Eastern Monetary System (EMS) and is a cross between cross and a float.

More Flexible : Managed float: The Central bank sets the rate, but sometimes varies it frequently. Adjustments are judgemental, usually based on a range of indicator, such as foreign exchange reserves, the real effective exchange rate, and developments in paralleled or black markets for foreign exchange.

More flexible : Independent float: Rates are market-determined. Most developed countries have floats, partial for the EMS countries, but the number of developing countries included in this category has been increasing in recent years.

Source : *IMF, International Financial Statistics (Various issues).*

flexible rates. In seven cases (five from Asia) the average inflation rates were somewhat higher for five. In India, in particular, the average inflation rates for the two periods were 4.5 and 8 per cent, respectively.

From the historical experience it is obvious that when a developing country faces BoP problems and cannot, or is reluctant to, devalue its currency, it will impose or expand import restrictions. This has been a pervasive features in the developing countries during their fixed, or reluctant exchange rate adjustment periods. Trade restrictions cannot substitute for the continuous depreciations of the exchange rate that are required when there is high inflation relative to trading partners, but they are at least imperfect substitutes for the real devaluations called for at various times by the real targets approach, as indicated by the classic internal-external balance model.[35] And when the developing countries were practising the new flexible rate regimes, the response to BoP problems was hardly ever to tighter restrictions, but much more commonly, actually to liberalize.

It is important to note that all episodes of significant trade liberalization have been associated with, or shortly preceded by significant devaluation

F. India's Exchange Rate Adjustments, July 1991 and After

India was of no exception. By 1990-91, it was evident that

both macro-economic policy and structural factors had contributed to a misalignment[36] (i.e. over-valuation or under-valuation in the exchange rate). The fiscal deficit grew at an alarming pace, creating a problem of monetary overhang and endangering price stability. There was a growing divergence in the parallel market rate of "hawala rate" from the official rate in spite of the frequent adjustments in the exchange rates effected by RBI. Among the structural factors, the striking ones relate to tariffs which were at an abnormally high level at around 300 per cent and stringent capital and exchange controls. Capital inflows from commercial sources started dwindling away following the successive downgrading of the country's credit rating by international agencies, and as the oil prices rise took place with the Gulf War crisis, leading to dangerously sharp decline in foreign exchange reserves, the international confidence began to ebb away resulting in a large outflow of capital particularly from the non-resident deposits. The cumulative effect of these factors was the unprecedented balance of payments crisis in 1991.

As part of the crisis management the Reserve Bank of India (RBI) effected a two-step discrete downward adjustment in the external value of the rupee in July 1991 instead of the usual gradual small step adjustment by virtue of which the rupee in order to gauge the reaction of the market, was adjusted downwards by 7-9 per cent against the five major currencies (the US dollar, the Deutche Mark, the Yen, the Pound Sterling and the French Franc) on July 1, 1991, and on July 3, 1991 the rupee was further devalued by about 11 per cent against these currencies. As a result, between June 28 and July 3, 1991, the value of the rupee declined by 17-19 per cent *vis-a-vis* the five major currencies while these major currencies appreciated *vis-a-vis* the rupee by about 21 to 23 per cent. This significant exchange rate adjustment was done with a view to quelling the destabilizing market expectations, restoring international confidence in the value of the rupee and stemming capital outflows, shoring up the level of reserves and improving the country's international competitiveness which was considered eroded in the global market due to high domestic inflation since October, 1990. After the two-step discrete devaluation of the rupee, the basket system was somewhat abandoned in favour of a dollar peg by keeping the value of rupee stable with dollar.[37]

A downward adjustment of the exchange rate undertaken in July 1991 cannot be taken repeatedly to tide over balance of payments difficulties, given the stance of competitor countries and the implied requirement of deflationary demand management policies. hence the need for a market-related exchange rate policy. The Liberalized Exchange Rate Management System (LERMS) was consequently introduced in March 1992. The LERMS was essentially a transitional mechanism. The introduction of LERMS implied a partially floating dual exchange rate with an official rate pegged to dollar and an inter-bank rate determined at the market. The dual exchange rate system involved surrender of 40 per cent of all foreign exchange remittances, whether earned through exports of goods and services or remittances at the officially fixed rate and the remaining 60 per cent to be sold at a market determined rate. The foreign exchange surrendered at the fixed official rate financed the import of essential items such as petroleum, oil products, fertilizers, defence and life-saving drugs and governmental departmental imports and the balance financed other imports like raw materials, components and also capital goods.

This arrangement was timely and constituted a considerable improvement over the earlier exchange rate system which involved in effect a multiple exchange rate system characterized by highly restrictive trade regime. The dual exchange rate was designed to liberalize trade, by a subsidising imports, and initiate a move towards convertibility of the rupee; this move towards partial convertibility of the rupee had cleaned up the trade system by eliminating licenses and the associated delays and inefficiencies over a wide range of current account transactions. At one stroke, the large number of import categories which required the issue of separate import-entitlements called "EXIM scrips" were eliminated and were made freely importable. Instead of the need to issue EXIM scrips for each transactions, the system was much simpler and operated through banks and authorized dealers on foreign exchange. It covered not just merchandise exports and a few services as in the case of EXIM scrips scheme, but covered the entire gamut of current account transactions including workers' remittances. It incorporated a self-balancing mechanism whereby total imports were automatically regulated by the availability of foreign exchange. The myriad of *"Appendices, Parts, and Lists"* which characterized the Indian trade policy for long was established in favour of just a simple *"negative list"* consisting of banned, restricted, and canalised items and all items not included in this list were made freely importable at the market exchange rate.

Although the dual exchange system represented an improvement of trade regime thus functioning effectively with the market determined exchange rate, and exhibited remarkable stability, it did not continue indefinitely because it involved an implicit tax on exports and allowed for the rationing of subsidized foreign exchange for certain inputs which could lead to distortions in resource allocation over time. Moreover this anti-export bias—the rupee price of exportables was lower than that of import substitutes—was hardly justifiable in the context of the need for a big jump in export growth in order to sustain the economic reform programme.[38] The process of dismantling the managed float regime which went hand-in-hand with substantial deregulation of exchange control, removal of trade restrictions and freedom to import bullion and to prevent a worsening of the current account, ultimately culminated in the unification of the official and market rates in March 1993, leading to the introduction of a market determined exchange rate regime. The combination of the earlier devaluations and the unification measure resulted in a real effective depreciation of the rupee of around 20 to 25 per cent in real terms between July 1991 and March 1993 and about 35 per cent in nominal terms. Since March 1993 the nominal exchange rate had been constant and there had been a small real appreciation. The rupee had been strong as a result of a dramatic current account improvement and a surge in capital inflows. The RBI had intervened and increased reserves substantially. From a competitive viewpoint, the rupee depreciation since June 1991 had been a step in the right direction.[39]

Another move towards reform of the exchange rate regime was the relaxation of controls over foreign exchange transactions. Significant among these was the abolition of the advance deposit scheme on imports on non-capital goods.

The rupee was floated thereafter and its value was set to the free market rate of above 31 per US dollar. These measures, aided with severe fiscal and import squeeze, enabled the government to tide over the payments crisis, raise foreign exchange reserves to a fairly decent $ 5.6 billion by March 1992 and considerably restore the confidence of international investors. It was however felt that for long-term BoP viability and for making a international transactions a potent instrument of economic growth, radical changes in both trade and exchange rate regimes were called for. It was also felt by the government that trade liberalization was not enough to ensure BoP viability of the country. The major issues in this context were examined by the High Level Committee whose recommendations formed the basis of the country's external sector policy stance since the early 1990s. The policy stance consisted in avoiding misalignment of the exchange rate; containing external debt-GDP ratio within prudential limits; reductions in short-term loans; encouraging non-debt capital inflows; maintenance of adequate forex reserves; and keeping the current account deficit at a sustainable level, in line with the country's absorptive capacity. However, the exchange rate remained more or less stable at Rs. 31.37 per dollar from March 1993 till the beginning of August 1995. But India's competitiveness in international markets was significantly eroded by the rate of inflation in India being higher than the rates of inflation in India's major trading partners. As a result the five-country trade weighted REER (Real Effective Exchange Rate, i.e., the trade weighted average nominal exchange rate *vis-a-vis* major partner countries adjusted for inflation rate differential) had appreciated in the order of 8 per cent between 1993-94 and August 1995. Had this erosion of India's competitiveness continued, it would have been adversely affected exports, the foreign trade balance and the overall BoP. In mid-October 1995, the rupee threatened to breach the Rs. 35 level. The nominal exchange rate fell to Rs. 35.65 per US dollar in terms of Foreign Exchange Dealers' Association of India (FEDAI) indicative rates, amplified by speculative factor and again in January and February 1996 when the two incidents put rupee under pressure in the wake of unfounded expectations about the external payments situation.

The widening of the current account deficit in the face of a rising trade deficit, an ebbing of capital flows and the pronounced appreciation of the US dollar against major international currencies triggered off market expectations and resulted in a depreciation of the rupee in the second half of 1995-96. The RBI came forward to take actions to quell persistent volatility or misalignment and to prevent speculative attacks on the exchange rate. The fluctuations in the exchange rate of the rupee has been limited since the beginning of 1996-97. The value of rupee stabilized.

There were some pressures on the rupee in August 1997 (the time when East Asian crisis broke out), by which time the REER of the rupee had appreciated by 13.4 per cent, the base year being 1993. The RBI intervened in view of the East Asian situation to avoid any possible contagion effect. In a sense, August 1997 was a turning point in Indian exchange rate management in that a policy of working towards a neutral REER started giving the authorities some top concern. Thereafter especially since August 1999, the REER had remained remarkably stable despite the fact that the period saw serious currency turmoils in different parts of the world. In order to prevent sharp swings in the exchange rate and keep it close to its long-term equilibrium, the Reserve Bank of India regularly intervened in the foreign exchange market mopping or adding to market supply of foreign currency, as and when required. However, during the 1990s, a judicious combination of aforementioned policies played a decisive role in ensuring "orderly behaviour" of the exchange rate and to maintain a relatively small current account deficits.

Allowing the Indian rupee to move in response to the changes taking place in global foreign exchange rate, India has been following a broadly market determined exchange rate policy for quite some time. The Rupee has indeed demonstrated adequate flexibility, which is evident from the pattern of its movement against major global currencies (i.e. the Euro, Pound Sterling, US dollar, Yen). The monthly exchange rate of the rupee moved in a range of Rs. 46.56 to Rs. 48.85 per US dollar during 2001-02, though the terrorist attack on September 11, 2001 in the United State made foreign exchange markets in

India volatile, with the rupee showing a depreciation of 1.3 per cent *vis-a-vis* US dollar during a ten-day period of September 10-20, 2001. For reducing volatility in the foreign exchange market, RBI announced some measures during September 15-25, 2001. They yielded desired result. At the end of January, 2002, exchange rate of the Rupee was 48.58 per US dollar. And it was Rs. 43.49 to Rs. 46.34 during 2003-04 and 2004-05. With a flexible exchange rate regime and interventions limited to maintaining orderly market conditions, the rupee exhibited considerable two-way movements in 2005-06 and 2006-07 in terms of movements in monthly averages. While the magnitude of appreciation or depreciation in nominal terms are indicative, the real impact on the economy is often assessed through the NEER and REER indices. Taking 1993-94, as the base year, the rupee has depreciated by 31.41 per cent in NEER terms in Nov. 2002, and in REER terms, the rupee stands appreciated by 2.05 per cent in November, 2002. The 5-country NEER (base 2000=100) composed of a basket of five currencies, viz., US dollar, Euro, Pound Sterling and Yen was seen to have depreciated from 1991-92 till 2004-05 to reach a level of 90.76 (Table 5.6). Thereafter it rose, on an annual basis, to 94.06. It depreciated steadily in 2006-07 till August 2006, reaching a low of 88.05, where after it has picked up and was at 91.31 in November 2006. The 5-country REER (base 2000=100) that indicated the real competitiveness by factoring the relative price level of competitors displayed some signs of appreciation. It rose steadily to reach 106.79 in 2005-06. (Table 5.6). Figure 5.1 shows the trends in NEER and REER since 1991-92. It is important to note that the RBI replaced its five—country effective exchange rates with six-country indices in December 2005 (*RBI Bulletin*, January 2008).

It is important to note here that between April 3, 2007, and February 6, 2008, the rupee appreciated by 8.9 per cent against the US dollar, following the mismatch between the demand for foreign exchange (debit side of BoP) and the supply of foreign exchange (credit side of BoP). The REER (6 country trade-based weights) appreciated by 7.8 per cent in April- Jan. 2007-08. With increased capital inflows and appreciating rupee, concerns about possible overvaluation of the currency and consequential loss of long-term competitiveness of exports in traditional and

TABLE 5.6
Exchange Rates Movements

Year/Month	*Ranges (Rupees per US $)*	*NEER five-country index*	*REER five-country index*
(1)	*(2)*	*(3)*	*(4)*
1991-92		178.27	107.01
1992-93		146.98	97.03
1993-94	31.21-31.49	136.52	96.54
1994-95	31.37-37.97	131.69	102.25
1995-96	31.37-37.95	120.82	99.00
1996-97	34.14-35.96	118.50	102.18
1997-98	35.70-40.36	117.74	106.31
1998-99	39.48-43.42	104.12	102.11
1999-00	42.44-44.79	100.78	100.76
2000-01	43.61-46.89	99.54	100.11
2001-02	46.56-48.85	98.47	103.45
2002-03	47.51-49.06	93.13	100.89
2003-04	43.45-47.46	92.07	103.06
2004-05	43.36-46.46	90.76	103.50
2005-06	43.49-46.34	90.06	106.79
2005-06 (P)			
April		92.22	104.91
May		93.36	106.52
June		94.58	108.98
July		95.96	110.12
August		94.81	108.44
September		94.16	106.95
October		93.56	105.51
November		92.81	105.39
December		92.81	104.88
January		94.37	105.48
February		95.29	107.48
March		94.78	106.81

(*Contd.*)

TABLE 5.6 (*Contd.*)

(1)	*(2)*	*(3)*	*(4)*
2006-07			
April		93.16	103.65
May		89.88	102.09
June		89.39	102.22
July		88.72	101.30
August		88.05	100.65
September		89.17	103.95
October		90.93	107.52
November		91.31	109.04

Source : *Economic Survey*, GoI (various issues).

goods sectors—popularly known as the "Dutch Desease" have already arisen (*Economic Survey, 2007-08*).

In what follows the authorities have not been able to prevent an appreciation of the REER of the rupee, nor been successful to evolve a transparent system under which any correction of the REER is brought about smoothly to avoid sudden volatility of the exchange rate. Thus a sensible and responsible exchange rate management policy is needed for smoothing excessive volatility in the exchange with no fixed rate target, for preventing the emergence of destabilizing speculative activities, and helping maintain adequate level of reserve, while allowing the underlying demand and supply conditions to determine the exchange rate movements in an orderly way. Towards this end the RBI should monitor closely the developments in the financial markets at home and abroad and carefully co-ordinate its markets operations with suitable monetary, regulatory and other effective measures, as considered necessary from time to time.

5.6.6 Convertibility Agenda: Towards Almost Full Convertibility on Current Account

We have traversed quite a long from a sterling peg to a basket system, to a partial float and then to a full float. Finally

FIG. 5.1
Trends in NEER and REER Since 1991-92

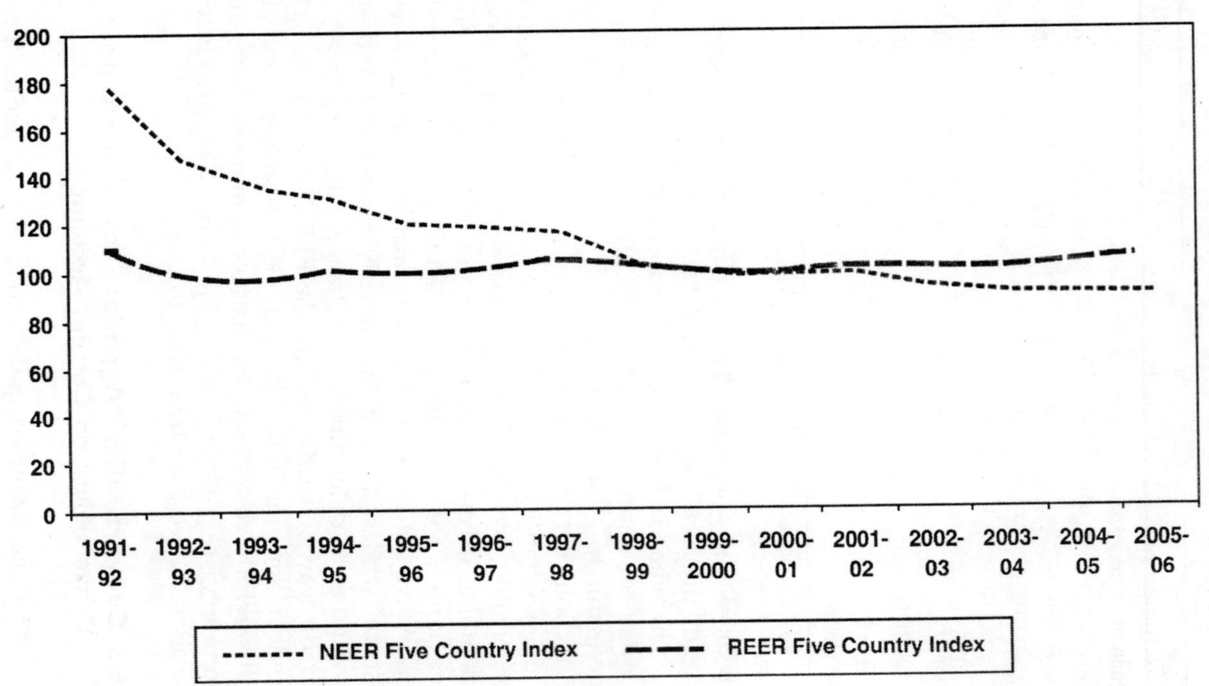

the exchange rate is now under a 'managed float' regime controlled by the Reserve Bank of India with the nominal exchange rate targeted, broadly speaking, to achieving the real exchange rate which yields a sustainable current account deficit. The rupee remains more or less stable, although at times there are signs of instability. We think this will continue to be a sensible strategy over the medium-term future in which capital movements are likely to be volatile.

Those who argue that India's inflation is driven mainly by agricultural production, money supply, growth and fiscal deficits, not by the exchange rate is not wholly correct. High fiscal deficits generate large money supply growth which, in turn, build up inflationary pressures in the economy. High inflation raises real effective exchange rate requiring the nominal effective exchange rate to be lowered to maintain export-competitiveness. High inflation also necessitates maintenance of a dear money policy to keep inflation down. Lower value of rupee raises import prices and this together with high interest rates raises the cost of production adversely affecting industrial growth and external competitiveness. Therefore, the exchange rate policy and management constitutes an important factor and it cannot been seen in isolation from other policy instruments such as fiscal and monetary policy and also the structural policies being pursued by the Government.

Turning to the objective of exchange rate policy in the 'managed float regime', we feel that the exchange rate should be maintained at such a level as to progressively reduce the current account deficit and eventually generate a current account surplus. The most crucial aspect of the balance of payments in India from a medium-term perspective is the prevalence of the relatively high international indebtedness and the debt service obligations. India has a huge external debt—to be serviced for which current account surpluses are to be generated. For that purpose, the authorities have to be alive to the need to maintain a competitive exchange rate meaning thereby that the possibility of the real appreciation of the rupee has to be prevented. Whatever be the reasons for a real appreciation of the rupee, be it occurred either on account on an appreciation of the nominal exchange rate or to a large inflation in India, the authorities need to intervene to offset real appreciation and should look into an appropriate exchange rate system (which includes the exchange rate arrangement and exchange rate policies) that will accommodate the diverse economic structures and institutional arrangements. In choosing an appropriate system for the country, the authorities may be guided by four criteria that, when applied, must take into consideration of the economic. characteristics and circumstances of the country. These criteria may be applicable to all other developing countries.

The first is : Does the system help or hinder macro-economic policy in pursuit of objectives? The important test of the appropriateness of the system is whether the variability in exchange rate impinge upon or facilitate the achievement of the ultimate targets of domestic economic policy like price stability, high employment and sustainable economic growth.

The second criterion is : How effective is the arrangement in promoting external payments adjustment under which the country's current account position can both be financed by normal capital flows without recourse to under restrictions on trade, special incentives to flow of capital, and disincentives to outflows of capital or wholesale unemployment and disequilibria in BoP over a reasonable time period can be eliminated through external payments adjustment.

The third criterion is: How does the arrangement affect the volume and efficiency of world trade and capital flows? As the global welfare is generally increased by an expansion of world trade and investment, this criterion refers to the efficiency of trade and investment.

Finally, the fourth criterion is : How robust or adaptable is the system to significant changes in the global economic environment? The rationale for this criterion is that there are substantial costs associated with changing an exchange rate system, especially under crisis conditions. Other things being equal, it is better to have an exchange rate system that is relatively robust or adaptable to changes in the global economic environment than one that is not. Under conditions of high international capital mobility or rapid or abrupt changes in comparative advantage, such a system may have to perform well.

A. India's Move from Exchange Control to Convertibility

Since 1950, licensing of imports, imposition of high duties and stringent foreign exchange controls were part of the package of policy measures in India. This import substituting self-reliance strategy of 1950-80 has not delivered significantly improved quality of life to the vast majority of population.

In the early and mid-1980s, policy changes were initiated. Relaxation of import controls enhanced export initiatives and reduced controls on selected industries marked the beginnings of modest economic liberalization. The exchange rate policy, too, for the first time, was flexibly administered, allowing steady depreciation of the real exchange rate through continuously downward adjustment in the nominated exchange rate.

During the 1990s and beyond, the exchange rate regime has undergone significant changes. From a managed floating system under which the exchange rate was officially determined, the regime has passed through several phases to reach a market-based system. The unification of the exchange rate and the removal of the exchange restrictions on imports through the abolition of foreign exchange budgeting in the beginning of 1994 constituted the first major step toward current account convertibility. The final step towards current account convertibility was taken on 20th August 1994, when India as the ninety-eighth country of the world adopted Article VIII of the IMF (Sections 2, 3 & 4), under which India was committed to forsake the use of exchange restrictions on current international transactions as an instrument in managing the balance of payments and thus established full convertibility on current account implying thereby that (except for a few items) there was no exchange control on trade in goods and services. Under full current account convertibility the holders set the right to convert this currency for any current account purpose, such as trade or foreign travel; but not for capital account purposes such as market loans or buying assets abroad. Moreover, holders need no official security for all foreign payments.

The rupee has been convertible on current account on the logic that it would minimize the need for enforcement. In a country where enforcement is weak, exchange control simply encourages black market (Hawala) transactions and corruption among enforcement officials. Therefore it is imprudent to have exchange controls which encourage currency smuggling and black money and an increase in Bhagwatian 'DUP' activities. Secondly, attracting foreign investments is impossible if there are far too many controls, licenses and permits. Importantly, if remittances of profits and interest receipts in the case of bank deposits and dividends/earnings from portfolio investments are subject to exchange controls, the regime will act as a disincentive for foreign investors in the present day scenario where there are other countries which are keen to offer better facilities and fewer restrictions. Thirdly, the trade and exchange control regime in India did not generate a healthy export growth until the late 1970s and 1980s. Both per capita export and the export to GNP percentage were both relatively low in India in comparison with China, Indonesia, South Korea, Malaysia and Thailand. Moreover, controls on exchange transactions imply an overvalued exchange rate that may help to draw the conclusion that the level of traded goods' prices was too low. The overvalued exchange rate prevailing—either at a formal level with different transactions taking place at different official rates and/or at an informal (frequently illegal) level with high 'black-market' rates coexisting with the official rate—may naturally dissuade exporters to reap the benefits of export earnings into the country and dampen domestic savings. Besides, a similar reasoning applies to inward remittances. The country lost billions of dollars through the so-called processes of under-invoicing of exports and over-invoicing of imports. Lastly, a market-based exchange rate and a well-functioning exchange market provides an appropriate benchmark prices for goods and services as well as promotes domestic economic efficiency, especially when currency convertibility is accompanied by trade liberalization.

The above arguments pointed to the need for convertibility on current account. However, export growth, inward remittances, FDI and allocative efficiency will not depend on currency convertibility alone; in most cases, other complementary measures suited to the context are needed. Trade liberalization in general is one such important complementary measure.

Current account convertibility has been successfully implemented in India since 1991. Now India has walked some steps towards the road to capital account convertibility. We address here to pros and cons for capital account convertibility in India.

5.6.7 Should There Be Full Capital Account Convertibility (CAC) in India?

The RBI set up a Committee on CAC and the committee submitted its reports at the end of May, 1997. Since then there has been an hotly debate on the issue. The issue that crops up in the context of the currency and banking crisis experienced by several countries of East Asia in 1997, as well as those seen in Russia in 1998 and Brazil and Euro-Zones most recently is that of CAC of the balance of payments (BoP) of developing countries. Among developed countries, the US was the first one that went in for CAC in 1974. Between 1979 till 1991, most of the European Countries, Japan, Australia and New Zealand also adopted full capital account liberalization although patterns as well as time taken varied between countries. The IMF nowadays proposes that all its member-countries should make their currencies freely convertible for all current as well as capital account transactions.

Here a brief sketch of the basic theoretical issues that have arisen in international discussions on CAC and India's standpoint in this issue in particular.

With the displacement of pegged exchange rates by a regime of floating rates in the 1970s, a new orthodoxy begins to campaign that free capital mobility is of utmost importance for maximizing global benefits from international trade and investments. The floating market determined exchange rate determined by the forces of demand and supply and the lifting of capital controls were considered essential steps in the establishment of an efficient international financial system. The argument was that full convertibility on capital account will bring about equilibrium in the external sector of developing countries by bringing in capital flow to finance whatever current account gap that may result in if the interest rates are kept high enough. This argument was in line with the Mundell-Fleming

Open Economy Model (*Mundell*, 1962 and *Fleming*, 1962) which extends the Keynesian Fix Price Model for well developed domestic financial markets, well integrated with the global financial markets.

The new orthodoxy is vociferous on capital mobility, but peculiar thing is that there has not grown any consensus on the exchange rate regime. The IMF defines CAC as the 'freedom from exchange controls on capital transactions in the BoP' within either a fixed or a flexible exchange rate regime. India has accepted the goal of capital account convertibility as part of the ongoing liberalization process. The Tarapore Committee (I and II), appointed by RBI has looked into the issues and prospects of undertaking CAC in India and have laid out a detailed road map for CAC, along with necessary safeguards. The Committee defines CAC as "the freedom to convert local financial assets to foreign financial assets and *vice-versa* at market determined exchange rates". In other words, it implies complete mobility of capital across countries. The Tarapore Committee recommended in May 1997 (RBI 1997) that CAC should be conditional on a set of stringent requirements, including fiscal consolidation, low inflation, strict supervision and regulation of financial institutions, and financial restructuring, besides keeping watch on BoP and the quantum of forex reserves. The absence of a fully open capital account places limits on large-scale capital transfers without short period of time. In recent years the Committee has recommended a five-year phase of fuller CAC, with 2006-07 being the first phase, 2007-09 the second phase, 2010-12 be the third and the final phase. On December 20, 2006, RBI completed the first phase of fuller CAC and allowed the Indian residents to remit USD 50,000 annually for any current and capital account transactions or a combination of both. In Phase II & III they will be allowed to remit USD 100,000 and USD 200,000 respectively. However, the Indian Investors are now free to buy property or share or any other assets abroad without any prior approval of the regulator, RBI. Now Indians are able to invest in any listed foreign entity. Additionally, this liberalization will offer individual to open, maintain and hold foreign currency accounts with a bank outside India without prior approval of the RBI. Currently only NRIs are allowed to invest in companies on Indian stock exchanges. The committee II recommended extension of this facility to all non-residents.

Here an attempt has also been made to deal essentially with the arguments for and against international capital mobility, with a brief sketch of the simple macroeconomics of BoP transactions, because an understanding of the link between the current and capital account is crucial to understanding the issues involved in discussion on CAC.

A. Debate Hovering Over the CAC in India

The essence of CAC is a liberalization of outflows for residence. Convertibility for non-residence on the capital account has all along been available. Discussion on liberalization of the capital account on the BoP essentially revolve around whether or not to restrict the free movement of capital across the national boundaries and, if a free flow is deemed a desirable objective, how and why it should be introduced in the context of an overall liberalization programme in India.

The basic issue of capital account liberalization has been to integrate the domestic capital market with the free working of the international capital market so that various policy induced distortions stemming from multitude of controls in the domestic capital market are eliminated and the law of arbitrage prevails in the capital account transactions. This again calls for systematic dismantling of controls and elimination of informational asymmetries such that arbitrage conditions prevail and the capital market functions smoothly.

One can easily point out that the present Indian situation is not ripen enough to go into for full convertibility on capital accounts on the account that full convertibility involves freeing capital markets. Unless and until the rupee is freely floated, this would complicate the task of the exchange rate management. With large capital flows there can be an unsustainable massive real appreciation of the rupee and when the market assessment is that the appreciation is unsustainable, there can be sudden capital outflows and an uncontrollable spiral of depreciation of currency. This will in fact destroy the countries tradable sectors which is undergoing a re-structuring process following the package of reforms undertaken in industrial, trade, and exchange rate policis.

The globalization of capital has had its discontents. In the aftermath of Asian crisis, many academics and policy-makers blamed volatile, speculative capital flows for the virulence of this crisis and their contagion effects. This crisis led to a breakdown of international finance and resulted in costly adjustment for those economies.

Besides, hasty capital account liberalization will lead to speculative attack on the exchange rate as it happened in South Asian Countries. Thirdly, financial openness index for the Indian economy is still very low in comparison to the other countries. Fourthly, the inadequate liberalization in the domestic financial and banking sector may cause to greater volatility. Finally, full capital account convertibility will put a pressure on the trade balance of the economy. Another thing may happen, following an increase in the interest rate structure in the developed countries with CAC as a step, like sudden withdrawal of foreign funds invested through the foreign financial institutions. This happens in India and now it is apprehended that the resources mobilized through the Mutual Funds have been channeled into the share market without adequate preparation resulting in an artificial upward trend in the share prices. As a consequence, there has been a crash as well as instability in the share market. This problem may have the implication of a distant thunder, and it may cause adverse effect on the unemployment situation. Another point that is to be noted is that India has had the past memories of an acute shortage of foreign exchange. Capital outflows by overseas deposits by Indian investors will fetch a lower return as well as a currency risk for the Indian investors. One must draw lessons from the recent history of Latin America where the outflow of capital pushed a number of countries into debt trap and towards "casino capitalism." Nay, a review of the international experience with CAC shows that liberalization of the capital account induces large capital inflows which can cause real appreciation in the exchange rate and erode the effectiveness of the domestic monetary policy. Moreover, an open capital account imposes tremendous pressures on the financial system and brings weaknesses in the financial system into sharper focus.

Thus the critics argue that in the absence of complementary macro-economic policies, full scale liberalization of capital account will pose much more danger to the Indian economy as is not comprehended by the Tarapore Committee (*Chatterjee*, 1998)

D.M. Nachane (2007) identifies types of risks attendant on a capital account liberalization programme. These risks may be classified into five categories: (i) Currency Risk, i.e., the possibility of a sudden precipitous devaluation of a country's currency without taking adequate safeguards in place, (ii) Capital Flight Risk that occurs when non-resident holders of liquid financial assets sell that holding *en masse*, (iii) Fragility risk that refers to the vulnerability of the borrowers (corporate and banks) to internal or external shocks, and (iv) Sovereignty Risk that pertains to the constraints that a domestic government may face in its stability to pursue independent national policies in the event of a crisis. Besides, the *trilemma* in question (*Bernanke*, 2005) i.e., the impossibility of maintaining in simultaneous operation (for a given country) of a policy regime of an open capital account, a fixed exchange rate, and an independent domestic monetary policy remains. The *trilemma*, therefore, needs to be interpretated as a move in one direction having to be compensated by a countervailing move along another dimension.

Now a pertinent question is whether there are any benefits from CAC. Advocates in its favour articulate that there would be some distinct advantages in the following manner:

- The Indian resident will be able to use the world capital market for risk diversification and maximize the return on their resources.
- Convertibility would enable aggregate saving and investment to be optimized.
- The cost of capital would come down as there will be large inflow of capital in the country.
- It has been noted that over a period of time capital controls turn ineffective, costly and even distorting.

- There will be gains from free inflow and outflow of capital. Indian residents, Indian banks, Indian mutual funds, Indian corporate, if the corporate finds it remunerative with joint ventures, would be able to enhance their earnings, by investing a part of their money and resources.
- There will be an availability of a large dose of capital at international prices to supplement domestic resources and if there is large capital inflows CAC would relieve pressure on the exchange rate, the monetary aggregates and thereby enhance the effectiveness of domestic policy.
- The spread of financial intermediaries will come down as a result of increased competition and as such the system would be more efficient.
- Tax evasion and capital flight will reduce since tax levels would come down to international level.
- The cost of government borrowing will come down as the rate of interest would be low and ultimately fiscal deficit will reduce.
- Capital outflows will propel Indian authorities to initiate corrective macroeconomic policies, for which Indian interest rates and stock prices would be highly attractive and Indian holding foreign financial assets abroad would find it attractive to invest in India.

In this perspective, the advocates also argue that India just can not remain isolated in an increasingly integrating world. If India does not plan for an orderly integration with the world economy, the world would integrate with it in a manner in which India would have no control over events. Thus, the question is whether or not we should move to CAC but whether we want an orderly or a disorderly transition to CAC.

B. Conceptional Issues

As we all know that gross national product (GNP) may be considered from either the product side (demand) or the factor payments side (supply). On the product side, we have:

$$Y=C+I+G+X-M$$

where Y is GNP, C is consumption, I is investment, C is government purchases, X is exports, and M is imports.

On the factor payments side, we have:

$$Y=C+Sp+T$$

where C is again consumption, Sp is private saving, and T is tax revenue.

We may obtain from above two equations :

$$O= (I-Sp) + [G-T] + [X-M]$$

Rearranging, we may identify the resource gap as:

$$M-X= (I-Sp) + (G-T)$$

Thus, the excess of imports over exports must equal the excess of investment over private saving plus the excess of government purchases over tax revenue. Considering that the government's fiscal balance is tax revenue minus government spending or T-G and that this balance may be thought of as government's saving (Sg) we now rewrite the resource gap as:

$$M-X=I-Sp-(T-G) =I-Sp-Sg=I-(Sp+Sg) =I-S$$

where S is the total of all saving, government plus private. Thus, the need for the external resources, and therefore the trade gap, equals the excess of domestic investment over total domestic savings. Similarly (X-M) is the surplus in the trade account. If we add to it invisible trade and unrequited transfer payments, we have the current account of BoP. If we assume for simplicity, that such receipts are zero, then the current account surplus has be matched by excess of saving over investment and the budget surplus. In this perspective, a deficit in the current account implies insufficient saving relative to investment and government spending.

Since the overall BoP balances, we now have to look towards the BoP in the capital account. The capital account records all international transactions that involve a resident of a country changing either his or her assets with, or liabilities to, a resident of another country and consists of short-term and long term private official towards, portfolio and direct investment, and changes in official resources. In fact, capital account transactions can involve changes in the composition of the national capital of the country. In what follows, a deficit in the current account will always imply a surplus in the capital account and *vice-versa* that also means inflow of foreign funds has to supplement domestic savings.

And the net inflow of foreign funds though the capital account meet the excess requirements of invertible funds over domestic savings in the economy. In fact, the following relationships hold between the current and the capital accounts, from two sides:

Current account deficit = capital account surplus + drawing down of reserves

Or

Surplus in the current account

$$(X\text{-}M) = S - I + T - G = \text{Change in Net foreign assets.}$$

This means that if a country has a deficit on its current account, the country has spent more abroad that it has earned during the specified period. This can be settled by international borrowing, or by seeking capital flows in the form of direct or portfolio investment or by depleting reserve accumulation of foreign currency that have built up over the years. Now any changes in the capital account of BoP, brought about by autonomous capital 'flows' get reflected through changes either in the current account position or the reserve position.

The decision to allow the free flow of direct and financial foreign capital across national boundaries can thus have serious implications for the national sovereignty of a country. A substantial inflow of capital sometimes distort the medium and long-term fundamental of an economy as it happened in case of Mexico in 1995, East Asia in mid-1997, and Euro-Zones during 1999-2003. Furthermore, even if macroeconomic fundamentals like high growth, relative stability in prices, healthy financial sector and high returns on investment, remain strong, a country may be highly vulnerable to speculative attacks with high current account deficits.

However, large capital inflows[40] or outflows affect the domestic economy in a variety of ways. For example, within a flexible exchange rate regime, capital inflows results in an appreciation of the domestic currency. This results in the possibility of an increasing current account deficit that can become unsustainable. On the other hand, capital outflows in a flexible exchange rate regime tend to depreciate the domestic currency and can cause inflationary pressures and can induce capital flight.

So choices regarding appropriate exchange rate and whether and how to control capital flows become crucial. Second, the maintenance of high interest rate concerning incoming of foreign portfolio flows can adversely affect productive investment directly and it also makes public debt servicing more expensive. Thus opening up of global portfolio flows may result in stagnation of the country since portfolio investment comes to a country when the BoP position of a country is good. Hence, the debate crops up whether a country should liberalize capital account transactions and, if they do so, how this should be done.

C. The Present Scenario

To pave the way for the success of Indian CAC ,the First and the Second Tarapore Committee provide a certain set of pre-conditions, sequencing and timing of measures. For example, India must maintain inflation rate at 3.5%, fiscal deficit at 3.5% of GDP, current account deficit at 1.6% of GDP, but the present statistics for India goes other way round. (Table 5.7) For example, average inflation rate at India is nearly 5% from 2001 to 2005/06, which goes against the Tarapore target rate. It is also difficult task before the Government to achieve Tarapore target of fiscal deficit to the tune of 3.5% of GDP, while the actual average fiscal deficit during 2000/01 to 2005/06 is found to be 5% of GDP. The CAC Committee has also recommended that the ratio of short term debt plus portfolio stock as a percentage of forex reserve should not exceed 60%. Recent RBI Annual Report has indicated that this ratio is around 75%. So we may articulate that India should embark on full CAC from a position of strength—a satisfactory real rate of growth, relatively low inflation and a high level of forex reserves, a low current account deficit in BOP and a falling debt service ratio. Besides, D.M. Nachane (2007) has pointed out that it is not very evident that especially Tarapore Committee II have really gone into a detailed examination of all the risks attached to CAC and devoted sufficient attention to measures such as TWSBs (Trip Wires—Speed Bumps Approach) which have recently been experimented with in several countries on ground for insulating economies from financial crises, without impinging seriously on the volume of FDI as well as in checking real currency appreciation.

To sum up CAC in India requires several prerequisites in terms of strong macroeconomic policy framework and soundness and efficiency of financial systems and markets. The management of the external sector must be accompanied here

TABLE 5.7

Precondition for Capital Account Convertibility in India : Tarapore I Vs Actuals

Item	*Recommendation of Tarapore Committee (1997) for 1999-2000*	*Actual Position in 2005-06*
Fiscal Consolidation		
Gross Fiscal Deficit (GFD) of the Central Govt. as % of GDP	3.5	4.1
The Rate of Inflation (Mandated)	3.0-5.0 (average for 3 years)	4.6 (average for 3 years)
Strengthening of the Financial System		
(i) Gross Non-performing assets (NPAs) as a percentage of total advances	5.0	5.2 (2004-05)
(ii) Average effective Cash Reserve Ratio for the banking system	3.0	5.0
Important macro-economic indicators		
Debt service ratio to be reduced to 20% from 25% of total exports		Debt service ratio declined to 10.2%
The Forex Reserves should not be less than 6 months of imports		14 months coverage

Source : RBI, Report on Currency and Finance, 2001-02 and RBI (2006) : Report of the Committee on Fuller Capital Account Convertibility.

by a flexible exchange rate, sustainable current account deficit, preference to non-debt creating resource flows, limits on the quantum, use and cost of external debt, and a highly restrictive approach to short term debt: the exchange rate not to be in any way out of alignment with the fundamentals for a prolong period of times. The currency must not be imbibed with over valuation as because overvaluation in that case could act as a catalyst when there will be a run on the currency. The speculator in that case will do the massacre for the economy. The liberalization of financial markets should be accompanied by an increase in regulation and supervision. Today's financial markets are very sensitive to new information and also exhibit risks and volatility. Under such circumstances, to meet the emerging challenges before India, a cautious and calibrated approach with enough regulatory and prudential safeguards is urgently called for towards moving to full CAC.

5.7 CONCLUSION

To conclude, the trade and payments policy regime in India as they have evolved since independence in line with the planned development process clearly reflect that the regimes has served as an important segment of India's overall economic policy to fulfil production, consumption and employment targets in different plans in pursuit of industrialization drive. And to fulfil these objectives the country is struggling hard to become internationally competitive by an effort to integrate its economy with the World Economy. Not much has been achieved in this direction so far, but the process has started in moving towards the right direction. The future performance of exports will strongly depend on the country's ability to adjust effectively with the management of trade and payments policy to changes in the world trading system, guided by the rules and regulations of WTO. The success of the structural adjustment in India thus should be judged not only by the stability on the balance of payments situation but also by the growth and structural transformation of the economy which require a lot of other institutional changes within the economy as well.

NOTES AND REFERENCES

1. In an open economy the national income accounting identity can be written as:
$GNP = C + I + G + X - M$ (i)
where all variables are at constant prices.
The total spending or absorption (A) by domestic residents can be expressed as :
$A = C + I + G$ (ii)
Equation (i) and (ii) give: $A = GNP - X + M$ (iii)
Following the monetary approach to the balance of payments theory the absorption function can be specified as :
$$A = Y + \varepsilon\left(\frac{M^s}{P} - \frac{M^d}{P}\right) \quad \text{(iv)}$$
where Y is GNP and e is the adjustment co-efficient of monetary disequilibrium whose value lies between zero and unity.
Equations (iii) and (iv) yield :
$$M - X = \varepsilon\left(\frac{M^s}{P} - \frac{M^d}{P}\right) \quad \text{(v)}$$
Taking the exponent of both sides in equation
$\log (M^d/P) = a\log y - bp^e$
where the above demand for money is expressed in the semi-logarithm form. M^d is the demand for nominal money balances, P is the price level, Y the real income or output, p^e the expected inflation, a and b are structural parameters. It shows the demand for money increases with the increase in real income and decreases with the increase in expected inflation. Thus we find:
$M^d/P = exp\ (a\log - bp^e)$ (vi)
where exp denotes the exponentiation operator.
Substitution of equation (vi) into equation (v) yields
$M - X = e\{M^s/P - exp\ (a\log y - bp^e)\}$ (vii)
It shows that the trade balance of country deteriorates with the increase in both the money supply and expected inflation and that it improves with the increase in real income.
2. In general, developing countries are small open economies. So far India is concerned, it is one of the small open economies in the world. The trade-to-income ratio is less than that of China or even Russia. Compared with East Asian or Latin American averages, India has a share almost with half a per cent in the world trade. In the absence of intervention the traded goods sector invariably accounts for a large share of total output or final expenditure. The exact composition of output would in turn be determined by factor endowments, technology and tastes and preferences. Economic Theory tells us that the allocation of resources across sectors, and the efficiency with which resources are utilized in a given sector, can be influenced by intervention. Governments have at this disposal a range of instruments which can be, and in general are used in an endeavour to direct resource utilization in a particular way.

These instruments are collectively referred to as trade policy, or more generally trade and industrial policy. (For details on the evidence, see Greenaway, David and Chris R. Milner (1993)—*Trade and Industrial Policy in Developing Countries* - Macmillian, London).

3. See Hussain, Abid 'Foreign Trade Policy in Indian Planning' in K. Banerjee, and Tarjani Vakil (eds) (1990): *India: Joining the World Economy,* Tata McGraw-Hill Publishing Company Ltd., New Delhi.
4. From the theoretical literature, it follows that if one calculates the effective exchange rate (EER) facing producers in the import substitutions sector and compares this with the exchange rate facing producers in the export sector and if one finds that the former is larger than the latter, then it can be said that the country is said to be following an import-substituting strategy; if the EERs are the other way around, the country is said to be following an export promotion strategy. This approach has been advocated by a number of analysis, including B. Balassa, (1982).
5. Throughout the post-War years, except the intensive reform period, import controls had become a normal feature of Indian economic life. The continued reliance on import controls as an instrument of balance of payments policy had rested on the belief that without these controls it would not be possible to ensure that the total claims on foreign exchange did not exceed the available receipts. However, import controls had in the process acquired some new functions such as that of influencing the volume and composition of private investment in accordance with developmental priorities. In countries where investment is often greatly dependent on the availability of imported equipment, and other instruments of influencing the volume and composition of private investment (such as monetary and fiscal policies) that cannot be used in a flexible manner, planners have found import controls a handy tool of planning.
6. See Cohen, Benjamin I. (1970) : 'International Development in India and Pakistan' in Robinson E.A.G. and Michael Kidron (eds.), *'Economic Development in South Asia'*. Proceedings of a Conference held by the International Economic Association at Kandy, Ceylon, Macmillian St. Martin's Press, London.
7. Bhagwati, Jagdish (1994) : 'Free Trade: Old and New Challenges' in the *'Economic Journal'* March 1994, Vol. 104, No. 423.
8. Bhagwati J.N. and T.N. Srinivasan (1976) : *Foreign Trade Regimes and Economic Development*, Macmillian Company of India Ltd., Delhi.
9. Bhagwati, J.N. and T.N. Srinivasan (1975) : *Foreign Trade Regimes and Economic Development : India*, New York, National Bureau of Economic Research (Special Conference series on Foreign Trade Regimes and Economic Development, Vol. VI).
10. Due to the uncompetitive cost-price structure of her non-traditional manufactured products, India was faced with the problem that an exchange rate appropriate to its traditional products was found to be overvalued for promoting exports of new manufactures. The response of the government was to institute a system of export subsidies, on a selected basis. The most important form was through the import entitlement schemes. Under these schemes, exporters of many

manufactured products were entitled to retain a part of the export earnings or the import of specified inputs and in certain cases the import entitlement could be sold to third parties. There was a general scarcity of products eligible for imports under these schemes and as a result import entitlement certificates enjoyed a considerable premium. Thus, for exporters of manufactured products, the effective export exchange rate was more favourable than the official rate. Since the entitlement rate varied from one product to another and in addition there were limits on transferability of entitlements, the schemes led to the creation of a larger number of differentiated exchange markets (for details, See Bhagwati, Jagdish, N. and T.N. Srinivasan (1970) : *India : Planning for Industrialization and Trade Policies since 1951*, London, OUP).

11. The production of food-grains fell from 89 million tons in 1964-65 to 72 million tons in 1965-66, and it rose only to 74.2 million tons in 1966-67. The availability of raw cotton (production and imports) fell from 9.4 million bales in 1964-65 (September-August) to 8.5 million bales a year in 1965-66 and 1966-67. The availability of raw jute fell from 10.4 million bales in 1964-65 (July June) of 9.1 million bales in 1965-66 and 9.4 million bales in 1966-67. The production of major oil seeds fell from 8.5 million tons in 1964-65 to 6.4 million tons a year in 1965-66 and 1966-67. See Govt. of India, *Economic Survey*, 1968-69. These figures relate to agricultural years.
12. Jalan, Bimal (1996) : *India's Economic Policy: Preparing For the Twenty-First Century*; Viking by Penguin Books India Pvt. Ltd. For a discussion of the influence of political economy factor in India's development policy, see Pranab Bardhan's *The Political Economy of Development in India*, (1984), Oxford : Basil Blackwell.
13. National Council of Applied Economic Research (NCAER) (1969) : 'Export Strategy for India', New Delhi.
14. In September 1975, the rupee was de-linked from the Pound Sterling, and devalued to the extent of 25.6 per cent between 1970 and 1975 on an export weighted basis (Wolf, 1982, Table 4.1, p. 8). For details on the evidence see Wolf, Martin (1982) *India's Exports*, New York, OUP.
15. Sood, Krishnalekha (1989), *Trade and Economic Development: India, Pakistan and Bangladesh*, Sage Publications, New Delhi.
16. For details see Narasimham, M. (1988) : *World Economic Environment and Prospects for India*, Sterling Publishers Private Ltd., New Delhi.
17. Ahluwalia, I.J. (1985) : Industrial Growth in India: Stagnation since the Mid-Sixties, Delhi, OUP.
18. Kelkar, V.L. (1977) : 'Evaluation of India's Trade Policies', *Economic and Political Weekly*, 18 June.
19. Singh, Manmohan (1976) : 'International Trade and Payments' in *A Survey of Research in Economics, Vol. II, Macro-economics*, ICSSR, New Delhi, Allied Publishers, New Delhi.
20. Balasubramaniyam, Y.N. and D.R. Basu (1990) : 'India's Export Promotion Policies and Export Performance' In Milner (ed.), *Export Promotion Strategies* (Helmel Hemosteade: Harvester Wheatsheaf).
21. Sen, Sunanda (1982) : 'Policy Planning in the Foreign Trade Sector: From Import Substitution to Export Promotion in India'. Proceedings of the ISI

Golden Jubilee International Conference on Review of the Indian Planning Process, Calcutta.

22. Alexander, P.C. (1978), Chairman, Report of the Committee on Import-Export Policies and Procedures, *Ministry of Commerce*, Government of India.
23. A liberalizing economy is defined as one with a rising import share in GDP, a falling proportion of tariffs in the total tax revenue and a low black-market premium. The conflict between various definitions of trade liberalization makes it difficult to assess the extent to which it has occurred. In general, liberalization has been equated with becoming 'more outward-oriented'. This may refer, however, to a move toward neutrality, liberality, or openness. A move towards neutrality involves equalizing incentives, on average, between the export and import competing sectors. A more liberal regime is one where the level of intervention has been reduced. Finally, an increase in openness is equated with an increase in the importance of trade in the economy (e.g., as a percentage of GDP). Trade Policy Reforms in Developing Countries since 1985 : a review of the evidence by Dean, J.S. Desai and J. Riedel (1994). World Bank Discussion Paper No. 267 holds the similar view. A policy action which reduced the scarcity premium attached to controls would be considered 'mild liberalization' .
24. The flow of Non-residents' deposits, which had been positive in September 1990, turned negative in October 1990. V. P. Singh, the then Prime Minister of India had tried to prevent the crisis of confidence by borrowing foreign exchange worth 11.7 billion rupees from the IMF, but this was of no avail. When Chandra Sekhar formed another minority government which was even more dependent of 'toleration' than V.P. Singh's government, he rushed back for help to the IMF in January 1991 and borrowed foreign exchange worth 33.3 billion rupees. But this did not restore confidence either. Chandra Sekhar's government was toppled down in February by Rajiv Gandhi, who then launched a vigorous election campaign in the course of which he was murdered by terrorists on May 21, 1991. The outflow of funds of non-resident Indians was at its peak from April to July 1991 (See Rothermund, Dietmar, 1991) : *An Economic History of India: From Pre-Colonial Times to 1991*, Routledge, New York).
25. Balasubramanyam, Y.N. (1995), "India's Trade Policy Review" in Arndt, S. and C. Milner, eds., (1995). *"The World Economy: Global Trade Policy"*: Blackwell Publisher, London.
26. Chatterjee, Biswajit and Sugata Marjit (1992), "Trade and Payments Policies in India: An Evaluation of Recent Changes and Their Implications" : *The Indian Economic Journal*, Vol. 39, No. 3, Jan.-March.
27. Karmakar, Asim K. (1993), "The Indian Economy—A March Towards Globalization" in Das, Debendra K., ed, *"Structural Adjustment in the Indian Economy"*, Vol. 2, Deep and Deep Publications, New Delhi.
28. Karmakar, Asim K. (1994), "External Value of the Rupee and India's Balance of Payments—A Macroeconomic Assessment". Conference Volume of the Indian Economic Association, Bombay.
29. Karmakar, Asim K. (1994), "Privatisation of Public Sector Enterprises in India: An Evaluation of Some Basic Issues" in Das, Debendra K. (ed.),

Privatisation of Public Sector Undertaking—Rationale and Feasibility, Deep and Deep Publication, New Delhi.
30. Chatterjee, Biswajit (1994) : 'An Economic Theorist's Tale of Trade Liberalization' in Das, Debendra, K. (ed.) *Structural Adjustment in the Indian Economy,* Vol. 1, Deep and Deep Publication, New Delhi.
31. Mathew Joseph (1992), *Exchange Rate Policy: Impact on Exports and Balance of Payments,* Deep and Deep Publications, New Delhi.
32. The decade of the 1970s saw the breakdown and disintegration of the Bretton Woods system. The best date to attach to the end of Bretton Woods is probably 15 August 1971 when President Nixon suspended the free convertibility of the US dollar into gold at the fixed rate agreed at Bretton Woods. This ended the era of fixed exchange rates and destroyed the foundation of even the truncated Bretton Woods which had emerged. The breakdown of the system was more immediately connected with the emerging payment imbalances between the industrial countries, but also with increasing concerns with 'overheating' of their economies and a consequent displacement of full employment by control of inflation as a priority objective. Thus the engine of growth which had supported the developing countries during the golden era began to shutter and then violently changed gear.
33. Corden, W Max (1993), "Exchange Rate Policies for Developing Countries", *The Economic Journal,* Vol. 103, No. 416 (January '93), pp. 198-207.
34. Exchange rate floats have normally been associated with substantial liberalization of current account transactions of the BoP, so that the exchange rate rather than controls becomes the mechanism by which foreign exchange is allocated between usuers. In many cases particularly in Africa capital account controls, have remained in force to prevent capital flight, where holders of domestic assets convert these into foreign exchange and take them abroad.
35. In the long run equilibrium, when all adjustment has been completed, an economy must be at both internal and external balance. Internal balance means that the demand for goods and services is equal to full capacity supply, external balance means that on the balance of payments the current account is exactly in balance, so the country is neither adding to nor subtracting from its net international wealth. Thus:

    INTERNAL BALANCE

    Capacity output = domestic demand + net exports.

    EXTERNAL BALANCE

    Net exports = interest on net foreign debt.

    Initially we ignore interest on foreign debt, which is a reasonable simplification of either net debt is small or if (real) interest rates are close to zero.

    In this special case, external balance requires that net exports are zero. Net export demand depends on income levels at home and abroad, and on competitiveness. Competitiveness depends on the real exchange rate. If P is the price of domestic goods, p* the price of foreign goods, and S the spot exchange rate (unit of foreign currency per unit of domestic currency), the real exchange rate R is given by PS/P*. A rise in the R makes the domestic country less competitive and reduces its exports.

In the long-run equilibrium, external balance requires that net exports are zero. Given zero net exports, internal balance then requires that domestic demand equals domestic capacity output.

Several observations follow from this simple description of long-run equilibrium. First, since the real exchange rate, like other real variables, is constant in long-run equilibrium, Purchasing Power Parity (PPP) holds. An excess of domestic inflation over foreign inflation must be continuously offset by depreciation of the nominal exchange rate precisely. to keep the real exchange rate constant, provided all other real things remain equal.

PPP holds when nominal variables are changing but real variables are not; it can not be hold when real variables are changing.

In short, the internal and external balance framework allows us to work through the long-run implications of any shocks we may wish to address. This framework enables us to think about the determinants of exchange rate in the long-run, also it plays an important role in the minds of short-term speculators who must hear the direction in which the exchange rate is eventually heading.

36. Misalignment is defined as the 'persistent departure of the exchange rate from its long-run equilibrium'. A misalignment can be brought about by two factors, viz. macro-economic policy and structural factors. Macro-economic policy-induced misalignment is the result of inconsistencies between monetary and fiscal policies, on the one hand, and official nominal exchange rate regime on the other. Structural misalignment has its source in structural factors like terms of trade, productivity, growth, tariffs, capital and exchange controls and capital flows.
37. Kumar, Rajiv and Mathew Joseph (1994), "External Value of the Rupee". Paper Printed and Presented at the Annual Conference of the Indian Economic Association held at Bombay University, Bombay during 19-21 February 1994.
38. See A. Vasudevan's article, "External Value of the Rupee: Issues for Discussion", Printed and presented at the Annual Conference of the Indian Economic Association held at Bombay University Bombay During 19-21 February 1994.
39. See Joshi & Little (1994), India : Macroeconomics and Political Economy 1964-91. Oxford University Press, Bombay.
40. Large capital flows may turn out to be a welcome as well as a worrisome macroeconomic development for India. Some of the positive features are (i) acquiring capital for higher economic growth; (ii) smoothing out consumption overtime and acquiring new technology and expertise through FDI. Concurrently, these inflows have posed major challenges for the conduct of monetary policy. There is a tendency for the real exchange rate to appreciate as a result of build up of foreign exchange reserves and associated expansion of monetary base, greater speculative activity on the part of the domestic asset markets and possible disruption associated with sudden reversal of flows. The money supply becomes endogenous in the presence of capital flows. Moreover, capital inflows lead to increased expenditure, some of which spill over onto tradable goods. This increases the trade deficits. Some expenditures will spill over onto the non-tradable goods sector, increasing the size of the non-

tradable sector at the expense of the tradable goods sectors. Besides, the sudden increase in the balance sheet on both the asset and liability sides for the banking system may make it possible to finance investment / consumption decisions that are not sustainable over the long-run, thus widening the current account, increasing the private sector's indebtedness and the emergence of non-performing assets. Unless sterilized, these accretions to the financial sector's balance sheet will lead to inflationary consequences and the build-up of international debt through recurrent current account deficits will undermine the country's creditworthiness.

APPENDIX

TABLE A 5.1
Major Events in India's Trade and Payments Policy Regime

Year/Period	*Major Events*
1947-55	India's trade regime was in practice free of restrictions. Capital controls were more restrictive than import controls. "Export pessimism" brought high export taxes and there was no modernization in the export sector; consequently, exports stagnated; and there was fast deterioration in India's forex reserves. This necessitated a reversal of trade policy. When the pound was devalued in 1949 the rupee-sterling rate remains intact at £ 1 = Rs. 13.33. In the first half of the 1950s inflation in India was low; so the real exchange rate (RER) depreciated modestly.
1956-60	The Second Five Year Plan launched in 1956 emphasized on foreign exchange intensive investment in the manufacturing and heavy industries. In response to a severe balance of payments and foreign exchange crises, the authorities introduced strict import and investment licensing schemes that shifted the investment pattern towards inward-oriented, capital intensive manufacturing industries centred on import substitution as a means of stimulating industrialization. Formally, the exchange rate regime was an adjustable peg Bretton-Woods-style regime. But in practice it was operated as a fixed nominal exchange rate. As the Second Plan did not alleviate the shortage of foreign exchange, foreign aid and official foreign borrowing increased substantially. Inflation in India was faster than inflation abroad; so the Rupee appreciated substantially and exports stagnated.
1961-66	This period could be hailed as **First Transition Period** that occurred in trade and payments policy regime involving "partial liberalization" in view of the export subsidization (that began in earnest around 1962 and intensified through the period on a whole range of exports) and growing resort to import duties as well as planned use of aid to expand domestic production of imported goods. Indian prices continued to rise faster than foreign prices and the RER appreciated. The appreciation was modest from 1960-63 but sharp in 1964 and 1965. In 1965 Indo-Pakistan war and

(*Contd.*)

TABLE A 5.1 (*Contd.*)

Period	*Major Events*
	drought brought about a crisis. Exports grew modestly from 1960 to 1963, stagnated in 1964, and collapsed in 1965.
1966	The World Bank forced India to devalue the rupee by 57.5 per cent in June 6, 1966 computed as the increase from Rs. 4.76 to Rs. 7.50 in the official rate on the dollar. Rupee-sterling parity changes, to £ 1 = Rs. 21. This was combined with some import delicensing and reductions in tariffs and export subsidies. Export taxes were also introduced. The twin objectives of devaluation: improving BoP position and replacing the cumbersome structure of import restrictions and export subsidies did not yield desired results.
1967-71	Pound devalued in November 1967 from \$ 2.80 to \$ 2.40; rupee sterling parity changes to £ 1 = Rs. 18. In 1968, Britain entered into agreement with India to restrict the drawing down of sterling reserves from September of the same year. In fact, after the devaluation of 1966 the nominal exchange rate was kept constant until 1971 when rupee pegged to the U.S. dollar on August 22, 1971. By 1968, the liberalization efforts had been largely reversed and import protection had been further intensified : QR protection was enhanced while import premia reached over 50 per cent of import values on an average. Export subsidies has been reinstituted and went up high levels. As might be expected, there was only a modest increase in exports.
1972-74	Pound floated on June 23, 1972; India's maintenance of parity with sterling remained unchanged. The first oil crisis came in 1973 and there were severe droughts in 1972 and 1974, leading to high inflation. But the sterling peg led not only to a nominal effective devaluation, but also to a real effective devaluation. Import controls were tightened in response to the oil crisis but export incentives were also encouraging. The behaviour of the RER helped exports to grow quite rapidly despite high inflation.
1975-79	India adopted a basket peg on September 25, 1975. Pound, however, continued as intervention currency. For two years from 1975, the NER was kept constant but was allowed to fall in 1978 and 1979.

(*Contd.*)

TABLE A 5.1 (*Contd.*)

Period	*Major Events*
	Since inflation to India was low in this period, the RER fell since export subsidies continued to increase. These changes brought about improvements in export competitiveness. The improvement in the foreign exchange position in 1975 was followed by some liberalization of imports. However, the liberalization was extremely cautious and gradual. Nevertheless, the change was important because from then on there had not been a major tightening of import controls even in the face of BoP difficulties. From 1975 to 1979 there was an export boom. This was mainly the result of the above developments.
1980-85	This period could be hailed as **Second Transition Period** in trade and payments policy regime, since there had been renewed thinking regarding liberalization of the industrial and trade regimes. Since the early 1980s, export incentives have been expanded. The main thrust of the reforms had been to ease the supply situation of important non-competitive inputs used by domestic industries. After the second oil shock, import controls were not tightened. There was no exchange rate depreciation. The nominal exchange rate was kept fixed and current account deficits were financed partly by running down reserves and partly by increased borrowing. Inflation was high and the RER appreciated about 12 per cent. Overall exports in real terms slowed down during 1980-82.
1985-90	Right from beginning of the mid-1980s, India witnessed **Third Transition Period** in her trade and payments policy regime. Between 1985 and 1990 the pattern of trade reform in India was one of moving toward a more neutral trade regime with much less progress toward liberality. Some selective reduction in QRs took place, as well as rationalization of the tariff structure and small reduction in tariff. Despite these changes, both tariff and QRs remained significant impediment to trade.
1991	As part of the crisis management the authorities effected sizeable (a two-step) discrete downward adjustment in the external value of the rupee against

(*Contd.*)

TABLE A 5.1 (*Contd.*)

Period	*Major Events*
	the five major currencies on July I and 3, instead of usual small step adjustment. As a result, between June 28 and July 3, 1991, the value of the rupee declined by 17-19 per cent *vis-a-vis* the five major currencies. This is for the first time that large discrete adjustments in the exchange rate are made after the adoption of the basket peg in September 1975. 'Permit Raj' had been mostly dismantled. Tariffs had been lowered using a 'tops down' approach. Another reform included liberalization of import licensing system as well as rules and regulations relating to FDI.
1992-97	After two massive doses of devaluation in 1991 and a brief period of EXIM scripts and the partial convertibility of the rupee with a two-tier system, the full convertibility of the rupee on current account BoP was made in August 1994, and capital account convertibility for Non-Residents had worked in favour of opening up of the economy and its integration with the world economy. From March 1993, there had been a prolonged stability in the exchange rate of the rupee, except in October 1995. In fact, the exchange rate regime became the managed float with the nominal exchange rate targeted to achieving the RER which yielded a current account deficit.
1997-2002	During this Ninth Plan the exchange rate of the rupee had broadly been market determined, except for occasional counter-cyclical operations by the RBI for stabilization of the domestic financial markets, foreign exchange and government securities market following the event of September 11, 2001 in the US. However, the exchange rate market had displayed reasonable stability with the rupee depreciated by 6.1 percent from the annual average of rupees 37.165 per dollar in 1997-98 to rupees 47.707 in 2001-02. During this period the export-weighted REER of the rupee had shown considerable amplitude, combining sharp depreciation with long periods of gradual appreciation. And the exchange rate management policy during this period, continued its focus on smoothening the excess volatility in the exchange rate with no fixed rate target. Besides, tariff reduction drive became an important

(*Contd.*)

TABLE A 5.1 (*Contd.*)

Period	*Major Events*
	component of the efforts at increasing competition and efficiency in the economy and making Indian exports more competitive.
2002-07	The then Union Commerce and Industry Minister on March 31st, 2002 announced the Exim Policy for the Five Year Period (2002-07) coinciding with the Tenth Plan Period. The main thrust of the policy was to create an expanding base of tradable goods and services. Various export policies had been formulated from time to time. SEZs were being set up to further boost the exports. The policy was geared towards the goal of attaining US $ 80 billion exports over the Tenth Five Year Plan by 2007. The Exim Policy 2002 meanwhile had removed all QRs on exports, except for a few sensitive items. Exchange rate was consequently viewed as an instrument to effect the behaviour of exports. With the introduction of almost full convertibility on the current account and also partial convertibility on the capital account, the exchange rate had been made more sensitive to the demand for and supply of foreign exchange in the economy. The country entered into ***Fourth Transition period*** onto her attempt to achieve international level of tariffs without too much disruption in view of the additional protection to the domestic industry during this Tenth Plan Period.

6

India's Trade Balance and Macroeconomic Policies—An Alternative Approach

The balance of payments of a country reflects varied interactions between its macroeconomic variables, and the factors governing foreign trade and trade policy regimes of the nation. For a developing economy like India, the behaviours of balance of payments and trade balance over time are also subject to the various constraints on the growth process of the economy that appeared from time to time. Identification of the key determinants of trade balance in the current account and of balance of payments as a whole for the entire time span, therefore, becomes important for understanding the growth process of the economy, and the underlying factors that shape the growth process. Our review of the theoretical literature on balance of payments adjustment and policies, and the studies on India's balance of payments, emphasize the significance of some such variables like GDP, stock of money supply, the inflation rate, foreign exchange reserves, the exchange rate, apart from exports, imports and net barter terms of trade, in specifying the exact macro-economic framework for an open economy, and in the context of a developing nation, one needs to look at the interactions of some such selected variables closely and carefully to avoid mis-specification errors. In this chapter, we shall attempt to test the statistical significance of the relationship between variables in terms of simple econometric methods. We shall adopt a holistic approach in integrating alternative theoretical strands while specifying different estimable equations. This will enable us to evaluate the importance of alternative factors separately in explaining the behaviour of India's balance of payments over the period.

6.1 OPENNESS OF THE INDIAN ECONOMY

Before we proceed to set-up econometric models for identifying the determinants of India's balance of payments and trade balance over the period, let us examine the degree of openness of the Indian economy. This is important for two reasons: (a) it measures the extent of dependence of the economy and its growth process on external transactions, and reflects the nature of trade and payments policy regimes which govern these transactions; and (b) it also signifies the importance of home market and hence the role of domestic macroeconomic variables and the policies affecting them in shaping the overall growth performance of the economy and the extent of external balance that such growth implies over the period. Table 6.1 presents the relevant data.

The degree of openness is measured by the trade orientation ratio (TOR), which has two definitions: (a) Exports/ GDP ratio, and (b) absolute value of the sum of value of export and imports as ratio of GDP at current prices. It is clear from Table 6.1 that (i) the degree of openness of the Indian economy remained consistently low for most of the periods under consideration, no matter which of the above definitions we use, (ii) The TOR exhibits a mild U-turn, although there is periodic fluctuations in both the phases, and this behaviour is found to be true in cases of both the definitions of TOR, and (iii) since 1991, there seems to be an accelerating tendency for the TOR, thus reflecting the response of the growth process of the economy to regime shifts in trade and payments policies towards greater globalization and liberalization. All these suggest that the development strategy adopted in India since the Second Five Year Plan which tends to emphasize import substitution and export pessimism clearly prevented the growth process of the economy from reaping the benefits of dynamic externalities that integration with foreign markets is supposed to generate. Naturally, for most of the periods of her growth process, the Indian Economy had to rely primarily on the domestic market and provide sheltered markets to indigenous producers under the garb of 'infant industry protections' through the adoption of restrictive trade and payments policies, compounded by the failure of macroeconomic management of the economy to tackle the twin problems of internal balance and external balance. The sluggish growth of exports, high growth of maintenance imports, despite mounting export subsidies and import protection (tariff plus non-tariff), and the consequent overvaluation of the exchange rate for the Indian rupee had their mainfestations in the periodic balance of payments crisis facing the nation during most of the period. Only after 1991, and mildly since 1985, there are attempts to orient the Indian growth strategy towards the signals of global markets, and this was reflected in a relatively sharp rise in her TOR. Another interesting feature that is revealed by the behaviour of trade orientation ratios is that the second measure gives a higher value of degree of openness of the economy and that it exhibits a much sharper V-turn than the first measure of TOR, namely, the Export-GDP ratio (TOR_1). This has an important implication for the integration of the Indian economy with the rest of the world. As the economy grew, its exports did not grow at a very high rate due to several factors, but its dependence on imports grew rather sharply, so that the degree of openness becomes larger when we take the second measure of trade orientation ratio (TOR_2). The fluctuations in imports, due to both domestic as well as international factors, and stability and growth in export values over the period are reflected in the behaviour of its current account trade balance. The identification of the factors that primarily influenced our exports and imports, and hence the current account trade balance, therefore, crucial in our understanding the prospects of economic integration with rest of the world and the policies which aim at these objectives. The

Table 6.1

Trade Orientation Ratios in India : 1951-52 to 1994-95

Year	TOR_1	TOR_2
1951-52	7.553	17.60
1952-53	6.182	13.50
1953-54	5.216	11.10
1954-55	6.201	13.70
1955-56	6.267	14.30
1956-57	5.216	13.60
1957-58	4.730	14.90
1958-59	4.380	11.70
1959-60	4.593	12.30
1960-61	4.201	12.60
1961-62	4.100	11.80
1962-63	3.980	11.50
1963-64	4.031	11.20
1964-65	3.551	10.20
1965-66	3.366	10.10
1966-67	4.224	12.70
1967-68	3.725	10.80
1968-69	4.001	10.70
1969-70	3.785	08.90
1970-71	3.866	08.70
1971-72	3.806	08.80
1972-73	4.241	08.90
1973-74	4.43	10.2
1974-75	4.965	12.40
1975-76	5.668	13.90
1976-77	6.718	14.30
1977-78	6.191	14.30
1978-79	6.099	14.30
1979-80	6.265	16.40
1980-81	5.491	16.90
1981-82	5.463	16.40

(Contd.)

TABLE 6.1 (Contd.)

Year	TOR_1	TOR_2
1982-83	5.542	15.80
1983-84	5.258	14.80
1984-85	5.652	15.10
1985-86	4.655	13.10
1986-87	4.789	12.60
1987-88	5.316	12.90
1988-89	5.736	13.70
1989-90	6.768	15.40
1990-91	6.813	15.90
1991-92	7.978	16.65
1992-93	8.554	18.65
1993-94	9.863	20.20
1994-95	9.874	20.56

Note : TOR_1 = Export/GDP × 100
TOR_2 = (Export + Import/GDP) × 100

Source : Estimated from data on value of exports, value of imports and GDP-all at current prices. The data are obtained from H.L. Chandhok and the Policy Group (1990)—Data Base of the Indian Economy and from Economic Survey, various issues, Government of India.

link between trade balance and domestic macro-economic variables provides important clues in this respect. This, coupled with the nature of growth regimes that we had instituted since 1951 and the shifts in this regimes from time to time due to policy shocks, constitute an integral part of the policy of balance of payments in our country. While one may venture to enquire into the nature of relationship between trade orientation ratio, the size of population and the GDP growth, the more important questions appear to be the scale of economic activities and the nature of utilization of resources depending upon the interplay of domestic macroeconomic variables as compared to the factors originating in the international economy. Our estimates of the significance of some such variables provide an idea of the forces that work in influencing the country's balance of payments and trade balance over the period, and thus affect the degree of openness of the economy.

In order to test the temporal behaviour of our trade orientation ratio (TOR_2), we have fitted the following second-degree polynomial:

$$TOR_2 = \alpha_0 + \alpha_1 \text{ TIME} + \alpha_2 \text{ (TIME)}^2 + U_t \qquad (6.1)$$

The data set spans from 1951-52 to 1994-95, and the estimated equation is given by:

$$TOR_2 = 0.144119 - 0.0033523 \text{ TIME} + 0.000963381 \text{ (TIME)}^2 \qquad (6.2)$$

The properties of these estimates are summarised in Table 6.2 (A, B and C).

It is clear that the estimates of, $\hat{\alpha}_0$, $\hat{\alpha}_1$ and $\hat{\alpha}_2$ are all statistically significant at 10%, 5% and 1% levels of significance. But the non-linearities in the actual behaviours of TOR_2, over 1951-52 to 1994-95, as reflected in the periodic fluctuations (Figure 6.1), makes this a relatively poor fit, as evidenced from low value of Adj-R^2.

TABLE 6.2
Regression of Trade Openness on Time

A. Model: Trade Ratio = $\alpha_0 + \alpha_1$Time + α_2Time^2 + U_t

Regressor	$\hat{\alpha}_0$	$\hat{\alpha}_1$	$\hat{\alpha}_2$
Coefficient	0.144119	-0.0033523	0.000963381
t-ratio	14.9121	-3.06706	3.74528

R^2 = 0.34393, Adj-R^2 = 0.308467, SEE = 0.0193622 F(2/42) = 9.6982, D.W. = 0.535391

Dependent variable is TOR_2. 44 observations are used for estimation from 1951-52 to 1994-95. All the coefficients are significant at 5%, 10% and 1% levels of significance.

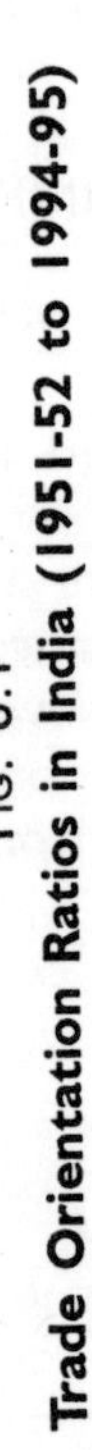

FIG. 6.1
Trade Orientation Ratios in India (1951-52 to 1994-95)

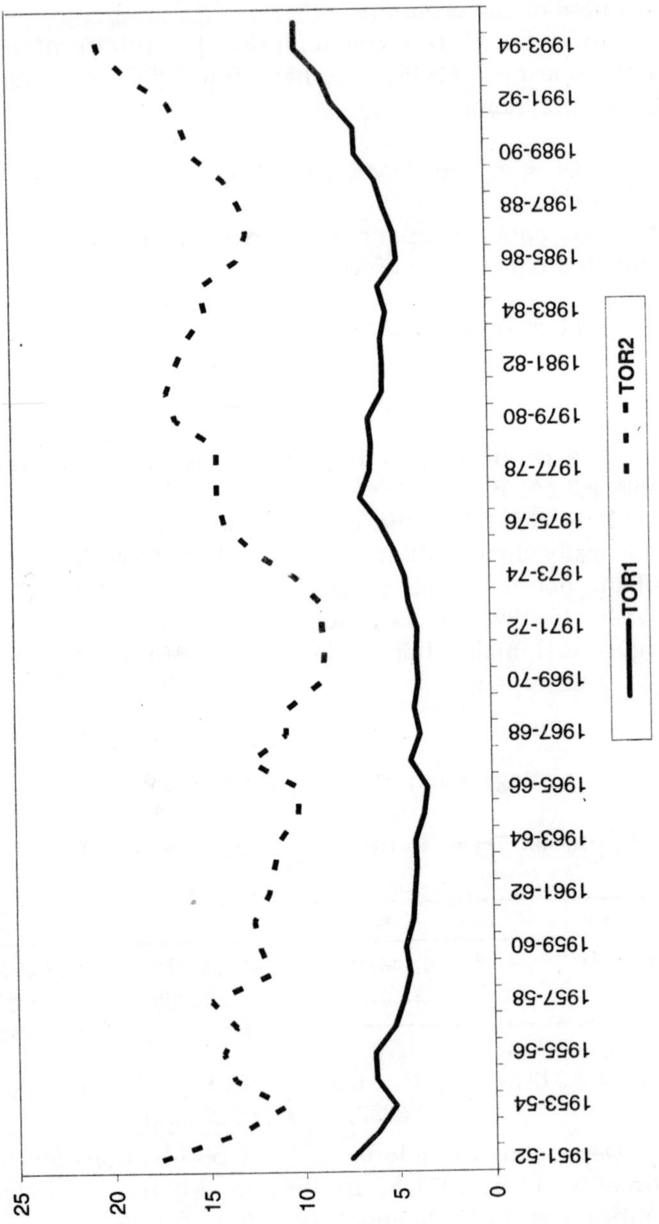

B. Analysis of Variance

Due to	*d.f. (Degrees of Freedom)*	*(Sum of Squares)*	*Mean Square=SS/df*	*F(df/42)*
Regression	2	.0072717	.00363582	9.6982
Residual	42	0.0138711	.000374896	
Total	44	0.0211428		

C. Variance—Covariance Matrix

	Time	*Time²*	*Constant*
Time	0.00000118252	-0.000000027127	-0.00000922548
Time²	-0.000000027127	-0.00000000661649	0.000000189848
Constant	-0.00000922548	0.000000189848	0.0000934046

6.2 BALANCE OF PAYMENTS AND FOREIGN EXCHANGE RESERVES

In an accounting sense, the balance of payments always balances. But if one is interested in identifying the major factors whose behaviours are reflected in the movements of a country's balance of payments over time, then one has to come out of the accounting framework and adopt a behavioural approach. Theory of balance of payments tells us that the movements in the balance of payments of a country are influenced by both the domestic and international factors and that both the flow and the stock variables exert their influences. In a well-specified macroeconomic model, the flows and stocks bear specific relationship among themselves as defined by theory. Since we are dealing with time series data for a long period of time, it would be difficult to identify a specific or single macroeconomic model, because the underlying behavioural equations would be subject to periodic shifts over time as a result of interplay of several factors. Rather we shall be interested in checking the associations of selected variables that appear important from different theoretical standpoints. Again, since the balance of payments of a country has both the current account and capital account transactions, the factors that influence both types of transactions are chosen for our regression exercises. In order to keep our analysis simple, we prefer to work with single - equation models, although the single behaviourial equations that we postulate as the basis of our estimation may be derivable from a set of equations of a macroeconomic framework. Our decision to include several explanatory variables, to explain the behaviour of India's balance of payments over time, is prompted by our holistic approach so as to include the insights of alternative theoretical strands. Dealing with several explanatory variables in time-series models to test the stationarity property is difficult, and not attempted here. This is done to keep the analysis comprehensible and make the message clear for purposes of policy design. We adopt a simple multiple regression framework using the technique of Ordinary Least Squares (OLS) with the help of the computer programme ASP.

In this section, we shall focus on India's overall balance of payments and the foreign exchange reserves that emanate from such a balance. First, we take the overall balance of payments. This is influenced by factors that govern both the current account and capital account transactions, and involve both domestic and foreign factors. The current account balance is influenced by domestic macroeconomic factors that govern domestic absorption, as well as by world exports in relation to domestic exports. The capital account transactions are influenced by domestic absorption parameters, particularly the rate of interest and domestic rate of inflation. In keeping with the theoretical traditions of the Keynesian, the Monetarist and the Portfolio balance approaches to balance of payments, we postulate the following two behaviourial models linking India's balance of payments (BoP) with India's exports as a percentage of world exports (*WE*), the bank rate (*BR*) as the proxy for domestic rate of interest, the annual rate of domestic inflation (*RI*) computed from the wholesale price indices and the combined budget deficits of the Central and the State Governments (BD). The period covers 1951-52 to 1990-91, i.e., 40 years. Model I postulates a linear regression relationship, while Model II links the log of the dependent variable, BoP, linearly with the log of explanatory variables. The estimable equations are:

$$\text{Model I : BoP} = \lambda_0 + \lambda_t \text{ WE} + \lambda_2 \text{ BR} + \lambda_3 \text{ RI} + \lambda_4 \text{ BD} + \text{U} \quad (6.3)$$

$$\text{Model II : log BoP} = \theta_0 + \theta_1 \text{log WE} + \theta_2 \text{log BR} + \theta_3 \text{log RI} + \theta_4 \text{log BD} + \text{U} \quad (6.4)$$

The estimated equations are:

Model I : BoP = 1373.59 –714.91 WE – 97.7915 BR –19.5718
(1.21119) (–1.18349) (–0.894505) (-1.06637)
R1–0.0462977 BD (6.5)
(–0.699039)

R^2 = 0.151714; Adj–R^2 = 0.0547668;
D.W. = 2.59029; F(4/35) = 1.56491.

The t-ratios of the estimated coefficients are given in brackets. All the estimated coefficients are found to be insignificant at 1%, 5%, and 10% levels of significance.

Model II : log BoP = 9.63024 – 5.94891 log WE – 5.71092
(1.02324) (–1.07845) (–0.906915)
log BR – 0.520237 log RI (6.6)
(–1.75643)
–0.332923 log BD
(–0.735861)

R^2 = 0.14751; Adj-R^2 = 0.0500825; D.W. = 2.14172, F(4/35) = 1.51405.

The t-ratios of the estimated coefficients are given in brackets. The estimated coefficients of log WE and log BR, i.e., $\hat{\theta}_1$ and $\hat{\theta}_2$ are found to be statistically significant at 1%, 5% and 10% levels of significance, while $\hat{\theta}_3$ and $\hat{\theta}_4$ are found to be insignificant at all levels.

From the estimates of Model I and Model II presented above, we may argue the following. First, all the estimated coefficients are found to be, statistically insignificant in Model I, and both R^2 and Adj-R^2 are very low, and so also the estimated F-statistic. The explanatory power of the regression in Model I is not changed much when in Model II we switch to linear relationship between the logarithms of the variables. The R^2, Adj-R^2 and F continue to be low in model II also. But the estimated coefficients of log WE and log BR turn to be statistically significant. This suggests that perhaps these two variables WE and BR do not possess linear relationship with the balance of payments. Secondly, the signs of the estimated coefficients in both the model specifications turn out to be negative. Although the regression results do not give us the confidence of a 'good fit' i.e., they do not support the postulated relationship with some degree of confidence, the signs of the estimated coefficients are worth noting. The signs of BD and RI are of expected nature—a higher budget deficit augments domestic absorption and thus worsens current account trade balance, while a higher rate of domestic inflation worsens both current account balance (as it raises domestic absorption in nominal terms) and also the capital account balance (as if depresses the real rate of return on capital inflow). When the domestic rate of interest rises domestic absorption should fall, and current account trade balance should improve, according to the Keynesian mechanism, and it should also attract capital inflow so that balance of payments should have improved, i.e., coefficients should have positive rather than negative signs. This suggests that the working of the Indian financial markets does not perhaps conform to the Keynesian mechanism of balance of payments adjustments. There are various imperfections/frictions in India's capital/financial markets which variations in the bank rate of the Central Bank failed to capture. The bank rate was more or less stable for sizeable periods during the 1950s and the 1960s and the RBI's intervention was confined to organize public sector financial institutions for most of the time, and hence did not have the kind of macroeconomic impact that the Keynesian theory would perhaps predict. Again, the impact of a rise in WE i.e., India's share of exports in world exports should expectedly be positive on the country's balance of payments, but the estimates are found to be negative. This is possible when a part of world exports that India imported rose faster than India's own exports to the rest of the world, while the overall WE exhibited upward tendencies. Some amount of multi-collinearity also seems inevitable, but we have checked them to be moderate, except the cases of WE and BR, where the signs are found to have been contrary to expectations. Tables 6.3 and 6.4 present the variance-covariance matrices for Model I and Model II respectively.

TABLE 6.3

Model I: BoP = –714.91 WE + –97.7915 BR + –19.5718 RI + –0.0462977 BD + 1337.59

Variance-Covariance Matrix Model I

	WE	*BR*		*RI*	*BD*
WE	364897	52773.9	3456.13	-17.7296	-645936
BR	52773.9	11951.9	196.428	-5.40981	-115744
RI	3456.13	196.428	336.86	-0.0939801	-6136.56
BD	-17.7296	-5.40981	-0.0939801	4.38647E-3	43.9283
Constant	-645936	-115744	-6136.56	43.9283	1.28615E6

TABLE 6.4

Model II: log BoP = –0.520237 log RI + –5.94891 log WE + –0.332923 log BD + –5.71092 log BR + 9.63024

Variance/Covariance Matrix of Model II

	log RI	*log WE*	*log BD*	*log BR*	*Constant*
log RI	0.0877281	0.0462706	0.0118504	-0.263322	0.394242
log WE	0.0462706	30.428	-0.127217	29.1132	-43.3889
log BD	0.0118504	-0.127217	0.204689	-1.08854	0.759769
log BR	-0.263322	29.1132	-1.08854	39.6533	-57.4017
Constant	0.394242	-43.3889	0.759769	-57.4017	88.5763

The above exercise, though not very helpful in explaining the overall balance of payments of India during 1951-52 to 1990-91, suggests the need to look to the current account trade balance, which constitutes the core of the country's balance of payments deficits and change in its foreign exchange reserves. It also becomes easier to relate the behaviour of variables like budget deficits to changes in trade balance and test the significance of the association. It is also possible to relate our exercises to some of the important past works in the field, which also concentrated on current account trade balance rather than an overall balance of payments position of the country. But before we proceed to a detailed investigation of the proximate determinants of India's trade balance during the period under consideration, let us check how the net capital account balance of the economy are related to flow variables that govern the current account balance. Since from an accounting requirement the need for capital account transactions arises as a residual to the adjustments in the country's current account trade deficits, Model III relating net capital account balance (NCAB) to the flows of Exports (EX), GNP at current prices (GNP_{CP}) and the gap between saving and investment (GAPSI) shows an interesting relation.

$$\text{Model III: } NCAB = \alpha_0 + \alpha_1 EX + \alpha_2\, GNP_{CP} + \alpha_3\, GAPSI + U \tag{6.7}$$

The estimated equation is:

$$NCAB = -91.6352 + 1.15642\ EX - 0.050325\ GNP_{cp} - 0.075441\ GAPSI \tag{6.8}$$

$$(-0.212354)\ (3.37491)\ (-1.88664)\qquad (-0.401323)$$

$R^2 = 0.816808$; Adj-$R^2 = 0.801542$; D.W. = 1.71628;
$F\ (3/36) = 53.5052$.

The t-ratios of the estimated coefficients are given in parenthesis. From the t-ratios, the estimated coefficient of Ex i.e. $\hat{\alpha}_1$ is found to be statistically significant at 1%, 5% and 10% levels of significance, while that of GNP_{CP}, i.e. $\hat{\alpha}_2$ is found to be significant only at 10% level of significance. The coefficient of GAPSI, i.e. $\hat{\alpha}_3$ is found to be insignificant at 1%, 5% and 10% levels of significance.

The estimates of Model III indicate that (a) the net capital account balance in India bears a positive association with her export earnings; (b) a higher GNP at current prices have been associated with lower NCAB, perhaps because it stimulated import of goods and out flow of financial capital much more than inflow on the capital account—an aspect that merits some detailed investigations, although the estimated value of the coefficient of $\hat{\alpha}_3$ is found to be significant only at the 10% level; and (c) the gap between domestic saving and Investment bears a very weak and inverse relation with NCAB and this relation is also found to be insignificant. Altogether, the Model III exhibits a good fit of the regression equation, as is evident from Adj-R^2 and F-value of the estimated equation. We may offer two comments in this connection. First, the positive sign of $\hat{\alpha}_1$ indicates that when the country's export earnings rise, not only does it improve the current account trade balance, but it also increases the confidence of foreign investors to flow their financial resources into the Indian economy thus a strategy of export promotion is helpful both on account of its favourable impacts on trade balance as well as on NCAB. Secondly, a higher GNP in the Indian case has been associated with import growth faster than the rise in our export earning, which, if our first hypothesis is correct, has tended to dampen the flow of capital account resources from abroad over time as our GNP in nominal terms rose substantially over the period under review, partly due to periodic acceleration of domestic inflation rates. This suggests that from the policy point of view, the management of the country's balance of payments must be linked with policies aimed at improving its trade balance over time.

The foreign exchange reserve of a country is the outcome of the combination of current account transactions and capital account transactions as they occurred in the past. It is essentially a stock defined at a point of time, but influenced by actual flows suitably lagged. How did this stock of foreign exchange reserves (FOREX) defined on March 31, every year relate to other stock variables of the Indian economy like money supply with the public, (MS) which we have taken to be M_3? Or, is it related to the functioning of the government sector, is measured by the combined budgetary deficit of the Central and State Governments (BD) over time, or simply the index of the success of demand management of the economy proxied by the annual rates of inflation (RI)? Models IV and V investigate these questions in terms of [near relationships between variables and also between the logarithms of the variables. Thus, we have:

$$\text{Model IV : FOREX} = D_1 + D_1 RI + D_2 BD + D_3\ MS + U \quad (6.9)$$

Model V: $\log FOREX = D_0 + D_1 \log RI + D_2 \log BD + D_3 \log MS + U$ (6.10)

The estimated equations are:

$$\text{Model IV: } FOREX = \underset{(2.55476)}{888.151} + \underset{(0.224844)}{7.74238\, RI} + \underset{(0.187966)}{0.0494868\, BD} + \underset{(3.38155)}{0.0384168\, MS} \quad (6.11)$$

$R^2 = 0.78532$; Adj-$R^2 = 0.767429$; D.W. = 0.482067; F(3/36) = 43.897.

The t-ratios of the estimated coefficients are given in brackets. The estimated coefficient of MS i.e. $\hat{D}_3$ is found to be statistically significant at 1%, 5% and 10% levels of significance, while that of $\hat{D}_0$ is found to be significant at 5% and 10% levels. The other coefficients $\hat{D}_1$ and $\hat{D}_2$ are found to be statistically insignificant at 1%, 5% and 10% levels of significance. Interestingly, the Adj-R^2 and the F-statistic indicate regression to be a reasonably good fit, although only one of the explanatory variables is found to have statistically significant estimate of the coefficient.

The estimated equation of Model V is given by :

$$\text{Model V: } \log FOREX = \underset{(-0.405757)}{-0.251144} \underset{(-1.93504)}{-0.0468743 \log RI} + \underset{(1.06146)}{0.039184 \log BD} + \underset{(9.96521)}{0.749532 \log MS} \quad (5.12)$$

R2 = 0.838889; Adj–R2 = 0.825462; D.W. =1.0737; F(3/36) = 62.4822.

The t-ratios of the estimated coefficients are given in parenthesis. The estimated coefficient of log MS, i.e. $\hat{D}_3$ is found to be statistically significants at 1%, 5%, and 10% levels of significance, while that of log RI, i.e. $\hat{D}_1$ is significant only at 10% level of significance. The rest of estimates are found to be statistically insignificant. The regression exercise continues to be a good fit, as is evident from the Adj-R^2 and F-statistic. In fact, Model V provides a better fit compared to Model IV as both

Adj-R^2 and F improve, when we postulate the relationship to be linear in the logarithms of the variables. Thus the fundamental relationship between the foreign exchange reserve and the explanatory variables are essentially non-linear in nature. The variance/covariance matrices for Models IV and V are given in Tables 6.5 and 6.6 below.

TABLE 6.5

Model IV: FOREX = 7.74238 RI + 0.0494868 BD + 0.0384168 MS + 888.151

Variance/Covariance Matrix Model IV

	RI	*BD*	*MS*	*Constant*
RI	1185.73	-1.1834	0.0299366	-6832.6
BD	-1.1834	0.0693137	-2.8387E-3	11.73
MS	0.0299366	-2.8387E-3	1.29066E-4	-0.94337
Constant	-6832.6	11.73	-0.94337	120857

TABLE 6.6

Model V: log FOREX = –0.0468743 log RI + 0.039184 log BD + 0.749532 log MS + –0.251144

Variance/Covariance Matrix Model V

	log RI	*log BD*	*log MS*	*Constant*
log RI	5.86798E-4	6.75518E-5	-5 .18427E-4	4.37257E-3
log BD	6.75518E-5	1 .36274E-3	-1 .70981E-3	8.49356E-3
log MS	-5.18427E-4	-1.70981E-3	5 .65728E-3	-0.0443154
Constant	4 .37257E-3	8.49356E-3	-0 .0443154	0.383101

Although from a theoretical standpoint (Keynesian or Monetarist), one would expect strong correlation between the explanatory variables, the problems of multi-collinearity is not found to be serious in the above two exercises. The problem of positive autocorrelation also diminishes in Model V compared to Model IV. The crucial point is to explain the positive association between money supply with the public and foreign exchange reserves of the country, a relationship that is found to be statistically significant in both the versions. The monetary approach to balance of payments suggests an inverse relationship under a fixed exchange rate regime, but a direct one in the reverse direction, i.e., a rise in foreign exchange reserves augmenting the stock of domestic money supply. Under a flexible exchange rate system with international mobility of finance capital between countries, a domestic monetary expansion would, however, tend to depreciate the exchange rate and exert favourable impact on a country's trade balance and hence on its foreign exchange reserves. For the Indian case the period under review was under both the varieties of exchange rate regimes, and domestic money supply always recorded a positive rate of growth, due to several factors including continued rise in budget deficits of the Central and State Governments over the period. While it is difficult to test the applicability of alternative approaches from our estimated equations of models IV and V, it may be noted that foreign exchange reserve constitutes a component of the base of domestic money supply in India, and this fact may have been reflected in the positive association between FOREX and MS in our exercises presented above.

The above analysis tends to suggest that searches for appropriate determinants of the country's balance of payments must begin with the current account balance, i.e., we should primarily check the alternative hypothesis to explain the temporal behaviour of India's trade balance. This is because the identification of the channels becomes blurred when we try to estimate relations involving highly aggregative categories like the BoP or the FOREX, with whom meaningful associations can be defended in theoretical terms only under specific assumed conditions. Therefore, we move in the next section to a study of India's trade balance in our efforts to identify its proximate determinants. We adopt a holistic approach in integrating alternative theoretical strands in an unified framework as far as practicable and postulate different relationships of India's trade balance or import surplus with selected explanatory variables.

6.3 TRADE BALANCE AND ITS DETERMINANTS— A HOLISTIC APPROACH

From the discussions in section 6.2, it is clear that an analysis of the movements in India's balance of payments and foreign exchange reserves would remain incomplete without an in-depth analysis of the determinants of trade balance of the country, since deficits in the current account trade balance had been primarily responsible for the overall deficits in India's balance of payments over the period. Theoretical approaches to balance of payments adjustments and balance of payments policies, as was reviewed in Chapter 2, tend to suggest the significance of a number of domestic and external factors in explaining the behaviours of trade balance, and some studies in the Indian context (also reviewed in Chapter 2) have selected some such factors as proximate determinants of her trade balance. In this section, we shall adopt a holistic approach in integrating the alternative channels through which domestic absorption and trade balance get affected in response to changes in domestic and foreign macroeconomic variables. We shall attempt to estimate alternative hypothesis on the basis of such an integrated framework, condensed into single equation multiple-regression framework and test the significance of the importance of different variables in influencing India's trade balance or import surplus (negative of trade balance) over time.

In a synthetic or holistic approach to balance of payments adjustments, the different channels of transmission mechanisms as suggested in alternative theoretical strands need to be integrated. Thus not only the channels of effective demand or domestic absorption through adjustments in income and expenditure as suggested by the Keynesian (Absorption) approach, but also other channels like interest rate effect, movements in the relative price of exports and imports, or the nominal exchange rate, and the real balance or the wealth effect, and/or temporal variations in government's budget deficits, also appear significant. For some variables like the rate of interest or the rate of inflation, the channel of adjustment would be mixed in nature in the sense that both the Keynesian and the Monetarist, and to a certain extent the Portfolio Balance mechanisms would perhaps be working simultaneously. The

Monetarist and the Portfolio balance approaches highlight the importance of wealth effect and the role of budget constraints of both the government and the private sectors through which the stocks and flows in the economy are related, and which have important bearings on a country's trade balance. The elasticity approach points to the importance of net barter terms of trade in shaping the country's trade balance and the correspondence between movements in the exchange rate and the relative prices. The stock of foreign exchange reserves, being a part of national wealth and a base for domestic money creation, may also exert influence on a country's trade balance, in a longer run time frame. All other factors like productivity growth, technological progress etc., may be captured by a trend factor t=Time. One may also disaggregate between the private sector and the government sector, so as to test the significance of budgetary deficits on the country's trade balances.

Models VI-XII relate the import surplus (IS) of India during the period to alternative set of explanatory variables in order to test the synthetic framework outlined above. It may be mentioned that our choice of alternative set of endogenous variables are prompted by different considerations to capture the effects of these variables on the country's import surplus. While overlaps/correlations between macroeconomic variables are not unlikely from theoretical standpoints, they do not pose significant problems to our estimates. Our estimates also broaden the estimates attempted by G.C. da Costa on earlier occasions. The similarity and difference between our estimates and his estimates will also be discussed. The estimable equations of Models VI-XII are as follows:

Model VI : $IS = \alpha_0 + \alpha_1 RI + \alpha_2\ WE + \alpha_3 BD + \alpha_4 BR + U$ (6.13)

Model VII : $\log IS = A_0 + A_1 \log RI + A_2 \log WE + A_3 \log BD + A_4 \log BR + U$ (6.14)

Model VIII: $IS = \beta_0 + \beta_1\ NBTT + \beta_2\ GNP\ CP + \beta_3\ FOREX + U$ (6.15)

Model IX : $\log IS = B_0 + B_1 \log NBTT + B_2 \log GNP_{CP} + B_3 \log FOREX + U$ (6.16)

Model X : $IS = \delta_0 + \delta_1\ GDP_{MP} + \delta_2 m_1 + \delta_3\ TIME + U$ (6.17)

Model XI : $IS = \theta_0 + \theta_1\ GDP_{MP} + \theta_2\ m_2 + \delta_3\ TIME + U$ (6.18)

Model XII : $IS = \delta_1 + \delta_1\ GDP_{MP} + \delta_2 m_2 + \delta_3\ NBTT + \delta_4\ TIME + U$ (6.19)

Here the variables are : IS = Import surplus (negative of trade balance); RI = Annual rate of inflation; WE = India's exports as a ratio of world exports; BD = Budget deficits of central and state governments; BR = Bank rate; NBTT = Index of net barter terms of trade; GNP_{CP} = Gross National Product at current prices; FOREX = Foreign exchange reserves; GDP_{MP} = Gross domestic product at market prices; $m_1 = M_3/P_1$, where P_1 is the GDP deflator with 1980-81 as the base year, TIME = time t in years (i.e., t=1 implies 1951-52 and so on); $m_2 = M_3/P_2$ where P_2 is the wholesale price index (WPI) with 1970-71 as the base year. Clearly m_1 and m_2 stand for real balances of the economy which is used to proxy the wealth effect. Model VII have the same variables as in Model VI except that the variables are expressed in logarithms. Similarly in Model IX, the same variables as in Model VIII are expressed in log forms. In models X through XII, we used GDP at market prices rather than GNP in that we want to concentrate on income generated in the Indian economy independent of the participation of foreign factors of production. It may be mentioned that we have chosen to ignore some other variables that might have influenced the country's trade balance or import surplus over time in order to keep the regression analysis simple and tractable. We have not introduced exchange rate explicitly as an explanatory variables in these exercises, as its influence on trade balance is likely to be reflected through movements in NBTT with which it has strong correlation. In Table 6.7, we present the estimates of the regressions of models VI to IX.

Certain observations may be made about the regression estimates of Models VI to IX. First, the estimated coefficients of BD and BR in Model VI are found to be significant at 1%, 5% and 10% levels of significance, while the estimate of the constant term a_0 is found to be significant at 5% and 10% levels of significance. The coefficients of RI and WE are, however, found to be insignificant at all the three levels of significance. The estimates of Adj-R^2 and F-statistic indicate a good fit of the

TABLE 6.7

Regression Estimates of Models VI to IX

Estimates	*Model VI*	*Model VII*	*Model VIII*	*Model IX*
Constant	-4149.12**	-3.41609	-134.023	-25.1368**
t-ratio	(-2.09346)	(-0.631374)	(-0.637382)	(-2.7417)
RI/log RI				
(a) Coefficient	4.27031	7.03E-03	—	—
(b) t-ratio	(0.133134)	(0.041274)	—	—
WE/log WE				
(a) Coefficient	1318.94	3.59744	—	—
(b) t-ratio	(1.24938)	(1.13442)	—	—
BD/log BD				
(a) Coefficient	0.57586***	0.0978748	—	—
(b) t-ratio	(4.97523)	(0.376304)	—	—
BR/log BR				
(a) Coefficient	635.821***	5.39619	—	—
(b) t-ratio	(3.3279)	(1.49061)	—	—
NBTT/log NBTT				
(a) Coefficient	—	—	-2.61725***	-0.390606**
(b) t-ratio	—	—	(-2.82669)	(-2.65697)
GNP_{CP}/log GNP_{CP}				
(a) Coefficient	—	—	0.0152912***	2.79735**
(b) t-ratio	—	—	(4.82726)	(2.51195)
FOREX/log FOREX				
(a) Coefficient	—	—	0.434763***	0.059848
(b) t-ratio	—	—	(3.49739)	(0.06583)
Adj-R^2	0.834034	0.00832832	0.9038	0.189631
D.W.	1.40988	1.91843	1.40058	2.30847
F	49.99691	1.08188	123.221	4.04208

*** indicates significant at 1%, 5% and 10% levels of significance.

** indicates significant at 5% and 10% levels of significance.

Sources : Estimated from the data available.

regression equation. But when we express the estimable equation in terms of the logarithms of the same variables, the estimated equation does not fit well, as both the Adj-R^2 and F-statistic diminish sharply in Model VII compared to in Model VI. None of the estimated coefficients are found to be statistically significant, and, therefore, the relationship between the variables in log form does not seem appropriate. Secondly, in Model VIII, the estimated coefficients of all the three explanatory variables, viz. NBTT, GNP_{CP} and FOREX are found to be significant at 1%, 5% and 10% levels of significance, and the Adj-R^2 and the F-statistic indicate a good fit of regression equation of Model VIII. However, when we express linear relationship between the same set of variables in the form of logarithms as in Model IX, the measure of goodness of fit diminishes sharply, which suggests that the relationship between import surplus and the explanatory variables NBTT, GNP_{CP} and FOREX can be approximated by Model VIII better than that of Model IX. The two variables NBTT and GNP_{CP} however, continue to exert significant influences on IS at 5% and 10% levels of significance, but FOREX looses its significance in favour of the estimate of the constant term, which in Model IX version becomes significant at 5% and 10% levels of significance. We, therefore, concentrate on Models VI and VIII in our subsequent discussion.

The signs of the estimated coefficients in Models VI and VIII need careful analysis. While the positive sign of $\hat{\alpha}_1$ is in tune with the expectation of economic theory, that of $\hat{\alpha}_3$ testifies our hypothesis that a part of world exports that India imported grew at a faster rate than the growth of India's exports. A higher budget deficit, along the Keynesian, Monetarist and the Portfolio approaches, is expected to augment the import, surplus, and we have found this influence to be significant. Similarly, a higher domestic rate of interest, by reducing domestic absorption faster than domestic income may augment the import surplus, and this turns out to be the case in India. Regarding the signs of estimated coefficients of Model IX, $\hat{\beta}_1$ and $\hat{\beta}_2$ indicate expected direction of associations, while that of $\hat{\beta}_3$ gives credence to the three-gap model's relevance in the Indian context, since relaxation of the foreign exchange constraint or greater availability of FOREX, in general had stimulated our import growth faster than that of exports, over the period, and thus enhanced our trade deficits.

The results of our exercises in Models VI and VIII can be compared to those of G.C. da Costa's (1986) study on the determinants of India's trade balance. We have used the series of NBTT rather than the real exchange rate in our model VIII, and contrary to da Costa's findings, we find the estimated coefficient of NBTT to be statistically significant. Since the NBTT is likely to have high correlation with real effective exchange rate, it is puzzling that da Costa did not find the former to be significant, while he found the latter to have exerted significant influence on India's trade balance. This is perhaps due to the fact da Costa used both GDP of industrial countries, and GNP of India at current prices along with NBTT in his estimable equations, and significant multicollinearity between these variables may have blurred the significance of NBTT, although the R^2 was found to be quite high. Secondly, G.C. da Costa's use of GNP_{CP} was defended to capture the effects of domestic monetary expansion, whereas in our exercise, this variable is expected to influence trade balance via nominal spending, which in effect combines the effects of growth of real output as well as of domestic inflation. It is not proper to estimate a single equation combining the explanatory variables of Models VI and VIII to find out the proximate determinants of India's trade balance overtime, since BD, BR and RI are expected to have strong correlation with GNP_{CP}, and RI is similarly likely to be correlated with NBTT. Because of specification of the relations in terms of a holistic vision of balance of payments, our exercises provide a clearer explanations of trade balance over the period than the ones by G.C. da Costa, and they also provide explanations for a longer time frame. The relative price effect as suggested by the elasticity approach, income effect as suggested by the absorption approach, the stock effect as suggested by the three-gap and portfolio approaches are reflected in our unified framework of Model VIII, while in Model VI, our estimates give importance to management of budget deficits of the government (fiscal policy) and management of domestic interest rate as a proxy for domestic rate of return on assets (monetary policy) in affecting the country's overall trade balance over time (a combination of Keynesian, Portfolio and Monetary approaches to balance of payments which emphasize the importance of macroeconomic policies in the domestic economy in shaping the country's trade balance).

We now turn to Models X to XII. The only difference between Models X and XI lies in the choice of the deflator to deflate M_3 so as to arrive at a measure of real balances in the economy. In Model X, we use $m_1 = M_3/P_1$, where P_1 is the GDP deflator with base 1980-81, while in Model XI, we use $m_2 = M_3/P_2$, where P_2 is the wholesale price indices calculated with base period 1970-71. Model XII is the most general form in that it includes NBTT as an extra explanatory variable. In order to capture effects of temporal shifts in the combination of factors, we have included TIME as the trend variable. Some element of interdependence between TIME and other explanatory variables are inevitable because we are dealing with time-series data so that trend factor affects all the variables to a certain extent. In Table 6.8, we present the estimates of the regression Models X to XII. The estimates of Model XII span the time period from 1969-70 to 1989-90, while those of others take the entire period 1951-52 to 1990-91. This is prompted by the availability of NBTT series since 1969-70.

The regression estimates of Models X to XII reveal some features which are worth noting. First of all, from the point of the absorption approach to balance of payments, the effect of a change in GDP at market prices on import surplus should be positive, whereas in Model X, the estimated coefficient $\hat{\delta}$ is found to be negative. Secondly, the real balance effect on a country's import surplus, according to the tenets of Keynesian and Monetarist approaches to balance of payments, is expected to be positive, but the estimates of m_2 in Models XI and XII are found to be negative, weak and statistically significant at 1% and 5% levels of significance. This calls for an alternative explanation. A rise in m_2, i.e. M_3 divided by the wholesale price, may worsen import surplus or improve trade balance when the rise in income exceeds domestic absorption or when expenditure is switched away from foreign goods. To test the validity of either of the adjustment mechanisms, one needs to develop suitably specified macroeconometric model for the Indian economy—a task that goes beyond the scope of the

TABLE 6.8
Regression Estimates of Models X to XII

Estimates	*Model X*	*Model XI*	*Model XII*
Constant term	-1203.28	-353.8623	-1878.616
t-ratio	(-1.092)	(-0.234)	(-0.823)
GDPmp:			
(a) Coefficient	-0.005823**	0.021994*	0.001710**
(b) t-ratio	(-0.623)	(6.134)	(0.174)
m_1:			
(a) Coefficient	0.145463	—	—
(b) t-ratio	(2.961)		
m_2:			
(a) Coefficient	—	-0.002914**	-0.000292**
(b) t-ratio	—	(-0.809)	(-0.069)
NBTT:			
(a) Coefficient	—	—	1.44159**
(b) t-ratio	—	—	(0.068)
TIME:			
(a) Coefficient	-75.712139**	24.72720**	457.017***
(b) t-ratio	(1.672)	(0.783)	(2.518)
Adj-R^2	0.8694	0.8397	0.8579
D.W.	0.972	0.779	1.01
F	79.32	62.46	24.81

*** Significant at 1%, 5% and 10% levels of significance.
** Significant at 1% and 5% levels of significance
* Significant at 10% level of significance.
Source : Estimated from data available.

present study. Thirdly, the influence of the trend variable TIME in all the three Models (X to XII) found to be statistically significant—at 1% and 5% levels of significance in Models X and XI and at 1%, 5% and 10% levels in Model XII. The size of the impact of TIME is also found to be quite high in all these three Models. Fourthly, NBTT in Models XI and XII is found to exert positive effects on IS in contrast to negative impacts in Models

VIII and IX, but this positive effect was found to be significant at 1% and 5% levels of significance. The measure of goodness of fit in Models X to XII are quite satisfactory as high values of Adj-R^2 and F-statistic indicate.

There are, however, certain inherent problems associated with the estimates presented in Table 6.8. The first thing that bothers about these estimates is the presence of multicollinearity among the explanatory variables. For example, in Model X, GDPmp and m_1 have positive high correlation because m} is arrived at by deflating M_3 by the GDP deflator which is contained in the estimate of GDPmp itself. When we replace m_1 by m_2, i.e. the deflator of M_3 changes from GDP deflator to wholesale price index, the severity of multicollinearity diministes as expected, but still remains quite high. The problem further eases in Model XII when we add NBTT as an additional explanatory variable. But since all the variables in Models X to XII are in time series, their correlation with TIME is bound to be high and this becomes inevitable given the formulation. The problem is particularly severe between GDPmp and TIME, because there is a clear time trend of gross domestic product at market prices in India over time. The second problem is one of positive autocorrelations as suggested by the D.W. statistic—but here again, the problem gradually diminishes, as we move from Models X to XI, and XII. As a result of these problems, the estimates in the regression Models X to XII do not satisfy all the properties of a good OLS estimator despite having high Adj-R^2 and F statistic. But on the whole, Model XII turns out to be least problematic amongst the three model estimates presented in 6.8.

So far we have not explicitly considered the movements in the nominal exchange rate. This is mainly because (i) the official exchange rate information is quarterly, and our entire analysis on other variables is based on annual figures, and (ii) the SDR rate which is obtained annually does not truly reflect market variability in the foreign exchange market. In what follows, therefore, we use the exchange rate (e), which measures the exchange rate of the Indian Rupee in terms of Dollar, as released by the Ministry of Finance, Government of India. In order to assess which of the macro-variables exert significant influences on 'e', we postulate a set of linear relationships in Models XIII to XVII using the time series data for an extended period from 1951-52 to 1994-95, i.e. 44 years including some years in the post 1991 liberalization phase.

The estimable equations of Models XIII to XVII are as follows:

Model XIII:

$$e = a_0 + a_1 \text{ BoP} + a_2 \text{ EDS} + a_3 \text{ GDPmp} + a_4 \text{ BD} + U \quad (6.20)$$

Model XIV :

$$e = b_0 + b_1 \text{ EDS} + b_2 \text{ GDPmp} + U \quad (6.21)$$

Model XV :

$$e = q_0 + q_1 \text{ BoP} + q_2 \text{ BD} + U \quad (6.22)$$

Model XVI:

$$e = A_0 + A_1 \text{ GDPmp} + U \quad (6.23)$$

Model XVII :

$$e = d_0 + d_1 \text{ BD} + U \quad (6.24)$$

Here e stands for the exchange rate of the Indian Rupee in terms of Dollar; BoP = balance of payments; EDS = External debt servicing (amortisation plus interest payments); GDPmp = gross domestic product at market prices; BD = combined budget deficits of central and state governments, and U = random disturbance/error term. It may be noted that external debt service obligations form a part of overall BoP of a country and further that BD similarly constitutes a part of GDP at market prices, so that presence of some elements of multicollinearity cannot be ruled out in these exercises, but we have checked with variance-covariance matrices of these regressions to find that the degree of multicollinearity is rather weak. The estimate of the parameters in Models XIII to XVII are given in Table 6.9.

Some interesting features may be observed from the estimates of Models XIII to XVII. First of all, the constant terms in all the regressions, barring Model XIII have estimates which are statistically significant and positive in sign. This suggests the existence of an autonomous term in all the postulated relations of Models XIV to XVII. Secondly, in Model XIII, where BoP along with EDS, and GDPmp along with BD are regressed on e, multicollinearity among these pairs of variables has affected the estimates to a certain extent with BoP and BD turn out to be statistically insignificant with wrong signs, although the overall

TABLE 6.9

Regression Estimates of Models XIII to XVII

Estimates	*Model XIII*	*Model XIV*	*Model XV*	*Model XVI*	*Model XVII*
(1)	*(2)*	*(3)*	*(4)*	*(5)*	*(6)*
Constant	5.39644 (0.274228)	5.37884 *** (20.2014)	5.74244 *** (9.3961)	5.03987 *** (18.1868)	5.7709 *** (9.43547)
BoP	-3.34117E-5 (-0.220634)	—	3.75718E-4 (1.0696)		
EDS	3.59113E-4*** (3.26182)	3.5053E-4*** (3.42987)	—		
GDP_{MP}	2.35983E-5*** (7.60205)	2.23024E-5*** (9.58594)	—	2.9707E-5*** (30.558)	
BD	-1.0177E-4 (-0.747394)	—	1.68798E-3*** (12.3006)	—	1.66283E-3*** (12.2782)
Adj-R^2	0.96365	0.964923	0.77768	0.955933	0.776917
DW	0.817073	0.766789	0.907024	0.711911	1.01321
F	285.989	592.436	76.2073	933.791	150.754

Note : Values in ( ) indicate the t-ratio of the estimates.

*** indicate significant at 1%, 5% and 10% levels of significance.

Source: Estimated from the data available.

regression explains more than 96% of the variations in e, and the F-statistic also indicates a high degree of acceptability. Thirdly, when we drop BoP and BD as explanatory variables, and regress e only on EDS and GDPmp, the R^2 and the F-statistic still improves and all the estimated coefficients turn out to be statistically significant at 1%, 5% and 10% levels of significance.

Interestingly, when we compare Model XIV with Model XVI, where only GDPmp is used as the explanatory variable, the Adj-R^2 equals 0.955933 compared to 0.964923 in Model XIV, such that GDPmp appears to have a dominant influence on the exchange rate of the Indian rupee compared to her overall EDS. Similarly, when we compare the estimate of Model XV with that of Model XVII, (where only BD is used as a explanatory variable), the Adj-R^2 declines only very marginally, and F-statistic improves substantially, and also the degree of positive autocorrelation decreases. Thus the estimate of BD which is statistically significant in both Models XV and XVII appears to exert a much more dominant impact on India's exchange rate than the size of her overall BoP deficit. All these estimates together imply that explanations on the external value of the rupee must primarily be linked with domestic macroeconomic management of the Indian economy wherein policies to manage the overall budgetary deficit of the government sector assume paramount importance.

6.4 EXCHANGE RATE AND TRADE BALANCE—TEST OF CAUSALITY

One of the major issues in the literature on India's balance of payments has been the effects of exchange rate adjustments on the country's trade balance. This concern had been expressed quite strongly whenever the Government of India had adjusted the par value of the Rupee through official declarations in response to balance of payments deficits. While some researchers have argued that exchange rate did matter in improving our trade balance over time, some others took the opposite view. Authors like Mathew Joseph (1992), Rajiv Kumar and Mathew Joseph (1994), Joshi and Little (1994) and H. Joshi (1996) have supported the case for exchange rate variations because India's export growth bears significant relation with her real effective exchange rate (REER), but authors like Prabirjit Sarkar (1992,97) does not seem to be convinced with this line of arguments. We have reviewed the debate in Chapter 3, and do not find unanimity amongst scholars over this important issue, although the majority seem to support the view that exchange rate did matter for India's trade balance. On the whole, we can argue that the behaviour of India's trade balance over time can be explained by a combination of set of factors, of which the exchange rate is an important one. Factors that govern the domestic macroeconomic management of the economy such that the budgetary deficits of the Union and the State Governments are also found to have exerted significant influences on India's trade balance or import surplus over time as we have discussed in section 6.3 above.

In order to assess the importance between exchange rate and trade balance in the Indian context for the period 1951-52 to 1994-95, we have attempted Granger's Causality Test between the two variables. A four-period annual lag structure is assumed for the two variables, viz, the exchange rate of the Rupee in terms of U.S. dollar (e_t) and India's trade balance (B_t) We postulate the following relations:

Model XVIII:

A. $e_t=f(e_{t-i}, B_{t-i})$: Restricted Form (6.25)

B. $e_t = f(e_{t-i})$: Unrestricted Form (6.26)

Again, we postulate that,

Model XIX :

A. $B_t = g(B_{t-i}\ e_{t-i})$: Unrestricted Form (6.27)

B. $B_t=g(B_{t-i})$: Restricted Form (6.28)

It is clear that part B of Models XVIII and XIX can be obtained by dropping the second variable from the estimable forms of part A of these models. Here i= 1, 2, 3, 4 stands for the lag in years. The estimable equations of Model XVIII and Model XIX are as follows:

Model XVIII:

A. Unrestricted Form with lag:

$$e_t = \theta_0 + \theta_1 e_{t-1} + \theta_2 e_{t-2} + \theta_3 e_{t-3} + \theta_4 e_{t-4} + a_1 B_{t-1} + a_2 B_{t-2} + a_3 B_{t-3} + a_4 B_{t-4} + U_t \quad (6.29)$$

B. Restricted Form with lag:

$$e_t = \theta_0 + \theta_1 e_{t-1} + \theta_2 e_{t-2} + \theta_3 e_{t-3} + \theta_4 e_{t-4} + V_t \quad (6.30)$$

Thus Model XVIII B is obtained by putting the restrictions $a_i = 0 \ \forall \ i = 1, 2, 3, 4$, in Model XVIII A.

Model XIX:

A. Unrestricted lag form:

$$B_t = \alpha_0 + \alpha_t B_{t-1} + \alpha_2 B_{t-2} + \alpha_3 B_{t-3} + \alpha_4 B_{t-4} + \beta_1 e_{t-1} + \beta_2 e_{t-2} + \beta_3 e_{t-3} + \beta_4 e_{t-4} + U_t \quad (6.31)$$

B. Restricted form with lag:

$$B_t = \alpha_0 + \alpha_t B_{t-1} + \alpha_2 B_{t-2} + \alpha_3 B_{t-3} + \alpha_4 B_{t-4} + V_t \quad (6.32)$$

When we put $B_i = 0 \ \forall \ i = 1, 2, 3, 4$, in Model XIX A, we get XIX B. The Null Hypothesis in Model XVIII is that B_t does not Granger cause e_t and that in Model XIX is that e_t does not Granger cause B_t Granger causality obtains when the Null-Hypothesis is rejected, i.e. the calculated F-statistic exceeds the tabulated value. This test is due to Granger (1969).

The estimated coefficients in Models XVIII and XIX are presented in Table 6.10 and the corresponding ANOVA estimates are presented in Table 6.11.

Before we present the test of Granger causality for the Models XVIII and XIX, we may make some observations about the estimates of the regression equations in these Models. In Model XVIII, both the restricted and unrestricted forms of the regression equations provide statistically significant estimates of the coefficients of the constant term and of e_{t-1} only, and the adjusted-R^2s are also not very high. But in Model XIX A, the estimated coefficients of $\hat{e}_{t-2}, \hat{e}_{t-3}, \hat{e}_{t-4}$ $\hat{B}_{t-1}$ and $\hat{B}_{t-2}$ are found to be statistically significant and in the restricted form of Model XIX B, the estimated coefficients of B_{t-1} and B_{t-2} are found to be statistically significant at 1%, 5%, and 10% levels of significance, and the adjusted-R^2s are also quite high in both the versions of Model XIX. Thus Model XIX provides a much more reliable

TABLE 6.10

Regression Estimates of Models XVIII to XIX

Estimates	*Model XVIII A*	*Model XVIII B*	*Model XIX A*	*Model XIX B*
Constant	3.95099***	3.13783***	294.417***	-344.024***
	(2.51692)	(2.45254)	(0.599224)	(-1.09679)
e_{t-1}	0.721073***	0.874481***	5.00721	
	(3.27755)	(5.862133)	(0.0727156)	
e_{t-2}	0.0321122	-0.0306161	-191.586***	
	(0.116696)	(-0.148916)	(-2.22441)	
e_{t-3}	-0.240941	-0.157644	205.064***	
	(-0.933972)	(-0.766799)	(2.53966)	
e_{t-4}	-0.0295601	-0.0101934	-124.577**	
	(-0.151111)	(-0.0666562)	(-2.03466)	
B_{t-1}	-6.3236E-4	—	0.522142***	0.442212***
	(-0.942675)		(2.48684)	(2.86204)
B_{t-2}	-5.47276E-5	—	0.373716***	0.799638***
	(-0.0793557)		(1.73131)	(4.83788)
B_{t-3}	2.02185E-4	—	-0.20067	-0.232849*
	(0.351769)		(-1.11546)	(-1.40886)
B_{t-4}	8.67312E-5	—	0.0301269	-0.144028
	(0.158273)		(0.17565)	(-0.932743)
Adj-R^2	0.555491	0.583786	0.778386	0.75001
DW	2.02524	2.00765	1.74493	1.9932
F	8.0294	16.7794	20.7524	34.7517

Notes : (a) The t-ratios of the estimated coefficients are given in parenthesis.
(b) *** indicates significant at 1%, 5% and 10% levels of significance;
** indicates significant at 5% and 10% levels, and
* indicates significant at 10% level of significance.

Source : Estimated from data available.

form of relationship between the variables than Model XVIII, as is also evident from the F-statistic of these two Models.

TABLE 6.11
ANOVA Tables for Models XVIII and XIX

Model XVIII A

	Sum of SQ's	D.F.	Mean SQ	F(8/37)
Regression	1488.85	8	186.106	8.0294
Residual	857.588	37	23.1781	
Total	2346.43	45		

Model XVIII B

	Sum of SQ's	D.F.	Mean SQ	F(8/37)
Regression	1456.63	4	364.157	16.7794
Residual	889.809	41	21.7026	
Total	2346.43	45		

Model XIX A

	Sum of SQ's	D.F.	Mean SQ	F(8/37)
Regression	3.76972E8	8	4.71215E7	20.7524
Residual	8.40143E7	37	2.27066E6	
Total	4.60987E8	45		

Model XIX B

	Sum of SQ's	D.F.	Mean SQ	F(8/37)
Regression	3.55988E8	4	8.8997E7	34.7517
Residual	1.04998E8	41	2.56094E6	
Total	4.60987E8	45		

From the ANOVA Table 6.11, we find that in Model XVIII (A and B), the estimated

$$F(4,37) = \frac{(RSS_B - RSS_A)/(41-37)}{RSS_A/37} = 0.3475378 \quad (6.33)$$

This falls short of the tabulated value at 10% levels of significance i.e., F(4/37) = 2.10. Hence the Null-Hypothesis H_0:B_t does not Granger cause e_t is not rejected. Therefore B_t does not Granger cause e_t.

On the other hand, from ANOVA Table we find that in Model XIX (A and B), the estimated

$$F(4,37) = \frac{(RSS_B - RSS_A)/(41-37)}{RSS_A/37} = 2.31 > 2.10 \quad (6.34)$$

(the tabulated F-statistic at 10% levels of significance). Therefore, the Null-Hypothesis H_0:e_t does not Granger cause B_t, is rejected, and exchange rate (e_t) does Granger cause trade balance (B_t).

Thus we find that in the Indian case, the direction of causality runs from exchange rate to trade balance, and not the other way round. Thus the views of Mathew Joseph, Joshi and Little, and Himangshu Joshi that exchange rate does really matter in analysing adjustments in India's trade balance, gets vindicated by our exercise.

This above result should not, however, be construed to mean that it is sufficient to tinker with the exchange rate of the Rupee in improving India's trade balance and balance of payments. Other domestic macroeconomic policies of stabilization, particularly the budgetary deficits of the central and state governments also exert significant influence on our trade balance, and care should be taken to pursue domestic macroeconomic policies in tune with the policy of exchange rate management. Balance of payments and trade balance of a country are essentially macroeconomic phenomena, and therefore policies to improve them must also be integrated macroeconomic in nature. This is the central message of the holistic approach adopted by us in this chapter. Unfortunately, in the Indian case, policies pursued by the government often were not based on such an integrated approach, and piecemeal interventions by the government from time to time did not provide long-term solutions to our balance of payments problems, which had shown strains of recurrent crises from time to time. In this exercise, we have adopted the holistic approach to balance of payments and trade balance to highlight the importance of co-ordinated policies to tackle balance of payments disequilibrium in our country from a long-term perspective.

6.5 INDIA'S BALANCE OF PAYMENTS AND MACRO-ECONOMIC BEHAVIOUR SINCE THE 1990s : AN EMPIRICAL ANALYSIS

Considering the serious worsening positions of the BoP on current account that arises usually when domestic expenditure or absorption exceeds domestic income thereby causing a deficit in the country's current account in international transaction question may crop up: what determines the domestic absorption or expenditure and thus trade balance? There are three major theoretical approaches in this regard. The traditional approach or the elasticity approach usually connected with exchange rate adjustments and devaluation as a method of redressing a country's BoP focuses on the importance of the relative price mechanisms between exportables and importables in the determination of equilibrium in balance of trade. This approach gives emphasis on expenditure switching rather than on expenditure reduction and relates the trade balance to variations in terms of trade. A rise in import prices *vis-a-vis* export prices (i.e. a decline in terms of trade) does not necessarily improve the trade balance—it also depends on the price elasticity of exports and imports. When the sum total of price elasticity of exports and import price elasticity exceeds unity, trade balance improves. Export price elasticity in India has been found to be less than the import price elasticity and together they do not add up even three-fourths of one percent, thus violating the Marshall-Lerner condition required for short run exchange rate stability.

In contrast to the elasticity approach, the 'Absorption Approach' refers to the income adjustment in correcting disequilibrium in a country's trade balance. It directly focuses attention on expenditure reduction as an essential way of reducing the trade balance, which is the difference between a country's national income and domestic absorption, i.e.

$$B= Y-E(Y) = Y-A \text{ with } 0<E_y<1$$

where $B<0$ implies $Y<A$ and $B>0$ implies $Y>A$

A rise in income, cet par, will improve trade balance if $0<E_y<1$. This is Sydney Alexander's absorption approach. A variant of the absorption approach is the monetary approach to the BoP theory. In this approach real value of asset is the prime determinant of trade balance. For simplicity, we can treat money to be the only asset. Then real money balances is a determinant of aggregate expenditure. Through its influence on aggregate spending, real money balances has an effect on the level of prices, income and trade balance.

We adopt a synthesis of the above three approaches to the BoP and try to relate the trade balance to net barter terms of trade (NBTOT), GDP at market prices and real balances. We also bring in time as a fourth explanatory variable, to take account of the miscellaneous factors which affect trade balance in the long run including policy shifts. We have approximated the real worth (assets of the economy) by the real balance of M3 deflated either by the GDP deflator (P_1) or by wholesale price index (P_2). The relative prices between homogeneous and foreign goods are measured by the NBTOT. Our integrated system defines trade balance as:

$$B = B(Y, M_3/P_1, TOT, \text{time}) \quad i=1, 2 \qquad (6.35)$$

$IS = -B(\ )$ where IS = import surplus with

$IS_1 > 0, IS_2>0, IS_3>0, IS_4>0$

This hypothesis is tested with the following regressions to find out the determinants of import surplus (i.e. negative of trade balance) to be worked out for the period form 1991-92 to 2004-05. In Model XX, we regress import surplus on GDP at market prices, real balances M_3/P_1 and time as an extra explanatory variable to accommodate the impact of the long-run variables like technological progress and other factors such as interest rate, exchange rate etc., and the policy parameters which have undergone substantial changes over the fifteen year period under review. The estimated values of coefficients and the related estimates are given below. In Model XXI, the import surplus being the dependent variable is hypothesized to be a function of GDP at market prices (X_1), real balances as measured by M_3 deflated by WPI (P_2) i.e. (X_2) and time (X_2).

The estimated values of coefficients and the related estimates are given below. In Model XXII, we have estimated the determinants of import surplus for the same period. The GDP at market prices (X_1), real balances with base year 1991-92 (X_2) and index of NBTOT (X_3) and time (from 1991-92 to 2004-05) (X_4) are treated as explanatory variables. The estimates are given below. The equations of the models are given below:

Model XX:

$$\text{Import Surplus} = \beta_o + \beta_1 \text{ GDPmp} + \beta_2 M_3/P_1 + \beta_3 \text{ time} + U_1 \quad (6.36)$$

where time = 1, 2,.... 15 (1991-92- 2004-05) and P_1 is GDP deflator base 1990-91.

and M_3 is deposit money of the public + currency with the public + time deposit with banks.

and U_t is a stochastic random term.

Model XXI:

$$\text{Import Surplus} = \alpha_0 + \alpha_1 \text{ GDPmp} + \alpha_2 M_3/P_1 + \alpha_3 \text{ Time} \quad (6.37)$$

where Time = 1, 2 15
and where M_3/P_1 = real balances deflated by WPI (P_2) with base and
other variables being the same as in model

Model XXII:

$$Y = A + B_1X_1 + B_2X_2 + B_3X_3 + B_4X_4 + U_t \quad (6.38)$$

where

Y= Import Surplus
X_1 = GDP at market prices
X_2 = Real balances M_3/P_1 (where P_2 = WPI base 1991-92)
X_3 = Index of NBTT
and X_4 = Time (from 1991-92 to 2004-05)

It may be noted that the terms of trade of a nation is closely related to the exchange rate which may be defined as the ratio between prices of traded goods and non-traded (domestic) goods, and under normal circumstances bear direct relationship. Hence we omit the use of exchange rate as a separate explanatory variable in Model XXII.

Results and Interpretations

After the estimation of the model we proceed with the evaluation of the results of calculation, i.e. with the determination of the reliability of the coefficients of the above economic relationships. The evaluation consists of deciding whether the estimates of the parameters are theoretically meaningful and statistically satisfactory.

Economic theory takes note of the signs and values of the parameters of the economic relationships. For the above economic relationship, the effect of GDP at market prices on import surplus (M-X) should be positive, so that the coefficient of the parameters is positive. Again, as real balances of an economy rises, people will go for more imported goods so that the import surplus of that country should rise, causing b_2 to become positive. Again, it is possible to take into account the influence of time on the dependent variables, measured by the number of observed period from a the starting year onwards, as an explanatory variable in the model. The meaning of such a time variable is that there is an autonomous trend experienced

TABLE 6.12

Summary Results of Regression Estimates of the determinants of India's Import Surplus (1991-92 to 2004-05)

	Estimated coefficient of the parameter X_1	Estimated coefficient of the parameter X_2	Estimated coefficient of the parameter X_3	Estimated coefficient of the parameter X_4	Adjusted R^2	F values	D.W
(1)	(2)	(3)	(4)	(5)	(6)	(7)	(8)
Model XX	β_1 -.00487 (-.176)	β_2^* -17.982 (-3.456)	β_2^* 5379.89 (3.904)		.825009	34	1.57
Model XXI	α_1 .0006750 (.787)	α_2^* -15.7062 (-2.773)	α_2^* 17820.85 (3.704)		.833167	35.96	.85
Model XXII	B_1^* .891166 (4.134)	B_2^* -12.5078 (-2.268)	B_3^* -259.753 (-3.228)	B_4^* 2428.06 (3.000)	.7874088	26.93	1.21

Note : Computed t-values appear in the parenthesis below the estimates of the regression coefficients.

* Significant at 1% and 5% level respectively.

by the dependent variable. Referring to the equation under Model XX, we see that the impact of time variable on import surplus is direct, i.e. as time passes, there is a continuous improving trend in the import surplus. Thus it confirms with the general trend of BoP during the last 15 years.

The sign of b_1 is expected to be positive, while the sign of b_2 is negative but b_3 is found to be positive in our model. We also see that the coefficient of adjusted multiple determinations $R^2 = 0.8250$ is quite high suggesting goodness of fit.

To test the null hypothesis $H_0 : b_i = 0$ against all alternatives, we use the two tailed t-test statistic and find that b_2 and b_3 are statistically significant at 1% level. The D.W. statistic $d = 1.57$ refers to the existence of positive autocorrelation to some degree in the system.

As regard to the Model XXI, the coefficients of the parameters are expected to be positive but we see that the signs of estimated a_1 and a_3 are consistent with our theoretical model while that of estimated a_2 is not.

But here the inclusion of the time variable is significant in that the effect of time variable on import surplus is direct, i.e. it satisfies the recent trend of India's BoP. The computed t-values of the estimated coefficients as reported give their statistical significance. Adjusted $R^2 = 0.8331677$ shows, being a high one that the greater percentage of variation in import surplus is explained by the given regression plane although it is higher compared to the Model XX. To test the null–hypothesis H_0: $a_i = 0$ against all alternative hypotheses, we use the t-test statistic and conclude that a_2 and a_3 are significant, while is not at 5% and 1% level of significance. D.W statistic, $d = 1.85$ signifies some degree of autocorrelation in the model, which is comparatively higher than the earlier model.

Again, referring to the Model XXII, we find the parameters B_1 and B_4 have the expected signs, while that of B_2 and B_3 are not. The time variable has a much greater positive impact on import surplus, thus satisfying the economic *a priori* criteria. As for the inclusion for the new variable net barter terms of trade, one of the real factors underpinning the current account, its effect on the import surplus is negative. To test the null hypothesis $H_0 : B_i = 0$ against all alternatives we use the t-test statistic and find that B_1, B_2, B_3 and B_4 are statistically significant.

The coefficient of adjusted multiple determination is $R^2 = .7874$, being a high one, signifies goodness of fit. The D.W statistic d = 1.21 signifies some degree of positive autocorrelation in the model.

Our conclusion from the above exercise is that since BoP is a macro economic phenomenon, it then requires macroeconomic interventions, apart from increasing the value of GDP or net barter terms of trade. Our macro-econometric exercise provides a simple integrated framework in terms of which we can test the significance of the influence of other variables. These factors could be alternative estimates of real wealth, the exchange rate, the size of government expenditure and the rate of interest etc. We want to test some of the important variables in the next.

6.6 FACTORS INFLUENCING THE EXTERNAL VALUE OF RUPEE

External value of a country's currency is determined by a number of factors. To a large extent, the balance of payments deficits, external debt, foreign exchange reserves may influence the external value. However, domestic factors like the internal value of the currency, growth of national income, excess of public expenditure over the public revenue are also likely to influence the external value of the currency. The extent to which and the direction in which these factors influence the external value of a currency may vary from economy to economy and from time to time. The rising burden of external debt and the resulting payments problems pose serious problems threatening to the stability of the external value of our currency. Under this circumstances, it would be of academic interest, if the factors influencing the external value of Rupee are identified in the light of our experience in the past. Here is an attempt to identify the significant variables influencing the external value of Rupee from the following variables: balance of payments, external debt, foreign exchange reserves, internal value of the currency, budget deficit, and GDP.

Most of the research works undertaken in the field concentrate on the verification and empirical testing of the purchasing power parity theory, during different periods of time and for different countries. This works examine the validity of PPP theory in explaining the determination of exchange rate under flexible and fixed exchange rate systems and also in short-run and long run.

Some other available works attempt to investigate the variations of exchange rate in association with different economic factors. A survey of the existing research works reveals the fact that attempts made to examine the trend of external value of Rupee and the influence of BoP, public external debt, forex reserve, internal value of Rupee, GDP and budget deficit seem to be vary rare and such works do not figure prominently in the literature.

The data used for this work are secondary data only. In the first part of the analysis, the trend of external value of Rupee is examined during the period from 1991-92 to 2004-05. To work out the external value, the average exchange rates of the different years have been taken. The data on exchange rate have been taken from RBI's Handbook of Statistics on Indian Economy and Economic Survey (various issues). To identify the factors influencing the external value of rupee the time period taken for analysis is a period of 15 years. Multiple linear regression model is used to identify the relationship between the external value of rupee and other factors taken into considerations. Using the consumer price index numbers, the internal value of rupee is worked out. Hence the model used for the analysis is :

Model XXIII

$$EVR = b_0 + b_1(BoP) + b_2(ED) + b_3(Forex) + b_4(IVR) + b_5(GDP) + b_6(BD) \quad (6.39)$$

where all items expressed in crores of rupees (except EVR),
EVR is the external value of rupee,
BoP is the balance of payments,
ED is the public external debt,
Forex is the foreign exchange reserves,
IVR is the internal value of rupee,
GDP is the value of gross domestic product at 1990 prices,
BD is the budget deficit.

The regression coefficients have been estimated through least squares method and the estimated regression coefficients have been tested under the null hypothesis so that their value is zero.

Results and Inferences

Table 6.13 presents the estimated values of the regression coefficients, their standard errors, levels of significance, etc. When all the six variables, viz, BoP, external debts, forex reserves, internal value of Rs. GDP and budget deficit are taken in the model, internal value of rupee, forex reserve become insignificant. They have not influenced much the external value of rupee during the period 1991-92 to 2004-05. However, the remaining four variables, viz. BoP, external debt, GDP and budgetary deficits are significantly affecting the external value of rupee. External debt is positively influencing the external value of the rupee. The absolute value of the regression coefficient of the internal value of the rupee seems to be the highest among the variables. All the six variables taken together help to explain 98% of the variations in the external value of rupee. Simple linear regressions run by taking the external value as the dependent variable and the other factors as independent variable also support the fact that forex reserves and internal value of the rupee do not help much in explaining the variations in the external value of rupee.

The major conclusions emerging from the above exercise are:

External debt is a major factor affecting the external value of Rupee. During the period under investigation, the external debt of the government has increased manifold. This bears evidence to the fact that external debt is the major factor deteriorating the external value of the rupee. In Indian case, debt service is exerting immense pressure on the BoP and if India is to sustain growth in the first decade of the new millennium and avoid sliding into a morass of debt, the country's debt burden be restructured to reduce service payments and exports be increased at a much faster rate.

TABLE 6.13

Results of the Linear Regression Models XXIII

Constant	BoP	External Debt	Forex Reserve	Internal value of Rupee	GDP Deficits	Budgetary	R^2	F
(1)	(2)	(3)	(4)	(5)	(6)	(7)	(8)	(9)
12.94	-.00006478	.000045669	-.00000143	.000854	.00009383	.0000645	.9845	84.70
(4.114)	(-2.832*)	(2.865*)	(-1.606)	(.089)	(2.804*)	(2.704*)		

Notes : Figures in parenthesis are t-values.

* Significant at five percent level.

GDP is another factor influencing the external value of rupee. However, GDP is positively related to external value of Rupee. This means that the rise in GDP helps to improve the external value of Rupee. However, the growth rate of GDP does not influence the external value of Rupee. Hence, if the growth rate of GDP is increased; it may help to improve the external value of Rupee. Growth of foreign exchange reserves will also help to improve the external value of the Rupee.

Internal value of rupee has a strong and positive influence on the external value of rupee. Hence, increase in the internal value of rupee is likely to improve the external value of rupee. This implies that rising domestic price level and consequent inflation is one of the significant factors responsible for the depreciation in the external value of the rupee. Substituting devaluation in this regard in Indian context may be a short-term rescue operation, but not for long-term solution. Hence strict fiscal discipline, reduction in borrowing and curbing inflation with a tight control over money supply are the need of the hour to maintain the stability in the external and internal value of the rupee.

6.7 DO EFFECTIVE EXCHANGE RATE INFLUENCE TRADE BALANCE?

In order to access the importance between real effective exchange rate (REER) (trade-weighted) and the trade balance in the Indian context from the post-reform period 1991-92 to 2004-05, we have attempted Granger's causality test between these two variables. The logic for taking real effective exchange rate is that it is the most important macroeconomic variable that influences international competitiveness in the present post-WTO era of increasing globalization. Besides, if it really affects the trade balance of the country, then prudent adjustment in it can resolve the BoP disequilibrium situation. For this exercise to perform, we have taken quarterly data. A four-period lag structure is assumed for the two variables, viz., the REER and India's trade balance (Bt). We postulate the following relation:

Model XXIV

A. $REER_t=f\ (REER_{t-i}, B_{t-i})$; Unrestricted Form (6.40)
B. $REER_t=f\ (REER_{t-i})$; Restricted Form (6.41)

Again we postulate that,

Model XXV

A. $B_t=g\ (B_{t-i}, REER_{t-i})$; Unrestricted Form (6.42)
B. $B_t=g(B_{t-i})$; Restricted Form (6.43)

It is clear that part B of the Models XXIV and XXV can be obtained by dropping the second variable from the estimable forms of part A of these models. Here i =1, 2, 3, 4 stands for the quarterly lag. The estimable equations of Model XXIV and Model XXV are as follows:

Model XXIV

A. Unrestricted Form with lag:

$$REER_t= \theta_0+ \theta_1 REER_{t-1}+ \theta_2 REER_{t-2}+ \theta_3 REER_{t-3}+ \theta_4 REER_{t-4}+ a_1 B_{t-1}+ a_2 B_{2-1}+ a_3 B_{t-3} + a_4 B_{t-4}+U_t \quad (6.44)$$

B. Restricted Form with lag:

$$REER_t=\theta_0+\theta_1 REER_{t-1}+\theta_2 REER_{t-2}+\theta_3 REER_{t-3}+\theta_4 REER_{t-4}+V_t \quad (6.45)$$

Thus Model XXIVB is obtained by putting the restrictions $a_i =0\ V\ i=1, 2, 3, 4$ in Model XXIVA

Model XXV

A. Unrestricted Form with lag:

$$B_t = \alpha_0 +\alpha_1 B_{t-1}+\alpha_2 B_{t-2}+\alpha_3 B_{t-3} +\alpha_4 B_{t-4}+ \beta_1 REER_{t-1}+\beta_2 REER_{t-2}+\beta_3 REER_{t-3}+\beta_4 REER_{t-4} U_t \quad (6.46)$$

B. Restricted Form with lag:

$$B_t = \alpha_0 + \alpha_1 B_{t-1} + \alpha_2 B_{t-2} + \alpha_3 B_{t-3} + \alpha_4 B_{t-4} + V_t \quad (6.47)$$

When we put b_I=0 V i=1, 2, 3, 4, in Model XXVA, we get Model XXVB. The Null Hypothesis in Model XXIV is that B_t does not Granger cause $REER_t$ and that in Model XXV is that $REER_t$ does not Granger cause B_t. Granger causality obtains when the Null-Hypothesis is rejected i.e., the calculated F-statistic exceeds the tabulated value.

TABLE 6.14

ANOVA Tables for Models XXIV and XXV

Model XXIVA

Residual sum of squares (RSS)	D.F.	F(7.51)	Adjusted R^2	D.W.
22473.12706	51	366.95	0.97786	1.10920

Model XXIVB

Residual sum of squares (RSS)	D.F.	F(7.51)	Adjusted R^2	D.W.
6946.335255	55	3028.31	0.99365	1.17001

Model XXVA

Residual sum of squares (RSS)	D.F.	F(7.51)	Adjusted R^2	D.W.
469805278	51	14.88	0.62627	1.08730

Model XXVB

Residual sum of squares (RSS)	D.F.	F(7.51)	Adjusted R^2	D.W.
803984876.5	55	83.66	0.81044	2.47196

From the ANOVA Table 6.14, we find that in Model XXIV (A and B), the estimated.

$$F(4, 51) = \frac{(RSS_B - RSS_A)/(55-51)}{RSS_A/51} = -88.21 \qquad (6.48)$$

This falls short of the tabulated value both at 1% and 5% level of significance i.e., in F (4, 51) = 2.53

Here the Null Hypothesis H_0:B_t does not Granger because $REER_t$ is not rejected. Therefore, B_t does not Granger cause $REER_t$.

On the other hand, from ANOVA Table we find that in Model XXV (A and B), the estimated

$$F(4, 51) = \frac{(RSS_B - RSS_A)/(55-51)}{RSS_A/51} = 20.54 > 2.53 \qquad (6.49)$$

(The tabulated F-statistic both at 1% and 5% levels of significance). Therefore, the Null Hypothesis H_0: $REER_t$, does not Granger because B_t, is rejected and the trade weighted real effective exchange rate ($REER_t$) does Granger cause trade balance (B_t). Thus we find that in the Indian case, the direction of causality runs from REER to trade balance, and not the other way round. Hence we can conclude that the exchange rate matters and here the changes in the real exchange rate will have an effect on the trade balance.

7

Concluding Observations and Policy Implications

We have traversed a long way on the path of post-independence India's balance of payments along with some aspects like BoP theories, researchers' contribution on India's BoP, India's BoP—a historical perspective as well as trade and payments policy in India and the attempt to identify the crucial factors that determine the course of BoP in India. In this journey we witnessed some of the major reforms in India towards the external sector. Among them, the major reforms to the overall policy environment concerning macroeconomic policies, trade and payments policies, exchange rate policies were initiated in 1991, though few of them had their roots in a partial reform measures initiated during the mid-1980s. There is no denying the fact that economic reforms in the early 1990s came as a rescue for the Indian economy. With integration of the Indian economy more or less with the global economy in a phased manner, the decade 1990s showed some signs of advances in different indicators of external development. International trade in general and exports in particular were given greater emphasis during the decade. Yet the decade was not without major challenges. The economy faced the BoP crisis of 1991 (which was essentially linked to the large and growing fiscal imbalances witnessed since the mid-1980s), the extra-ordinarily eventful challenges like the surges in private capital flows in 1993-94 to 1994-95, thus complicating the operation of macroeconomic policy, the external debt management, the risk of contagion from East Asian crisis, the management of huge pile-up of foreign exchange reserves as well as issues and options in exchange rate management faced in the emerging scenario of globalization and liberalization. The new millennium had no doubt brought to the fore some of the strength, resilience and the stability of the country's external sector reflected by a steady accretion to foreign exchange reserves, moderate and sustainable level of current account deficit, changing composition of capital inflows with a significant reduction in the external debt to GDP ratio and moderate rise in the level of short-term debt. For example, in the last two years of the new millennium, the current account deficit to GDP ratio (averaged 1.2 per cent of GDP) was considerably lower than in the 1990s (which was 1.8 per cent of GDP) and the 1980s (which was at around 2-3 percent of GDP). But in the new millennium also, the economy continued to face newer problems like Dutch Disease, the earlier problems of managing the excess of net capital inflows over the current account deficit in a new form, particularly that of balancing the contradictions in the trilogy of objectives (a relatively open capital account, monetary policy independence and flexible exchange rate), though capital flows, as a proportion of GDP, reached a high of 5.1 per cent in 2006-07 thus exhibiting an outcome of the improved investment climate and recognition of robust macroeconomic fundamentals. Even as the external environment remained conducive, the problems of managing a more open capital account with increasing inflows and exchange rate appreciation surfaced. Hence a search for an appropriate policy mix for balancing these items is urgently called for.

There is also no denying the fact that the twin processes of globalization and liberalization are shaping a new system of international economic situations in which the changing pattern of investment, production and trade, the global pace of finance and the central role of technology are dominant. The sky-rocketing pace of liberalization and globalization in the world economy has no doubt increased opportunities, while at the same time it added new complexities and risks in the management of global interdependence. India is a player in this game. Her ability to influence the pace and direction of global policy initiatives is still weak, while their vulnerability to the economic policy decisions taken by major developing developed and developed countries has increased. In this context to have a benefit from globalization, India as a developing country will need to engage herself more actively in shaping the contours of the international economic order. Otherwise India will be lagging behind in its economic performance.

A robust growth in exports remains one to the most critical factors in the long term viability of her external sector. Uneven performance of merchandise exports will introduce a structural weakness in the BoP. So strategies for export growth need to be designed to put export growth on a higher and sustainable growth trajectory. On the import side, the economy needs to be insulated from continuing volatility.

Sound macro-economic policies with sustainable fiscal deficits and realistic exchange rate are a prerequisite of progress. Large government budget deficits absorb domestic savings and foreign funds that could otherwise be channeled to private sector. Crowding out productive investment by farmers, entrepreneurs and large business, government deficits place the financial system under great strain, often they induce rapid inflation which in turn exacerbate the deficit, creating vicious circle. Deficits also lead to over valued exchange rates, which stifle exports, damage domestic producers and create pressures for protectionism. Evidence is accumulating from country experience of widespread ill-effects of large fiscal deficits. A distinguishing feature of some successful country-experience is that the public sectors exercised discipline in its spending: such discipline is essential to ensure that rents from government intervention are kept to a minimum. Fiscal discipline was practised in different ways. Most South East Asian economies managed to keep their macro-economic policies on course and their broad economic performance has benefited accordingly.

They had a fiscal surplus during a large part of their high growth period. A fiscal surplus also have had the ability to contribute to an increase in a nation's global wealth holdings. Thus it appears that a persistent government fiscal deficit is the surest route to economic failure. One study made by Chatterjee and Karmakar (1998) clearly shows that particularly the fiscal deficits of the Central and States Government in case of India exerts significant influence on India's trade balance. It is a great hope for the Indian economy that with the structural adjustment programme initiated in 1991, the fiscal deficit of the Centre as a proportion of GDP came down from 7 per cent in 1990-91 to 3.4 per cent in 2006-07 and 3.3 percent in 2007-08 respectively.

If a persistent government fiscal deficit is the surest route to economic failure, an artificial overvalued exchange rate must be the runner-up. Underlying such overvaluation are expansionary fiscal and monetary policies, excessive borrowing and inadequate trade and exchange rate policies. Overvaluation leads to the rationing of foreign exchange, which is invariably associated with its discretionary allocation and appropriation by government officials. Overvaluation also creates pressures for layer after layer of controls on import, capital flow. And it destroys emerging export industries, perhaps the most important foundation for growth that any developing country enjoys and caters to balance of payments difficulties. So to tinker with the exchange rate of the Rupee in improving trade balance and balance of payments is one of the essential elements in external balance for the Indian economy as in Indian case, the direction of causality runs from exchange rate to trade balance and not the other way round. That is why care should be taken to pursue domestic macro-economic policies—a judicial mix of fiscal and monetary policies in tune with the policy of exchange rate management. Balance of payments and trade balance of a country are essentially macro-economic phenomena and therefore policies to improve them must also be integrated macro-economic in nature. It is a fact that BoP equilibrium, a major macro-economic target, should be attained primarily by letting the exchange rate move flexibly under the influence of market forces affecting both current and capital account transactions. Unfortunately in the Indian case, policies pursued by the government often were not based on such an integrated framework and piecemeal interventions by the government from time to time did not provide long term solution to India's balance of payments problems, which had shown a strain of recurrent crisis from time to time.

India's progressive globalization and liberalization episode have led to increasing inflows of foreign investment, both in terms of FDI as well as FPI. These inflows have been instrumental in strengthening the BoP and provided strength to debt management. To have the sustainability of external debt indicators of the country, several new initiatives like pre-payments of identified high cost debt, refinancing of costly debts and measures to actively managed sovereign debt of the country would be helpful in the long run.

In sum, for India's external sector to be strengthened—a satisfactory real rate of growth, relatively low inflation, an optimum level of foreign exchange reserves with at least a foreign exchange assets-to-currency ratio of 40% to be prescribed by law, a low current account deficit in BoP and a falling debt-service ratio as well as a realistic exchange rate buttressed by appropriate monetary policy measures that will prevent undue volatility, is highly warranted. Moreover, an orderly liberalization of the capital account may be pursued after fulfilling the prerequisites on its onward march towards capital account convertibility, as it is essential to reap the benefits of globalization. Isolating an economy and living in a protective cocoon are hardly an optimal solution.

Bibliography

Abid Hussain Committee (1984), *Report of the Committee on Trade Policies,* Government of India, Ministry of Commerce, New Delhi.

Agosin, M. (1994), "Saving and Investment in Latin America," *UNCTAD Discussion Paper,* No. 90.

Ahluwalia, I.J. (1985), *Industrial Growth in India, Stagnation Since the Mid-Sixties,* Delhi, Oxford University Press.

Alexander Committee (1978), *Report of the Committee on Import and Export Policies and Procedures,* Ministry of Commerce, Government of India.

Alexander, Sidney S. (1952), "Effects of a Devaluation on a Trade Balance", *International Monetary Fund Staff Papers,* 2, 263-78.

Alexander, Sidney S. (1959), "Effects of a Devaluation: a Simplified Synthesis of Elasticities and Absorption Approaches, *American Economic Review,* 49, 22-42.

Allen, Polly R. and Peter, B. Kenen (1980), *Asset Markets, Exchange Rates and Economic Integration: A Synthesis,* Cambridge University Press.

Asher, Mukul G. (2006), "India's Rising Role in Asia", Vera Anstey Memorial Lecture, delivered at 89th Annual Conference of the Indian Economic Association, December 27.

Avramovic, D., *et al.* (1964), *Economic Growth and External Debt,* Bultimore, John Hopkins Press.

Bacha, Edmar L. (1990), "A Three Gap Model of Foreign Transfers and GDP Growth Rate in Developing Countries", *Journal of Development Economics,* 32:279-96.

Backus, David K. (1984), "Empirical Models of the Exchange Rate: Separating the Wheat from the Chaff," *Canadian Journal of Economics*, 17, 824-46.

Bagchi, A.K. and Prabirjit Sarkar (1993), "Trade and Exchange Rate Policy for India", *Economic and Political Weekly*, September 18.

Balassa, B. (1978), "Exports and Economic Growth: Further Evidence", *Journal of Development and Cultural Changes*, Vol. 36.

Balasubramaniyam, V.N. (1995), "India's Trade Policy Review" in Arndt, S. and Milner, C., eds., (1995), '*The World Economy: Global Trade Policy*': Blackwell Publisher, London.

Balasubramaniyam,V.N. and D.R. Basu (1990), "India's Export Promotion Policies and Export Performance" In Milner (ed.). *Export Promotion Strategies* (Helmel Hemosteade : Harvester Wheatsheaf).

Banerjee, Anindya *et. al.* (1992), Recursive and Sequential Tests *of* the Unit Root and Trend Break Hypotheses: Theory and International Evidence, *Journal of Business and Economic Statistics*, Vol. 10, No. 3, July.

Bardhan, P.K. (1962), "Case Against Devaluation", *The Economic Weekly*, 14 September 1962.

Bardhan, P.K. (1984), *The Political Economy of Development in India*, Oxford University Press.

Barro, R. (1989), "A Cross Country Study *of* Growth, Saving, and Government", *Working Paper No.* 2855 (NBER, Cambridge).

Beanstock, Michael (1990), "Exchange Rate Dynamics" in Llewellyn, David T. and Chris Milner (eds.) *Current Issues in International Monetary Economics*, Macmillian Press Ltd., London.

Bernanke, B.S. (2005), "Monetary Policy in a World of Mobile Capital", *Carlo Journal*, Vol. 25(1).

Bhaduri, Amit (2005), *Development with Dignity: A Case for Full Employment*, National Book Trust of India.

Bhagwati, Jagdish (1962), "The Case for Devaluation", *The Economic Weekly*, 14 August, 1962.

Bhagwati, Jagdish (1994), "Free Trade" Old and New Challanges, *Economic Journal, March* 1994, Vol. 104, No. 423.

Bhagwati, Jagdish and Padma Desai (1970), *India Planning for Industrialization: A Study of India's Trade and Industrialization Policies (1950-66),* Oxford, 1970.

Bhagwati, Jagdish N. and T.N. Srinivasan (1975), *Foreign Trade Regimes and Economic Development: India,* National Bureau of Economic Research, New York.

Bhandari, I.S., R. Driskill, and J.A. Frenkel, (1984), "Capital Mobility and Exchange Rate Overshooting", *European Economic Review,* 24:309-20.

Bhattacharya, B.B. (1995), "Stabilization, Adjustment and Growth in India", published in the Conference Volume of the *Indian Economic Journal,* Chandigarh.

Bhattacharya, P.C. (1966), The Case of Devaluation, *RBI Bulletin,* July 1966, p. 728.

Bickerdicke, C.F. (1920), "The Instability of Foreign Exchange", *Economic Journal,* 30, 118-22.

Blackburn, Keith and Martin Sola (1993), "Speculative Currency Attacks and Balance of Payments Crises", *Journal of Economic Surveys,* 7, 119-44.

Blanchard O.J.S. and O. Fisher (1989), *Lectures on Macroeconomics,* MIT Press, Cambridge, Mass.

Blejer, M. and M.S. Khan (1984), "Government Policy and Private Investment in Developing Countries", *IMF Staff Papers,* 31:3279-403.

Bokil, S.V., V. Chitre and R. Murthy (1981), "A Structural Study of India's Trade Dependence (1956-75)", *Artha Vijnan,* March.

Boughton, J.M. (1988), "The Monetary Approach to Exchange Rates: What Now Remains?", Princeton Essays in International Finance, Princeton, No. 171, (October).

Brahmbhatt, M., T.G. Srinivasan and K. Murrel (1996), *India in the Global Economy,* Policy Research Working Paper No. 1681, World Bank, November.

Branson, W.H. (1976), 'Asset Markets, and Relative Prices in Exchange Rate Determination', *Institute for International Economic Studies, Seminar Paper,* No. 66, Stockholm.

Branson, William H., Hannu Hattunen and Paul Masson (1977), "Exchange Rates in the Short Run: The Dollar Deutshe-mark Rate", *European Economic Review,* 10, 303-24.

Branson, William H. (1984), "A Model of Exchange Rate Determination with Policy Reaction: Evidence from Monthly Data", in P Malgrange and P.A. Muet, (eds.), *Contemporary Macroeconomic Modelling* (Oxford: Basil Blackwell).

Branson, William H. and Dale W. Henderson (1985), "The Specification and Influence of Asset Markets", in R.W. Jones and P.B. Kenen (eds.), *Handbook of International Economics* (Amsterdam: North-Holland).

Branson, William H., Hannu Hattunen and Paul Masson (1979), "Exchange Rates in the Short Run: Some Further Results", *European Economic Review,* 12, 395-402.

Buiter, W.H. and M, Miller (1981), "Monetary Policy and International Competitiveness": The Problem of Adjustment, in W.A. Letis and P.J. Sinclair (eds.), *The Money Supply and the Exchange Rate,* Oxford University Press, Oxford.

Chandhok, H. L. and the Policy Group (1990), *India Data Base—The Economy—Annual Time Series Data,* Volume I and II.

Chandrasekhar, C.P. and Jayati Ghosh (1999), 'India's External Debt : Are we out of the Woods yet ?' *Business Line,* June 15, 1999.

Chatterjee, Biswajit (1994), "An Economic Theorist's Tale of Trade Liberalization in a Developing Economy" in Das, Debendra K. (ed.), *Structural Adjustment in the Indian Economy,* Vol. I, Deep and Deep Publications, New Delhi.

Chatterjee, Biswajit (1997), "Globalization of the Indian Economy": The Tasks Ahead, *Occasional Paper* No. 5, Economics Department, Rabindra Bharati University, 1997.

Chatterjee, Biswajit and Asim K. Karmakar (1995), "Trade Balance and Domestic Absorption in India: An Examination of Basic Issues" in Dr. S. Murty (ed.), *India's International Trade and Rupee Exchange Rate,* RBSA Publishing, Jaipur.

Chatterjee, Biswajit and Asim K. Karmakar (1998), "India's Trade Balance and Macroeconomic Policies" in Chatterjee, Biswajit (ed.), *Economic Liberalization in India,* Allied Publishers Pvt. Ltd, Kolkata.

Chatterjee, Biswajit and Asim K. Karmakar (1998), "Balance of Payments Position in India" in *Economic and Social Change,* A Quarterly Journal of Economic Development, New Delhi.

Chatterjee, Biswajit and Sugata Marjit (1992), "Trade and Payments Policies in India : An Evaluation of Recent Changes and Their Policy Implications", *The Indian Economic Journal,* Vol. 39, No. 3, Jan.-March.

Chaudhuri, Kausik (2005), " Is Devaluation Working? Evidence from India in Phase of Economic Liberalization", *Journal of Quantitative Economics,* Vol. 3, No. 2, July.

Chenery, Hollis B. and A.M. Strout (1966), "Foreign Assistance and Economic Development", *American Economic Review,* 56: 679-733.

Chenery, Hollis B. and M. Bruno (1962), "Development Alternatives in an Open Economy : The Case of Isreal", *Economic Journal,* 72:79-103.

Claassen, Emil-Maria (1996), *Global Monetary Economies,* Oxford University Press.

Cline, William R., (1994), *International Economic Policy in the 1990s.* The MIT Press. (Washington, D.C. : Institute for International Economics, mimeographed, July).

Cohen, Benjamin I. (1964), "The Stagnation of Indian Exports, 1951-61", *The Quarterly Journal of Economics,* November, 1964.

Cohen, Benjamin I. (1970), "International Development in India and Pakistan" in Robinson, E.A.S. and Michael Kidron (eds.), *'Economic Development in South Asia'*. Proceedings of a Conference held by the International Economic Association at Kandy, Ceylon, Macmillian, St. Martin's Press, London.

Corbo, Victoria and Andres Solimans (1991), "Chile's Experience with Stabilization Revisited", in Michael Bruno *et. al., Lessons of Economic Stabilization and its Aftermath,* Cambridge, Mass: MIT Press, 1991.

Cumby, R.E. and M. Obstfeld, (1984), "International Interest Rate and Price Level Linkages Under Flexible Exchange Rates: A Review of Recent Evidence", in J.F.O. Bilson and R.C. Marston (eds.), *Exchange Rate Theory and Practice* (Chicago: University of Chicago Press).

Currie, D.A. (1976), "Some Criticisms of the Monetary Analysis of Balance of Payments Correction", *Economic Journal*, 87, pp. 771-3.

Da Costa, G.C. (1965), "Elasticities of Demand for Indian Exports", *The Indian Economic Journal*, 13 September, 1965.

Da Costa, G.C. (1986), "India's Trade Balance During the Seventies", *Economic and Political Weekly*, March 8-15, 1986, 433-42.

Da Costa, G.C. (1988), "India's Balance of Payments : Heading Towards a Crisis"? *R.M. Joshi Memorial Lecture*, Sydenham College of Commerce and Economics, Bombay, December 21, 1988, Printed in Bhuleskar, A.V. and Dawood Mithani (eds.), (1990) *Structural Changes and Issues of Indian Economy* Himalaya Publising House, Bombay.

Da Costa, G.C. (1990), *India's Balance of Payments in the Seventies and the Eighties*, Himalaya Publishing House, Bombay.

Dagli Committee (1979), *Report of the Committee on Controls and Subsidies*, Government of India, Ministry of Finance, New Delhi.

Das, Kaushik (2006), "Issues and Insights—Capital Account Amnesia", *Business Standard*, May 31.

Dasgupta, A.K. (1962), "Export Promotion Through Devaluation", *The Economic Weekly*, 7 September 1962.

Datt, Ruddar (1996),, 'Windowdressing India's External Debt', *Mainstream*, March 2, 1996.

Desai, Padma (1969), *Tariff Protection and Industrialization", A Study of the Indian Tariff Commission at Work, 1946-65*, Delhi, 1969.

Desai, Padma (1972), *Import-substitution in the Indian Economy: 1951-63*, Hindustan Publishing Corporation India, Delhi.

Dornbusch, Rudiger (1975), "Exchange Rates and Fiscal Policy in a Popular Model of International Trade", *American Economic Review, 65*, 859-71.

Dornbusch, Rudiger (1976), "Expectations and Exchange Rate Dynamics", *Journal of Political Economy*, 84, 1161-76.

Dornbusch, Rudiger (1980), "Exchange Rate Economics: Where Do We Stand?", *Brookings Papers on Economic Activity*, 143-85.

Dornbusch, Rudiger (1982), "Stabilization Policies in Developing Countries: What Have We Learned"? *World Development*, 10, 701-8.

Dornbusch, Rudiger (1983a), "Real Interest Rates, Home Goods and Optimal External Borrowing", *Journal of Political Economy,* 91, 141-53.

Dornbusch, Rudiger (1983b), "Exchange Risk and the Macroeconomics of Exchange Rate Determination", in Robert G. Hawkins, Richard M. Levich (eds.), *The Internationalization of Financial Markets and National Economic Policy*, Greenwich, Conn : JAI Press, 3-27.

Dornbusch, Rudiger (1992), "Lessons from Experiences with High Inflation", *World Bank Economic Review,* 6, 13-31.

Dornbusch, Rudiger and Jacob A. Frenkel (1984), "The Gold Standard Crisis of 1847", *Journal of International Economics* 16, 1-27.

Dornbusch, Rudiger and Jeffrey Frankel (1988), "The Flexible Exchange Rate System: Experience and Alternatives", in Silvio Borner (eds.), *International Finance and Trade in a Polycentric World*, New York: St. Martin's Press 151-97.

Dornbusch, Rudiger and Stanley Fischer (1980), "Exchange Rates and the Current Account," *American Economic Review,* 70, 960-71.

Downes, P. and R. Vaez-Zadeh (1991), *The Evolving Role of Central Banks,* IMF : Washington, D.C.

Dutta, Bhabatosh and S. Chakraborty, M. Bhattacharya, and Gouri Ghosh (1962), *Economic Development and Exports,* The World Press, Calcutta.

Dutta, M. (1964), "A Prototype Model of India's Foreign Sector", *International Economic Review,* 5(1) *January*.

Easterly, W., C. Rodriguez and K. Schmidt- Hebel (eds.), (1994), *Public Sector Deficits and Macroeconomic Performance,* Washington, DC: World Bank.

Edwards, Sebastian (1983), "Floating Exchange Rates, Explanations and New Information", *Journal of Monetary Economics,* Vol. II, pp. 321-36.

Edwards, Sebastian (1982), "Exchange Rates and 'News' : A Multi-Currency Approach", *Journal of International Money and Finance,* 1, 211-24.

Eichengreen, Barry, Michael Mussa and others (1998), 'Capital Account Liberalisation—Theoretical and Practical Aspects:, *IMF Occasional Paper,* No. 172, IMF, Washington D.C.

Fischer, S. (1993), "The Role of Macroeconomic Factors in Growth", *Journal of Monetary Economics* 32; 485-512.

Fleming J. Marcus (1962), "Domestic Financial Policy Under Fixed and Under Floating Exchange Rates", *International Monetary Fund Staff Papers,* 12, 369-80.

Flood, Robert P. and Peter M. Garber (1984), "Collapsing Exchange Rate Regimes: Some Linear Examples", *Journal of International Economics,* 17, 1-13.

Flood, Robert P. and Peter M. Garber (1991), "The Linkage Between Speculative Attack and Target Zone Models of Exchange Rates", *Quarterly Journal of Economics,* 106, 1367-72.

Frankel, J. A. and K.A. Froot (1989), "Chartists, Fundamentalists and Trading in the Foreign Exchange Market", *American Economic Review,* Papers and Proceedings, Vol. 80, pp. 181-5.

Frankel, Jeffrey A. (1979), "On the Mark: A Theory of Floating Exchange Rates Based on Real Interest Rate Differentials", *American Economic Review,* Vol. 69, pp 610-22.

Frenkel, J.A. and C.A. Rodriguez (1982), "Exchange Rate Dynamics and the Overshooting Hypothesis", *IMF Staff Papers,* 29: 1-30.

Frenkel, Jacob A. (1982), "Flexible Exchange Rates, Prices and the Role of 'News': Lessons from the 1970s", in R.A. Batchelor and G.E. Wood, (eds.), *Exchange Rate Policies,* London, Macmillan.

Frenkel, Jacob A. and Assaf Razin (1987), "The Mundell-Fleming Model a Quarter Century Later: a Unified Exposition", *International Monetary Fund Staff Papers,* 34, 567-620.

Frenkel, Jacob A. and Morris Goldstein (1986), "A Guide to Target Zones", *International Monetary Fund Staff Papers* 33, 633-73.

Gadgil, D.R. (1958), "Rephasing the Second Plan", *The Indian Economic Journal,* April, 1958.

Gandolfo, G. (2002), *International Finance and Open-Economy Macro-Economics,* Berlin Heidelberg, New York : Springer-Verlag.

Ganesh-Kumar, A., Kunal Sen and Rajendra Vaidya (1999), "India's Export Competitiveness and Finance" in Parikh, Kirit (ed.), (1999) : *India Development Report,* 1999-2000, OUP, Delhi.

Ganguli, B.N. (1960), *The Devaluation of the Rupee,* 1966, Ranjit Printers and Publishers, Delhi.

Ghosh, Jayati (1990), "Exchange Rates and the Trade Balance: Some Aspects of Indian Experience", *Economic and Political Weekly,* 25(9):441-45.

Girton, L. and D.W. Henderson, (1977), "Central Bank Operations in Foreign and Domestic Assets Under Fixed and Flexible Exchange Rates", in P.B. Clark, D.E. Logue, and R.J. Sweeny, (eds.), *The Effects of Exchange Rate Adjustment* (Washington: Govt. Printing Office).

Goldar, B. (1986), "Import Substitution, Industrial Concentration and Productivity Growth in Indian Manufacturing", *Oxford Bulletin of Economics and Statistics, May.*

Government of India, Ministry of Finance, *Economic Survey,* Various Years, New Delhi.

Granger, C.W.J. (1969), "Investigating Causal Relationship to Econometric Models and Cross Spectral Methods", *Econometrica,* Vol. 34 , 424-38.

Greenaway and Chris R. Millner (1993), *Trade and Industrial Policy in Developing Countries,* London.

Greenspan, Alan (1999), "Currency Reserves and Debt", Remarks before the World Bank Conference on Recent Trends of Reserves Management, Washington, D.C., April.

Griffin, Keith (1989), *Alternative Strategies for Economic Development,* Macmillion Press Ltd., London.

Gupta, S.P. (ed.) (1993), *Liberalisation : Its Impact on the Indian Economy,* Macmillan India Limited.

Habermeier, Karl, (2000), "India's Experience with the Liberalization of Capital Flows since 1991, in *IMF Occasional Paper* (17 May 2000), p. 81.

Harberger, Arnold, C. (1950), "Currency Depreciation, Income, and the Balance of Trade", *Journal of Political Economy,* 58, 4760.

Harrod, R.F. (1993), *International Economics,* Cambridge University Press, Cambridge.

Hume, D. (1752), 'Of the Balance of Trade', in D. Hume, *Political Discourses,* Edinburgh.

Hussain, Abid (1995), "Foreign Trade Policy in Indian Planning" in Banerjee, K. and Tarjani Vakil (eds.), : *India: Joining the World Economy.* Tata Mcgraw-Hill Publishing Ltd., New Delhi.

International Monetary Fund (IMF), Various Years, *International Financial Statistics Yearbook*, Washington, D.C.

International Monetary Fund (IMF), Various Years, *World Economic Outlook*, Washington, D.C.

Israd, Peter (1995), *Exchange Rate Economics: Cambridge Survey of Economic Literature*, Cambridge University Press.

Jalan, Bimal (1992), *The Indian Economy: Problems and Prospects*. Viking Penguin Books India Pvt. Ltd., New Delhi.

Jalan, Bimal (1996), *India's Economic Policy: Preparing for the Twenty-first Century*, Viking, Penguin Books India Pvt. Ltd.

Jadhav, Narendra (2005), 'Capital Account Liberalization in India' in Tseng, Wanda and David Cowen (eds.), *India's and China's Recent Experience with Reform and Growth*, Palgrave Macmillan.

Jha, R. (2001), " Macroeconomics of Fiscal Policy in Developing Countries," *WIDER 2001/71 Discussion DP*, Helsinki: UNO-WIDER.

Johansen, S. and K. Juselius, (1990), "The Full Information, Maximum Likelihood Procedure for Inference on Cointegration", *Oxford Bulletin of Economics and Statistics*, Vol. 52, 1990.

Johnson, Harry, G. (1961), "Towards a General Theory of the Balance of Payments", in H.G. Johnson, *International Trade and Economic Growth: Studies in Pure Theory*, Cambridge, Mass: Harvard University Press, 153-68.

Johnson, Harry, G. (1972), "The Monetary Approach to Balance of Payments Theory", *Journal of Financial and Quantitative Analysis*, 7, 1555-72.

Johnson, Harry G. (1976), "Money and the Balance of Payments" *Banca Nazinale Del Lavro Q Rein*.

Johnson, Harry G. (1977), "The Monetary Approach to the Balance of Payments: A Non-technical Guide", *Journal of International Economics*, 7, 251-68.

Joseph, Mathew (1992), *Exchange Rate Policy: Impact on Exports and Balance of Payments*, Deep and Deep Publications, New Delhi.

Joshi and Little (1996), *India's Economic Reforms, 1991-2001*, Oxford University Press.

Joshi, Himanshu (1996), "Responsiveness of India's Exports to Exchange Rate Changes: A Cointegration Analysis". Paper presented at the 32nd Annual Conference of *The Indian Econometric Society* held at Bangalore, 1996.

Joshi, Vijay and I.M.D. Little (1994), *India: Macroeconomics and Political Economy,* 1964-91, Oxford University Press, Bombay.

Kaldor, Nicholas (1979), "Equilibrium Theory and Growth Theory", in M. Baskia (ed.), *Economics and Human Welfare,* New York: Academic Press.

Kaldor, Nicholas (1984), "An Exchange Rate Policy for India", *Economic and Political Weekly* 19(28), 1093-95.

Karmakar, Asim K. (1993), "The Indian Economy—A March Towards, Globalization" in Das, Debendra, K., (ed.), "*Structural Adjustment in the Indian Economy*" Vol. 2, Deep and Deep Publications, New Delhi.

Karmakar, Asim K. (1994), "External Value of the Rupee and India's Balance of Payments—A Macroeconomic Assessment", Conference Volume of the *Indian Economic Journal,* Bombay, 19-21 February.

Karmakar, Asim K. (1994), "Privatisation of Public Sector Enterprises in India : An Evaluation of Some Basic Issues" in Das, Debendra K. (ed.), *Privatisation of Public Sector Undertaking—Rationale and Feasibility,* Deep and Deep Publications, New Delhi.

Karmakar, Asim K. (1996), "Contribution of Alfred Marshall to International Trade Theory and Policy", *Indian Economic Journal,* Vol. 43, No. 3.

Karmakar, Asim K. (1998), *Balance of Payments and Economic Development—The Indian Experience During the Period 1951-52 to 1990-91,* Ph.D. Dissertation (unpublished), Jadavpur University.

Karmakar, Asim K. (2007), "Capital Account Convertibility in India—Some Theoretical Issues And Policy Prescriptions", *Artha Beekshan,* Vol. 15, No. 4, March.

Karmakar, Asim K. (2007), *Balance of Payments and Macroeconomic Behaviour in India Since 1990s,* Completed UGC Sponsored Minor Research Project under SEED Support for Potential for Excellence, Jadavpur University.

Karmakar, Asim K. (2007), "India's Foreign Exchange Reserves : A Synoptic Review", *Rabindra Bharati University, Journal of Economics*, Volume: I, March, 2007.

Karmakar, Asim K. (2008), "India's External Debt—An Evaluation of its Status during the Reform Period", *Rabindra Bharati University Journal of Economics*, Volume II, March, 2008.

Kearney C. and R. MacDonald (1986), "A Structural Portfolio Balance Model of the Sterling-Dollar Exchange Rate", *Weltwirtschaftliches Archiv*, 122:3, 478-96.

Kearney C. and R. Mac Donald (1985), "Asset Markets and the Exchange Rate: A Structural Model of the Sterling Dollar Rate", 1972-82, *Journal of Economic Studies*, 12:3, 3-20.

Kelkar, V.L. (1977), "Evaluation of India's Trade Policies", *Economic and Political Weekly*, 18 June.

Kenen, P.B. (1982), "Effects of Intervention and Sterilization in the Short Run and the Long Run", in R.N. Cooper, P.B. Kenen, J.V. Machedo and I.V. Ypersele (ed.), *The International Monetary System Under Flexible Exchange Rates*. (Cambridge Mass: Ballinger).

Kohli, Renu (2005), *Liberalizing Capital Flows: India's Experiences and Policy Issues*, Oxford University Press, New Delhi.

Kouri, Pentti, J.K. (1976), "The Exchange Rate and the Balance of Payments in the Short Run and the Long Run: A Monetary Approach", *Scandinavian Journal of Economics*, 78, 280-304.

Kouri, Pentti, J.K. and Michael G. Porter (1974), "International Capital Flows and Portfolio Equilibrium", *Journal of Political Economy*, 82, 443-67.

Krueger, Anne O. (1995), "Increased Capital Mobility and Policy Reform in Developing Countries", *Ramaswamy Memorial Lecture*, 14 December, Delhi School of Economics, Delhi.

Krugman, Paul (1979), "A Model of Balance of Payments Crises", *Journal of Money, Credit and Banking*, 11, 311-25.

Krugman, Paul (1990), "Equilibrium Exchange Rate", in William H. Branson *et. al.* (eds.), *International Policy Coordination and Exchange Rate Fluctuations*, Chicago: University of Chicago Press, 159-87.

Krugman, Paul (1991), "Target Zones and Exchange Rate Dynamics", *Quarterly Journal of Economics*, 106, 669-82.

Krugman, Paul and Lance Taylor, (1978), "Contractionary effects of Devaluation", *Journal of International Economics,* Vol. 8, 445-56.

Krugman, Paul and Marcus Miller (1993), "Why Have a Target Zone"? *Carnegie-Rochester Conference Series on Public Policy* 38, 279-314.

Krugman, Paul and Maurice Obstfeld (1991), *International Economics: Theory and Policy,* New York: Harper Collins.

Krugman, Paul and Richard E. Baldwin (1987), "The Persistence of the U.S. Trade Deficit", *Brookings Papers on Economic Activity,* 1-43.

Kumar, Nagesh (1998), "Liberalization and Changing Pattern of FDIs : Has India's Relative Attractiveness as a Host of FDI Improved ?" *EPW,* Vol. XXXIII, No. 22, May 30.

Kumar, Nagesh (1998), "East Asian Economic Crisis and South Asian Growth Prospects : A Note", *RIS Digest,* Vol. 14, September.

Kumar, Rajiv (1993), "The Walk Away from Leadership: India" in Tussie, Diana and David Glover (eds.), *The Developing Countries in World Trade Policy and Bargaining Strategies,* Lynne Rienner Publishers Inc., USA.

Kumar, Rajiv and Mathew Joseph (1994), "External Value of the Rupee". Paper presented and published at the Conference Volume of the *Indian Economic Journal,* Conference held at Bombay University, Bombay during 19-21 February 1994.

Lakdawala, D.T. (1964), "Aspects of Trade Policy in India", *The Indian Economic Journal,* October-December, 1964.

Lall, S. (1999), "India's Manufactured Exports: Comparative Structure and Prospects," *World Development,* 27 (10); 1769-86.

Laursen, S. and L.A. Metzler (1950), "Flexible Exchange Rates and the Theory of Employment", *Review of Economics and Statistics,* 32, 281-99.

Lerner, Abba P. (1944), *The Economics of Control,* London: Macmillan.

Levich, R.M. (1978), "Tests of Forecast Models of Market Efficiency in the International Money Market", in J.A. Frenkel and H.G. Johnson, *The Economics of Exchange Rates* (Reading, Mass: Addison Wesley).

Little, I.M.D., Richard N. Cooper, W. Max Corden, and Sarath Rajapatirana (1993), *Boom, Crisis and Adjustment: The Macroeconomic Experience of Developing Countries*, New York: Oxford University Press.

Lucas, Robert E.B., (1998), "Demand for India's Manufactures Exports", *Journal of Development Economics*, Vol. 29(1).

MacDonald, R. (1983), "Some Tests of the Rational Expectations Hypothesis in the Foreign Exchange Market," *Scottish Journal of Political Economy*, Vol. 30, pp. 235-50.

MacDonald, R. (1988), *Floating Exchange Rates: Theories and Evidence* (London: Unwin Hyman)

Machlup, F. (1950), 'Three Concepts of the Balance of Payments and the So-called Dollar Shortage,' *Economic Journal*, 60, 46-68.

Magee, Stephen P. (1973), "Currency Contracts, Pass-through, and Devaluation", *Brookings Papers on Economic Activity*, No. 1, 303-23.

Marjit, S. and Ajitava Ray Chaudhuri (1997), *India's Exports*, Oxford University Press, Delhi

Marshall, Alfred (1923), *Money, Credit and Commerce*, London: Macmillan.

Marwah, K. (1969), "Measurement of Devaluation Impact: Indian Case", *Indian Economic Journal*, Vol. 17.

McCombie, J.S.L. and A.P. Thirlwall (1992), "Comment: The Re-emergence of the Balance of Payments Constraint" in T. Michie (ed.), *The Economic Legacy*, 1979-1992. Acadamic Press, London.

McCombie, J.S.L. and A.P. Thirlwall (1994), *Economic Growth and the Balance of Payments Constraints*, London: Macmillan.

McKinnon, R. (1964), "Foreign Exchange Constraints in Economic Development and Efficient Aid Allocation", *Economic Journal*, 74 : 388-409.

Meade, James E. (1951), *The Theory of International Economic Policy, Volume One: The Balance of Payments*, London : Oxford University Press.

Meese, R.A. and K.J. Singleton, (1982), "A Note on Unit Roots and the Empirical Modelling of Exchange Rates", *Journal of Finance*, Vol. 37, pp. 1029-35.

Meese, Richard A. and Kenneth Rogoff (1984), "The Out-of-Sample Failure of Empirical Exchange Rate Models:

Sampling Error or Misspecification?", in J.A. Frenkel (ed.), *Exchange Rates and International Economics*, Chicago: Chicago University Press.

Meese, Richard A. and Kenneth Rogoff (1983), "Empirical Exchange Rate Models of the Seventies: Do They Fit Out of Sample?", *Journal of International Macroeconomics*, 14, 3-24.

Meese, Richard A. and Andrew K. Rose (1991), "An Empirical Assessment of Non-linearities in Models of Exchange Rate Determination?" *Review of Economic Studies*, 58, 603-19.

Mehta, Rajesh (1997), "Trade Policy Reforms, 1991-92 to 1995-96 : Their Impact on External Trade", *EPW*, 32(13):779-84.

Mehta, Rajesh (1998), *Tariff and Non-Tariff Barriers of the Indian Economy : A Profile, Study Report* submitted to the Tariff Commission, Government of India.

Metzler, Lloyd A. (1949), "The Theory of International Trade", in Howard S. Ellis (ed.), *A Survey of Contemporary Economics*, Philadelphia: Blakiston, 210-54.

Metzler, Lloyd A. (1951), "Wealth, Saving, and the Rate of Interest", *Journal of Political Economy*, 59, 930-46.

Ministry of Finance (1995), *India's External Debt—A Status Report*, December, 1995.

Mittelman, J.R. and Mustapha Kamal Pasha (1997), *Out from Underdevelopment Revisited: Changing Global Structures and the Remaking of the Third World*, Macmillan Press Ltd. London.

Muellbauer, J. and A. Murphy (1990), "The UK Current Account Deficit", *Economic Policy*.

Mukherjee, A. (1983), "The Effects of Terms of Trade on the Trade Balance with Emphasis on Devaluation: General and Sectoral Cases", *Indian Economic Journal*, Vol. 30.

Mundell, Robert A. (1960), "The Monetary Dynamics of International Adjustment Under Fixed and Flexible Exchange Rates", *Quarterly Journal of Economics*, 74, 227-57.

Mundell, Robert A. (1961a), "The International Disequilibrium System", *Kyklos*, 14, 152-70.

Mundell, Robert A. (1961b), "Flexible Exchange Rates and Employment Policy", *Canadian Journal of Economics and Political Science*, 27, 509-17.

Mundell, Robert A. (1962), "The Appropriate Use of Monetary and Fiscal Policy for Internal and External Stability", *International Monetary Fund Staff Papers,* Vol. 9, 70-9.

Mundell, Robert A. (1963), "Capital Mobility and Stabilization Policy under Fixed and Flexible Exchange Rates", *Canadian Journal of Economics and Political Science,* 29. 475-85.

Mundell, Robert A. (1968), *International Economics,* (London: Macmillan).

Nag, A.K. and G. Upadhya (1994), "Exchange Rate and Trade Imbalance", *Economic and Political Weekly,* April 2.

Narasimham, M. (1988), *World Economic Environment and Prospects for India,* Sterling Publishers Private Ltd., New Delhi.

National Council of Applied Economic Research (NCAER) (1969), *Export Strategy for India,* New Delhi.

Nayyar, Deepak (1976), *India's Exports and Export Policies in the 1960s,* Cambridge: Cambridge University Press.

Nayyar, Deepak (1982), India's Balance of Payments, *Economic and Political Weekly,* Annual Number, April 1982.

Nayyar, Deepak (1994), *Migration, Remittances and Capital Flows: The Indian Experience,* Oxford University Press.

Obstfeld, Maurice (1980), 'Imperfect Asset Substitutability and Monetary Policy under Fixed Exchange Rates', *Journal of International Economics,* Vol. 10, 177-200.

Obstfeld, Maurice (1986), "Rational and Self-Fulfilling Balance-of Payments Crisis", *American Economic Reviewm,* 76, 72-81.

Page, Sheila (1990), *Trade, Finance and Developing Countries: Strategies and Constraints in the 1990s.* Harvester, Wheatsheaf, London.

Panchamukhi, V.R. (1965), "Import Substitution in Relation to Technical Change and Economic Growth", *Arthaniti,* 8, 114-39.

Panchamukhi, V.R. (1967), "Planning for Import Substitution-Some Methodological and Empirical Results", *Arthavijnana,* 1967.

Panchamukhi, V.R. (1968), "The Terms of Trade Effects and the Balance of Payments (Factual Analysis for 1949-63)", *The Indian Economic Review,* April, 1968.

Panchamukhi, V.R., Jagdish Bhagwati, and Padma Desai (1970), *Effective Rate of Protection in India: Trade and Industrialization,* OECD, Ch. 17.

Patil, Surendra, J. (1959), "Export Prospect and Economic Growth: India", *The Economic Journal,* September, 1959, *490-506.*

Patnaik, Prabhat (2003), 'On the Economics of "Open Economy" De-Industrialization', *V.V. Giri Memorial Lecture* delivered at 45th Annual Conference of the Indian Society of Labour Economics, Organised by Jadavpur University, Kolkata, December 16.

Pilbeam, Keith (1992), *International Finance,* The Macmillan Press Ltd., London.

Pomfret, Richard (1996), *Asian Economies in Transition,* Edward Elgar, U.K.

Pursell, Gary (1992), "Trade Policies in India", in D. Salvatore (eds.), *National Trade Policies,* New York : Greenwood Press, pp. 423-58.

Pursell, Gary (1996), "Indian Trade Policies since the 1991-92 Reforms", *Mimeo,* World Bank.

Rakshit, Mihir Kanti (1994), "Issues in Structural Adjustment of the Indian Economy" in Edmar L. Bacha (ed.), *Economics in a Changing World,* Vol. 4, International Economic Association.

Rakshit, Mihir Kanti (2005), "Using Forex Reserves for Infrastructural Investment", *Special Lecture* delivered at the Indian Econometric Society on 20.1.2005 at Jadavpur University.

Rakshit, Mihir Kanti (2006), "Some Economics of Capital Account Liberalization", *Special Lecture* delivered on February 17 at Visva Bharati University in the 26th Annual Conference of Bengal Economic Association.

Rakshit, Mihir Kanti (2006), "On liberalizing Foreign Institutional Investment", *EPW,* March 18-24, Vol. XLI, No. 11.

Rakshit, Mihir Kanti (2007), Services-Led Growth: The Indian Experience, *Artha Beekshan,* Vol. 15, No. 4, March.

Raman, Rakesh (2003), *The Monetary Approach to Balance of Payments and its Policy Implications : A Case Study of India,* Ph.D. Thesis of B.R. Ambedkar Bihar University, Muzaffarpur.

Rangarajan, C. (1990), "The Balance of Payments Scenario", *7th G.L. Mehta Memorial Lectures,* IIT, Mumbai.

Rangarajan, C. (1991), "Recent Exchange Rate Adjustment: Cases and Consequences", *RBI Bulletin* Mumbai, September, pp. 905-9.

Rangarajan, C. (1994), "India's Balance of Payments", The Emerging Dimensions", 16th G.B. Pant Memorial Lecture, *RBI Bulletin*, January 1994.

Rangarajan, C. and A. Prasad (1999), "Capital Account Liberalisation and Controls—Lessons from the East Asian Crisis", *ICRA Bulletin—Money and Finance,* April-June.

Reddy, Y.V. (2006a), "Dynamics of Balance of Payments in India", *The First Diamond Jubilee Lecture* delivered at the Department of Commerce, Osmania University on December 16, 2006.

Reddy, Y.V., (2006b), "Reflections on India's Economic Development', Address at the Council on Foreign Relations, New York, May 12.

Reinhart, C.M. (1995), "Devaluation, Relative Prices and International Trade", *Staff Papers,* IMF, Vol. 42, No. 2, 1995.

Reserve Bank of India, Various Years, *Reserve Bank of India Bulletin*, Mumbai.

Reserve Bank of India, Various Years, *Report on Currency and Finance,* Mumbai.

Reserve Bank of India, Various Years, *Annual Reports*, Mumbai.

Reserve Bank of India, Various Years, *Handbook of Statistics on Indian Economy*, Mumbai

Rishi, Meenakshi and James Boyce (1990), "The Hidden Balance of Payments : Capital Flight and Trade Misinvoicing in India, 1971-86", *Economic and Political Weekly,* 25 (50): 1650-48.

Roach, Stephen (2006), 'Global Imbalances Matter More than Ever', *Morganstanley.com,* May 5.

Robinson, Joan (1947), "The Foreign Exchanges," in Robinson, *Essays in the Theory of Employment,* Oxford: Basil Blackwell, 134-55.

Rodrik, Dani (1998), "Who Needs Capital Account Convertibility?" in *Should the IMF Pursue Capital-Account Convertibility? Essays in International Finance,* Princeton University.

Rothermund, Dietmar (1991), *An Economic History of India—From Pre-Colonial Times to 1991*, Routledge, New York.

Roy, Mohua, Rekha Misra and Sangita Misra (2006), "A Review of Cross-Country Experience in Capital Account Liberalisation", *RBI Occasional Papers,* Vol. 27, Nos. 1 & 2.

Sandesara, J.C. (1979), "Size of the Factory and Concentration in the Factory Sector in India, 1951 to 1970", *Indian Economic Journal*, Oct.-Dec.

Sarkar, Prabirjit (1992), "Rupee Depreciation and India's External Trade and Payments since 1971", *Economic and Political Weekly,* June 13-20, 1992.

Sarkar, Prabirjit (1994), "Indian Balance of Payments and Exchange Rate Behaviour since 1971 : A New Approach", *Economic and Political Weekly,* January 1-8, 1994.

Sarkar, Prabirjit (1995), "Indian Economy Since 1991—Trade Price and Exchange Rate Behaviour", *Economic and Political Weekly*, Vol. 30, No. 20, May 1995.

Sarkar, Prabirjit (1997), "Foreign Trade and Real Exchange Rate Behaviour, 1980-96", *Economic and Political Weekly*, Vol. 32, Nos. 20 & 21. May 17-23/24-30.

Sarkar, Prabirjit (1999), "India's Balance of Payments Crisis : Is there any recovery under the New Economic Policy", in Oshikawa Fumiko (Ed.), *South Asia Under the Economic Reforms*, JCAS Symposium Series 6, Osaka, Japan.

Sarma, Y.U.K. (1989), "Indian Balance of Payments 1948-49 to 1984-85 : A Survey", *Journal of Indian School of Political Economy,* Vol. 1, No. 2, July-December, 1989.

Sathe, Dhanamanjiri (1996), "A Review of India's Balance of Payments : 1985-86 to 1993-94", *Journal of Indian School of Political Economy*: Vol. 8, No. 4, Oct.-Dec. 1996.

Sau, Ranjit (1992), "Making of a Payments Crisis: India 1991", *Economic and Political Weekly,* August 15.

Sen, Pronab (1986), "The 1966 Devaluation in India: A Reappraisal", *Economic & Political Weekly,* Vol. XXI, No. 30, July 26, 1986: 1322-28.

Sen, Pronab, Ashima Goyal and Srinivasan Varadarajan (2006), "Full Rupee Convertibility: Good, Bad or Ugly?" *The Economic Times,* March 28.

Sen, Sunanda (1982), "Policy Planning in India's Foreign Trade Sector: From Import Substitution to Export Promotion in India". *Economic and Political Weekly, Annual Number,* 1982.

Sen, Sunanda (2006), 'Drive with Caution', *The Telegraph*, May 9, 2006.

Sen, Sunanda and Hiranya Mukhopadhyay (1994), "Devaluation, Liberalization and Structural Linkages Between India's Foreign Trade and National Income", *Economic and Political Weekly*, Vol. 19, No. 30, September 3, 1994.

Sengupta, Anindita (1996), "A Design of Stabilization Policies for Low Inflation and High Foreign Exchange Reserves : An Experiment for India Using a Small Macro Econometric Model", Paper Presented at the 32nd Indian Econometric Conference held in Bangalore during 21-23, March 1996.

Senhadji, A.S. (1998), 'Dynamics of the Trade Balance and the Terms of Trade in LDCs: The S-Curve, *Journal of International Economics*, 46, 559-82.

Sesadri, R.K. (1993), *From Crisis to Convertibility: The External Value of the Rupee*; Orient Longman, Calcutta.

Seth, Asok and R.N. Bharadwaj (1994), "Current Account Balance, Real Exchange Rate and Budget deficit: An Empirical Study of Indian Economy", Paper presented at the 75th Conference of the Indian Economic Association, held at Bombay on 19-21 February, 1994.

Shah, V.C. (1970), "Devaluation—The Indian Case", *The Indian Economic Journal*, July-September, 1970.

Sharan, Vyuptakesh (1998), 'Recent Trends in FDI in India', *International Capital Markets*, 18 (4).

Shenoy, B.R. (1958), "The Indian Economic Scene", *The Indian Economic Journal*, April, 1958.

Sikorshi, Trevor M. (1996), *Financial Liberalization in Developing Countries*, Edward Elgar Publishing Ltd., UK.

Singh, D. (1986), *Economics of Exchange Rate Management*, Criterion Publications.

Singh, Manmohan (1964), *India's Export Trends and the Prospects for Self-Sustained Growth*, Clarendon Press, 1964.

Singh, Manmohan (1970), "Trade Policies and Economic Development", in R.A.G. Robinson and M. Kidron (eds.), *Economic Development in South Asia*, London, 1970.

Singh, Manmohan (1976), "International Trade and Payments - A Trend Report" in *A Survey of Research in Economics*, Vol. II, Macro Economics, ICSSR, New Delhi, Allied Publishers, Calcutta.

Sinha-Roy, Saikat (1998a), 'Post-Reforms Export Growth in India: Exploration into the Issue of Disparity in Structures', *Mimeo, RIS, New* Delhi.

Sinha-Roy, Saikat (1998b), 'Post Reforms Export Growth in India: An Exploratory Analysis,' Paper Presented at the conference *'Development, Displacement & Disparity : India in the Last Quarter of the Century'* held at the Centre for Studies in Social Sciences, Kolkata, 17-19 December, 1998.

Sood, Krishnalekha (1989), *Trade and Economic Development: India, Pakistan and Bangladesh,* Sage Publications, New Delhi.

Srinivasan, T.N. (1998), 'India's Export Perfromance : A Comparative Analysis' in I.J. Ahluwalia and IMD Little (eds.), *India's Economic Reforms and Development : Essay for Manmohon Singh.*

Stein, Jerome L. (1990), The Real Exchange Rate,' *Journal of Banking and Finance,* 14:1045-78.

Stein, Jerome L. (1995), 'The Natural Real Exchange Rate of the United States Dollar, and Determinants of Capital Flows,' in J.L. Stein, P. Reynolds Allen and Associates, *Fundamental Determinants of Exchange Rates,* Oxford University Press.

Stein, Jerome L. (1999), 'The Evolution of the Real Value of the US Dollar Relative to the G 7 Currencies, in R. Macdonald and J.L. Stein (eds.), *"Equilibrium Exchange Rates,* Dordrecht: Kluwer Academic Publishers.

Sundararajan Srinivasa, S. and Ganti Subrahmanyam (1995), "Three-Gap Theory of Investment and Growth", Paper Presented at the 31st Annual Conference of the Indian Econometric Conference held at Pune during May, 1995.

Sundararajan Srinivasa, S. and LM. Bhole (1989), "The Functional Form of the Effects of Exchange Rate Changes on Trade Balance and Balance of Payments in India", *Prajnan,* Vol. 17, No. 1.

Swan, Trevor W. (1963), "Longer-Run Problems of the Balance of Payments", in Heinz W. Arndt and Max W. Corden (eds.), *The Australian Economy: A Volume of Readings,* Melbourne: Cheshire, 384-95.

Tandon Committee (1980), *Committee on Export Strategy 1980s: Final Report,* Ministry of Commerce, New Delhi.

Tarapore, S.S. (2003), *Capital Account Convertibility: Monetary Policy and Reforms*, UBSPD Pvt. Ltd., New Delhi.

Taylor, L. (1993), "A Three Gap Analysis of Foreign Resource Flows and Developing Country Growth" in Lance Taylor (ed.), *Rockey Road to Reform: Adjustment, Income and Growth in Developing World"*, MIT Press, Cambridge.

Taylor, M.P. (1988), "A Dynamic Model of Forward Foreign Exchange Risk, with Estimates for Three Major Exchange Rates", *The Manchestor School*, Vol. 56, pp. 55-68.

Thirlwall, A.P. (1979), "The Balance of Payments Constraint as an Explanation of International Growth Rate Differences", *Banca Nazionale del Lavoro Quarterly Review*, 1979, 128, pp. 45-53.

Thirlwall, A.P. (1986), *Balance of Payments Theory and the United Kingdom Experience*, Macmillan, London.

Tinbergen, Jan (1952), *On the Theory of Economic Policy*, Amsterdam : North-Holland.

Tomlinson, B.R. (1993), *The New Cambridge History of India: The Economy of Modern India*, Cambridge University Press.

Trivedi, Puspa (1992), "The Impact of Recent Policy Measures on India's Balance of Payments : An Analytical Exercise", *Indian Economic Journal*, No. 3, Jan.-March, 1992.

Tsiang, S.C. (1961), "The Role of Money in Trade Balance Stability: Synthesis of the Elasticity and Absorption Approaches", *American Economic Review*, 51, 912-36.

Turnovsky, Stephen J. (1995), "Endogenous Growth in a Dependent Economy with Traded and Non-Traded Capital", *Mimeo*, Washington University, Discussion Series, September 1995.

Upadhyaya, K.P. and D. Dhakal (1997), 'Devaluation and the Trade Balance: Estimating the Long Run Efect,' *Applied Economics Letters* 4, 343-45.

Vasudevan, A. (1994), "External Value of the Rupee: Issues for Discussion", Published at the Annual Conference Volume of the *Indian Economic Journal*, Conference held at Mumbai During 19-21 February 1995.

Virmani, Arvind (1991), "Demand and Supply Factors in India's Trade", *Economic and Political Weekly*, 26(6), 9 February.

Weiss, John (1995), *Economic Policy in Developing Countries—The Reforms Agenda*, Harvester Wheatsheaf, London.

Weisskof, T.E. (1972), "Econometric Test of Alternative Constraints on the Growth of Underdeveloped Countries", *Review of Economics and Statistics*, 54:67-78.

Williamson, John, (1977), *The Failure of World Monetary Reform*, Nelson, Sunbury-on-Thames.

Williamson, John, Amitava Krishna Dutt and others (2006), 'Capital Account Convertibility—A Debate', *Economic and Political Weekly*, May 13.

Wolf, Martin (1982), *India's Exports*, Oxford: Oxford University Press.

World Bank, Various Years, *World Debt Tables*, Washington D.C.

World Bank, Various Years, *World Development Reports*, New York, Oxford University Press.

World Trade Organisation (WTO), *GATT Trade Policy Review*, Various Countries.

Yesuthasen, P. (2006), "Road to Freedom: Capital Account Convertibility", *Economic Times*, May 10.

Zuang, Juzhong (1996), "Estimating Distortion in the Chinese Economy: A General Equilibrium Approach," *ECONOMICA*, Vol. 63, No. 252.

Index